CASS LIBRARY OF VICTORIAN TIMES

No. 9

General Editor: Anne Humpherys
Herbert H. Lehman College, New York

PROSTITUTION

Considered in its Moral, Social, and Sanitary Aspects

CASS LIBRARY OF VICTORIAN TIMES

No. 1. Frances Trollope
The Life and Adventures of Michael Armstrong, the Factory Boy (1840).
New Impression

No. 2. Henry Mayhew and John Binney
The Criminal Prisons of London and Scenes of Prison Life (1862).
New Impression

No. 3. Henry Mayhew
London Labour and the London Poor. A cyclopaedia of the conditions and earnings of those that will work, those that cannot work, and those that will not work (1862).
New Impression

No. 4. James Phillips Kay Shuttleworth
The Moral and Physical Condition of the Working Classes employed in the Cotton Manufacture of Manchester (2nd ed., 1832).
With a new preface by Dr. W. H. Chaloner.
New Impression

No. 5. Thomas Beames
The Rookeries of London. Past, Present and Prospective (2nd ed., 1852).
New Impression

No. 6. Octavia Hill
Homes of the London Poor (2nd ed., 1883).
New Impression
together with
   Andrew Mearns
The Bitter Cry of Outcast London. An Inquiry into the Condition of the Abject Poor (1883).
With notes on the authors by Dr. W. H. Chaloner.
New Impression

No. 7. Augustus Mayhew
Paved With Gold or The Romance and Reality of the London Streets. An Unfashionable Novel (1858).
With a new introduction by Anne Humpherys.
New Edition

No. 8. Hector Gavin
Sanitary Ramblings, being Sketches and Illustrations of Bethnal Green. A Type of the Condition of the Metropolis and Other Large Towns.
New Impression

PROSTITUTION

CONSIDERED IN

ITS MORAL,
SOCIAL, AND SANITARY
ASPECTS

IN

London and other Large Cities and Garrison Towns

WITH

PROPOSALS FOR THE CONTROL AND PREVENTION
OF ITS ATTENDANT EVILS

BY

WILLIAM ACTON

With a new biographical note by
PROFESSOR ANNE HUMPHERYS
Herbert H. Lehman College, New York

FRANK CASS : LONDON

Published by
FRANK CASS AND COMPANY LIMITED
67 Great Russell Street, London WC1B 3BT

Distributed in the United States by
International Scholarly Book Services, Inc.
Beaverton, Oregon 97005

Library of Congress Catalog Card No. 75–171265

ISBN 0 7146 2414 4

First edition	1857
Second edition	1870
Reprint of Second edition with a new biographical note	1972

Printed in Great Britain by Clarke, Doble & Brendon Ltd.
Plymouth and London

Biographical Note

William Acton was a man of science whose specialization—the study of human sexuality—was an unmentionable subject for most Victorians. Paradoxically, Acton himself was very Victorian in many of his attitudes, believing, for example, that masturbation led "if carried far enough, to early death or self-destruction" *(The Functions and Disorders of the Reproductive Organs . . .).* Nevertheless, he insisted, frequently with the zeal of a social reformer rather than that of a doctor, that the results of officially ignoring the sexual drive in men were not in the best interests of society. "I am," he says in his Preface to the Second Edition of *Prostitution,* "an advocate of RECOGNITION. . . . I propose to show that concentrated effort, sanctioned by authority, can alone stay the ravages of a contagious and deadly disorder, and that only by methodical and combined action, and by gradual and almost imperceptible stages, can any moral cure be effected." Thus, his great work on prostitution is a combination of scientific observation and analysis, sound social criticism, and open propaganda, a compound not untypical of the best Victorian social documents.

Acton had an excellent background to prepare him for this work. He was born in 1814, the second son of a clergyman in Shillingston, Dorset. At 17, he went to London to begin his studies for a medical career, and was an articled pupil of Charles Wheeler, the apothecary to St. Bartholomew's hospital, until 1835, when he went to Paris to serve as an "externe" (a non-student) at the women's venereal hospital in Paris. During this period he laid the scientific foundations for his life-long subject of research, studying under one of the foremost men in the field of venereology, Philippe Riccord. Acton served as Secretary of the Parisian Medical Society in 1839.

In 1840, he returned to London, becoming a member of the Royal College of Surgeons, and building up a fashionable practice in George Street, Hanover Square until 1843, and in Queen Anne Street in Cavendish Square thereafter. In 1845–1846, he served as surgeon to the Islington Dispensary. Until his death in 1875, he was an active writer of articles on a variety of medical problems, by far the largest number dealing with the physical and social problems related to venereal diseases. Some of these articles were reports of observations on social problems, such as "Observations on illegitimacy in the London parishes of St. Marylebone,

St. Pancras, and St. George's, Southwark during the year 1857 . . ." (*Journal of the Statistical Society*, 1859). Others dealt with medical questions such as "On the best means of disguising the taste of nauseous medicines" (*Lancet*, 1846). Some articles are tantalizingly unclassifiable—"Child-murder and wet-nursing" (*British Medical Journal*, 1861).

Acton's first book, *A practical treatise on diseases of the urinary and generative organs*, was published in 1841. His most popular work was *The Functions and Disorders of the Reproductive Organs, in Childhood, Youth, Adult Age, and Advanced Life, Considered in their Physiological, Social, and Moral Relations*, first published in 1857, and reaching a sixth edition in 1875. For the modern reader, however, Acton's greatest work is rather his expansively titled *Prostitution, Considered in its Moral, Social and Sanitary Aspects, in London and Other Large Cities: with Proposals for the Mitigation and Prevention of its Attendant Evils*, published in 1857 but substantially revised for the second edition in 1870.

The differences between *The Functions and Disorders* and *Prostitution* are instructive. In *The Functions and Disorders of the Reproductive Organs*, described by Steven Marcus as "part fantasy, part nightmare, part hallucination, and part madhouse" (*The Other Victorians*, p. 13), Acton tried to give scientific justification to the prevailing attitude to masturbation and sexual intercourse, namely that, to quote Marcus again, "sex is . . . a universal and virtually incurable scourge" (op. cit., p. 28). But in *Prostitution*, Acton aimed to attack rather than support prevailing ideas about sex, to inculcate a more humane and reasonable response to a social problem which he knew did not improve with ignorance. Among other pet Victorian assumptions, Acton attacked the belief that all prostitutes end up destitute and brutalized. "I prove," he says in the Preface, "that the great mass of prostitutes in this country are in the course of time absorbed into the so-called respectable classes." Though Acton's work was favourably received by the press when it appeared, such home truths were perhaps too strong for the book to be acceptable to the general Victorian reader. It is just this quality of honest observation, however, as well as Acton's insistence that the problem must be faced, which ensures the book's continuing interest for the modern reader. It proves to us once again that the complex Victorians defy generalization.

1971   A.H.

PROSTITUTION,

CONSIDERED IN

ITS MORAL, SOCIAL, AND SANITARY ASPECTS,

IN

London and other Large Cities and Garrison Towns.

WITH

PROPOSALS FOR THE CONTROL AND PREVENTION OF ITS ATTENDANT EVILS.

By WILLIAM ACTON, M.R.C.S.

FORMERLY EXTERNE TO THE FEMALE VENEREAL HOSPITAL IN PARIS ; LATE SURGEON
TO THE ISLINGTON DISPENSARY ;
FELLOW OF THE ROYAL MEDICAL AND CHIRURGICAL SOCIETY ; ETC. ETC.

SECOND EDITION.

LONDON:
JOHN CHURCHILL AND SONS,
NEW BURLINGTON STREET.
MDCCCLXX.

PREFACE.

TWELVE years have elapsed since I submitted to public consideration the first edition of this work. I entered upon my labours
with feelings far different from those which induce me to resume
them. Then, the attempt to rouse attention to a question that
seemed to myself one of national importance, appeared almost
hopeless. Now, the mind and conscience of the nation are
awakened, and opinions which would have been formerly dismissed as idle dreams, are deemed worthy of serious attention.
During the intervening period prostitution, with its attendant evils, has been the subject of anxious inquiry. In 1864 the
Secretary of State for War, and the Board of Admiralty, appointed a Committee to report on the best means of protecting
the army and navy from the ravages occasioned by venereal
disease, and in 1866 an Act having this end in view — now
well known as the Contagious Diseases Act of 1866 — passed
through the legislature. The results achieved by means of
this Act, and the subject of prostitution generally, have also
been reported on by two Select Parliamentary Committees—
one of the House of Lords, in 1868, the other of the House of
Commons, in 1869, and the legislature has seen fit to extend the
scope of the Act of 1866, by an Act of the last session (32 and
33 Vic. c. 96). The working of this Act, and the public attention
called to the subject, has been attended with the happiest
results, both as regards the health of our army and navy, and
the sanitary and moral improvement wrought in the unhappy
women who have come within the scope of its provisions. So

much so, that we read in the report of the above-mentioned
Committee of the House of Commons :—

"4. Although the Act has only been in operation two years and
a half, and at some stations only seven months, strong testimony
is borne to the benefits, both in a moral and sanitary point of
view, which have already resulted from it.

"5. Prostitution appears to have diminished, its worst features
to have been softened, and its physical evils abated."—P. iii.

This Act, however, is something more than a means of imparting
health both physical and moral, it forms the commencement of
a new legislative era, being a departure from that neutral position previously held by English law with respect to venereal
diseases, and admits that there is nothing in the nature of prostitution to exclude it from legislative action; but that, on the
contrary, it may be necessary to recognise its existence, and to
provide for its regulation, and for the repression, so far as possible, of its attendant evils; it is, in fact, the adoption—so far as
it goes—of the principle for which I have always contended, that
prostitution ought to be an object of legislation.

I believe I may claim, without vanity, to have in some measure
paved the way for, and guided the progress of this change, and I
hail with satisfaction the advent of the time which has at length
arrived when we may contemplate work accomplished, and, guided
by the experience gained from results attained, consider what
more remains to be achieved.

Although the benefits that have resulted from the recent
legislation — as regards this special class of disease — are undoubted, there is great unwillingness in certain quarters to
extend them from a class to the nation, and a radical distinction is sought to be drawn between the case of the army
and navy and that of the civil population. Strange as it
may appear, the same arguments that were urged against interference by the legislature with venereal maladies previously to
the passing of the Contagious Diseases Bill—of whose futility
that measure is the strongest possible acknowledgment—are
still put forward with as much confidence as though they had
never received such authoritative refutation, and must still
be met and answered, so far as the civil population is concerned.
Opposition to legislative interference is still based mainly on

religious and moral grounds, the risk of encouraging sin, and
the injustice of curtailing individual freedom. I yield to no man
in my love of liberty and regard for religion. I am therefore
especially careful in the following pages to show that the interference which I propose with personal liberty is unhappily necessary both for the sake of the community at large, and of the
women themselves. Such interference is, in fact, not special—
it is the extension to venereal disorders of the principle on which
the Government endeavours to act in dealing with other forms
of preventable disease, nor have the objections on religious
grounds to the course which I propose any real foundation;
on the contrary, religion is on my side.

The fresh phase assumed by the question discussed in the ensuing pages has necessitated considerable changes and modifications on my part, and I find that much of the matter contained
in my first edition may now be conveniently omitted. The whole
work has been carefully revised and remodelled, and to a great
extent re-written; moreover, sources of information formerly
closed or unknown, are now open to me. My statistics are no
longer solely dependent on my own opportunities for investigation. I have been enabled to make use of the researches of
others, and much official assistance has been accorded to me. I
have described the actual state of prostitution at home and
abroad, and have shown the different methods of dealing with it
employed in this and other countries, thus rendering easy the
comparison between the state of things existing in England and
on the Continent, and the rival systems of legislation prevailing
here and there.

It will be seen that on a great part of the Continent the necessity for the RECOGNITION of prostitution by the State, and the
adoption of remedial and preventive measures, has long been
acknowledged, while in England such recognition has been, till
within the last few years, steadily refused, and is now conceded
only in the exceptional case of the army and navy. The Continental
system, owing to the way in which police supervision is there
carried out, has been termed the licensing system; the English,
under which prostitutes, except in districts to which the Contagious Diseases Act applies, are left to themselves, has been
termed the voluntary system.

In considering the attitude which it becomes us to assume towards prostitution, one fact must be carefully borne in mind, that it is no evanescent evil, but that it has existed from the first ages of the world's history down to the present time, and differs but little, and in minor particulars, in this the nineteenth century, from what it was in the earliest times. The records of the human race, from the Book of Genesis downwards, through the whole range of ancient and mediæval literature to the writings of our own day, bear witness to the perpetual presence among men of the daughters of shame. Kings, philosophers, and priests, the learned and the noble, no less than the ignorant and simple, have drunk without stint in every age and every clime of Circe's cup; nor is it reasonable to suppose that in the years to come the world will prove more virtuous than it has shown itself in ages past. From time to time men's purer instincts, revolting from the sin, have striven to repress it; but such efforts have too often ended in failure, and entailed disasters more terrible than those from which relief was sought;* and it is evident that it would be unreasonable to expect any other result. Equally irrational is it to imagine that this irrepressible evil can exist without entailing upon society serious mischief; though incapable of absolute repression, prostitution admits of mitigation. To ignore an ever-present evil appears a mistake as fatal as the attempt to repress it. I am, therefore, an advocate of RECOGNITION.

It is high time for us to get the better of "a fear that starts at shadows." This word RECOGNITION may sound very dreadful, and be regarded by many as the precursor of a coming deluge of continental immorality. But what is the real fact? Is not recognition already accorded by society? Who are those fair creatures, neither chaperons nor chaperoned, "those somebodies whom nobody knows," who elbow our wives and daughters in the parks and promenades and rendezvous of fashion? Who are those painted, dressy women, flaunting along the streets and boldly accosting the passers-by? Who those miserable creatures, ill-fed, ill-clothed, uncared for, from whose misery the eye recoils, cowering under dark arches and among bye-lanes? The picture has many sides; with all of them society is more or less acquainted.

---

* At Berlin, repeatedly, see page 139.

Why is the state—that alone can remedy a condition of things that all deplore—alone to refuse recognition ? The voluntary system has been tried long enough with its affected ignorance and empty parade of hospitals, penitentiaries, and asylums. Individual efforts are powerless to effect either the cure of disease or the reformation of the prostitute. The nation's weakness can be assisted only by the nation's strength; and I propose to show that concentrated effort, sanctioned by authority, can alone stay the ravages of a contagious and deadly disorder, and that only by methodical and combined action, and by gradual and almost imperceptible stages can any moral cure be effected.

To the licensing system of the continent I am as strongly opposed for the reasons given in the text as I am to the voluntary system hitherto adopted in England—the necessary consequence of the neutral position assumed by the legislature. My examination of the character of prostitution—the causes that produce, and the evils that result from it—leads me to this conclusion, that the consequences of RECOGNITION must be threefold, and embrace PREVENTION, AMELIORATION, and REGULATION. For the sake of greater clearness I have devoted a separate chapter to each of these three divisions.

Although some of the causes of prostitution are undoubtedly beyond the reach of legislation, others are clearly amenable to it. To these last I address myself in the chapter on Prevention. Thus I propose to diminish the amount of prostitution by putting an end so far as possible to the over-crowding of families, and making better provision for the relief and suitable employment of women. With this object also I propose to remodel the laws relating to seduction, making the seducer substantially responsible for the support of his bastard offspring,—providing facilities for procuring affiliation orders—and assisting the pregnant woman during her confinement. Such legislation would, I am fully persuaded, diminish the number of seductions by increasing the responsibility thereto attaching, and would as a necessary consequence decrease the amount, not only of prostitution but also of ILLEGITIMACY and INFANTICIDE. With this object, I demand that the funds of the Foundling Hospital, producing as they now do an annual revenue of the present value of £11,000, and an assured income within the present century (according to the

Charity Commissioners) of £40,000 a year, shall for the future be applied more in accordance with the intention of the founder than they are at present.

I could hardly have avoided, had I wished to do so, alluding to the kindred subjects of ILLEGITIMACY, BABY-FARMING, and INFANTICIDE, following as they do, with prostitution, in the wake of seduction. It seems to me that all these forms of evil, germane to and dependent on each other, should be the subjects of legislation, and I have gladly availed myself of the opportunity of pointing out the direction which that legislation should in my opinion take. It seems to me that the mischiefs attendant on SEDUCTION, PROSTITUTION, and ILLEGITIMACY, require careful and comprehensive handling. These evils are all to a certain extent preventable, and the agency to which any one of them is amenable is capable of dealing with all the rest. I propose the formation of a GOVERNMENT BOARD, to which might be intrusted the working of the amended bastardy laws and the Contagious Diseases Act, the care of illegitimate children, and the amelioration of fallen women. By this means the various evil consequences of seduction would be subjected to that methodical and organised action which it seems to me essential to provide, if we desire to deal effectually with evils too vast and too difficult for private enterprise. To the preventive measures advocated in the following pages I apprehend little hostility, as it is agreed on all hands that the temptations to adopting a life of prostitution should be removed as far as possible ; but when I insist upon the duty of REGULATION and AMELIORATION, I find that my more timid friends fall away from me, and accuse me of countenancing sin, and of encouraging people in immorality by making the consequences of their evil ways less painful and degrading. I repudiate this unjust accusation as a cruel calumny, and am sure that no impartial reader, after examining my proposals, and the reasons by which I support them, will consider it to be well founded. It seems to me vain to shut our eyes to the fact that prostitution must always exist. Regret it as we may, we cannot but admit that a woman if so disposed may make profit of her own person, and that the State has no right to prevent her. It has a right, however, in my opinion, to insist that she shall not, in trafficking with her person, become a medium of communicating disease, and that, as she has given herself up to an occupation dangerous to herself and others, she must, in her own interest and that of the community, submit to supervision. My proposals go to this extent, and no further,—viz., to make the evil that we cannot repress as little injurious as possible. I desire to protect both society at large, and the individual, from the permanent injury at present inflicted by a highly contagious and virulent disorder. I desire also to heal the sick prostitute, and to cleanse her moral nature. The State must moreover set its face against any one, man or woman, making a profit of another's prostitution. I may here observe that it unhappily appears necessary to extend toleration to persons who keep accommodation-houses, otherwise hotels, coffee-houses, and other places of public resort will become debased.

If, in spite of all the precaution that can be taken, the woman becomes a prostitute, our next object should be to attempt to ameliorate her condition, so as to enable her to pass through this stage of her existence with as little permanent injury to herself and as little mischief to society as possible. This is the more important because I prove that the great mass of prostitutes in this country are in course of time absorbed into the so-called respectable classes, and I maintain that in proportion as they are assisted or neglected during their evil days will they assume the characters of wives and mothers with a greater or less degree of unsoundness in their bodies and pollution in their minds. Notwithstanding the incalculable importance of working such reformation as may be possible in these unhappy women, no adequate effort in this direction has ever yet been made, and it is a lamentable fact that while the penitentiaries and asylums on the one hand effect but little good, and are at once expensive and useless, on the other the present hospital system is inadequate to the task of coping with the diseases incidental to prostitution.

To give access to and control over the woman whose amelioration we desire to accomplish, it seems to me absolutely necessary that the Contagious Diseases Act should be extended to the civil population, for by means of its machinery alone can we discover and detain till cured the women afflicted with syphilitic diseases, and in no other way that has occurred to me can the supervision necessary for enabling us to work a gradual improvement in their lives be obtained. In our efforts to ameliorate the prostitute, we must doubtless tolerate much that we would willingly discountenance, but of two evils we must choose the least.

In the consideration as to the advisability of extending the above-mentioned Act, the expenditure that must be thereby incurred, though not a primary, is undoubtedly an important element. I have entered fully into the necessary calculations, and I believe that the figures which I have placed before my readers will convince them that the expenditure will be moderate, when weighed with the benefits obtained.

The reader who is a conscientious parent must perforce support me; for, were the sanitary measures I advocate once in operation, with what diminished anxiety would he not contemplate the progress of his boys from infancy to manhood? The statesman and the political economist are mine already, for are not armies and navies invalidated—is not labour enfeebled—is not even population deteriorated by the evils against which I propose we should contend? The sympathies of all who can look kindly upon the sick, the sorry, and the fallen, must gain new impulse from the study of the facts, figures, and deductions, possibly new to them, which I have here marshalled for their use.

I shall have occasion, in the body of the text, to express my thanks to several gentlemen whose communications I have turned to good account. My public acknowledgment is more especially due to Lord Stanley, who—with the ready appreciation of a true statesman—at once saw the importance of the continental information I sought for, and willingly instructed our Ministers at the different Foreign Courts to collect the statistics which my readers will find fully set out in Chapter V., on Prostitution Abroad.

To the Registrar General, and to my kind friend, Dr. Farr, I beg to tender my thanks for the correction of Tables, which, without their assistance, I could not have obtained. To Captain Harris, Assistant Commissioner of Police, I here acknowledge my indebtedness, and to many others to whom I have submitted my proof-sheets, and who, in authenticating the correctness of their statements, have added so much to the value of this book.

17, QUEEN ANNE STREET,
November, 1869.

TABLE OF CONTENTS.

ERRATA.

Page 13, line 22, *for* "live" *read* "lived."

,, ,, 3rd line from bottom, *for* "remains" *read* "remained.

,, 58, line 19, *for* "this" *read* "these."

,, 68, line 40, *for* . *read* ?

,, 83, line 24, *for* "209" *read* "155."

,, 85, line 20, *for* "by which means" *read* "by means of."

,, 109, head-line, *for* "des filles" *read* "de filles."

,, ,, line 33, no accent over "engage."

,, 113, "for females" in brackets.

,, 128, 6th line from bottom, *for* "soda" *read* "sodæ."

,, 257, line 8, *for* 1,100 *read* 1,400.

,, ,, line 9, *for* 14,300 *read* 16,800.

,, ,, line 10, *for* 10,400 *read* 9,600.

,, ,, Also, read note thus :

* Thus, according to the calculations of page 254, the annual expense for the metropolis would not exceed £56,000, and might fall as low as £34,300 (even if all the beds
provided were always occupied), instead of amounting to £100,000, as estimated by
Mr. Simon.

CHAPTER I.

PROSTITUTION DEFINED.

ETYMOLOGY would, of course, at once suggest a "standing forth, or plying for hire in open market," as a definition of the word prostitution. Charitable and refined persons instinctively recoil from its general use, under the very natural impression that the essence of "prostitution" is not so much *the receipt of consideration* as *community;* but, on the other hand, many forcible divines and moralists have maintained that all illicit intercourse is prostitution, and that this word is as justly applicable as those of "fornication" and "whoredom"* to the female who, whether for hire or not, voluntarily surrenders her virtue. According to them, her first offence is as much an act of prostitution as its repetition.

For the purpose of the politico-statistical researches which the French administrators have, since the time of the first Republic, made into prostitution, as well as everything else, they arrange disorderly women under two heads, *femmes débauchées* and *prostituées.* The former, instead of being, as would at first sight appear, a generic term, seems to distinguish the numerous group known as *femmes galantes* and *filles clandestines,* and corresponds with the "kept mistresses" and more reserved class of prostitutes in this country. Over it, while a certain degree of self-respect is preserved, the police neither assert nor can maintain control. Its members enjoy to the full extent their civic rights, and a maxim of law is acknowledged in their favour, which their sisters of this country are obliged to maintain for themselves,—often to the disgust, and occasionally to the amusement, of the public. "Mulieris, quæ non palam sed passim et paucis sui copiam facit, actio competit adversus eum qui eam meritricem vocavit."

Into the second class, which answers to our common street-walkers, the French authorities do their best to drive such of the first as they consider to have forfeited their independent position. It is held that the legally established and repeated exercise of fornication as a calling, combined with public notoriety thereof, arrest *in flagrante,* proved by witnesses other than the informer or the police agent, constitute the "prostitute." The prostitute has been more particularly described by a French author as the woman who abjures society, repudiates its laws, and forfeits all claims upon it, by adopting those "habitudes scandaleuses hardiment et constamment publiques," through which she passes into "cet état de brutalité scandaleuse dont l'autorité doit réprimer les excès."†

---

* *Whore,* is past tense of verb to *hire,* means *one hired.*—HORN TOOKE.
  Dutch, *Hoer;* Swedish, *Hoera;* German, *Hure;* Anglo-Saxon, *Hure;* Danish, *Hore.* Derived from *Hyran, conducere,* to hire. "W" has been idly prefixed, it is said.
† Parent-Duchâtelet, troisième édition, tom. i. p. 25.

According to the Board of Public Morals at Berlin, all voluntary sexual abandonment for a consideration is held to be prostitution. The necessity of defining not only "a prostitute" but "a common prostitute" may be seen from a perusal of the evidence on which is formed the report of the Select Committee on the Contagious Diseases Act, printed by order of the House of Commons, and lately published (July, 1869) :—

158. To the question by the Chairman, The Hon. T. C. Vivian,] What other new clause would you propose ?—Mr. Sloggett, Visiting Surgeon to the Devonport Lock Hospital, replies: I think that a new clause should be introduced defining more exactly the term "common prostitute."

159. What clause is there in this Bill which defines the term "common prostitute" ?—There is no such clause.

160. How would you propose to define a common prostitute ?—I would first define them as women who habitually gain their livelihoods, partly or wholly, by the proceeds of prostitution.

161. Sir John Pakington.] Is there in the law of England no definition of a prostitute ?—I think not.

374. Again, Dr. Brewer asks,] What is your definition of a prostitute ? To which Mr. Parsons, Visiting Surgeon to the Portsmouth Lock Hospital, replies : Any woman whom there is fair and reasonable ground to believe is, first of all, going to places which are the resorts of prostitutes alone and at times when immoral persons only are usually out. It is more a question as to mannerism than anything else.

375. Must she be making her livelihood by it ?—Yes, she ought to be ; but, if you confine yourself to that definition, all I can tell you is, that your Act will never succeed. The amount of clandestine prostitution is very large. I think the definition here, of "common prostitute," is very objectionable, inasmuch as I have heard it stated, by those who wish to object to the Act, that you have no right to bring under the provisions of the Act what may be called the better class of prostitutes, who, they say, are not common prostitutes.

Mr. John Simon, the Medical Officer of Health to the Privy Council, said, in reply to a question (1301) put to him :—" I do not see any practical definition of prostitution which could include women wishing to practise clandestinely. How are you to prove clandestine prostitution ? Would those who propose such things take a woman on the mere ground of her having had sexual relations with more than one man, and put two and two together, and produce their evidence in a police court ? It seems to me to be a thing which could not be done. The only kind of prostitution which can be dealt with, I suppose, is prostitution carried on by women who make it their calling, and live in gangs in brothels, or who publicly solicit men."

Leaving those on whom the duty of passing Acts of Parliament devolves to discover the definition necessary for their purpose, I shall here content myself with a definition sufficiently accurate to point out the class of persons who ought, in my opinion, to become the objects of legislation, and shall assume, for the purpose of my present inquiry, that the fact of "hiring," whether openly or secretly, whether by an individual or a plurality in succession, constitutes prostitution.

CHAPTER II.

PROSTITUTION IN ENGLAND.

1. Extent of in London, Aldershott, &c.
2. Life and Career of Prostitutes.

To obviate the possibility of misapprehension, I remind the reader that I regard prostitution as an inevitable attendant upon civilized, and especially closely-packed, population. When all is said and done, it is, and I believe ever will be, ineradicable. Whether its ravages, like those of disease and crime, may not be modified by unceasing watchfulness—whether it may not be the duty of the executive, as a French writer suggests, to treat it as they do such ordinary nuisances as drains, sewers, and so forth, by diminishing its inconvenience to the senses, and, in fact, rendering its presence as little noticeable as possible, it will be my business to inquire in a future chapter. In the present I shall offer as complete a survey of that portion of it which stalks abroad, *tête levée*, in this metropolis, and other parts of the kingdom, as the facts at any English writer's disposal admit of.

The number of prostitutes in London has been variously estimated, according to the opportunities, credulity, or religious fervour of observers, and the width of interpretation they have put upon the word. To attempt to reconcile or construct tables upon the estimates I have met with would be a hopeless task. I can merely give a few of the more moderate that have been handed down by my predecessors. Mr. Colquhoun, a magistrate at the Thames Police Court, rated them at 50,000 some sixty years ago. The Bishop of Exeter spoke of them as reaching 80,000 ; Mr. Talbot, secretary of a society for the protection of young females, made the same estimate. The returns on the constabulary force presented to Parliament in 1839, furnished an estimate of 6,371—viz., 3,732 "known to the police as kept by the proprietors of brothels," and 2,639 as resident in lodgings of their own, and dependent on prostitution alone for a livelihood. It was estimated by the Home authorities in 1841, that the corresponding total was 9,409—which, I need hardly point out, does not include the vast numbers who regularly or occasionally abandon themselves, but in a less open manner.

I am indebted to the courtesy of Sir Richard Mayne, the late Chief Commissioner of Metropolitan Police, for the subjoined return, as well as for those of 1837 (made up in 1841) :—

A Return of the number of Brothels* and Prostitutes within the Metropolitan Police District, as nearly as could be ascertained at that date (May 20th, 1857).

Division	Number of Brothels					Number of Prostitutes			
	Where prostitutes are kept.	Where prostitutes lodge.	Where prostitutes resort.	Total.	Total returned in 1841.	Well dressed, living in brothels.	Well dressed, walking the streets.	Low, infesting low neighbourhoods.	Total.
A	—	—	—	—		—	—	—	—
B	—	135	18	153	181	16	144	364	524
C	14	92	46	152	83	168	150	—	318
D	10	113	16	139	93	49	188	289	526
E	30	110	54	194	206	74	85	387	546
F	26	—	19	45	181	60	120	300	480
G	3	77	72	152	360	26	165	158	349
H	209	217	45	471	289	132	420	1251	1803
K	—	402	17	419	882	13	435	517	965
L	—	184	193	377	275	108	329	365	802
M	12	138	28	178	178	13	71	583	667
N	53	98	34	185	152	87	142	216	445
P	3	33	29	65	56	63	67	98	228
R	46	66	36	148	122	69	116	216	401
S	—	52	36	88	96	8	90	133	231
T	—	12	—	12	107	—	12	94	106
V	4	37	6	47	4	85	82	92	209
Total	410	1766	649	2825	3325	921	2616	5063	8600
Do. 1841	933	1544	848	3325	—	2071	1994	5344	9409

A. Whitehall, the Parks, Palaces, Government Offices.
B. Westminster, Brompton, Pimlico, part of Chelsea.
C. St. James's, Regent-street, Soho, Leicester-square.
D. Marylebone, Paddington, St. John's Wood.
E. Between Oxford-street, Portland-place, New-road, and Gray's-inn-lane.
F. Covent Garden, Drury-lane, St. Giles's.
G. Clerkenwell, Pentonville, City-road, Shoreditch.
H. Spitalfields, Houndsditch, Whitechapel, Ratcliff.
K. Bethnal-green, Mile-end, and from Shadwell to Blackwall.
L. Lambeth and Blackfriars, including Waterloo-road, &c.
M. Southwark, Bermondsey, Rotherhithe.
N. Islington, Hackney, Homerton, &c.
P. Camberwell, Walworth, part of Peckham.
R. Deptford, Greenwich, and neighbourhood.
S. Kilburn, Portland, Kentish and Camden Towns to Cattle Market.
T. Kensington, Hammersmith, North End, Fulham.
V. Walham-green, Fulham, Chelsea, Cremorne.

* The word brothel, or rather the French word bordel, is said to come from *bord et eau*, because houses of ill-fame were at first established on the borders of rivers or close to baths. This is corroborated by old records of London, which prove that such houses, called stews, were excluded from the city of London, but were allowed over the water in Southwark. Jeannel thus describes one—"For the brothel it is the sign, and in default of the sign it is notoriety. It is the incoming and outgoing of strange men which constitute public acts giving cause for the intervention of the police."—JEANNEL, de la Prostitution, p. 214.

The headings of the above tables demand a few explanatory observations. It is, in the first place, desirable that the reader should understand the distinction between the three classes of houses, termed by the police, brothels. The first, or "houses in which prostitutes are kept," are those whose proprietors overtly devote their establishments to the lodging, and sometimes to the boarding, of prostitutes, and prostitutes only. At first sight it might appear that, by the phrase employed, were indicated houses in which prostitutes are harboured, fed, and clothed at the cost of speculators, who derive a revenue from the farm of their persons. Such is, however, not the intention of the framers of the document. The houses last mentioned are, doubtless, included in the first column of the above returns, but as will be seen from the last return, (page 6), these have now almost disappeared from the Metropolis.

By "houses in which prostitutes lodge," the reader must understand those in which one or two prostitutes occupy private apartments, generally with, though perhaps in rare cases without, the connivance of the proprietor. It often occurs, it must be remembered, that females of no virtue, are so desirous of preserving the appearance of it before those among whom they reside, that they will not introduce their paramours to their apartments; but both they and their domicile, being generally known to the police, both figure on the return. "Houses to which prostitutes resort" represent night houses —the brothels devoted to casual entertainment of these women and their companions, and the coffee-shops and supper-shops which they haunt.

The "well-dressed, living in lodgings" prostitute is supposed to be the female who, though to all intents and purposes common, extending her pursuit of acquaintances over the town at large, or limiting it to the places of public recreation, eschews absolute "street-walking."

The "well-dressed, walking the streets" is the prostitute errant, or absolute street-walker, who plies in the open thoroughfare and there only, restricting herself generally to a definite parade, whereon she may always be found by her friends, and hence becomes, of course, "perfectly well known to the police."

The "low prostitute, infesting low neighbourhoods," is a phrase which speaks for itself. The police have not attempted to include—in fact, could not have justly included, I might almost say—the unnumbered prostitutes, whose appearance in the streets as such never takes place—who are not seen abroad at unseemly hours—who are reserved in manners, quiet and unobtrusive in their houses or lodgings, and whose general conduct is such that the most vigilant of constables could have no pretence for claiming to be officially aware of their existence or pursuits. The recent (1869) Report on the Contagious Diseases Act enables us for the first time to show the proportions of common prostitutes to soldiers at Aldershott. Thus, Inspector Smith gave in a report proving that there were in June, 1869, 243 recognised prostitutes to about 12,000 troops. This paucity of prostitutes, according to Dr. Barr, causes some of them to have intercourse with 20 or 23 men in one night. Page 41.

I am further indebted to the good offices of Captain Harris, Assistant Commissioner of Police, for the subjoined return made up in 1868 :—

METROPOLITAN POLICE.

ABSTRACT RETURN OF THE NUMBER OF BROTHELS AND PROSTITUTES IN EACH DIVISION.

Police Division.	Number of Brothels and Places.					Number of Prostitutes.			
	Where Prostitutes are kept.	Where Prostitutes lodge.	Where Prostitutes resort.	Coffee Houses or other Places where Business is ostensibly carried on, but which are known to the Police to be used as Brothels or places of accommodation for Prostitutes	Total.	Well-dressed living in Brothels.	Well-dressed living in Private Lodgings.	In low Neighbourhoods.	Total.
A. or Whitehall	...	141	2	18	161	...	167	310	477
B. Westminster	...	106	1	21	128	...	227	10	237
C. St. James'	...	7	3	15	25	...	128	162	290
D. Marylebone	...	171	8	12	191	10	371	136	517
E. Holborn	1	...	1	21	23	1	2	427	430
F. Covent Garden	1	86	35	12	134	...	29	235	264
G. Finsbury	...	126	2	11	139	...	...	623	623
H. Whitechapel	...	350	9	16	375	...	133	799	932
K. Stepney	...	149	34	21	204	...	144	228	372
L. Lambeth	...	19	23	19	61	...	14	314	328
M. Southwark	...	127	...	15	142	...	247	186	433
N. Islington.	...	43	1	4	48	...	...	65	65
P. Camberwell	...	125	6	12	143	...	144	415	559
R. Greenwich	...	...	...	5	5	...	128	45	173
S. Hampstead	...	193	1	4	198	...	236	110	346
T. Kensington	...	12	...	...	12	...	33	85	118
V. Wandsworth	...	27	...	1	28	...	23	53	76
W. Clapham	...	23	1	6	30	...	61	50	111
X. Paddington	...	51	5	16	72	...	68	96	164
Y. Highgate	...	...	...	...	...	...	...	...	...
Total	2	1756	132	229	2119	11	2155	4349	6515

Metropolitan Police Office, 4, Whitehall Place,
19th November, 1868.

THOMAS KITTLE,
Superintendent.

The falling off (amounting almost to extinction of the class) of the number of "houses where prostitutes are kept," which is shown by the table of 1868, cannot fail to strike the reader, the number given being two only as against 410 in 1857 and 933 in 1841. It appears that of the eleven prostitutes returned, as inhabiting such houses, one only resides in one of these houses, and ten in the other; this latter is kept by a French woman. It is satisfactory to find that this class of house is, if we may trust the police, rapidly disappearing from London. It is not too much to say that the Brothel where prostitutes are kept is an institution alien to English feelings, and that even if the Government should sanction the maintenance of such houses, which is far from probable, public opinion may be confidently expected to work their extinction. I may here call attention to a lesson taught us pretty clearly by these returns, which is, that to attempt to put down prostitution by law is to attempt the impossible. Notwithstanding the numerous prosecutions and parish raids which have been directed against prostitutes and their dwellings during the past few years, there were in the year 1868 1756 houses where prostitutes lodge, against 1766 in 1857. What can show more strongly the impossibility of, by the arm of the law, suppressing prostitution? Eleven years ago I pointed out that if a prostitute is prosecuted for plying her trade in one parish, she will only move into another; the result has proved the truth of my prediction, and recent failures add their testimony to that of world-wide experience, and prove the impolicy of making attempts of this nature, except in cases when the houses proceeded against are shown to be productive of open scandal, or a cause of intolerable annoyance.

I must observe that these returns give but a faint idea of the grand total of prostitution by which we are oppressed, as the police include in them only those women and houses whose nature is well and accurately known to them. There can be little doubt that numbers of women who live by prostitution lead apparently respectable lives in the lodgings or houses which they occupy; but all such are necessarily excluded from the returns.

Were there any possibility of reckoning all those in London who would come within the definition of prostitutes, I am inclined to think that the estimates of the boldest who have preceded me would be thrown into the shade. A few figures from the census tables may furnish material for more thought on this head than would be due to a wilderness of random conjectures.

In the year 1851, 42,000 children were born alive in England and Wales upon a total of 2,449,669 unmarried women, among whom widows were included for the purposes of calculation, between the ages of fifteen and fifty-five, or 1·7 per cent. Each of these mothers has taken the first step in prostitution; and, conceding to each the trifling expectation of five years of unreformed life, we shall find that 210,000, or one in twelve, of the unmarried females in the country above the age of puberty have strayed from the path of virtue. This approximation may be objected to as erroneous, inasmuch as one woman may have two, three, or four illegitimate children; but this is balanced by the un-

doubted fact that an enormous number of illicit connexions are un-
fruitful, or result in premature or unregistered births.

The Government commentator upon the Census argues from the
above figures, that if as many unmarried women are living irregularly
to every child born out of wedlock, as there are *wives* to *every child* born
in wedlock—viz., 1000 to 212—then 186,920, or 1 in 13, of the unmarried women must be living so as to contribute as much to the births
as an equal number of married women.

The registered births in 1851, out of 212,293 unmarried women in
London, were 3203. The application of the first of the above formulæ
gives 16,331, and of the second, 15,000 as the irregular indigenous connexions of this city, but affords no guide to the extent of its *common*
prostitutions.

In the census of England and Wales for the year 1861, I find the
following suggestive remarks :—

"BACHELORS AND SPINSTERS.

" While the number has increased, the proportion of bachelors and
of spinsters at all the ages between 20 and 40 has decreased ; and the
husbands and wives at those prolific ages have not only increased in
number, but in proportion. Thus the wives of the age of 20—40 were
1,608,216 in 1851, and 1,846,514 in 1861, the increase having been
nearly two hundred thousand.

The spinsters of the age of 20—40 were 1,229,051 in 1851, only
60,665 more than the numbers unmarried at the same ages ten years
ago. The bachelors of the age of 20—40 were 1,198,050 in 1851, and
so rapidly do they abandon this state, that their numbers are scarcely
increasing ; they amounted to 1,201,576 in 1861.

Those who dread the depopulation of England, will observe with
satisfaction the resources which the country commands in this reserve
both of spinsters and bachelors, while the economists will see that prudence is exercised to an extent which Malthus scarcely anticipated.
Besides 944,714 girls of 15, and under 20, there were more than a
million and a half (1,537,314) spinsters of the age of 20 and upwards
in England, including 643,366 of 20—25, and 307,633 of 25—30, and
168,100 of 30—35, and 109,952 of 35—40 ; at 40—60 their numbers
fell to 223,205, at 60—80 to 78,618, at 80—100 to 6,440. Twenty of
these spinsters were centenarians. To 100 men of the age of 20 and
upwards, 28 are bachelors ; to 100 women of the corresponding ages,
27 are spinsters. Between the ages of 20—40 of 100 women, 39 are
spinsters, 58 wives, and 3 are widows.

"WOMEN LIVING IN CELIBACY AND OTHERS.

" To complete this view of the population, it is right to bring into
account the number of unmarried women who bore 423,171 children in
the ten years 1851—60, when 6,048,479 children were born in wedlock
by an average number of 2,757,705 wives of the age of 15, and under
55.

" 42,317 children of unmarried women are registered annually.
Now, 100 wives of the age of 15—55 bear 22 children, 21,933 annually,

consequently 192,938 married women of the age of 15—55 would bear 42,317 children. The inference is probable, then, that as far as child-bearing women are in question, 192,938 must be added to the wives and deducted from the spinsters. Of women of the age of 15—55, about three millions are married, or are otherwise to the same extent as married women bearing children, and one million are living in a state of celibacy.

"While out of 100 married women of the age of 15—55, full 21—9 bear children annually. 100 unmarried women bear children in the proportion of 1·7.

"If the mothers of all the children are of the ages 20—40, then 35·0 in 100 married women, and 3·3 unmarried women, bear children annually; one in three married women of the age 20—40 bears a child annually; and of the unmarried women of that age the proportion is one in 30. Allowing for unregistered births, this proportion is not overstated."*

Having briefly called attention to the vast extent of the evil with which we have to contend, I will now endeavour to supply the reader with some general idea of the unfettered domestic life and haunts of London prostitutes, which, in default of better experience, we can presently bring to bear, with what information we may have as to the present state of our law, towards estimating the practicability of assimilating it to any of the laws which prevail abroad, or otherwise improving it. For the sake of clearness, I shall briefly notice under separate heads :—

1. HOMES—viz., *dress houses; houses in which prostitutes lodge.*

2. HAUNTS—viz., *introducing houses; accommodation houses; casinos and pleasure gardens; the public streets.*

Dress Houses.—The description of brothels called dress houses was much more prevalent a few years ago than is the case at present. It appears from the police returns for 1868, that there are now only two such houses in the Metropolis, containing between them 11 inmates.† They were maintained to some extent by persons who furnished board, lodging, and clothes to a number of prostitutes whom they sent out into the streets under guard of servants, or kept at home to receive visitors. The girls, who, it is needless to say, were of the most utterly degraded class, received but a small share of the wages of their sin; their condition was almost as abject as the *filles numérotées* of the Continent in general, and they were far more unprotected than those of Berlin, especially against persons speculating in them. The spread of venereal taint was not, as might be imagined, more favoured by this most revolting phase of the evil than by any other. The brutalized woman-farmers had, it is true, no more bowels of compassion for the male sex than for their stock-in-trade, and would drive into the streets with taunts and curses the diseased unfortunate. But the evil reputa-

---

* Vol. III. General Report, p. 21.

† I am informed that the exception in London is the rule in Edinburgh. It will appear in a subsequent chapter, there is less disease in brothels conducted on the French principle than among isolated prostitutes. I do not know whether the Scotch brothels can boast a similar advantage.

tion which an establishment might acquire by being a focus of disease, induced them to adopt a certain degree of care and precaution. To show, however, the dangers to which the unwary might be exposed under that system, I may mention a case that came under the notice of a friend of my own :—

In the year 1858 his sympathy and curiosity were awakened by the behaviour of a very handsome girl, who, seemingly against her will, was very urgently forced upon his notice by a brothel-keeper, who was hawking her about the streets. Acquiescing in the offer of her company and paying the demands of the house, he put some searching questions to the girl. She at first half confessed slight indisposition, but on his avowing himself a medical man, and showing clearly enough that his curiosity like his gift was dictated by mere charity, she submitted to a superficial examination. No more was required to prove that she was a mass of syphilis.

The rouged and whitewashed creatures, with painted lips and eye-brows, and false hair, accustomed to haunt Langham Place, portions of the New Road, the Quadrant, the Peristyle of the Haymarket Theatre, the City Road, and the purlieus of the Lyceum, were the most promi-nent gangs of this description in London. They were watched by persons of their own sex, employed purposely to prevent their abstrac-tion of the lodging-house finery, and clandestine traffic with men. These wretched women, virtually slaves, though nominally free, with bodies and time no longer their own, were restricted, for the con-venience of the real proprietors, to certain parades or beats, and from year's end to year's end might be observed on the same side of one particular street, and within a few hundred yards or less of one par-ticular spot. If their solicitations proved unsuccessful, their exertions were stimulated by the proprietor in person, who would sally forth from her den to aid the canvass, to admonish and to swear ; and some-times by the sentinel in charge, who assumed for the time being these functions of authority.

Women under like sad conditions may still be observed in some of the principal streets of London, but I am happy to say a great improve-ment has taken place in this respect during the last twelve years. There still exist establishments in which the women live with their landlady, by whom they are provided with food, dress, and lodging, all which are charged to the women at an exorbitant price, and the landlady usually contrives to keep them in her debt ; they have, however, the right of receiving and retaining their own money, and the privilege of accepting or declining, at their own discretion, the attentions offered by their visitors.

Houses in which Prostitutes Lodge.—I must now briefly notice the domi-ciliary arrangements of the various classes of independent prostitutes. These are so influenced, like our own homes, by the resources and taste of the individual—have so little local colour—and are besides so exceedingly well understood among men, that accurate pictures at any length would be as superfluous as fancy sketches would be out of place.

If we enter the house, or apartment, in a suburban neighbourhood—where, perhaps, the occupier of the shop below is non-resident—of the first-class prostitute, we find it neat or slovenly, plain or elegant, according to its mistress's income, the manners and tastes of her admirers, and her tendency to sobriety or the reverse. We have cheap and respectable lodgings, in reputable quarters of the town, wherein young and pleasing women of unambitious temperament will reside for years, receiving no visitors at home, anxiously guarding their characters there, and from choice involving themselves in no more sin than will serve to eke out their modest earnings, or provide a slender maintenance, which they may have been precluded from earning in their normal walk of life by the first false step. This numerous band, who, keenly alive to their painful position, willing to do better, unwilling— even for the sake of those wondrous magnets, dress and admiration— to join the ranks of the flashy and dissipated, are the proper objects of sympathy. London holds hundreds of them, not too far gone for true, permanent reform; and success would richly reward a far larger expenditure than can be expected at the hands of private charity.

These present us with the least degraded aspect of prostitution, but both in the western and eastern districts, especially in the latter, are to be found a great number of lodging-houses crowded together, in certain neighbourhoods of no fair fame, and called generically, in police reports, "notorious brothels," devoted especially to the reception of prostitutes. They are clean or dirty—comparatively well or ill-furnished, according to the capital embarked in them. From houses in St. John's Wood, Brompton, and Pimlico, to the atrocious slums of Blackfriars and Whitechapel, there are, of course, many steps, and with the rent at which the proprietors offer their apartments varies, of course, the style of the sub-tenants. In point of morality, there is, naturally, no difference; and in the general internal propriety, little enough. The most decently-minded woman who takes up her quarters in a circle of prostitutes, and, though she has a private apartment in which to receive visitors, betakes herself for society and distraction (as do always the inmates of such houses) to the common kitchen, must speedily fall to the common level. She finds that modesty and propriety are considered offensive hypocrisy. Liquor, in the intervals of business, is insisted upon by her companions and by the landlady, who makes a profit on the supply. Her company is sought for novelty's sake when she is a new comer, and her absence or reserve is considered insulting when she is fairly settled; so, if she had any previous idea of keeping herself to herself, it is very soon dissipated. She finds, when she has no male visitors, a sort of communism established in her rooms, which she can only avoid by resorting to the common hall in the dirty kitchen. There is no making head against this practice in lodging-houses generally, and hence the remarkable uniformity in the habits, manners, dress, and demeanour of the three or four sub-sections of their inhabitants.

They are usually during the day, unless called upon by their followers, or employed in dressing, to be found, dishevelled, dirty, slipshod and dressing-gowned, in this kitchen, where the mistress keeps her *table d'hôte*. Stupid from beer, or fractious from gin, they swear and chatter brainless stuff all day, about men and millinery, their own schemes and adventures, and the faults of others of the sisterhood. As a heap of rubbish will ferment, so surely will a number of unvirtuous women thus collected deteriorate, whatever their antecedents or good qualities previously to their being herded under the semi-tyranny of this kind of lodging-house. In such a household, all decency, modesty, propriety, and conscience must, to preserve harmony and republican equality, be planed down, and the woman hammered out, not by the practice of her profession or the company of men, but by association with her own sex and class, to the dead level of harlotry.

From such houses issue the greater number of the dressy females with whom the public are familiar as the frequenters of the Haymarket and the night-houses. Here they seem to rally, the last thing, from other parts of the town, when general society, and the most decent as well as lowest classes of prostitutes, are alike housed for the night. Here they throw the last allures of fascination to the prowler and the drunkard—hence wander to their lairs, disgusted and weary if alone—noisy and high-spirited if chance has lent them company.

To form an idea of the sort of life these women lead, we must listen to the evidence given at police courts. I extract the following from a leader in the *Times* for April 10, 1858, on evidence taken at the trial of an Italian, Giovanni Lani, who murdered one of these women for the sake of her jewelry :—

" The house appears to have been well tenanted, and was, no doubt, a lucrative investment for Madame Levi's capital. ' Three or four women lodged in the house. They provided their own dresses and jewelry.' Madame Silvestre was one of these lodgers. She was not a *femme galante*, but still had a habit of walking the streets late at night. She lived in the front room of the second floor with her friend M. Théophile Mouton, by whose commercial profits she was supported. Madame Silvestre returned home on the night in question at one o'clock, and Héloise Thaubin, leaving the prisoner in her room, came down and had supper with her friend in the room where M. Mouton was in bed. About half-past two o'clock she went back to her own room, and at this seasonable hour Madame Silvestre, wishing for amusement, went up and borrowed a book from Héloise, which the prisoner, in his shirt, handed out at the door. ' I then,' she says, ' went to bed, got up the next morning about twelve, and had breakfast at one.' Madame Silvestre, though not a *femme galante*, not only walked the streets, but was visited by male friends. ' When this occurred M. Mouton was generally out at his work.' This work M. Théophile Mouton tells us was the business of a commission agent. ' My business consists of selling every article that is intrusted to me. I have no offices, and never receive any business letters, because I am only a clerk, and have no business on my own account. I formerly used to deal in jewelry. The articles I sold were gilt or false jewelry.' Such is the account M. Mouton gives of his own professional pursuits. Besides these persons ' another man named Disher lived in the house. He carried on the business of a tailor. A woman lived with him who was called Mrs. Disher.' Mr. and Mrs. Disher quarrelled on the night of the 23rd of February, and it was in consequence of the latter leaving her room and sitting on the stairs all night that she was able to hear the deceased's groans, and to recognise Lani as he came down laden with the murdered woman's spoils.

"We have given this brief sketch of the house and its inmates, because No. 8, Arundel Court, was probably only a specimen of scores of other houses tenanted by this class of foreign adventuresses. They all seemed to have lived together with as little decency as brute animals. The last vestige of modesty which belongs even to the fallen seems to have been erased from the character of these cold, hard, money-grasping prostitutes and their paramours. They are well off, they wear their watches and chains and 'four rings on two fingers,' they are 'proud of showing their jewelry,' and they refuse 10 francs with disdain. The gentlemen lead an easy life. When the deceased's bed-room was broken open and her corpse found M. Théophile Mouton had not long returned home. 'He had been out for a walk with Mr. Disher during the day, and he brought home something for dinner.' In short, we are introduced to a community which is existing in the most self-complacent manner on the wages of infamy, and in which each individual has the air of considering that he or she is doing nothing in the world to be ashamed of."

The keepers of the old dress houses were mostly females of extreme avarice, and often ferocious manners—the former sharpened by the unprincipled atmosphere in which they live, and the latter by the necessity of preserving discipline among their tenants and dependents. They were ordinarily persons who had been bred to the business from youth, as relatives or old servants of their predecessors. Such an establishment was considered to be too lucrative to permit the idea of its dispersion upon the death or retirement of a proprietor ; and as a matter of fact, the lease, goodwill, and stock-in-trade of a brothel were, in such an event, disposed of like those of any other lodging-house. Women who had been themselves kept or frequented by men of property were sometimes able to found or purchase one or more of them. A large share of their tenants' earnings passed through their hands, and a liberal portion always remained there. They were highly paid for liquors and eatables they procured on account of male visitors ; and several instances are well authenticated of their having left ample means behind them, or having retired wealthy into private life. Things are, doubtless, changed.

It is to be feared, however, as we see, that there still exists a system analagous to that of woman farming, and resembling it only too closely, and that the dress house has merely given place to an institution too similar, viz., the dress lodging. Still the difference, though at first sight it may appear but one of name, is really one of degree. The dress girl was, as we have seen, the serf—the white slave of her proprietor, dependent on the latter for food and clothes and shelter, having no property of her own, or power over her own actions, but forced to fulfil the evil will of another by whom the fruits of her infamy were received. No property, no rights, no will, no hope—not one attribute, in short, of independent existence ; the right alone remains to suffer and decay, while wretches more vile even than herself grew rich by her ruin. The dress lodger, like the dress girl, receives from the owner of the house in which she resides, clothes, and board and lodging, but the wages of her guilt are paid to herself. She obtains from the man whom she has enticed to the house as much money as she can, and the proprietor's interest in the booty amounts either to a part or the whole, according as her skill in extortion is small or great. Like the dress girl, she is exposed to the tender mercies of a brutal tyrant, who expects the surrender to herself of the gains of her corruption, but to her is, at least, conceded the acknowledgment of separate rights and independent existence.

Introducing Houses.—The establishments of certain procuresses (Latin, *proxenetæ* ; French, *proxénète* : brokers, go-betweens, match-makers), vulgarly called "introducing houses," which resemble, to some extent, the *maisons à parties* kept for a similar purpose by somewhat used-up *lorettes* of the first water in Paris, are worth notice as the leading centres of the more select circles of prostitution here. Unobtrusive, and dependent upon great exterior decency for a good connexion, they concern us as little from a sanitary as from a police point of view, but are not without an influence upon the morals of the highest society. Their existence depends upon the co-operation and discretion of various subordinate accomplices, and on the patronage of some of the many wealthy, indolent, sensual men of London, who will pay any premium for assurance against social discredit and sanitary damage. Disease is therefore rarely traceable to such a source, and notoriety and scandal almost as seldom ; although impolitic economy on the gentleman's part, or indiscreet bearing towards any of the characters among whom he cannot be a hero, will induce them occasionally to hunt him and his follies into daylight, as a warning to others, not against the lusts of the flesh, but against sentiments which horse-leeches might consider illiberal. He usually obtains for his money security, comfort, and a superior class of prostitute, who is, according to his knowledge of the world or desires, presented to him as maid, wife, or widow—British, or imported direct from foreign parts. The female obtains fairly liberal terms, either directly from the paramour, or from the *entrepreneuse* (who, of course, takes good care of herself), the company of gentlemen, and when this is an object with her, unquestionable privacy. A number of the first-class prostitutes have relations with these houses, and are sent for as occasion and demand may arise. I have heard of one establishment at which no female is welcome who has not some particular accomplishment, as music or singing. I am told these establishments are much more common in New York than in London.

A stranger might be long in London—as he might, indeed, in Paris, where the *dame à parties* is a more prevalent institution—without hearing of, and still longer without gaining access to, this aristocracy of brothels. Their frequenters are often elderly, sometimes married, and generally men of exclusive sets, upon whom it would not be to the proprietor's interest to impose even unseen association with the stranger or the *roturier*. The leading persons in this line of business, who keep up regular relations with certain men of fashion, and sometimes means, make known to their clients their novel and attractive wares, one might almost say, by circular. A. finds a note at his club, telling him that a charming arrival, *de la plus grande fraicheur*,* is on view at Madame de L.'s. If he has no vacancy for a connexion, he may answer that a mutual friend, C., a very proper man, will call on such and such a day in —— road, or that Madame —— may drive the object round to his rooms at such another time; but that he has no great fancy at present for anything but a thoroughly warranted—in fact, an all-but modest person. All parties handle the affair with mock refinement. Sometimes money passes direct, as third persons have to be arranged with; at others, the broker, or procuress, ventures her capital, and leaves recompence to the honour of her friends—some of whom, of course, fleece her, others do what is considered fair, and now and then may be so generous that she is, on the whole, perhaps, better off than if she traded on strict cash principles only. The pungent anecdotes which occur to me respecting such houses and their frequenters, would, if properly disguised, go little way in proof of their existence—which, by the way, must be patent enough to those who habitually read law reports—and as their unvarnished recital here would give my pages an air of levity quite foreign to my intentions, I must suppress them, and request the reader to take for granted, for the purpose of this survey, the existence of these superior haunts of London prostitution.

Accommodation Houses.—Accommodation houses for casual use only, the *maisons de passe* of London, wherein permanent lodgers are not received, are diffused throughout the capital; neither its wealth nor poverty exempting a district from their presence. I have not, and I believe that no other person has, any guide to their numbers or classification. I have seen various numerical estimates of these and other houses in print, some of them professing to be from public sources; but I attach in this respect little value to even those I have obtained from the police, as their framers seem neither to have settled for themselves or for the public the precise meanings of terms they employ. In the restricted sense in which I have employed the words "accommodation house," I believe their number is limited. Few persons to whom I have spoken are now aware of more than four or five within two or three west end parishes, and as they almost invariably name the same, I am strengthened in my opinion that these lupanaria are few. It were more desirable, indeed, that they should multiply than either class of the brothel proper above described; or that clandestine prostitution should be largely carried on in houses devoted to legitimate trades, and inhabited presumedly by modest females. The thorough elasticity of prostitution is shown in this as well as other ways; that there being a demand for more numerous and dispersed places of transient accommodation than at present exists, within the last few years numerous coffeehouses and legitimate taverns, at which in former days no casual lodgers would have been admitted, without scrutiny, now give accommodation of the kind, for the part openly, or when not exactly so, on exhibition of a slight apology for travelling baggage. This appears very clearly from the return for 1868, in which, for the first time, these houses are noticed, and in which they reach the important figures of 229. In

* Sic in orig.

addition to these coffee-shops, there are many restaurants at which people can obtain private rooms by ordering refreshments. Many abandoned women also are occupiers of houses, and though they do not receive lodgers, will, for a consideration and by arrangement, permit their rooms to be made use of by other women for immoral purposes. They naturally have a large acquaintance among prostitutes of their own class, so that it may be reasonably supposed that a large amount of illicit intercourse is in this way carried on; at the same time these houses are so quietly kept, that police supervision is, as regards them, impossible. The number of houses in the occupation of prostitutes has, it is true, materially decreased of late years, but is still considerable, Pimlico being the chief centre around which these women congregate. Formerly accommodation houses abounded, and were to be found in all parts of the town, some streets being entirely filled with them. Among others, I may mention Oxendon Street, close to the Haymarket; the front doors of the houses in this street were habitually left half open. King's Court was another locale in which several houses had existed from time immemorial; the narrow thoroughfare of Wych Street had also acquired an evil notoriety, the houses in this street, though ostensibly shops, being in reality all used for purposes of prostitution. Parish prosecutions have achieved the closing of most of these dens of iniquity, and the police returns show that the number of such houses throughout the metropolis has decreased to 132, against 649, in 1857, and 848 in 1841.*

The few accommodation houses of London are generally thronged with custom, and their proprietors are of the same order as, and perhaps make even more money than, those of the lodging-houses. Their tariffs are various, and the accommodation afforded ranges between luxury and the squalor of those ambiguous dens, half brothel and half lodging-house, whose inhabitants pay their twopences nightly. I believe that disorder is rarely encountered or courted by any casual frequenters of such places, and that in all of them but the vilest of the vile, the proprietors would be for their own sakes the last to countenance it, and the first to call in the aid of the law. This prosecution by parishes has had the effect of increasing the expense of using such of these houses as still exist. At the date of the introduction of the former edition of this work, the average sum charged for the hire of a room was about five shillings, but now the sum exacted for similar accommodation is never less than ten shillings, in the West End of London. In the East End and over the water, the numbers and the tariff remain as small as they were twelve years ago.

PLEASURE GARDENS AND DANCING ROOMS.

The Garden at Cremorne.—It might seem rather late in the day to argue, on the grounds of its entertaining prostitutes among others, against the most beautiful public garden London can boast for the

---

* There can be no doubt of the advantages arising from the closing of such places, if only the demand for them was on the decline, but while public morals are what they are, the policy of closing them is, as I shall endeavour to show in a subsequent page, at least questionable.

amusement of her people, and which, like many others of its kind, has taken, despite of strong objections, a position among the *faits accomplis* of the age. The union of Terpsichore and Melpomene, long forbidden by puritanism, has now for some time been sanctioned by the magistracy ; large capital has been invested in providing local habitations for the young couple, and these are frequented without risk of more than nominal damage by great crowds of both sexes, all ranks, and all ages. No less than fifteen thousand people have been known to be present at Cremorne, on the occasion of the manager's benefit, and the nightly visitors during the fine season amount to between 1500 and 2000. As my present business, however, is with the demeanour of London prostitution, I must unwillingly limit myself to the consideration of public out-door amusements, with reference to that common feature only, and state some impressions of travel on a pleasant July evening from Charing-cross to Chelsea. As calico and merry respectability tailed off eastward by penny steamers, the setting sun brought westward Hansoms freighted with demure immorality in silk and fine linen. By about ten o'clock, age and innocence, of whom there had been much in the place that day, had seemingly all retired, weary with a long and paid bill of amusements, leaving the massive elms, the grass-plots, and the geranium-beds, the kiosks, temples, " monster platforms," and " crystal circle" of Cremorne to flicker in the thousand gas-lights there for the gratification of the dancing public only. On and around that platform waltzed, strolled, and fed some thousand souls—perhaps seven hundred of them men of the upper and middle class, the remainder prostitutes more or less *prononcées*. I suppose that a hundred couples (partly old acquaintances, partly improvised) were engaged in dancing and other amusements, and the rest of the society, myself included, circulated listlessly about the garden, and enjoyed in a grim kind of way the " selection" from some favourite opera and the cool night-breeze from the river.

The extent of disillusion he has purchased in this world comes forcibly home to the middle-aged man who in such a scene attempts to fathom former faith and ancient joys, and perhaps even vainly to fancy he might by some possibility begin again. I saw scores, nay hundreds, about me in the same position as myself. We were there—and some of us, I feel sure, hardly knew why—but being there, and it being obviously impossible to enjoy the place after the manner of youth, it was necessary, I suppose, to chew the cud of sweet and bitter fancies ; and then so little pleasure came, that the Britannic solidity waxed solider than ever even in a garden full of music and dancing, and so an almost mute procession, not of joyous revellers, but thoughtful, care-worn men and women, paced round and round the platform as on a horizontal treadmill. There was now and then a bare recognition between passers-by—they seemed to touch and go, like ants in the hurry of business. I do not imagine for a moment they could have been aware that a self-appointed inspector was among them, but had they known it never so well, the intercourse of the sexes could hardly have been more reserved—*as a general rule*, be it always understood. For my part, I was occupied, when the first chill of change was shaken off, in

quest of noise, disorder, debauchery, and bad manners. Hopeless task !
The pic-nic at Burnham Beeches, that showed no more life and merri-
ment than Cremorne on the night and time above-mentioned, would be
a failure indeed, unless the company were antiquarians or undertakers.
A jolly burst of laughter now and then came bounding through the
crowd that fringed the dancing-floor and roved about the adjacent sheds
in search of company ; but that gone by, you heard very plainly the
sigh of the poplar, the surging gossip of the tulip-tree, and the plash of
the little embowered fountain that served two plaster children for an
endless shower-bath. The *gratus puellæ risus* was put in a corner with
a vengeance, under a colder shade than that of chastity itself, and the
function of the very band appeared to be to drown not noise, but still-
ness.

The younger portion of the company formed the dances, and enjoyed
themselves after the manner of youth, but I may fairly say, without
offence to the most fastidious eye or ear. The *Sergent de Ville*, so necessary—if the semblance of propriety is to be preserved at all—to repress
the effervescent indecorum of the *bal Mabille* at Paris, would have been
here an offensive superfluity. The officiating member of the executive,
Policeman T, had taken up an amiably discreet position, where his
presence could in no way appear symptomatic of pressure, and the
chances seemed to be, that had he stood so posed until his interference
was necessary on behalf of public order, he might have been there to
this day.

Lemonade and sherry seemed to please the dancers, and the loungers
indulged the waiters' importunity with a rare order for bitter-beer. A
strongish party of undergraduates in drinking—all males—were deep-
ening their native dulness in a corner with bottled stout, and more
seasoned vessels struggled against depression with hot grog. In front
of the liquor-bar, called, in the language of the billographer, "the gas-
tronomic department," two rosy capitalists (their wives at Brighton or
elsewhere) were pouring, for mere distraction's sake, libations of fictitious Möet, to the memory of auld lang syne with some fat old *dames
de maison*, possibly extinct planets of the Georgian era. There was no
drunkenness here to take hold of. As I have before recorded, there
was among the general company barely vivacity, much less boisterous
disorder. Let me try the assembly for immodest, brazen-faced solicitation by women. I declare my belief that I never saw the notoriously
anti-sociable habit of English people more rigorously adhered to. Of
the character of the female visitors—let me always say *with some exceptions*—I could have little moral doubt, but it was clear enough that
self-proclamation by any great number of them was out of the question.
It was open to the male visitors to invite attention and solicit acquaintance. No gentlemanly proposition of the kind would have been
rebuffed, no courteous offer of refreshment, possibly, declined, but I am
firmly of opinion, that had the most eligible men present tarried in
hopes of overtures from the other side, they might have been there yet,
with Policeman T.

As to the costumes of the company I have little more to say, than
that pretty and quiet dressing was almost universal, and painted cheeks

a rarity; but one or two physical characteristics seem worth mentioning. I saw many an etiolated eye and blanched chlorotic complexion, due to want of sun and air, and general defibrinization, but not more noticeable here than in Mayfair. There was here and there a deplorable hectic flush, distinguishable enough from carmine; and I noticed a great prevalence of sunken eyes, drawn features, and thin lips, resulting from that absorption of the cellular tissue which leaves mere threads of muscle stretched upon the skull. Inasmuch as within my recollection women of the town had a well-known tendency to stoutness, and they now live no worse than heretofore, I am inclined to attribute these symptoms not so much (as is the vulgar error) to the practice of prostitution, as to the dancing mania, which has been the only remarkable change of late years in their mode of life, superadded in many instances to the action of early privations, and perhaps hard work in domestic service and millinery factories, upon naturally delicate or defective organizations.

There are other pleasure gardens in or about the London district, such as the gardens at North Woolwich, Highbury Barn, and Rosherville, but they do not call for any special notice, as, except that their frequenters are drawn chiefly from a lower class, they differ in no material respect from Cremorne.

The principal dancing-rooms of London are the two casinos known respectively as the Argyll Rooms and the Holborn. Formerly there was a striking difference between these two places, the one receiving the upper, the other the under, current of the fast life of London; now, however, there is little of this distinction noticeable, and the visitor in quest, not of amusement, but of information, may feel assured that a visit to one is for all practical purposes a visit to both. They are open for music and dancing every evening, except Sunday, from half-past eight o'clock to twelve. The visitor, on passing the doors, finds himself in a spacious room, the fittings of which are of the most costly description, while brilliant gas illuminations, reflected by numerous mirrors, impart a fairy-like aspect to the scene. The company is, of course, mixed. Many of the men resorting to such places seek no doubt the opportunity of indulging their vicious propensities; but the majority of the better class go merely to while away an idle hour, because, unblessed by home ties, and weary of the cold monotony of their club, they find it pleasant to consume the "*post prandial* weed" in some place where, while chatting with friends, they can hear good music and see pretty faces. The women are of course all prostitutes. They are for the most part pretty, and quietly, though expensively dressed, while delicate complexions, unaccompanied by the pallor of ill-health, are neither few nor far between. This appearance is doubtless due in many cases to the artistic manner of the make-up by powder and cosmetics, on the employment of which extreme care is bestowed. Few of these women, probably, could write a decent letter, though some might be able to play a little on the piano, or to sing a simple song. Their behaviour is usually quiet, little solicitation is observable, and all the outward proprieties of demeanour and gesture are strictly observed.

The proprietor, indeed, is careful to maintain the appearance, at least, of decorum among his visitors. Should any woman misconduct herself, she is pointed out to the door-keepers, with instructions not to admit her again to the rooms. No punishment could be heavier, no sentence more rigorously carried out. She will attempt in vain by disguise to avoid recognition, or by bribes to soften the watchful janitor. Her efforts will be met with some such rebuke as this : " It's no use trying it on, Miss Polly ; the gov'nor says you are not to go in, and, of course, you can't !' Her only chance of obtaining remission of the sentence is to induce some friend to plead with the proprietor on her behalf, who may, but does not always, re-admit her after an exile of three months, and on her promising to behave herself in the strictest manner for the future.

On the whole, judging of the women who frequent these rooms by their dress, deportment, and general appearance, the visitor might be inclined to suppose them to belong to the kept mistress rather than the prostitute class. This is, however, not the case, as, with a few exceptions, they fall within the latter denomination. Many of them, no doubt, have a friend who visits them regularly, and who makes them a fixed allowance, not sufficient to keep them altogether, but substantial enough to make them careful in selecting their customers, and careless about accepting the company of a man in any way objectionable. This arrangement is perfectly understood by the " friend" who pays his periodical visits, and to whom, of course, the woman is always at home. The sum expected by one of these women in return for her favours is about two or three sovereigns. Many will expect those who desire their company to stand them refreshment without stint, not only at the casino, but at some house of call later on in the night suggesting champagne or " phiz" as agreeable to their palate, and will be indisposed to return home until they have had their full evening's amusement. One woman merits a passing notice here, who has achieved a sudden notoriety, and given to the casino (previously to her appearance at it the least fashionable) a pre-eminence over its rival. There she holds a mimic court, attired unlike the rest of the frequenters, who come in their bonnets in full ball dress. She is surrounded by a crowd of admirers, idlers, and would-be imitators, and gives the tone to the establishment that she patronises. It is said that the diamonds worn by this woman are worth £5000. She is supplied daily from a florist in Covent Garden with a bouquet of the choicest flowers, amid which are interspersed specimens of the most beautifully coloured beetles, the cost being about 30s., and her habit on entering the rooms is to present this really splendid trifle to the female attendant at the wine bar, as a mark of her condescension and favour. On permission to visit her being requested, she would probably, like another celebrated " *fille de joie*," take out her pocket-book and, after a careless glance at it, reply that she was full of engagements, but that if the petitioner would call at her house at a given hour that day week, she would, perhaps, spare him some twenty minutes of her society, for which favour she might expect the modest sum of £25.

The casinos, music-halls, and similar places are closed at twelve o'clock; after that hour the search for dissipation must be extended to other places, and loose persons of both sexes may be found congregated in the divans and night houses situate in the Haymarket* and adjoining

* Although the aspect of the Haymarket is somewhat improved of late years, its condition is still disgraceful, and the following description of it by Albert Smith, in "Household Words," of the 12th September, 1857, is still, to a great extent, applicable:—

"About the top of this thoroughfare is diffused, every night, a very large part of what is blackguard, ruffianly, and deeply dangerous in London. If Piccadilly may be termed an artery of the Metropolis, most assuredly that strip of pavement between the top of the Haymarket and the Regent Circus is one of its ulcers. By day, the greater part of the shops and houses betray the character of the locality. Some there are, indeed, respectable; but they appear to have got there by chance, and must feel uncomfortable; the questionable ones preponderate. Observe the stale, drooping lobsters, the gaping oysters, the mummified cold fowl with its trappings of flabby parsley, and the pale fly-spotted cigars; and then look into the chemist's windows, and see, by the open display, in which direction his chief trade tends. Study the character of the doubtful people you see standing in doorways—always waiting for somebody as doubtful as themselves—and wonder what the next 'plant' is to be, which they are now cogitating. It is always an offensive place to pass, even in the daytime; but at night it is absolutely hideous, with its sparring snobs, and flashing satins, and sporting gents, and painted cheeks, and brandy-sparkling eyes, and bad tobacco, and hoarse horse-laughs, and loud indecency. Cross to the other side of the way, go out into the mud, get anywhere rather than attempt to force your passage through this mass of evil; for it will most probably happen—as if this conglomeration of foul elements was not enough to stop the polluted stream trying to flow on—that a brass band has formed a regular dam before the gin-shop, so dense that nothing can disturb it, except the tawdry bacchantes blundering about the pavement to its music. I am not an ultramoralist. I have been long enough fighting the battles of life upon town, to stand a great deal that is very equivocal, unflinchingly: but I do say, that this corner of the Haymarket is a cancer in the great heart of the Metropolis, and a shame and a disgrace to the supervision of any police. A convivial 'drunky,' who inclines to harmony as he goes home at night, when there is not a soul in his way to be annoyed, by expressing his confidence, through all changes, in dog Tray's fidelity, has been quieted, before this, by a knock on the head from a truncheon. A poor apple-woman, striving to earn a wretched pittance against the birth of an infant evidently not far off, is chased from post to pillar by any numbered letter of the alphabet; but here, wanton wickedness riots unchecked. The edge of the pavement is completely blockaded. If you happen to be accompanied by wife, daughter, sister, any decent woman, and to be waiting, or not waiting for one of the omnibuses that must pass there—go anywhere, do anything, rather than attempt to elbow through the phalanx of rogues, and thieves, and nameless shames and horrors.

"From an extensive continental experience of cities, I can take personally an example from three quarters of the globe; but I have never anywhere witnessed such open ruffianism and wretched profligacy as rings along those Piccadilly flagstones any time after the gas is lighted.

"It is during the weeks of Epsom, Ascot, and Hampton, that the disciples of Thurtell's school of pursuits hold high festival. Two or three years back, there were various betting houses here, with their traps always set open to catch their prey; but although these are abolished, something of the kind is still going on, which the police know (or pretend to know) nothing about. The swarm of low sporting ruffians hovering about here, at all times, is incredible. You know they have all figured, are figuring, or will figure, in card-cheating cases and dirty bill transactions. They have all the bandy legs and tight trousers, the freckled faces and speckled hands, and grubby, dubby nails that distinguish this fraternity. Theirs are the strong-flavoured cigar and highly-coloured brandy, the snaffle coat-links, and large breast-pin, the vulgar stock, and the hat-band—always the hat-band; is it a last clinging to respectability, to show that there was somebody belonging to them once? And when to this unsavoury locust-cloud the closing casino adds its different but equally obstructive

streets. These places are for the most part small, ill-ventilated rooms, at which wine and other liquor, and also solid refreshment, can be procured. Here there is no amusement except such as the visitors can provide for themselves. Much of the restraint on the part of the women observable at the other places to which I have referred is, therefore, laid aside, and a very general *abandon* in conversation and behaviour on the part both of men and women is freely indulged in, while the opportunity of soliciting custom is certainly not neglected. The early closing bill gave a blow to these places, from which, notwithstanding the present unsatisfactory state of the law, they have not recovered ; they are, however, neither so numerous nor so much frequented now as they were a few years ago.

Fast life in London has greatly changed during the last thirty years. It was the fashion formerly for those wishing to see life, as it is called, to go to the Theatre Royal, and between the acts to stroll into the saloons, and there look at the stout, over-dressed women who frequented these places, and resided in houses of ill-fame in the neighbouring slums. It was the correct thing to be taken after the theatre to Mother H.'s, and then to go to the "Finish," having previously visited the notorious saloon in Piccadilly. From all these dens the police were excluded, and scenes were enacted very different from those now witnessed at the casinos.

Some shades of prostitution unknown to the more fashionable West are to be discerned in the East End of London. To acquaint myself with these, I made a pilgrimage in company with Captain Harris, Assistant Commissioner of Police, to the notorious Ratcliffe Highway. We were attended by the Superintendent of the Executive Branch of the Metropolitan police, and two Inspectors. The night being very wet, the streets were comparatively empty, and therefore I can say little or nothing from personal observation about the condition of street prostitution in this district. I understand that it in no respect differs from what we see elsewhere. The first house we entered was one in which prostitutes reside. It was kept by a dark, swarthy, crisp-haired Jewess, half creole in appearance, who stated that she was a widow, and that having married a Christian, she had been discarded by her own people. To my inquiry whether she knew of many Jewesses who led a life of prostitution, she replied in the negative, giving as a reason that the Jews look after their people better than Christians, and assist them when in distress. The Police Inspectors corroborated her

---

swarm, and they all flutter about in the lamp-lights, amidst an admiring audience of pickpockets, flower-sellers, rich country fools, who think they are 'seeing life,' and poor scamps who show it to them, such a witch's cauldron is seething in the public eye, and splashing in the face of decency, as is quite intolerable in this land at this date.

"I entreat the intelligent magistrates in whose division ROGUES' WALK lies, to leave their dinner-tables some evening, and go and judge for themselves whether it is anybody's business to do anything towards the correction of this scene of profligacy. Why should no quiet person be able to walk upon its skirts, unmolested, and why should all modest ears and eyes be shocked and outraged in one of the greatest thoroughfares of this Metropolis ?"

statement, which seems to contradict the prevalent notion that houses of ill-fame are frequently kept by Jewesses.* We went upstairs, and saw the rooms, eight in number, which were let out to as many women. The landlady told us that they pay 2s. when they bring home a visitor, and she thought that on an average they are lucky when they bring two each in the course of the evening. This woman was clearly indisposed to let us into her secrets, seeing us accompanied by the Inspectors, and entered into a rambling statement as to the care and leniency with which she treated her lodgers when they were "out of luck." She asserted, and the statement was corroborated by the girls, that they kept themselves ; two may chum, or sleep together, when disengaged ; but they receive the money they earn, and are not farmed out. The utmost pressure put upon them is, perhaps, that they are induced to go out and persevere in prostitution when otherwise indisposed to do so. When ill, they apply to the hospital, and St. Bartholomew's appeared to be the favourite establishment. This house may be taken as a fair sample of the brothels existing in the East End of London.

The Inspectors next introduced us into a long, dirty room, behind a public-house. In the distance was a German band, such as one often sees in the streets. Several couples were waltzing, and other visitors were arranged round the room, smoking long pipes and drinking beer. We were next ushered into a large music-hall connected with a public-house. On the stage some interesting drama was going on, while the spectators drank and smoked ; the majority were men, but they were in many instances accompanied by their wives and sweethearts. To make observations on the latter was my object, and I noted that in and out of the passages and bar were passing crowds of well-dressed women, according to East End fashions ; some were prostitutes, but many were married women, according to the belief of my informants. This curious amalgamation—this elbowing of vice and virtue—constituted a very striking feature, and was to me a novel one. It is brought about, I presume, by the modern plan of these public-house amusements, enabling the mechanic, his wife and his daughters, to rationally spend the evening, as it is called, in witnessing plays, hearing music, and seeing dancing, at the same time that the man can smoke his pipe and drink his beer by the side of his wife. The landlords—two brothers, Jews, who told us they had been in Australia—assured us that they took the greatest pains to maintain order and decorum. My chief interest lay in considering the effect produced upon married women by becoming accustomed at these *réunions* to witness the vicious and profligate sisterhood flaunting it gaily, or "first-rate," in their language—accepting all the attentions of men, freely plied with liquor, sitting in the best places, dressed far above their station, with plenty of money to spend, and denying themselves no amusement or enjoyment, encumbered with no domestic ties, and burdened with no children. Whatever the purport of the drama might have been, this actual superiority

* On inquiry, I find that there are twenty houses of ill-fame where prostitutes either lodge or resort, that are kept by Jews or Jewesses ; five of the proprietors are males, and fifteen females.

of a loose life could not have escaped the attention of the quick-witted sex.

What the result may be remains to be seen, but the enormous increase of establishments similar to the above must, I think, tend to the spread of immorality both in the East and West End of London. One explanation that I have received of the phenomenon, and it seems to me a plausible one, is that it is not unusual for the mechanic's wife to have sisters who are frail, and to these are accorded the greatest measure of kindness, and a sort of commiseration, which not unfrequently culminates in their having a "drop o' gin" together, and so forgetting for a time their mutual troubles—for the mechanic and the mechanic's wife have their troubles, and very serious ones, in providing for their daily wants, and any persons connected with them whom they see well-dressed, and with money in their pockets, command a kind of respect, although the source from whence the means are obtained may be a disreputable one. This same mingling of vicious with presumably respectable women is also noticeable at the Alhambra and other music-halls at the west end of London, and in this respect they seem to me to exercise a more evil influence on the public morals than the casino, as to these last the notoriously profligate only resort.

It would be an endless task to examine into the features exhibited by prostitution in the different provincial towns throughout the kingdom. There may be slight differences in details, but the broad features are identical with those already presented to us in the Metropolis. Two places there are exceptionally circumstanced, and in them some special features will be looked for. Oxford and Cambridge have, through their Universities, one great cause of prostitution, viz., the presence in their midst of a floating population of unmarried males. Owing, however, to the restraints on indulgence imposed by university discipline, the amount of local prostitution is but little, if at all, in excess of the usual average of towns of similar dimensions, and it presents no features specially worthy of notice. I may, therefore, now pass on to another place where a large floating population of unmarried males is present, but the inducements to restraint above mentioned are absent. With the sanction of Sir Richard Mayne, and with an introduction to Dr. Barr, I made a visit to the camp and town of Aldershott to witness for myself the condition of prostitution at this great military centre, and to inquire on the spot into the state of things existing at the present day under the operation of the Contagious Diseases Act, which was applied to this district in April, 1867, though periodical examinations were not instituted until April, 1868. We were assisted in our investigations by Police Inspector Smith, whom I found a most useful cicerone in making my rounds in corners and places, that it would have been impossible to see or venture into without his support. There appears to exist a sort of tacit understanding between these women and the authorities that they shall be suffered to pursue their calling unmolested so long as they abstain from acts of flagrant indecency. Neither is there here any third party to make a traffic of their bodies, and grow rich on the wages of their guilt. The prostitute is free to exercise her calling, and to receive the profits of it for herself. She obtains lodgings at the rate of about 3s. 6d. a-week, payable *die in diem*, for the daily accruing quota of which the landlord calls upon her every morning. One of these lodgings into which I was introduced by the inspector may be taken as a fair specimen of the class. It was a small room on the first floor of a cottage, approached by a steep narrow staircase, furnished in the most primitive manner, containing only a bed with the usual covering, one or two rough chairs, and the other commonest necessaries of a bed-room. One only condition beyond punctual payment of the rent is attached to the tenancy. The landlord is usually the proprietor of a beer-house or some other place of public entertainment, which the lodger must patronise during her stay. She is required to spend her evenings there until the tattoo sounds at 9.30, after which hour she is free to go where she pleases. She is also expected to aid the landlord in the sale of liquor, both by inducing the soldiers to drink, and by accepting whatever drink may be offered to her by them. Most of the girls have or acquire a habit of drinking: some few abstain, and while accepting, find means to avoid partaking of the refreshment offered to them. They are sneered at by their more debased companions, but are distinguished by their superior dress, and greater neatness, spending, in fact, in this manner the money that they would otherwise squander, like their companions, in the beer-houses. There is at Aldershott no street prostitution permitted, the woman's hunting grounds are the above named public rooms. The daily gains are not large. The generous and prodigal son of Mars who has lately received his pay or his loot money will, perhaps, bestow half-a-crown in return for the favours granted to him, but the usual honorarium is 1s. For this poor pay, these wretched women are content to surrender their persons. To obtain a subsistence, a woman must take home with her about eight or ten lovers every evening, returning to her haunts after each labour of love—as a French woman would say having *fait son commerce*, to dance or drink beer until a fresh invitation to retire is received by her. As night approaches, each woman usually seeks her room, carrying with her ale or other stimulating liquor, which she shares with her fellow-lodgers, and wakes in the morning languid from the night's debauch to breakfast off beefsteaks and beer. Thus are her vile earnings grossly squandered, with nothing saved for an evil day. For help when her own resources fail her, she depends on the contributions of those of her companions whom chance has for the time being more befriended ; and in justice to these women, it must be said that they are always ready to afford each other this mutual assistance. I visited with the inspector the different public rooms, which were crowded with soldiers and women. To my surprise I saw no instance of drunkenness, no riot or romping, and heard no indecent jests or songs. This propriety of conduct may have been due to the word having been passed that the inspector was making his rounds with the two doctors ; if drunkenness or other disorderly conduct had been indulged in previously to our arrival, traces of it would, I should think, have remained. The lodgings before referred to are attached, or at least contiguous to the public rooms owned by the different landlords. They naturally do not afford sufficient accommodation for the

vast mass of Aldershott prostitution. Many of the women, therefore,
live in lodgings in the town, and as these apartments are at a considerable distance from the soldiers' haunts, they take their temporary
companions to rooms in their immediate neighbourhood that can be
hired for a short time for this purpose. We entered one of these dens.
In a room, opening on to a court, reached by a dirty street, and looking
more like an old rag and bottle shop than anything else, sat an old man,
huddled close up to the fire, surrounded by candlesticks ready for use,
while in a trussel bed, covered up with shawls and flannel, and propped
up by pillows, sat a woman, who must have been in her day remarkably
handsome, but on whom the hand of disease lay heavily. She had been
an out-patient at the Brompton Consumption Hospital, and had obtained
some relief there, but her complaint being incurable, she returned
home, though the bleak air of Aldershott did not agree with her ; and
truly as she lay there coughing and wheezing and grumbling, she
seemed a doomed being, whose life was not worth a week's purchase.
But what had these people to do with prostitution ? All and everything ! The inspector pointed out to me a range of cottages, with lights
in their windows ; each room contained a man and woman, and the
cottages all belonged to this aged and decrepit couple. It seems that
any woman desiring to use a room would come in for a candle to the
old man, who, in a few minutes, would crawl furtively to get his two
pence for the use of the room, which he would bring back to the old
woman lying at the receipt of custom, as above described. The daughter
of this precious pair was, at the time of my visit, in the hospital, under
treatment. She hires a room of her parents, paying them the rent
every morning, and is as noted a prostitute as any other wretched fre-
quenter of her father's miserable rooms. In a house of a similar nature
that we visited, we found the landlady engaged in washing, with her
two little children lying in bed asleep, with the happy smile of childhood on their faces, unconscious of the surrounding depravity, while
two boys scarcely in their teens were employed to collect the twopences
from their parents' customers. Thus is it that some, at least, of our
population are brought up, and a constant supply maintained of recruits
for the dangerous classes.

Having now surveyed the extent of prostitution, together with the
more salient points connected with the life and habits of its victims, it
will not be without profit to consider attentively, and at some length,
the condition to which these unhappy women are reduced, paying especial regard to two points of considerable importance—viz., whether the
effects produced are permanent, and how far the facts ascertained with
regard to prostitution bear out the notions generally prevailing on this
subject.

When the licentious epoch of the Restoration, due itself to the
national recoil from the abortive attempt of the Puritans to enact
religion and morality, was succeeded by the austerity of the Roman
Catholic James and the decorous court of William and Mary, and while
the fixed and floating population of the capital was increasing with the
facilities of travel, the growth of trade, and the general wealth, there
is no doubt that long rampant immorality—incurable at short notice—

was but held repressed, and compelled to hide its head. A remarkable impetus was therefore given to comparatively secret prostitution, corresponding to the decrease in adultery and overt concubinage which about that time ceased to be indispensable qualifications of the man of parts and fashion.

When I consider that genteel society was passing during the period of the Augustan essayists from a political and moral delirium towards a state of repose, and the artificial scarcity of trained intellects which yet recent events had created among the class for whom they wrote—I am not surprised that earnest authors, careful of administering strong meat to babes, should have elected to work upon the public mind, as they did, with types and parables. But I do wonder that so many able men, from that period to our own day, who might have touched moral pitch without the fear or imputation of defilement, have, whether through moral cowardice or considerations of expediency, still as it were by concert, been content to do little more than retouch and restore the pictures of the ancient masters, adding, from time to time, perhaps, some horrid feature. Thus has been painfully built up a sort of "bogie" in a corner cupboard, unheeded by the infant, terrible to the aged, the untempted, and others whom it concerned not; while the flower of the people have rushed into the streets and worshipped the immodest Venus.

Thus, I believe, was firmly rooted—if it did not thus originate—and thus has mightily prospered, remaining even to our day an overshadowing article of almost religious belief, the notion that the career of the woman who once quits the pinnacle of virtue involves the very swift decline and ultimate total loss of health, modesty, and temporal prosperity. And herein are contained three vulgar errors :—

1. That once a harlot,* always a harlot.

2. That there is no possible advance, moral or physical, in the condition of the actual prostitute.

3. That the harlot's progress is short and rapid.

And the sooner fearless common sense has cleared the ground of fallacy, the sooner may statesmen see their way to handle a question of which they have not denied the importance.

It is a little too absurd to tell us that "the dirty, intoxicated slattern, in tawdry finery and an inch thick in paint"—long a conventional symbol of prostitution—is a correct figure in the middle of the nineteenth century. If she is not apocryphal, one must at least go out of the beaten path to find her. She is met with, it is true, in filthy taps, resorts of crime, and in the squalid lairs of poverty—rarely courting the light, but lurking in covert spots to catch the reckless, the besotted,

---

* Harlot, from Welsh, *Herlawd*, a stripling, *herlodes*, a hoiden, a word composed of *her*, a push or challenge, and *llawd*, a lad. This word was formerly applied to males as well as females.

"A sturdie harlot—that was her hostes man."—*Chaucer's Tales.*

"He was a gentil harlot and a kind."—*Ditto.*

The word originally signified a bold stripling or a hoiden.
A woman who prostitutes her body for hire, a prostitute, a common woman.
OGILVIE'S IMPERIAL DICTIONARY, Vol. I.

and the young of the opposite sex. And though such may be even numbered by hundreds, it must, on reflection, be conceded by those who have walked through the world with open eyes, that, considering the square mileage of the metropolis, and the enormous aggregate I am treating of, they are but as drops in an ocean. The Gorgon of the present day against whom we should arm our children should be a woman who, whether sound or diseased, is generally pretty and elegant —oftener painted by Nature than by art—whose predecessors cast away the custom of drunkenness when the gentlemen of England did the same—and on whose backs, as if following the poet's direction, *in corpore vili*, the ministers of fashion exhibit the results of their most egregious experiments.

The shades of London prostitution—the previous definition at pages 1 and 2 being kept in view—are as numberless as those of society at large, and may be said to blend at their edges, but no further. The microcosm, in fact, exhibits, like its archetype, saving one, all the virtues and good qualities, as well as all the vices, weaknesses, and follies.

The great substitution of unchastity for female honour has run through and dislocated all the system ; but it must not be imagined that, though disordered and for a time lost to our sight, the other strata of the woman's nature have ceased to exist.

The class maintain their notions of caste and quality with all the pertinacity of their betters. The greatest amount of income procurable with the least amount of exertion, is with them, as with society, the grand gauge of position ; and each individual, like her betters, sets up for private contemplation some ideal standard with which she may compare, deeming most indispensable to beauty and gentility the particular elements she may best lay claim to.

I see the *monde* and *demi-monde* as shy of one another among the prostitutes of London as in other classes. I see, too, the arrogance of bran-new, short-lived prosperity, that has dashed from the ranks, and the jealous writhing of the beaten ruck. I see the active sinfulness and passive heedlessness of one set, and the patient hope and bewildered entanglement of another. But not admitting such salient differences between this fraction and the mass of the community as justify its political severance, I cannot see that it presents material for a special physiology ; and as such a task would be neither profitable to the reader nor congenial to myself, I will, as nearly as I may, avoid it. A writer who could analyse and catalogue the combinations of the kaleidoscope may some day, perhaps, be found to undertake the equally useless task of dissecting to each filament this twisted yarn of everyday virtue, vice, and good and evil qualities—variegated by degree of education—stained foully by one predominant vice and its ancillary failings—interwoven from end to end of the piece with one half of society, and supposed by courteous fiction to exist without the cognizance of the other. We can well afford to wait his coming, for we have not put to use one-half our present stock of knowledge.

The order may be divided into three classes—the " kept woman " (a repulsive term, for which I have in vain sought an English substitute), who has in truth, or pretends to have, but one paramour, with whom she, in some cases, resides ; the common prostitute, who is at the service, with slight reservation, of the first comer, and attempts no other means of life ; and the woman whose prostitution is a subsidiary calling.

The presence of the individual in either of these categories may of course depend upon a thousand accidents ; but once in either rank, as a general rule her footing is permanent while her prostitution, in any sense of the word, continues. There is, although the moralist insist otherwise, little promotion, and less degradation. The cases of the latter are quite exceptional ; those of the former less rare, but still not frequent. The seduction and primary desertion of each woman who afterwards becomes a prostitute is an affair apart ; and the *liaison* of a woman with her seducer is generally of the shortest. This over, her remaining in the ranks of honest society, or her adoption of prostitution, becomes her question. Some few voluntarily take the latter alternative. Domestic servants, and girls of decent family, are generally driven headlong to the streets for support of themselves and their babies ; needlewomen of some classes by the incompatibility of infant nursing with the discipline of the workshop. Those who take work at home are fortunate enough, and generally too happy, to reconcile continuance of their labours with a mother's nursing duties, and by management retain a permanent connexion with the army of labour, adopting prostitution only when their slender wages become insufficient for their legitimate wants.

Thus the *ouvrière* class—corresponding to the *grisette* of the French writers—and the promiscuous class of prostitutes—answering to their *lorettes*, are accounted for. Our first, or superior order, recruits its ranks as follows :—

1. From women cohabiting with, or separately maintained by, their seducers.

2. From kept women who are, as it were, in the business, and transfer their allegiance from party to party at the dictates of caprice or financial expediency.

3. From women whom men select for a thousand and one reasons, from promiscuous orders—or, as commonly said, " take off the town."

4. From women similarly promoted from the *ouvrière* class.

The prominent or retiring position the individual occupies in these three divisions—allowing, of course, for exceptions influenced by her idiosyncrasies—depends mainly upon gaiety or gravity of temperament. These characteristics exaggerated, on the one hand, into boisterous vulgarity, on the other, into nervous retirement—both chequered, more or less, at times, by extreme depression and hysterical mirth—pervade the devotees to this calling, and influence their whole career. A woman endowed with the one may, for a time, by force of circumstances, assume the other—but for a time only. The spring recoils, and the natural character asserts its sway. It is superfluous almost to allude, among men of the world, to the arrogant and offensive conduct into which some prostitutes of the upper class, and of mercurial temperament, will be betrayed, even when permitted to elbow respectability

and good conduct in public places ; or to their intense assumption of
superiority over their less full-blown sisters, on the strength of an
equipage, an opera box, a saddle-horse, a Brompton villa, and a visiting
list. This is the kind of woman of whom I said just now that the loss
of her honour seemed to have intensified every evil point in her character. She it is who inflicts the greatest scandal and damage upon
society, and by whom, though she is but a fraction of her class, the
whole are necessarily, but injudiciously, if not cruelly, judged. This is
the flaunting, extravagant quean, who, young and fair—the milliners'
herald of forthcoming fashions—will daily drag a boyish lover (for
whose abject submission she will return tolerable constancy, and over
whose virtue she presides like another Dian), will he, nill he, like a
lacquey, in her train to Blackwall parties, flower shows, and races—
night after night to the " select ballet balls," plays, or public dancing
saloons—will see him gaily, along with jockeys who are no gentlemen
and gentlemen who are all jockey, through his capital or his allowances,
and then, without a sigh, enlist in the service of another—perhaps his
intimate friend—till she has run the gauntlet as kept mistress through
half-a-dozen short generations of men about town.

Descend a step to the promiscuous category, and trace the harlot to
whom a tavern-bar was congenial instead of repulsive on her first
appearance there—say at sixteen or eighteen years of age. At thirty and
at forty you will find her (if she rises in the scale) the loudest of the
loud, in the utmost blaze of finery, looked on as " first-rate company"
by aspiring gents, surrounded by a knot of " gentlemen" who applaud
her rampant nonsense, and wondering, hotel-sick, country men of business, whose footsteps stray at night to where she keeps her foolish court.
She is a sort of whitewashed sepulchre, fair to the eye, but full of inner
rottenness—a mercenary human tigress ; albeit there exists at times
some paltry bull dog, nursed in the same Bohemian den, who may light
up all the fires of womanhood within her—some rascally enchanter, who
may tame her at the height of her fury, when none else human may
approach her, by whispering or blows. Exigeant of respect beyond
belief, but insufferably rude, she is proud and high-minded in talk one
moment, but not ashamed to beg for a shilling the next. The great
sums of money she sometimes earns, she spends with romantic extravagance, on her toilette partly, and partly circulates, with thoughtless
generosity, among the lodging-house sharks and other baser parasites
that feed upon her order.

Should such a light-minded woman descend in the scale of promiscuous
prostitution, which of course is a matter of possibility, though not so
likely as her rise, she will still be found the same. As no access of fortune will do much towards humanizing, so no ill-luck will soften or
chasten her. She will be in Lambeth or Whitechapel as I have
described her in Soho or the Haymarket—a drunken, brawling reprobate—but in a lower orbit.

On the other hand, the sad career in prostitution of the softer-minded
woman, in whatever rank she may be, will be marked and affected by
that quality. Whatever befal her in this vale of tears, the gentle-
minded woman will be gentle still ; and with this native hue will be

tinged all her dealings with the sisterhood, and with the rough rude males whom ever and anon it is her fate to meet. If fortunate enough to have the acquaintance of some quiet men of means, she will not be puffed up with vain-gloriousness, but seeking comfort in obscurity, and clinging fast to what respect she may gain of others, will profess—what I dare say she really often feels—disgust at brazen impudence, and all the pomps and vanities. Whether this eschewal be from real delicacy, or considerations of economy, or because any sort of notoriety, instead of cementing, as in the case of others mentioned, would be fatal to their particular *liaison*, it is hard to say ; but, however that may be, it is no less true that hundreds of females so constituted are at this moment living within a few miles of Charing Cross, in easy if not elegant circumstances, with every regard to outward decorum and good taste, and shocking none of the public who will not attempt unnecessarily close investigation, but for all that " in a state of prostitution." The ease and comparative prosperity that inflates the lighter woman into a public nuisance have no such effect upon such a one as I have spoken of last. They but cause her to prize each day more highly peace and quietness— more sadly to regret the irrevocable past—more profoundly to yearn after some way out of the wilderness.

Among the promiscuous prostitutes of the milder order will be found a numerous band, who, unlike the magnificent virago of the supper-shops, rarely see the evening lamps. Sober, genteelly dressed, well ordered, often elegant in person—such girls have the taste and the power to select their acquaintances from among the most truly eligible men whom the present false state of society debars from marriage. Their attractions, indeed, are of the subdued order that neither the hot blood of the novice nor the prurient fancy of the used-up rake could appreciate. Of course, they take the chances of their calling. They know that a short acquaintance often turns their sorrow into joy, and opens out a better, happier future. They know, too, that one unlucky hour may make them scatterers of pestilence. What wonder, then, that woman's tact, sharpened by uses of adversity, should induce them to prefer the respect and counsel of well-bred men of settled character to the evanescent passion of mere youths. From the former they get lessons, rarely thrown away, on the value of repose and thrift ; from the latter, only new proofs of folly and fickleness. With the one they may for a time forget their occupation ; with the other, only sharpen memory. They exhibit at times the greatest respect for themselves, and for the opinions, scruples, and weaknesses of those with whom they are connected, and whom they love to call their " friends ;" and, above all, they are notable for the intensity of love with which they will cling to the sister, the mother, the brother—in fact, to any one " from home" who, knowing of their fall, will not abjure them, or, ignorant of their present calling, still cherishes some respect and regard for them. The sick man is safe in their hands, and the fool's money also. There is many a tale well known of their nursing and watching, and more than will do so could tell of the harlot's guardianship in his hour of drunkenness. I have seen the fondest of daughters and mothers among them. I fancy that where they have that regard for men which they are too pleased to return for mere politeness, they are well-meaning, and not always foolish friends—no abettors of extravagance, and, so far as absolute honesty is concerned, implicitly to be relied on.   They are more dupes than impostors—more sinned against than sinning—till the play is played out, the pilgrimage accomplished, and they who have long strained their eyes for a resting-place quit the painful road—as I say they mostly do—for a better life on earth; or, leaving hope behind on their discharge from the hospitals, issue to an obscurity more melancholy and degraded than ever.   For of such on whom has fallen the lot of foul disease, or whom a loss of health or beauty has deprived of worthy associates, are the abject maundering creatures who haunt the lower dens of vice and crime.   Deficient in mental and physical elasticity to resist the downward pressure of intermittent starvation and undying conscience, they are pulled from depth to lower deep, by men who trample, and women of their class who prey upon them.   Liquor, which other organizations adopt as a jovial friend and partner of each gleam of sunshine, is to these the medicine and permanent aggravation of dejected misery. Cruelly injured by the other sex, they moodily resolve to let retribution take its course through their diseased agency ; trodden under foot by society, what can society expect from them but scorn for scorn ?*

The woman, the castle of whose modesty offered stoutest resistance to the storm of the seducer, often becomes in time the most abiding stronghold of vice.   Saturated with misery and drink, perhaps then crime and disease, dead long in heart, and barely willing to live on in the flesh—ceasing to look upward, ceasing to strike outward, she will passively drift down the stream into that listless state of moral insensibility in which so many pass from this world into the presence of their Judge.

"And here"—I can fancy some reader interrupting—" here ends your catechism.   You have led us a painful pilgrimage through the obscurest corners behind the scenes of civilized society, casting, by the way, a glare on matters from whose contemplation mature refinement would gladly be spared, and the bare conception of which should be studiously shut out from youth and innocence.   At the end of all you show us the heroine of your prurient sympathy overtaken by her doom.   We have seen by turns reflected on your mirror the pampered concubine and the common street-walker—the haunts of dissipation and the foul ward ; but you dissent from our religious, and at least venerably antique belief, that between these stages there is an organized progression. You cast your lantern ray at last upon a guilty, solitary wreck, perishing, covered with sores, in some back garret, in a filthy court; and you ask us to believe that this is not retribution."

I do, in truth.   For if this fate were general—inevitable, unless by direct intervention of Providence, or arrest of its decree by perverse interposition of science, I might admit the truth of my opponents' creed. But I maintain, on the contrary, that such an ending of the harlot's life

* I must be understood as not attempting to sketch other than oscillatory prostitution. The systematic concubinage which is stated, I believe with truth, to prevail among the lowest class in this city and in the manufacturing districts is an institution out of my scope.

is the altogether rare exception, not the general rule ; that the down-ward progress and death of the prostitute in the absolute ranks of that occupation are exceptional also, and that she succumbs at last, not to that calling, nor to venereal disease, but in due time, and to the various maladies common to respectable humanity.

I hope to show fair grounds for these conclusions, and for my opinion that the doors of escape from this evil career are many ; that those who have walked in it do eagerly rush through them, neither lingering nor looking behind ; that the greatest and most flagrant are not stricken down in the pursuit of sin, nor does the blow fall when it might be of service as an example. If in the following pages I can do something towards this, it may be more justly argued, I think, that an all-wise, all-merciful God has provided these escapes, than that those whom fate overtakes within the vicious circle are selected by His design. And if so, it justly follows that those are less impious and erring, than further-ing God's will, who would widen the gates of the fold of penitence and rest, gather by all possible means yet another crop to the harvest of souls, and claim the Christian's noble birthright of rejoicing over more and yet more repentant sinners.

To those who may ask, " What can it matter to us what becomes of them ? The subject may be statistically interesting, but no farther. The interests of society demand that a disgusting inquiry should be dis-couraged, lest by chance the eyes of youth should be polluted ;"—I have this much to say. That the Utopian epoch being long since passed, if indeed it ever had a beginning, when the book of evil could be sealed to the people, it is time that the good and wise, not flinching from the moral pitch, should emulate the evil and the crooked-minded in their attempts to guide the public.

The streets of London are an open book, and very few may walk therein who cannot and will not inquire and read for themselves. Shall those who of right should be commentators for ever leave an open field to the bigoted and the sinful, with the idea of fostering a degree of purity to which the state of society precludes a more than fictitious existence ? Shall dirt be allowed to accumulate, only because it is dirt?

A few stubborn figures may perhaps assist the candid reader toward, at least, a partial removal of impressions he may have received, in common with a large portion of the public, as to the causes of mortality among prostitutes.

Some years ago, in 1851, the Registrar-General, Major Graham, with his usual politeness and at considerable trouble, extracted for me the number of deaths ascribable to venereal diseases which occurred in the Metropolis during the years 1846—7—8, and again in the year 1868 I am further indebted to him and Dr. Farr for the additional tables, and from them I have compiled the following :—

Table, distinguishing the Males from the Females, their Ages, and the Forms of the Disease of which they died in London.

	FEMALES.						MALES.						Male and Female aged 15—65.
—	15 to 25.	25 to 35.	35 to 45.	45 to 55.	55 to 65.	Total aged 15—65.	15 to 25.	25 to 35.	35 to 45.	45 to 55.	55 to 65.	Total aged 15—65.	
Syphilis	3	12	5	7	2	29	4	4	2	—	4	14	43
Phagedænic disease..	2	3	—	—	—	5	2	—	—	—	—	2	7
Disease of bone ...	—	1	1	—	1	3	—	1	—	1	—	2	5
Ulceration of larynx .	1	2	—	—	—	3	1	5	—	—	—	6	9
Venereal disease ...	—	3	1	—	—	4	1	2	—	—	—	3	7
Consumption	2	6	1	—	—	9	1	6	—	2	1	10	19
Chest affection... ...	1	2	—	—	—	3	1	1	—	—	1	3	6
Paralysis	—	—	—	1	—	1	—	1	—	—	—	1	2
Cachexia and debility	2	2	3	1	—	8	—	—	1	3	—	4	12
Erysipelas	5	1	2	—	—	8	3	5	1	—	—	9	17
All diseases	16	32	13	9	3	73	13	25	4	6	6	54	127
Syphilis,* in the three years, 1864, 1865, and 1866	35	37	24	11	4	111	15	25	20	11	7	78	189

The first thing that strikes the reader here is the paucity of fatal cases. Notwithstanding the frequency of the complaint in the Metropolis, as shown in subsequent pages, only 127 deaths are noted during 156 weeks, out of a population amounting to more than 3,000,000, or on the average less than one a week.

The above table, I think, disposes of the hypothesis that any large number of females, whether prostitutes or not, die annually of syphilis. It exhibits only 73 women to 54 men; and this proportion is more striking when we consider that the female population of London is to the male as 120 to 100, or six to five.

In order to corroborate my assertions made some years ago, that syphilis was not a fatal disease, I again applied, in May, 1857, to Major Graham, and he kindly forwarded me the annexed table, which is curious as showing how large a proportion of the female mortality from syphilis falls upon infants and children under five years of age :—

In a letter, dated 1868, with which Dr. Farr has favoured me, that gentleman says :—" It is probable that at least a portion of the increase in the number of cases of syphilis is due to improved and more accurate registration."

---

   * Under this head, " Syphilis," are included cases variously returned as phagedænic disease from syphilis, ulceration of larynx from syphilis, cachexia and debility in syphilitic subjects, &c., &c.

Deaths from Syphilis of Females at Different Ages in England and Wales, and in London, in the years 1855, 1866, *and* 1867.

	England and Wales.	London.	England and Wales.	London.	England and Wales.	London.
	1855.	1855.	1866.	1866.	1867.	1867.
Under one year	269	54	556	166	582	170
One year	28	4	43	4	38	9
Two years	11	—	9	3	6	1
Three years	7	—	4	3	3	—
Four years	3	1	3	—	2	—
Total under five years... ...	318	59	615	176	631	180
Five and under ten years	5	—	4	1	1	—
Ten and under fifteen years	4	1	1	—	1	—
Fifteen and under twenty years ...	16	2	13	7	7	2
Twenty and under twenty-five years...	18	3	39	10	42	6
Twenty-five and under thirty years	25	2	75	12	68	13
Thirty and under thirty-five years	25	3				
Thirty-five and under forty years	20	3	42	6	51	7
Forty and under forty-five years	11	3				
Forty-five and under fifty years	13	1	20	5	26	2
Fifty and under fifty-five years	5	—				
Fifty-five and under sixty years	4	1	9	1	10	1
Sixty and under sixty-five years	3	—				
Sixty-five years and upwards... ...	1	—	9	1	3	1
Total, all ages	468	78	827	219	840	212

Let persons who have been through the syphilitic wards of hospitals call to mind the stamp of women to be seen there. The fact of a girl's seduction generally warrants her possession of youth, health, good looks, and a well-proportioned frame—qualifications usually incompatible with a feeble constitution. She, at least, meets the world with power of resistance beyond the average of women in her station. Notwithstanding all her excesses (and legion is their name), the prostitute passes through the furnace of a dissipated career less worse from wear than her male associates ; and when she withdraws from it—as withdraw she will in a few years, for old prostitutes are rarely met with—she is seldom found with her nose sunk in, her palate gone, or nodes upon her shins.

Nay, more, experience teaches that frequently the most violent and fatal cases among women take their rise during the period of comparative innocence, before their adoption of prostitution, and their consequent acquirement of worldly knowledge. I grieve to say that there are systematic seducers so unutterably base as not only to pollute the mind of modest girls, but simultaneously to steep their bodies in most lamentable corruption. Their want of knowledge and ingenuous sense of shame induce, in cases such as these, aggravation of suffering from which the experienced prostitute is comparatively exempt.

So rare is death from uncomplicated syphilis, that many a surgeon has never witnessed a single instance ; and those attached to hospitals where venereal diseases are specially treated have so few opportunities of witnessing post-mortems of persons who have succumbed to them, that it becomes interesting to inquire how they produced death. This is answered by the return from the Registrar-General. In the first place, erysipelas may attack the sores of *all* patients entering an hospital, and a certain number of syphilitic patients, as of other classes, die from this cause. Syphilis, therefore, acted but a secondary part in producing the fatal termination of the 17 cases of erysipelas in the above table.

We sometimes, in the present day, meet with death from sloughing phagedæna, but rarely without complication. I lately, for instance, saw it in a man who died, not from its severity, but from debility and loss of blood at stool, which nothing could check, and which was found to depend upon ulceration in the intestines. I allude hereafter, at p. 69, to the phagedæna, once so prevalent at St. Giles's Workhouse. I find that this form of the disease is now unknown there, and the preceding table records only seven deaths from phagedæna throughout London in three years. Whilst these pages were passing through the press, an epidemic of this affection was spreading to such an extent through the foul wards of St. Bartholomew's Hospital (having already caused the death of, I believe, three women), that the authorities were most reluctantly obliged to close them for a time against syphilitic patients, in order to arrest what might have proved a frightful scourge.

Dr. MacCarthy tells us*—"In Paris, out of nine patients affected with phagedænic serpiginous chancre, four died from the progress of the disease and colliquative diarrhœa, and on opening these I found violent inflammation of the entire colon and rectum, and I observed the mucous membrane sprinkled over with ulcerations. It is not uninteresting to compare this fact with the frequency noted by Dupuytren of the occurrence of ulcerations in persons who have died from the effects of severe burns."

Ormerod mentions† that a patient died at St. Bartholomew's from the giving way of a vessel in the upper part of the vagina.

In Wild's work on the "Institutions of Austria," I find seven deaths reported as having taken place in Vienna; five the result of bubo, probably sloughing; one from sore-throat; and one from general secondary symptoms. Of these, three were males, and only four females.

The whole mortality of prostitutes at St. Lazare, the female venereal hospital at Paris, was but 16 in 1853, and 17 in 1854. The deaths were principally caused by non-syphilitic affections, the germs of which they had contracted before coming into hospital.

In the year 1855, there were 14 deaths at the Lourcine Hospital out of 1384 patients admitted, and of these only one was attributed to syphilis.

But if syphilis be retributive, it would appear to be visited on the children with far greater severity than on the parents; for out of 85 infants, who in 1854 were born at the Lourcine, or, being under two years of age, were admitted with their mothers, I find that no less than 24 perished from its effects. Out of 60 children at the same hospital in 1855, there were 10 deaths.

Death from primary or secondary symptoms is of very rare occur-

* Thesis, p. 17, 1844. † Clinical Observations.

rence. I do not, in fact, very well see how it could be produced, unless erysipelas, fever, or acute inflammatory disease set in and destroyed the patient.

Syphilis is most frequently fatal when it has reached the tertiary form, in the neglected cases of which we observe its greatest ravages. Patients are destroyed by the deposit of bone, which, pressing on the brain, produces paralysis, convulsions, and other nervous phenomena. In other cases caries of bones takes place, and exhaustion causes death. Occasionally the cartilages of the larynx fall in, and the patient dies asphyxiated. Lastly, the hopeless and intense form of tertiary syphilis, known as syphilitic cachexia, sometimes comes on, and gradually leads to a fatal termination, as in the following instance :—

I was called to see a young girl who was stated to be very ill, at King-street, Islington. I found my poor dispensary patient living in an attic, in one of the small streets off the Lower Road, attended by her mother, without fire or furniture, almost without clothing. She lay, doubled up in the corner of this bare room, on an old mattress stuffed with shavings, with no bed-linen but a thin patched quilt and a few rags. She was covered with rupia, and attenuated to the last degree, though bearing marks of having been a very pretty girl.

She had never left her mother's roof for twenty-four hours; but had nevertheless been seduced, diseased, and deserted—sad and frequent story—and, as long as she was able, had in secret attended at an hospital. Her mother had never left her, and—so *naïve* had she remained in this city of licentiousness—was apparently unaware of the nature of her child's disorder. Never applying to the parish, she had obtained a bare subsistence by her needle, until her ministering office had shut out even this precarious support. She had parted with her every property, till, indeed, no warmth could be obtained except by creeping close together under their miserable counterpane.

At once, seeing the nature of the case, and the impossibility of my being of material service to this poor creature, I spoke of the hospital, but neither mother nor daughter would hear of it ; they had never been separated, and never would be. Persuasion was in vain. Assistance was procured ; still the debility increased, and I was absolutely obliged to threaten the interference of the parish officers. At last the patient consented to be carried to the hospital, but at such a stage of the complaint this could only be effected with the greatest difficulty. She was, however, admitted into St. Bartholomew's, and the comforts which that noble institution so liberally furnishes to its sick, at first caused her to rally, but an immense abscess formed in her thigh, and she sank in a short time under " syphilitic cachexia."

Who could have seen that hapless, unoffending victim to her woman's trust and man's barbarity, hurried to an early grave, without asking himself could such a one have been marked out for example and for punishment by a discerning Providence, as some would tell us ?

As it was a principal object with me twelve years ago to show that prostitutes did not die of syphilis, so in 1869 I am enabled to show that the statistics now kept by the larger hospital fully bear out my assertions, and controvert the public and popular notion that by deaths in hospitals we rid ourselves of the immoral female population. I extract the following returns from the last report (1868) of St. Bartholomew's Hospital, an institution that has 650 beds for the reception of patients, and admits nearly 6,000 persons :—

1	M.	...	15—25	Syphilis, Primary...	Phagedæna in Groin. Hæmorrhage from Femoral Artery, 9th week.
1	M.	...	15—25	,, Secondary	Exhaustion, 9th week.
1	M.	...	45—55	,, ,,	Typhoid Fever, 11th day.
2	...	F.	15—25	Gonorrhœa	Int. Hæmorrhage, 8th week, and Phthisis, 3rd month.

Not a single female died from syphilis, although some of the worst cases are admitted to the wards, and the most accurate accounts are kept.

I have now furnished the data whence I argue that syphilis is the fate neither of the bulk, nor of an important fraction, of prostitutes; and to meet the hypothesis that, if such is not the fact, they may at least fall victims to suicide, intemperance, or complaints incidental to an irregular course of life, I have made special inquiries among the medical attendants of hospitals, penitentiaries, as well as well-informed private practitioners, and certain parish authorities. Their replies seem to corroborate my impressions that the combined operation of all these agencies, in addition to venereal complaints, is inadequate to extirpate, as alleged, a generation of prostitutes every few years, and that no other class of females is so free from general disease as this is. I find that in 1867 83 females committed suicide; 7 of these were under 20 years of age; 76 were aged 20 and upwards. There was no reason to believe that even one-half were prostitutes.*

Parent-Duchâtelet, in treating of Parisian prostitution, was able, as follows, to account for a portion of the mortality among those who died in harness. "It extends," he says, "principally to women between twenty and thirty years of age, whose constitutions have been used up at a great pace by excesses. They say of themselves, that a girl in one of the low houses lasts three years. When we consider that such women are constantly drunk, and that they commit the sexual act from fifteen to twenty times a day, can we be surprised that they cannot hold out for ever?"

The same remark holds good, in truth, of a considerable class of women in this city, but we know that here, as in Paris, it is extremely

* It has been supposed that many prostitutes become insane. We find little evidence corroborative of this opinion. In Dr. Hood's statistics of insanity at Bethlam Hospital, from 1846 to 1856, I read "SENSUALITY." Here again, as in the case of intemperance in stimulating drinks, it is very difficult to arrive at any correct conclusion for want of accurate data. In the Bethlam tables, however, the mental disorder is referred to "Onanism" in 12 cases, and to "sexual excess" in 11 cases. M. Esquirol says that one-twentieth of the lunatics in the Saltpetiere had been prostitutes. But it is a question whether grief, anxiety, and broken hours may not have had a greater share in dethroning the reason than sensuality.

restricted. The records of our civil courts have recently proved how hard it is to kill a person of fine constitution, supplied designedly with unlimited liquor and relays of pot companions; and we know again, that by the thorough prostitutes the sexual act is generally performed with the least possible exertion, and that her visitor is not uncommonly himself debauched, and, for the time being, impotent. On the other hand, the same writer again observes; "All that I have said on the chances of contracting disease to which prostitutes are exposed, confirms the truth of the position taken by surgeons and others who have had their charge;—viz., that, notwithstanding all their excesses and exposure to so many causes of disease, their health resists all attacks better than that of the ordinary run of women who have children and lead orderly lives. They have (as some one has remarked) iron bodies, which enable them with impunity to meet trials such as would prove fatal to others."

If we compare the prostitute at thirty-five with her sister, who perhaps is the married mother of a family, or has been a toiling slave for years in the over-heated laboratories of fashion, we shall seldom find that the constitutional ravages often thought to be necessary consequences of prostitution exceed those attributable to the cares of a family and the heart-wearing struggles of virtuous labour.

How then is the disparition of this class of women to be accounted for, as they are neither stricken down in the practice of harlotry, nor by their own hands, nor by intemperance and venereal disease, nor would seem to perish of supervening evils in any notable proportion? Do they fall by the wayside, as some assume, like leaves of autumn, unnoticed and unnumbered, to be heaped up and to rot? Do unknown graves conceal, not keeping green the lost one's memory, and the obscure fallible records of the pauper burials at last confound all clue and chance of tracing her? Is she filtered again into the world through a reformatory? or does she crawl from the sight of men and the haunts of her fellows to some old homely spot in time to linger and to die?

I have every reason to believe, that by far the larger number of women who have resorted to prostitution for a livelihood, return sooner or later to a more or less regular course of life. Before coming to this conclusion I have consulted many likely to be acquainted with their habits, and have founded my belief upon the following data. Whatever be the cause of a female becoming a prostitute, one thing is certain—before she has carried on the trade four years, she has fully comprehended her situation, its horrors and its difficulties, and is prepared to escape, should opportunity present itself. The constant humiliation of all, even of those in the greatest affluence, and the frequent pressure of want attendant on the vocation of the absolute street-walker, clouding the gaiety of the kept woman, and driving the wedge of bitter reflection into the intervals of the wildest harlot's frenzy, are the agencies which clear the ranks of all but veterans who seem to thrive in proportion to their age.

Incumbrances rarely attend the prostitute who flies from the horrors of her position. We must recollect that she has a healthy frame, an excellent constitution, and is in the vigour of life. During her career, she has obtained a knowledge of the world most probably above the situation she was born in. Her return to the hearth of her infancy is for obvious reasons a very rare occurrence. Is it surprising, then, that she should look to the chance of amalgamating with society at large, and make a dash at respectability by a marriage? Thus, to a most surprising, and year by year increasing extent, the better inclined class of prostitutes become the wedded wives of men in every grade of society, from the peerage to the stable, and as they are frequently barren, or have but a few children, there is reason to believe they often live in ease unknown to many women who have never strayed, and on whose unvitiated organization matrimony has entailed the burden of families.

Others who, as often happens, have been enabled to lay by variable sums of money, work their own reclamation as established milliners, small shop-keepers, and lodging-house keepers, in which capacities they often find kind assistance from *ci-devant* male acquaintances, who are only too glad to second their endeavours. Others, again, devote their energies and their savings to preying in their turn, as keepers or *attachées* of brothels and other disorderly establishments, upon the class of male and female victims they themselves have emerged from.

The most prudish will doubtless agree with me, that an important fraction of ex-prostitutes may be accounted for in the last of these categories. Such, indeed—as reformatories of the kind hitherto opened have been notoriously restricted in their operation—has been the customary theoretical disposition of all, or almost all, who were supposed not to die in the ranks or of supervening illnesses. On reflection, too, the reader may, perhaps, acquiesce in some occasional re-entrances into society through the portals of labour. Emigration also, under its present easy conditions, may be admitted to be an outlet to a certain extent.

When, however, I suggest an enormous and continual action of wedlock upon prostitution, I am quite prepared for the smile of incredulity and the frown of censure from many whose notions of caste, propriety, and so forth, preclude their entertaining for a moment a proposition which would to them appear fraught with scandal, and because scandalous, preposterous. But let me tell the sceptic that this is a matter which, though heretofore it has attracted the attention of a few, will hereafter speak to society as with the voice of a trumpet. " Suum est cui proximus ardet," and few may say how soon or how near the fire may not approach them. The ball is rolling, the Rubicon has been crossed by many who have not been drowned in the attempt, nor found a state of things on the other side more distasteful than compulsory celibacy; and I apprehend that if some of our social marriage enactments are not repealed by acclamation or tacitly, I shall live to see a very large increase in concubinage and the marriages of prostitutes.

There are thousands of fathers, and what is worse, mothers of families, in every rank and occupation of life, who have done much evil, I fear, by the attempt to set up the worship of society in association with that of Mammon. Wholesale dealers in so-called respectability, but screwing out scanty halfpenny-worths of brotherly love, they have passed a marriage code in the joint names of these false divinities, which renders day by day more difficult the union of youth and love unsanctified by money and position. As this goes on, we see more and more of our maidens pining on the stem of single blessedness, more and more of our young men resigning themselves first, for a time, to miscellaneous fornication, then to systematic concubinage, and, of course for all this, none the richer or more eligible in the eyes of society, at last to a *mésalliance*.

I need not enlarge upon the social offence of one who thus practically lessens the number of prostitutes. All reflective men must appreciate in common the sad distress and shame which may accrue to his family, the depravity of his taste, who could consider it a triumph to bear off a battered prize from other competitors, and his insanity, who should dream of avoiding detection, or indulge the hope that, after detection, his false step could be forgotten or forgiven by the world. All can compassionate the temporary weakness of a mind which could esteem the permanent possession of a tainted woman worth the sacrifice of home and social ties. All are at liberty to predict his future sadness, if not misery ; though we are apt to err in supposing that the woman purchased at this sacrifice has no affection to return to him, no gratitude, no feeling, no good taste. And, I confess, I have occasionally joined the very worldly and immoral cry against the folly of a man who contrives to make an indissoluble bond of a silken thread which he might have rent at his own will and pleasure—who pays so dearly for the ownership of that which, by a little management, he might have occupied from year to year at will, for next to nothing. These are all every-day platitudes, and unfortunately in such common request that men may gather them at the street corners. I need not tire the reader by their useless amplification, but will briefly touch on a less hackneyed theme—I mean the circumstances which in general prelude such matches, and which, I fancy, will continue to induce them, until the advent of some healthy change in the management of the marriage booth in Vanity Fair.

Take a gentleman, A or B, of any income you please, so it be adequate to the support of two persons, and of any social position—from the *sangre azur* of May Fair to the " young man" of the East-end warehouse —and you may hear the gossips in society (behind his back, of course) remark, " How very singular it is that So-and-so has never married !" Here is a man in the prime of life, of ascertained position, or with every requisite for success, yet with no apparent intention of what is called " settling." The *commères* are at fault. The medical adviser, chosen probably by A or B because a perfect stranger to the rest of the family, could alone, perhaps, really enlighten them upon points which the principal devoutly conceals from others, not knowing what might turn up, and remembering the every-day truth of the good old saw—*Il y a je ne sçais quoi de plaisir dans le malheur d'autrui.* The man, in truth, is settled. For the fact is, often, that though A or B cultivates assiduously the forum, club, counting-house, or the factory—frequents the leisure-haunts where men of his own pursuits most congregate,—dines, smokes, and plays whist with them—appears even, on occasion, in my lady's drawing-room, or at public gatherings—his real bower of rest is in some unpretending retreat, perhaps a suburban cottage, or perhaps a London lodging.

Here lives a lady, of more or less education and refinement—often young and handsome, sometimes of the ambiguous age " de Balzac," and plain but interesting—with or without incumbrances—avowedly widow, wife, or maid, as the case may be. One sees more or less taste and pretension about the establishment according to the means of its master. He, if ostensibly a husband engaged in a profession, will be strictly domesticated at one time, and at another his habits, or other considerations, will induce him to adopt the guise of a travelling merchant, engineer, or other nomad calling, and thus excuse to servants and neighbours his continual absence from home.

If, on the other hand, he visit only in the character of a relative, next friend, trustee, executor of deceased husband, godfather to the children, or what not, the intercourse is necessarily more restricted— less falsehood and trouble are entailed—and both parties are less apprehensive of an *eclaircissement*, and more independent. While tradespeople and servants are well dealt by, the persons concerned are saved the unpleasantness of hearing in the parlour the tittle-tattle which of course takes place at the side-door. The gentleman has obvious reasons against unnecessarily attracting the notice of the world about him ; and the female (as contact with her neighbours is inevitable) will generally do her best to gain their respect and avoid all cause of scandal. Little educated, as a matter of course, and generally unaccomplished, she appreciates no literature beyond small journals, smaller stories, and the smallest poetry. Her position with " her friend" and her neighbours, depending on respectable demeanour, she avoids vulgarity, evil company, and the attentions of strange men, and falls back, if childless, upon the domestic pursuits of gardening, needlework, cookery, and scrupulous housewifery. If a mother, she is, as mothers are, devoted— mourning sadly her inefficiency as a trainer, passionately desirous for the respect as well as love of her offspring, as well as solicitous that they shall walk in the way of virtue and propriety.

Now, as years roll on, and the A or B in question gets no younger, he is the less disposed to alter habits that have grown upon him, perhaps, from youth. In the plurality of cases he has been disgusted in society, or has never cultivated any but that of men. He may even have been crossed in a legitimate love, or have had a proposal *de convenance* thrown back in his teeth. He is sick and tired of an atmosphere of deceit or mystery in which he has spent one-half of his time. He is fond of himself and of ease, and he has found it, affection, and consideration of his every whim, at the hands of this woman—he may really, in course of time, have conceived for her that amount of respect which is necessary to the composition of a perfect love. For his sake, she tells him—sometimes falsely, sometimes truly—she has rejected offers of position. Cases are handy of unfaithful wives legitimately wooed and won—her constancy without the tie should be rewarded. He knows, or maybe thinks he knows, by heart, the woman who has shared his bed and board for years, while he argues that all regular courtships are no better than tedious shams—a series of organized impositions on both sides—and that marriage à la mode is a lottery. His inclinations sometimes even press conscience into an alliance, and conscience seems to say it must be wrong to cast from his bosom down the winds of fortune the woman whose attractions he had enjoyed while the days of her youth sped from her, without a thought bestowed by either of them on her future. Maybe she has children—to whom he is much attached—and shall he?—no! he will not send them illegitimate upon the world. He could do nothing less than keep them all, whatever came to pass; and if he married suitably, their very life would be a cloud upon his future. He asks himself, Has he philosophy to break the chain if a reputable marriage were open to him? And inclination replying—as she sometimes does—in the negative, conscience warns him not to peril the happiness of a wife, besides his own and his paramour's. Considerations such as these combine at length, and deepen into a quasi-religious conviction, which is little to be wondered at where a man has been the original seducer of his mistress; and which, wondrous or not, very frequently operates—especially where the latter is a woman of tact—to change the most irregularly contracted liaison into the indissoluble bond of marriage.

The above arguments are capable of a thousand combinations, with some of which men of all ranks and temperaments are apt to back up their inclinations, and attempt the after justification of their proceedings. There are, however, many other marriages of this description susceptible of no defence, which, originating in a very different manner, are planned at haste, and produce their bitter fruit, sometimes forthwith, sometimes at leisure.

A banished prodigal, a spendthrift greenhorn, a discarded lover, will often rush headlong into matrimony to provoke his respectable relatives, to spite his mistress, or in a frenzy of jealousy and intoxication. I have known a man of family, position, and fortune carry a prostitute to church almost against her will, and, reckless of all consequences—without the slightest prospect of ever gaining her affections, but in the mere mad hope of securing her person from his rivals. I have known a month's acquaintance, born at a casino, nourished at Vauxhall, to terminate at the altar of St. George's, with little other object in the maniac bridegroom's head than to add fresh fuel to the fire of a father's anger, and "to do," as he said, "something worth a shilling legacy." I have known a man—of taste and elegance before his lunacy—take for better or worse a thorough strumpet, that he might wound more deeply still a virtuous heart he had already withered. The annals of the class could tell us of the man of fashion who ran the passionate tradesman neck and neck for the possession of their common favourite —how he only won her by the wedding-ring—and how his disconsolate rival took to poetry and travel. Full many a simpleton has conceived a passion in course of a night's debauch which, needing no spur of rivalry or spite, could not be assuaged except by marriage in hot haste, without even a preliminary state of probation.

If "society" would consider the numberless and inscrutable phases of which this marriage mania is susceptible—the beauty, and often the shrewdness of the women—the immense concourses of marriageable males at the height of their passions, who, from various causes, seek female society more in the streets than in the boudoir, and who are, at the same time, utterly deficient in physico-moral training—it would, as I do, marvel less at the occasional explosion of these flagrant cases than at their rarity.

The following case is, of course, violently exceptional; but it is no less true that, some time back, a gentleman of family, on his road to a country jail, to which he had been committed for misdemeanour, invited and accepted the recommendation of a wife from the driver of the vehicle. He absolutely married her, led subsequently a miserable life, and is since dead. This painful story needs no illustration, and no comment.

I speak advisedly—and many persons of experience will bear me out —when I state my firm belief that hardly a prostitute in London has not, at some period of her career, an opportunity of marriage almost always above her original station. It is no rare occurrence for a woman comparatively public to have one or two lovers on her list, who, with a full knowledge of her situation, will hold their hands for a length of time at her disposal. She will keep them dangling, as her betters do their swains, while she sows her wild oats, from a reluctance to desert some more cherished acquaintance who will not or cannot afford to marry, or some wealthy admirer from whom she may have, not merely income, but expectations.

A friend of mine was some time ago attending a very ladylike person, living in the first style. She was well known to be unmarried, and to receive the attentions of three gentlemen, of whom two had considerable property, while the third, although well placed, was not so well off. From an affection of the uterus, her health declined; and, after some ineffectual attempts at cure, she was advised that her recovery must depend upon the dismissal of her lovers and the adoption of an extremely quiet life. I am not prepared to detail the mechanism of the plot; but suffice it to say, that when I next heard of this lady, she was rid for ever of two of her lovers, and had married the last, to whom she was an excellent and affectionate wife.

There are individuals who, from sheer idleness, nervousness, want of leisure or of wit, prefer the sociability, ample choice, and facility of making acquaintance which characterize the dancing-master's " select assemblies," to the straightness and frigidity of more orthodox avenues to matrimony. And it must be remembered—as I am speaking of all conditions of men—that such gatherings as would appear to the higher orders to be thoroughly promiscuous, are, in the eyes of a very large number of our young people, as genteel and select, and to others as inaccessible, as are Almack's balls to the bulk of the middle classes. They are certainly as well conducted, generally speaking. And thus a fraction of the shoals of amiable girls, whose fall from modesty has been achieved by the kind of " gentlemen" who regularly prowl in search of prey at such assemblies and the pleasure gardens, very prudently gather, *en revanche*, the flower of safety from the self-same bed of nettles, and, withdrawing in time from the outskirts of prostitution and the prospective horrors of the absolute *pavé*, make excellent wives to men, sometimes in, and often above their own rank of life, who, being unconscious of their antecedents, neither suffer in mind nor can aggravate any after difficulties by cruel and unavailing reproach.

The ranks of prostitution, again, are to some extent reduced by men who, not exactly in search of wives, are yet prepared for marriage, and flutter, as do moths about a light, round the Circes of the marine parade, the boarding-house, the *pension-bourgeoise*, and the table-d'hôte—Circes for whom the education-mongers have contracted (on a somewhat sandy base) to set one up complete with deportment and accomplishments to match. The fate of such a bachelor, who should too long dally at Florence, Paris, Baden, Tours, Boulogne, or Brighton, among the elegant and experienced company I have seen there, is like the egg-trick of the conjuror Columbus—no problem when found out. Matches like these, of course not every day, but not uncommonly, relieve the pocket and the conscience of some ancient lover, and make a pair of speculators indifferently happy.

I remember a very laughable one, improvised at a water-cure, between a notorious dilapidated fortune-hunter and a pretended officer's widow. Appearances justified each in considering the other a capitalist. The wedding was splendid and charming—the honeymoon gay and expensive; but when the hour of payment came, their resources turned out to be an accurately fashionable toilette on either side, and a joint income of £150 a-year. The lady's share had been settled recently upon her by an admirer of her younger days, and the gentleman's was a life interest. The explosion was painful; but these defeated adventurers, after chafing at the collar for a while, very wisely joined their talents for the common good, and make a head against the world, I hear, successfully.

Nor is the union of the wealthy man's dependent with the pensioned mistress, by consent of all three, by any means less common in the world than is represented in plays and story-books. Upon the temperament and original social position of the female, and also the degree of luxury in which she has lived, must depend the position to which she will stoop; for it may be relied on she will, to all appearance, be the condescending party. The gentleman's means and sympathy naturally fix the limit to his generosity, and decide the style of husband purchaseable. As men of every grade, and with every sort of maintenance at their disposal, from the Government clerkship to the gamekeeper's lodge, have every year to disembarrass themselves of ties such as we speak of—nothing, I confess, seems to me more proper than that the suitor *ex machinâ*, who (having had perhaps his own full share of trouble) can set at rest two uneasy consciences, and the anxieties, it may be, of a whole family without violence to his own feelings, should be very handsomely provided for. Nothing seems more natural than that he should, if possible, be quartered upon the public—failing that, upon the family estate, or the business—or last of all, be set up in a cigarshop, an inn, or "the general line" in a country village. The transaction is not blazoned in the columns of the "Morning Post," nor announced by sound of bell at the market-cross; and, with a world of excuses to choose from, it is hard if the actors in this venial plot cannot account for their parts so as to answer all but that impertinent curiosity which at once encourages and richly merits deception.

As long as such events occur, they were better not made needlessly public property; but their number is certainly too important to be discarded from such a calculation as mine.

It is, I believe, an undisputed, though perhaps unparalleled, anecdote, that a once celebrated sporting character, who, with a well-intentioned view to some such ultimate disposal of a person he was connected with, and mindful, too, how fugitive are speculative gains and good intentions, had made a considerable settlement upon her—was not sorry, in an after time of pressure, to re-acquire, as husband, the funds he had placed beyond his own control by a fortunate liberality of more prosperous days.

It is no uncommon thing, again, for the smart London girl, who has contrived to maintain some relations with her home—and I never heard of one who did not cherish in her heart of hearts that tie—to go occasionally on a visit of sufferance to her country friends. The virtuous sisters, or the stepmother, who would ruthlessly close the door against the penitent, will yet permit their dulness to be enlivened for awhile, perhaps even under protest of some members of the family, by the bearer of new London scraps and fashions. " My daughter," or " my sister from town," is—for all the neighbours know—a milliner's improver, a nursery governess, or a lady's companion. Lively, well-dressed, a first-rate dancer, and as modest-looking as the best, she not unfrequently attracts a country suitor, whom she may accept at once, or bind to an apprenticeship, while she takes a parting sip at the cup of pleasure, and fortifies her good resolutions by a little more dissipation and a little more trouble. Another campaign, too, may give the opportunity of a little diplomatic arrangement for a settlement or a *bonne main*, according to the style of subsisting connexions.

I can by no means close this lengthy analysis of prostitution-marriage without including the very imaginable category of matches for love on both sides; and protesting against the vulgar error which denies susceptibility of love to the woman of pleasure. The " Arthur" of French light literature, the man for whom she keeps what heart she may, while her person is public, is not so common a personage here as elsewhere, because the independence of the English character will not suffer such youths as a gay woman of pretension would adopt, to step forward as candidates for her unpurchased affection ; but it may be relied on that the story of the much-abused *Dame aux Camelias* is, I might almost say, an every-day one. I have seen a London sultana, whose expenditure could not be less than from two to three thousand a year, and the future of whose children only partially provided for, cut off by degrees all her superfluities and luxuries, as her affection for a poor merchant's clerk made her craft from day to day more distasteful, and forced her to cashier, one by one, her opulent admirers ; and in my opinion, half the wildest women in our town would, to the extent of their power, go half way, and farther, to meet the genuine love of any man. The prostitute knows well enough to distinguish the furious evanescent flame of an emancipated schoolboy, or the business-like indifference of the practised man about town, from the passionate affection and sympathy which chance sometimes brings to her feet. Should she herself receive the flame, what wonder can there be that with the terrible sword of jealousy ever ready to her hand, beside all the smaller weapons of the female arsenal, she should gain any amount of ascendency where she would not wed; and where she would, a rapid victory over every consideration of reason and expediency.

It may, I dare say, be objected that in preceding pages I have lent myself to a gross slander upon the public at large, by setting at so grievous a discount the popular estimation of virtue and propriety. But it is not to a fervid imagination, but hard memory and the experience of our profession, that I owe the preceding facts and analysis; and, when I reconsider what I have written,. I confess I can see no single statement or opinion that can surprise the major part of readers conversant with London, although their juxtaposition be new, and favour startling inferences. If we consult the experiences of the clergy, who are the best of authorities upon the social condition of both urban and manufacturing communities; or men who, like the Brothers Mayhew,* have sifted to the dregs the lower orders in capital cities, and in this metropolis particularly, we find that female honour by no means holds its theoretical position in public esteem.† In parts of the manufacturing and mining districts, again, where the infant labour produces an early addition to the parents' resources, it is considered unthrifty and unnecessary to marry a woman who has not given evidence of fertility. She who cannot at least show fair prospect of adding young piecers, tenters, or hurriers, as well as her own person, to the common stock, is no better than an unproductive incumbrance. "If thou houd'st, I wed thee; if thou doesn't, thou'rt none the waur," is a north country proverb, familiar enough to many southerners, and acted upon to an immense extent, as I have been repeatedly and seriously informed by reliable authorities.‡

It is within the memory of politicians, that among the causes of the change in the bastardy clauses of the old Poor Law, was the prevalent fact, that a woman who had had several children, perhaps by different men, was in some parts of the country considered a more eligible match

---

* On the last day of the last week of the first quarter of 1854, there were 13,893 able-bodied women in the workhouses in England and Wales. Of these, 1904 were of dissolute and abandoned character, and 3593 were mothers of illegitimate children, but were not of dissolute or abandoned habits. The estrayals of women which bore fruit, and were avowed by registration of the infants, were in 1852 no less than 55,000. I should imagine that if the cases of seduction-bastardy not brought to light through nonregistration, unfruitfulness, miscarriages, and abortions could be calculated, their numbers would be as three to one of those which transpired as above.

† Mr. Mayhew says but one in twenty of the "street folk" who live as man and wife are married. The couples of the working population who cohabit in town are not married, and in many agricultural provinces cohabitation before marriage is systematic, and a matter of public understanding.

‡ I am not speaking on my own authority, but on that of credible witnesses, when I say that in a midland county, families are unable to keep female domestics virtuous for any length of time; and I am able of my own experience to assert that in the home counties the same occurs, and that the best of servants are often found among those who have children to support.

than the virtuous village girl who had no fruit of sin to her marriage portion; and the numbers of our lower orders whom the philanthropic clergy have found willing to accept of gratuitous marriage, but who adhered pertinaciously to concubinage until the Church gave up her fees, demonstrates clearly enough that the equivalent of a few gallons of beer consumed during the honeymoon, suffices with their order to kick the beam between morality and immorality, religion and irreligion, decency and indecency, present gratification and care for the future.

How little can these men prize the honour of wives or the credit of offspring—how little these females thought of their virtue, or of the rights of married women, the non-appreciation of maidenhood, the ramifications of prostitution. The more I reflect on these things, the more am I convinced that vast masses from top to bottom of our people, have not the proper poetical or theoretical appreciation of female virtue, and are, at present, most indifferent to those laws of society and religion by which they are supposed to be swayed. I am of opinion that these masses must, and obviously may be, dealt with by statesmen for their good, but constitutionally, and as far as they are concerned, without the slightest fear of jarring with an imaginary refinement which they do not possess.

Prostitution diffuses itself through the social fabric, though it is perceptible for a time only, as is the moorland stream which stains but for a space the bluest river. The masses I have spoken of, then, and those who to the third and fourth generation may have a concern in the actual harlot of to-day, are by far too great and important that they or their interests should be ignored or set aside, only through fear of grating on the fanciful belief of poetical men and ladylike politicians, or breaking down their plaster images of a perfectly genteel and virtuous polity. True religion says this must not be.

There are persons who deem the Haymarket and the Argyll Rooms—because, I presume, being adjacent to the Opera House, these places come betwixt the wind and their fine susceptibilies—at once the Alpha and the Omega of prostitution, and would exterminate the vice and its practitioners at one fell swoop, by a bonfire, in the Regent Circus. These will clamour, that the evil is over-magnified when each harlot is called a harlot, because this enlargement of the field of operations puts an end to all nonsensical proposals of high-handed suppression. I use none but their own weapons, when I marshal in the ranks of prostitution each woman who, in a pure society, would properly be so construed. But the accumulation to be dealt with thus becomes so frightful, that all who can read and think will agree with me, that management and regulation of "the greatest social evil" by the bâton or the pillory, grateful though it might be to Exeter Hall, would be neither effective nor perhaps politic.

The hand of an Englishman should be as withered before it advocated the forcible suppression of this vice, as must be the foolish brain that could plot it. Virtue and vice, as we all know, are no subjects for enactment. To protest against the latter's concentration is as futile and absurd as to argue against the herding of nobles or *parvenues*, tradesmen or manufacturers, criminals or paupers. Secrecy would be more fraught than publicity with danger to individuals and the public; diffusion would be lunacy on grounds both of morals and policy. The existing regulations are adequate for public protection and order, which are all the judicious can at present hope for; anything farther in that direction we are certainly not prepared for. The Home Secretary who should attempt anything like coercion would soon have his hands full indeed. We are already *policés* enough—we are already on the verge of excess. The shivering scorn with which the million utterly unaffected by the measure he was advocating, received the Puritan legislator's prescription of a "six-pounder's tail on the pavement," as a plaster for public discontent, should be a lesson, "when found to be made a note of," by such as would play incautiously with the screw of power.

I repeat that prostitution is a transitory state, through which an untold number of British women are ever on their passage. Until preventive measures, previously hinted at, to which I shall presently refer, shall have been considerately adopted—and thereafter, too, if needful, for I am no nostrum-monger—it is the duty, and it should be the business of us all, in the interest of the commonwealth, to see these women through that state, so as to save harmless as much as may be of the bodies and souls of them. And the commonwealth's interest in it is this—that there is never a one among all of these whose partners in vice may not some time become the husbands of other women, and fathers of English children; never a one of them but may herself, when the shadow is past, become the wife of an Englishman and the mother of his offspring; that multitudes are mothers before they become prostitutes, and other multitudes become mothers during their evil career. If the race of the people is of no concern to the State, then has the State no interest in arresting its vitiation. But if this concern and this interest be admitted, then arises the necessity for depriving prostitution not only of its moral, but of its physical venom also.

When the first edition of this book was published, it would have been in vain for me to have sought for any corroboration of these (at that time startling) views, but now that it is the habit of the different local government medical officers to study the natural history of the prostitute, I find plenty of corroborative evidence of these my original statements. Thus, in the recent report from the Select Committee on Contagious Diseases, Mr. Sloggett says, in reply to question 112, [Mr. Percy Wyndham.] Is it not the fact that a very large number of women who have at one time of their lives followed prostitution at Devonport, subsequently marry ?—A large number. Of those 1,775 (the number at Devonport), 250 have married.

Mr. Parsons, in speaking of Portsmouth, adds, in answering question 369, When you speak of so many women having married, have you found that for the most part they marry respectably ?—Many do; it is my own statistics that tell me the fact. I could not have believed it myself, but many of them marry exceedingly well.

CHAPTER III.

DISEASES THE RESULT OF PROSTITUTION.

I HAVE now to consider one or two of the most ordinary consequences of promiscuous intercourse. In passing through (as she generally does, whether rising or falling in the scale) this phase of her career, the prostitute almost inevitably contracts some form of the contagious (*vulgo* "infectious") diseases, which in medicine we term "venereal."* How these are passed from sex to sex and back again, *ad infinitum*, it were superfluous here to illustrate. I have treated at length elsewhere,† under the head of specific disease, of the laws which govern these complaints, and of the influences which favour their diffusion, and the reader will, I dare say, gladly dispense with the introduction of those topics here. I propose, however, in the following pages, to offer some idea of their importance, as being the first and foremost of the effects of prostitution coming under the notice of the surgeon.

When the first edition, in 1857, of this work was published, the London hospitals printed no statistical tables of their patients; but, fortunately for the public, now in the year 1869 a writer possesses materials which are of great value in judging of the prevalence of any form or type of existing disease. And I take advantage of the opportunities these statistics give me to illustrate the prevalence of venereal complaints among the hospital patients of London.

LONDON CIVIL HOSPITAL EXPERIENCE.

St. Bartholomew's Hospital.

This hospital contains 75 beds specially given up to venereal cases. There are 25 beds devoted to males and 50 for females. The statistical

---

* Venereal diseases are affections more or less directly the consequence of sexual intercourse. They embrace two grand divisions—viz., " specific" and "non-specific." Under the former I include syphilis and its sequelæ ; under the latter come gonorrhœa and its train of evils.

† A Practical Treatise on Diseases of the Urinary and Generative Organs in both Sexes. Third edition. 8vo.

tables now annually published enable me to give the following summary of the admission into these venereal wards :—

ST. BARTHOLOMEW'S HOSPITAL.
Report for 1868.

General Diseases.	Total patients under treatment.	Discharged cured and relieved.	Discharged unrelieved.	Discharged for other than medical reasons.	Died.	Per-centage of deaths to number of patients of each disease.	Per-centage of deaths to mortality from all	Nature of Complications, and Remarks.
Syphilis—								
(a) Primary ...	151	133	...	17	1	·66	·55	Sloughing phagedæna, 1 ; delirium tremens, 1 ; hæmorrhage, 1.
(b) Secondary.	204	180	1	20	3	1·49	1·65	Pyæmia (after tracheotomy), 1 ; typhoid fever, 1.
(c) Inherited...	4	4	...	...	...	...	...	
Gonorrhœa, incl. Bubo and Phymosis ...	238	206	...	30	2	·84	1·1	Scarlatina, 2 ; typhoid fever, 1 ; pleurisy, 1 ; rheumatism (acute), 2.
	597	523	1	67	6	2·99	3·30	

I am indebted to Mr. Callender, assistant-surgeon to the hospital, for the following information on the surgical out-patients seen by him July 21, 1869 ; and, at my request, he has separated the venereal from the non-venereal patients :—

Gonorrhœa	33
Swelled testis	5
Simple chancres	15
Indurated sore	10
Secondary symptoms	19
Tertiary symptoms	8
Infantile syphilis	3
Stricture	2
Total venereal cases	95
Total non-venereal cases	92*

Owing to circumstances of a temporary nature, the number of out-patients is at present unusually large.—G. W. C.

Until I pointed out the data, some twelve years ago, neither the profession nor the public recognised the fact that one-half the out-patients at our leading public hospitals came there in consequence of being affected with venereal diseases. The following statistical tables, which I published, are now admitted to have brought about the change in legislation which I shall have hereafter to chronicle; and I should have omitted the following tabulated cases, did I not feel convinced that future writers on the frequency of venereal complaints might thereby lose valuable means of comparison, from which to draw their conclusions, and show how these complaints have from time to time become modified and ameliorated.

The following table gives the symptoms of twenty-nine female patients examined by Mr. Stanley, as candidates for admission into St. Bartholomew's Hospital, on Thursday the 12th of November, 1840 :

1. Condylomata, the elevated form.
2. Condylomata, flattened, excoriated.
3. Tubercular eruption, covering the whole body.
4. Condylomata, elevated, much excoriation around.
5. Ulceration of the buttock, very extensive.

---

* These and the following tables have been drawn up on a very simple plan, which I proposed in the following words many years ago, and are very simply constructed :— "Divide a sheet of ruled foolscap paper into two equal columns. Appropriate one of these to the more usual forms of venereal diseases, written down in order ; and the other to non-venereal affections *en masse*. As each patient is inspected, make a cross upon the proper line, and, when the consultation is over, you will have a tabulated view of the forms of disease it has presented to your notice. Each of the above cases was classed according to its most salient symptom, although it frequently happened that a patient presented several forms of the same disease. Thus any one, at very small cost of trouble, may prepare elementary papers for statistics ; and I venture to impress upon medical readers, without pretending to elaborate a scheme, and I dare say only following in the track of all judicious professors, that if they will adopt the habitual preparation of similar forms, carefully dated, and return them to some of the medical or statistical associations, some very valuable tables might, in course of time, be constructed, which could not fail to be advantageous to the profession and to humanity. The results of the table are such as any one conversant with the working of syphilis in large capitals would have anticipated."

6. Enormous excoriation of and around the genital organs.
7. Chancres, excoriations, and large condyloma.
8. Condylomatous swelling, and phymosis of the præputium clitorides.
9. Tubercular eruption, sore (superficial) throat.
10. Condylomata.
11. Abscess in the clitoris.
12. Condylomata, open bubo (slight).
13. Tubercular eruption, condylomata, ulcerated.
14. Condylomata, superficial ulceration of the throat.
15. Superficial ulceration of the throat.
16. Excoriation of the genital organs, sore throat (superficial).
17. 1, Longitudinal fissure of the tongue ; 2, bald patches.
18. Small tubercular eruption (universal).
19. Gonorrhœa, bubo in left groin.
20. Sores around the anus.
21. Gonorrhœa, excoriation very extensive.
22. Tubercular eruption, iritis, sore throat (superficial).
23. White phagedænic ulceration of the internal part of vulva (very severe).
24. Sores on the labium.
25. Raised condylomata around the anus (clean, without excoriation).
26. Large condylomata.
27. Condylomata, tubercular (red), eruption around the genital organs.
28. Condylomata, tubercular eruption.
29. Condylomata, between the toes, sore throat (superficial).

Twenty-four female patients, classed as under, presented themselves to Mr. Lawrence, for admission into the same hospital, on Thursday the 26th of November, in the same year (1840) :—

1. Bubo, sore at the entrance of vagina.
2. Sores.
3. Condylomata, excoriation.
4. Itch, gonorrhœa, excoriation.
5. Suppurating bubo, gonorrhœa.
6. Warts, gonorrhœa.
7. Very large sores on thighs.
8. Two large sores on vulva, two buboes.
9. Gonorrhœa, excoriated tongue.
10. Excoriations around the anus.
11. Condylomata of the vulva (very red), two buboes.
12. Very large condylomata, excoriation of the throat.
13. Condylomata, itch, and a curious eruption.
14. A small sore on vulva, eruption on body, sore throat.
15. Discharge from vagina, raised condylomata.
16. Sores on the labium, perhaps primary.
17. Condylomata.
18. Eczema, itch, phagedænic sores.
19. Condylomata, excoriation very extensive.
20. Very large condylomata, white excoriation between toes, and on throat.
21. Condylomata, very extensive affection of tongue.
22. Condylomata.
23. Discharge from vagina, superficial ulceration.
24. Two buboes, condylomata.

In 1849, I made an analysis of the surgical out-patients of Messrs. Lloyd and Wormald, at that time assistant-surgeons to St. Bartholomew's Hospital.   They amounted to 5327 during the year; of whom 2513, or nearly half, suffered from venereal diseases :—

	Venereal men.	Venereal women and children.	Total.
Mr. Lloyd's patients.........	1009	245	1254
Mr. Wormald's ditto........	986	273	1250
Total	1995	518	2519

Hence it appears that about one in every five out-patients was a woman or a child.

In the "Medical Times" for 1854, page 587, I find in a report made by Mr. Coote on his out-patients at St. Bartholomew's during four months, he stated that out of 493, the whole number, 212 or 43 per cent. were venereal cases. Of these 155 were males and 57 females, which would seem to favour an approximate calculation, that one female infected on an average three males.

Feeling the importance of presenting the experience, brought down to this date, of this hospital, which took, as it still takes to this day, in 1857, as in 1840, the lead of all others in the comprehensiveness of its relief, I availed myself of the politeness of Mr. Holmes Coote, who has favoured me with the following notes of applicants' cases. I may hereafter have occasion to allude to a fact which I will now state broadly—viz., that in no continental capital could such frightfully aggravated forms and complications of the venereal disease be found as present themselves, I may say weekly, to the surgeons of St. Bartholomew's, in the generally very healthly metropolis of England. This indication of the severity which the complaint is permitted to attain, in a country whose climate would not favour it, was particularly commented upon by M. Ricord, when he inspected the hospitals of London with me a few years ago.

Cases Examined for Admission into St. Bartholomew's Hospital (June, 1857) by Mr. Holmes Coote.

Cases.
1. Gonorrhœa, simple 1
2. Gonorrhœa, with flattened and excoriated mucous tubercles 3
3. Superficial sores of the labia, discharge from the vagina 4
4. Ulcerated verrucæ 2
5. Gonorrhœa, superficial ulceration of labia and nymphæ, œdema of the external organs... 3
6. Ulcerated bubo... 2
7. Superficial ulceration of external organs, with discharge, and bubo in each groin 1
8. Groups of papulæ over the face, trunk, and limbs, upon an inflamed base, thickening of the mucous membrane of the tongue, inflammation and probable ulceration of the mucous membrane of the throat 1
9. Superficial ulceration of the tonsils and soft palate 2
10. Primary sore, with indurated base the size of a shilling on the labium ... 1
11. Mucous tubercles occupying the whole entrance of the vagina ... 1
12. Chronic discharge, ulceration on the os tincæ (speculum) 1

Thus proving that venereal disease presented the same features in London hospitals in 1857 that it did seventeen years before, when the first table was compiled.

It so happens that when these notes were taken, the applicants were far less numerous than on the occasions above referred to. I am enabled to state, however, on the very best authority, that in 1857, whatever progress modern surgery might have made against the intensity of venereal complaints, it had made none against their frequency.

On the 21st of April, 1857, a cold and wet day, therefore reducing to somewhat below the average the attendance of applicants for relief, I saw Mr. Paget treat his out-patients at St. Bartholomew's: 123 men, women, and children, passed under my eye, and out of these there were 59 venereal and 64 non-venereal cases.

From this it would appear, *primâ facie,* that in 1857, as in 1849 and 1854, nearly one-half of the surgical out-patients treated at St. Bartholomew's should be classed under the former of these headings. But Mr. Paget very properly called my attention to a fact, which, by the way, should be taken into consideration by those who undertake the construction of such tables as I have recommended, that syphilis is a complaint of long duration, and the patient suffering from it is constantly coming to the out-patient department, whereas the non-venereal cases are generally disposed of in a few visits. I therefore took occasion to distinguish the new cases, and I found that eight of them were venereal, and sixteen non-venereal—say 33 per cent. of the former, and 66 per cent. of the latter.

Mr. Paget's Out-patients, Male and Female, St. Bartholomew's Hospital, April 2nd, 1857.

Gonorrhœa ...	4
Swelled testis	1
Simple chancres	4
Indurated ditto	6
Secondary symptoms	27
Tertiary ditto	12
Infantile syphilis	1
Stricture	4
Total venereal cases ...	59
Total non-venereal cases	64

The very scanty appearance of gonorrhœa in the above tables, is to be accounted for by its being treated in another department of the hospital, the casualty ward. The paucity of primary syphilis, again, among Mr. Paget's cases, may be due to the fact that one of his colleagues, who is at the present time occupied in syphilitic investigations, might have obtained a temporary preponderance of such cases from the receiving ward.

The heavy proportion of secondary symptoms, under various forms, is worthy of notice. There were 27 cases of secondary, and 12 of tertiary symptoms, which must all have originated months previously. This fearful tenacity of the disease is not peculiar to one surgeon's cases or one hospital. Mr. Coote, in his Treatise on Syphilis (p. 15), observes:—"In the month of October, 1856, out of 93 venereal cases seen by myself and one of my colleagues, there were 19 cases of gonorrhœa and 74 of syphilis. Of these syphilitic cases, 35 were primary sores, and 39 constitutional affections. In the month of September there were, out of 81 patients, 34 cases of gonorrhœa, 23 cases of primary syphilis, and 29 of constitutional syphilis.

Royal Free Hospital.

As I was desirous of knowing the class of out-patients, and the proportion of venereal cases seeking the aid of an institution that really opens its doors and gives gratuitous advice to all comers, I gladly accepted the invitation of Mr. de Meric, and visited this institution on the 23rd day of October, 1868.

The results of the attendance on that day are shown in the following table :—

MEN.

Balanitis	1
Gonorrhœa	17
Chancre	6
Indurated chancre	1
Bubo	4
Secondary symptoms	13
Tertiary affections of skin	3
Orchitis	2
Total	47
Non-venereal Men	17

WOMEN AND CHILDREN.

Gonorrhœa	5
Secondary symptoms	7
Tertiary syphilis of face	1
Warts	1
Bubo	2
Tertiary affections of skin	1
Infantile syphilis	1
Chancre	1
	19
Non-venereal	12

It would appear, then, that two-thirds of the male applicants for relief at this institution have recourse to it on account of venereal affections ; and it would seem probable that this has been going on for twenty-six years at the least.

Before leaving the hospital, I had some conversation with the other surgeons to the Royal Free, namely, Mr. Weedon Cooke and Mr. Gant. They agree that the proportion of venereal diseases is very large, and that even the physicians see among their cases a large proportion of syphilitic complaints, affecting not only the external but the internal parts of the body.

To show how little syphilis has diminished, or rather how much it has increased, at this hospital, let me draw my reader's attention to other statistics furnished by this hospital 26 years ago.

In the year 1842 I visited, for the purpose of investigating the frequency of venereal diseases, the out-patient department of the Royal Free Hospital, in company with my friend, Mr. Gay, and I computed the following table as the result of my observations, published in a former edition of this book :—

Mr. Gay's Out-Patients (Males) at the Royal Free Hospital, August 9th, 1842.

Balanitis	6
Gonorrhœa	32
Swelled testis	4
Urinary fistula	1
Primary syphilis	10
Secondary ditto	6
Tertiary ditto	1
Bubo	2
Total venereal	62
Total non-venereal	19

The excessive proportion of gonorrhœa cases here is remarkable, amounting, as it does, to 50 per cent. of the whole. The non-venereal complaints presented nothing unusual.

In the year 1857 I again attended this hospital to see the male patients of Mr. de Meric, my engagements not allowing me to wait and see the females.

Mr. de Meric's Out-Patients (Males) at the Royal Free Hospital, March 3rd, 1857.

Balanitis	3
Paraphymosis	1
Gonorrhœa	18
Warts	2
Swelled testis	1
Spermatorrhœa (onanism)	2
Chancre	9
Indurated chancre	3
Phagedænic chancre	3
Bubo	1
Secondary symptoms	18
Tertiary syphilis of face	2
Tertiary affections of skin	1
Total venereal	64
Non-venereal, total	23

Out of 87 males, 64 were the venereal cases tabulated above, and 23 mixed diseases, such as bad fingers, ulcerated legs, and so on. Among the former, I found gonorrhœa and secondary symptoms equally abundant. These will always be the most frequent forms among masses of men who neglect themselves. I did not tabulate the various forms of secondary symptoms, but affections of the skin and tongue were rife.

I noticed only one case of rupia, and one of iritis. Papular eruptions were common.

I am disposed to attribute some share in the diminished virulence of venereal complaints to the opening of this and other perfectly free institutions, together with a slight increase of cleanliness among the poor—though by no means proportional, as yet, to the increase of water supply,—the institution of public baths, and the greater cheapness of soap and clothing.

The forms of chancre I witnessed were not serious, and phagedæna was rare, although the patients I saw were mostly from the very dregs of society. I should add, that the weather had been mild and dry for the previous three weeks, both very favourable conditions for the cure of this class of out-patient disease.

MILITARY HOSPITAL EXPERIENCE.

The influence of the different classes of disease, in causing sickness and mortality in the United Kingdom, is shown in the following table from the latest Army Medical Department Report, published in 1869 :—

Average Strength, 70,292.	Admitted into Hospital.	Died.			Ratio per 1,000 of Mean Strength.			
		With the Regiment.	Absent from the Regiment.	Total.	1866.		1860—5.	
					Admitted.	Died.	Admitted.	Died.
Venereal Diseases, now called En-thetic	18,170	11	—	11	258·5	·16	325·6	·11

It appears, then, from this and subsequent statistics, that about one in three soldiers suffers from some venereal complaint. My readers will be surprised when they come, subsequently, in Chapter V., to compare the proportions in the French army, to find that at present only 97 per 1000 men come into hospital for these venereal affections, showing that these complaints are 2½ times more common in England than in France, not one in ten suffering abroad, instead of one in three as in England ; and in Belgium we shall find the proportions even less. Let us hope that the measures I recommended twelve years ago, and now on the point of being carried out in our garrison towns, may render the English soldier as free from such complaints as his continental confreres.

ARMY MEDICAL DEPARTMENT REPORT FOR 1866.

APPENDIX.

ABSTRACT, showing the Admissions into Hospital, Deaths, and Invaliding among the Troops in the United Kingdom in 1866.

Diseases.	Household Cavalry.			Cavalry.			Royal Artillery.			Military Train.			Foot Guards.			Infantry.			Cavalry Depôt.			Roy. Art. Depôt Brigade.			Infantry Depôt Battalions.		
Strength	1,209			7,694			7,873			1,422			5,524			19,545			1,020			2,606			12,865		
	Admitted.	Died.	Invalided.	Admitted.	Died.	Invalided.	Admitted.	Died.	Invalided.	Admitted.	Died.	Invalided.	Admitted.	Died.	Invalided.	Admitted.	Died.	Invalided.	Admitted.	Died.	Invalided.	Admitted.	Died.	Invalided.	Admitted.	Died.	Invalided.
Enthetic:																											
Syphilis primaria	69			444			568			154			872			1445			110			228			803		
,, secundaria	28			181			232			51			96		2	442	2	6	40		2	65			268	1	19
Iritis syphilitica	1		1	11		1	8	2	12	4		1	8			16	2	1	5			1	1	1	26		5
Bubo	13			118		1	140			29			117			498			34			32			285		
Gonorrhœa	53			438			735			132			352			2054			124			376			1618		
Phymosis, &c.	1			18			10						10			38			1			7			35		
Orchitis (Gonorrhœal)	11			30			36			5			37			88			16			16			68	2	
Strictura urethræ				13			21		1	1			14		1	37			16			10			46		
Verrucæ	1			14			14		1	8			20			15		3	10			12			33		4
Cachexia syphiloidea													2		3												
Ulcus penis				30			8									46						1			17		

ALDERSHOT DISTRICT.

Return showing the Number of Soldiers admitted to Hospital suffering from Contagious Diseases, the Number of Men constantly under Treatment, and Number of Days Lost to the Service, with the Number of Men in Garrison for each Week during the Year, June 1868 to May 1869, inclusive.

| WEEK ENDED. | Number of Patients Admitted into Military Hospital. | | | | Total Number Admitted who contracted the Disease within the District. | Average Number constantly under treatment in Military Hospital. | Number of Days lost to the Service. Soldiers. | Number of Men in Garrison. Soldiers. |
| | Primary Sores and Gonorrhœa. | | Other Venereal Diseases. | TOTAL. | | | | |
	Contracted in District.	Contracted Elsewhere.						
1868:								
5 June	7	36	15	58	7	155	1,085	13,138
12 ,,	24	24	18	66	24	171	1,197	13,141
19 ,,	16	14	21	51	16	160	1,120	13,213
26 ,,	17	43	32	92	17	178	1,246	14,606
3 July	25	13	25	63	25	190	1,330	15,912
10 ,,	24	17	21	62	24	173	1,211	15,694
17 ,,	43	26	14	83	43	188	1,316	16,136
24 ,,	33	16	11	60	33	210	1,470	15,769
31 ,,	33	6	11	50	33	198	1,386	15,746
7 August	38	4	13	55	38	188	1,316	15,331
14 ,,	32	5	13	50	32	178	1,246	12,970
21 ,,	39	7	13	59	39	171	1,197	12,966
28 ,,	33	3	21	57	33	175	1,225	12,981
4 September	28	6	14	48	28	174	1,218	12,316
11 ,,	41	5	9	55	41	167	1,169	12,228
18 ,,	31	1	13	45	31	165	1,155	10,817
25 ,,	31	11	13	55	31	153	1,071	10,825
2 October	23	3	7	33	23	151	1,057	10,111
9 ,,	29	3	13	45	29	142	994	10,094
16 ,,	25	3	9	37	25	139	973	10,106
23 ,,	25	1	13	39	25	132	924	10,118
30 ,,	19	2	9	30	19	127	889	10,116
6 November	36	1	8	45	36	128	896	10,112
13 ,,	22	1	8	31	22	136	952	10,101
20 ,,	28	25	14	67	28	153	1,071	10,784
27 ,,	24	3	11	38	24	142	994	10,781
4 December	20	10	8	38	20	143	1,001	10,790
11 ,,	25	4	4	33	25	128	896	10,788
18 ,,	31	7	6	44	31	124	868	10,817
25 ,,	19	2	6	27	19	129	903	10,827
1869:								
1 January	45	10	7	62	45	134	938	10,825
8 ,,	38	4	12	54	38	165	1,155	10,805
15 ,,	31	7	16	54	31	157	1,099	10,802
22 ,,	26	5	14	45	26	166	1,162	10,809
29 ,,	23	7	4	34	23	154	1,078	10,816
5 February	22	8	7	37	22	136	952	10,765
12 ,,	30	6	6	42	30	134	938	10,703
19 ,,	24	6	12	42	24	134	938	10,705
26 ,,	19	1	17	37	19	136	952	10,708
5 March	15	6	10	31	15	124	868	11,465
12 ,,	14	2	7	23	14	118	826	11,434
19 ,,	31	7	12	50	31	114	798	11,217
26 ,,	15	4	7	26	15	113	791	11,469
2 April	21	23	9	53	21	130	910	11,359
9 ,,	22	9	10	41	22	122	854	11,387
16 ,,	14	22	18	54	14	112	784	12,303
23 ,,	17	11	8	36	17	127	889	13,078
30 ,,	22	10	6	38	22	130	910	13,301
7 May	29	7	17	53	29	135	945	13,704
14 ,,	28	6	8	42	28	149	1,043	12,240
21 ,,	16	6	10	32	16	145	1,015	12,220
28 ,,	20	37	7	64	20	143	1,001	16,229

The last table (which I extract from the Report (1869) of the Committee on the Contagious Diseases Act) for the first time will enable the public to see the effect of venereal disease upon a large body of troops concentrated at Aldershot, and doubtless had a great influence in urging that committee to extend the Act to a larger area.

To enable my readers to compare the present with former conditions of the Army, I shall republish a table which appeared in the former edition of this book.

Admissions into Hospital from Venereal Disease and Deaths among the Dragoon Guards and Dragoons, the Foot Guards, and Infantry of the Line serving in the United Kingdom from April 1st, 1837, to March 31st, 1847.

	Cavalry.	Foot Guards.	Infantry.	Total.	Deaths.	Artillery.
Aggregate strength... ...	54,374	40,120	160,103	254,597	...	—
Syphilis primitiva	1,396	4,769	6,157	12,322	1	—
Syphilis consecutiva ...	462	536	2,085	3,083	8	—
Ulcus penis non syphiliticum	2,920	883	13,380	17,183	1	—
Bubo simplex	1,495	989	6,635	9,119	1	—
Gonorrhœa	3,725	2,198	12,988	18,911	...	—
Hernia humoralis	1,019	558	2,768	4,345	...	—
Strictura urethræ	131	92	198	421	4	—
Cachexia syphiloidea ...	5	...	7	12	2	—
Phymosis et paraphymosis...	52	18	217	287	...	—
Total...	11,205	10,043	44,435	65,683	17	463
Number of men per 1000 of strength admitted during ten years	206	250	277	257	—	—

Dr. Balfour, who, with Sir Alexander Tulloch, drew up the report from which this table was compiled, has kindly favoured me with the following particulars, which may serve to illustrate it :—

In answer to the inquiry why this distinction is made between the foot-guards and infantry, he informed me that the line contains a large proportion of recruits, and of men returning from foreign service ; whereas in the foot-guards there is usually a much greater proportion of soldiers who have arrived at maturity on the one hand, and who, on the other, have not served in foreign climates.   As these circumstances were likely to have affected the amount of sickness and mortality, the returns of the two classes were kept separate in preparing the tables.

Dr. Balfour also remarks, that the meaning of the distinct classification of " Syphilis primitiva" and " Ulcus penis non syphiliticum," is not in pursuance of any written regulation or printed direction.   The surgeon is at full liberty to enter his cases under either title.   In answer to my doubt—resulting from the discrepancy of the table with my preconceptions—whether all cases of gonorrhœa were noted in the army, he told me that, so far as his experience went, no great number of them escaped notice, as health inspections were made once a week, which was the general rule in the service.* If a soldier was found at inspection to be labouring under disease, he was reported for having concealed it to his superior officer, who ordered him punishment-drill on his discharge from hospital. In order to induce him to apply early for relief, the soldier was told that if he did so, he might probably be only a few days instead of several weeks under treatment.

It was and is still contrary to the rules of the service to treat men out of hospital; even were it otherwise, the habits of the soldier and the accommodation in barracks would not favour celerity of cure.

I called Dr. Balfour's attention to the large number of cases followed by hernia humoralis, the proportion of which exceeds, as given in the above table, what we are accustomed to see in private or in hospital practice. It follows about one case in four of gonorrhœa in the army generally, and one in three in the cavalry; and Dr. Balfour informed me it probably arose among the latter from the effects of horse exercise, and, speaking of the army generally, from the secret use of injections to check discharge, and the exercise taken at drill when the man had not reported himself in the very earliest stage of the disease. As regards relapses among soldiers, it is as difficult to say as in private practice whether they are genuine or, in fact, fresh attacks.

The cases of syphilis primitiva among the household infantry seem enormously to outnumber those in other corps, being one to every ten soldiers of the former against one in twenty-six of the infantry at large. The proportion of syphilis consecutiva throughout the army is large, being as one to four cases of syphilis primitiva. In the brigade of Guards, though the average of syphilis primitiva is heavy, as above stated, only 11 per cent. of the cases are followed by secondary symptoms, which, however, follow 33 per cent. of the cases in the Line. It is not improbable, I apprehend, that some portion of the heavy mortality attributed to secondary syphilis would have been more accurately classed under the head of cachexia syphiloidea.

I understand that a mild mercurial treatment is usually pursued in the army, for hard sores especially. Some surgeons give no mercury; but this depends upon the discretion of the individual. Sir James M'Grigor, the late Director-General of the Army Medical Department, issued a circular some years ago, soon after the publication of Mr. Rose's work, in which attention was called to the subject: but full discretionary power was left in the hands of the surgeon.

An apparent increase will be observed in the number of diseased soldiers during the period antecedent to 1837. The annual number of diseased cavalry in the former seven years was 181; and in the second 206 per 1000 men. This increase would appear enormous; and it is quite an open question whether, in truth, it represents an aggravation of dissipation and disease, in spite of the advances of science and more careful

---

* As will be seen hereafter, these health inspections had been very generally abandoned in the army, to the no small detriment of the soldier. I am pleased to add, however, that the Committee of the House of Commons have recently (1869) recommended that these health inspections be re-introduced.

army management, or, as Dr. Balfour, who drew up these valuable
tables, suggested, is apparent only, resulting from more painstaking and
systematic collection of returns, for the continuation of which I shall
look with anxiety.

It must be remembered, also, that the same man may be in hospital
several times in a year, and thus figure upon paper as several patients ;
but, making every allowance, the documents before us show amply how
great is the enemy we have to deal with.

It is cheering, nevertheless, to observe that the absolute deaths in the
last decennial period upon an aggregate of 254,597 men numbered only
17; and happily, also, we now rarely meet with those losses of the palate,
nose, or portions of the cranium which our museums show must formerly
have been frequent.

NAVY EXPERIENCE.

Statistical Report of the Health of the Navy for the Year 1865.

Summary.—The total force in 1865 was 51,210 ; and the total number of men sick daily, 2,730·4, which is in the ratio of 53·3 per 1000.
In 1864, the ratio was 54· (page 377).

Four thousand three hundred and thirteen cases of syphilis were
under treatment, of which 130 were invalided. The daily loss of service occasioned by it was equal to 468 men, and the total days' sickness
on board ship and in hospital gave an average duration to each case of
39.6 days. In 1864 the daily loss of service was equal to 460 men, and
the average duration of each case 38·3 days (page 377).

*Table showing Comparative Prevalence of Venereal Disease on the different
Stations in* 1864 *and* 1865, *per* 1000 *Men.*

STATIONS.	SYPHILIS.		GONORRHŒA.	
	1864.	1865.	1864.	1865.
Home	96·6	97·1	25·7	30·3
Mediterranean	35·3	35·2	10·2	17·1
North America and West Indies	52·4	53·4	15·8	15·2
Brazils	45·2	36·1	22·6	16·1
Pacific	48·7	61·2	19·4	18·2
West Coast of Africa	22·9	42·3	22·3	40·
Cape of Good Hope and East Indies ...	63·7	65·5	23·2	23·8
China	177·7	165·3	37·2	35·3
Australia	17·2	16·	6·8	9·8
Irregular Force	127·6	130·9	20·1	45·7*

* Page 377.

Table* showing the Proportion of Venereal Diseases of Total Force.

DISEASE OR INJURY.	Number of Cases.	Ratio per 1000 of Force.	Number Invalided.	Ratio per 1000 of Force.	Number dead.	Ratio per 1000 of Force.
Disease of the Bladder and Kidneys... }	100	1·9	13	·2	3	—
Syphilis	4,313	85·1	130	2·5	—	—
Gonorrhœa	1,387	27·3	1	—	—	—

* Page 381.

Table* showing the Number of Days' Sickness from each Disease of Total Force.

DISEASE OR INJURY.	Number of Days' Sickness on Board.	Number of Days' Sickness in Hospital.	Total Number of Days' Sickness.	Average Number of Men Daily Sick.	Ratio per 1000 of Force.
Disease of the Bladder and Kidneys . ... }	1,091	1,056	2,147	5·8	·1
Syphilis	83,158	87,670	170,828	468·	9·1
Gonorrhœa	20,778	4,697	25,475	69·7	1·3

* Page 385.

Table* showing the Proportion of Venereal Diseases on Home Station.

DISEASE OR INJURY.	Number of Cases.	Ratio per 1000 of Force.	Number Invalided.	Ratio per 1000 of Force.	Number Dead.	Ratio per 1000 of Force.
Disease of the Bladder and Kidneys . }	47	2·2	3	·1	1	—
Syphilis	2,039	97·1	28	1·3	—	—
Gonorrhœa	636	30·3	—	—	—	—

* Page 23.

Table* showing the Number of Days' Sickness from each Disease on Home Station.

DISEASE OR INJURY.	Number of Days' Sickness on Board.	Number of Days' Sickness in Hospital.	Total Number of Days' Sickness.	Average Number of Men Sick Daily.	Ratio per 1000 of Force.
Disease of the Bladder and Kidneys . ... }	211	590	801	2·1	·1
Syphilis	25,727	57,005	82,732	226·6	10·8
Gonorrhœa	7,746	3,116	10,862	29·7	1·4

* Page 25.

In the Report of the English Navy for 1865, page 16, we read—

" These diseases (venereal) appear as a certain sequence of leave, and the loss of service from this cause is very great, not only at the time, but frequently by leaving the constitution in a cachectic state, and thus rendering the men more susceptible to the causes of other diseases. Our men contracted the disease in Plymouth and Portsmouth, and a few cases occurred after leave at Cork ; but none appeared after leave in the French ports, or in Lisbon, Portland, or Berehaven."

To show how prevalent is syphilis in the navy, the following extract from the Navy Report of 1865 is given (page 18) by Surgeon Sloggett, as an example, on board H. M. vessel the Edgar, on the Home Station :—

" In the past six months of the year, sixty-seven men have been affected with primary syphilis, and of these certainly sixty contracted the disease at Portsmouth. As out of this time six weeks had been spent at sea, it follows that in four months and a half this number of men contracted the disease. Deducting officers, boys, and those of the older, more respectable, and married men, who never exposed themselves (at least 250) there remain 550 men, out of whom sixty became infected in four months and a half, being a proportion of nearly thirty per cent. per annum, rendered unfit for service by this scourge of our seaport towns" (page 18).

The surgeon, Dr. Bowden, in speaking of the disease on board the Prince Consort, on the Home service, says—

" Of the whole ship's company 27·7 per cent. have been affected by some form of these complaints ; they represent 4·9 of the total cases of sickness on board, and 5·1 of the total days' sickness. The average duration of treatment on board was 9·7 days. Of the 161 cases sent to hospital, ninety-five were due to this cause.

The naval returns for 1865 give a very lamentable account of the complaint in Japan. Surgeon Loney says—

" Soon after the ship was released from quarantine on the disappearing of the small-pox, general leave was given to the ship's company, as they had been confined on board for some time. One unfortunate consequence which followed this indulgence was, after a time, the addition to the sick-list of twenty cases of syphilis and several of gonorrhœa, all contracted at Yokohama. The syphilitic disease proved of the most intractable character, much exceeding in virulence our previous experience of the same disease in the East Indies. The primary sore was not formidable, healing for the most part readily enough under treatment, and in none of our cases on board taking on a sloughing action ; but all of them were followed by secondary symptoms of the most inveterate nature. The soft parts were first attacked, the skin being covered with coppered-coloured and pustular eruptions, and occasionally with rupia ; then ulceration of the throat and larynx took place ; and this was followed by pseudo-rheumatic pains in the bones, periostitis, nodes, and caries. Emaciation progressed very rapidly, and the men from being strong and robust, were so worn out by the virulence of the disease, and the want of sleep from nocturnal pains, that in a short time they were reduced nearly to skeletons, and all had sooner or later to be sent home invalided. The brothels in Japan are a peculiar institution, under the regulation and supervision of the Government Japanese officials, who receive, it is said, great portion of the profits. The women are collected into one large building, which is open to all comers, and is visited in Yokohama by a mixed crowd of Chinese, and sailors, and adventurers of all nations; and whether it is owing to the effect of this indiscriminate, unclean, and common intercourse, or to some concentrated specific form of syphilitic poison existing amongst the Japanese themselves, shut up as they have been so long from communication with the external world, the poison not having been modified and weakened as in Europe by transmission through multitudes, certain it is that the disease contracted in Japan is about the worst form of syphilis known, and followed by the most lamentable consequences" (page 310).

It is not for me perhaps to question these facts, but I may suggest that the previous attack of small-pox and the condition of the vessel may have something to do with the severity of these attacks. The most curious circumstance in my opinion is the extraordinary frequency of severe rheumatism following these syphilitic affections—for I read at page 305 :—

" That rheumatism, unaccompanied by any form of skin affection, or sign of constitutional disease, appears in 26 per cent. of the cases recognised as non-infecting, and in 33 per cent. of the infecting sores, being, in the latter class of cases, commonly associated with a more or less ill-marked roseola-like syphilide, but in other instances appearing alone without any indication of secondary infection" (page 305).

These attacks resemble the epidemic of the fifteenth century.

I further add the returns of the navy for 1833, in order to enable my readers to draw comparisons between the present return and those of former periods.

It appeared from official returns extending over the seven years from 1830 to 1836, inclusive, and relating to an aggregate of 21,493 men employed in the "home service,"—that is to say, in our ports and about our coasts,—that 2880, say 134 per thousand, or 13·40 per cent., were attacked with venereal affections during that period.

In the year 1851 the following report was published, carrying on the experience from 1837 to 1843, both years inclusive :—

Report of the Health of the Navy (Home Service) for the Seven Years from 1837 to 1843.

—	1837.	1838.	1839.	1840.	1841.	1842.	1843.	Total.	Ratio per 1000 men.
Gonorrhœa..	93	82	101	122	200	207	205	1010	31·9
Stricture ...	4	6	12	19	24	17	4	85	2·6
Orchitis......	20	8	13	25	50	33	86	235	7·6
Syphilis......	118	122	132	175	320	275	314	1456	46·1

It appears from another table in the same report, that on board of ships employed "variously"—*i.e.*, not exclusively on the "home" service (when the men are apt to give way to excesses in foreign ports and with a variety of seriously affected women), the proportions of syphilis nearly double those given above, being 73 against 46 per thousand men, while the patients suffering from gonorrhœa were 44 against 31 per thousand.

Venereal diseases, then, are more common among soldiers than among sailors, owing, probably, to the more limited opportunities of becoming infected which the profession of the latter exposes them to.

MERCHANT SERVICE EXPERIENCE.

Dr. Rooke has kindly furnished me with the following returns.

Table of Cases of Venereal Disease treated in the "Dreadnought" Hospital Ship from 1864 to 1868.

	Number of In-patients treated for Venereal.	Total number of In-patients treated for all diseases.	Number of Out-patients treated for Venereal.	Total number of Out-patients treated for all diseases.	Total number of cases of Venereal.
1864...	721	2,129	430	1,315	1,151
1865...	690	1,918	384	1,134	1,074
1866...	656	2,175	380	1,125	1,036
1867...	573	1,980	339	1,044	912
1868...	648	1,875	396	1,193	1,044
	3,288	10,077	1,929	5,811	5,217

From these returns we may infer that in the merchant service, one in every three patients who applies to the hospital suffers from venereal disease.

In 1851 Mr. Busk, at that time Surgeon to the "Dreadnought," furnished me with similar data, published in the first edition of this book, and the coincidence and the proportions of their complaints is very curious. During the preceding five years, 13,081 medical and surgical cases were admitted, of which no less than 3703 or 28 per cent. were venereal, proving what I have advanced elsewhere, that venereal complaints have not diminished in frequency, although milder in form than they were formerly.

As far, then, as we may judge from the data above cited, venereal diseases are still very common among large bodies of otherwise healthy males engaged in the public service. At the same time, scurvy and hospital gangrene have nearly disappeared from the reports. The returns do not enable us to arrive at any accurate conclusion how far they incapacitate their victims from duty. Dr. Wilson, who must be supposed to be a competent judge, inasmuch as he has compiled the returns, told me in 1857 that on an average each man so affected is incapacitated from doing duty for a month. In the army, his stay in hospital has been averaged at six weeks. In the return furnished by Mr. Busk, the average stay in hospital is stated to be twenty-two days; this is similar to that in the army; and during five years the expense of venereal patients was £4165.

I doubt whether venereal complaints, although evidently more severe formerly, were ever more common than at present, or whether, since syphilis was first treated in hospitals, the large proportion here noticed, namely two out of three out-patients at the Free Hospital, nearly one in two at St. Bartholomew's, one out of every three at the "Dreadnought," one out of four in the army, one out of seven in the navy, at any former period suffered from venereal disease,—and yet many believe that the disease is declining. That such is not the case, if number be any criterion, must be admitted by all who weigh well the above statistics, and compare them with the statements met with in nearly all the books that have treated of syphilis. I think the surgeon to Queen Elizabeth, who nearly three centuries ago penned the following words, could he rise from his grave to see the present condition of the complaint, would corroborate my opinion:—

"If I be not deceived in mine opinion (friendly reader), I suppose the disease itselfe was never more rife in Naples, Italie, France, or Spaine, than it is this day in the Realme of England. I may speake boldly because I speake truly; and yet I speake it with griefe of minde that in the Hospital of Saint Bartholomew, in London, there hath been cured of this disease, by me and three others, within five years, to the number of one thousand and more. I speake nothing of Saint Thomas Hospital, and other houses about the citie, wherein an infinite multitude are daily cured. *It happened very seldom in the Hospitall of Saint Bartholomew's whilst I stayed there, amongst every twenty diseased that were taken into the said house, which was most commonly on the Monday, ten of them were infected with Lues Venerea.*"—*A briefe and necessary Treatise tovching the cvre of the disease now vsvally called Lves Venerea,* by W. Clovves, one of her Maiesties Chirurgions, 1696, p. 149.*

If my inferences are correct, that venereal diseases, though decreasing in virulence, are numerically as prevalent as ever, where single men are massed together, is it not time to consider, whether in the present advanced state of civilization, some methodical steps should not be taken still farther to mitigate and, as nearly as may be, eradicate the evil, more especially as we have so successfully operated against many others of "the thousand natural shocks that flesh is heir to."

Truth demands the acknowledgment that the individual affections both in England and on the Continent, are less severe in the present day. In but few cases do the symptoms run high, or is the patient permanently crippled by the disease. I myself can testify to enormous changes in this respect during the last twenty years. The frightful cases, attended with the loss of the nose, palate, &c., which formerly were really not uncommon, are now very rare either in hospitals or in private practice. The weekly average of deaths from syphilis in London,

---

* A copy of this work can be seen in the library of the Medico-Chirurgical Society.

within the last ten years, varies from 1·6 to 4·3. Phagedæna, or "the black lion of Portugal," was formerly to be met with weekly in our hospitals. It is now an exceptional case. Sir Astley Cooper states, that in the St. Giles' Workhouse at one time and in one room there were seven of these terrible cases, of which five were fatal. I need not say that, thanks to the improved treatment, and the many channels of relief available to the poor, these wholesale calamities are put a stop to, although an isolated case, as the Registrar-General's tables tell us, may every now and then result in a fatal termination.

LONDON.

Deaths registered from Syphilis in corresponding weeks of eleven years.

Week.	1858.	1859.	1860.	1861.	1862.	1863.	1864.	1865.	1866.	1867.	Mean. Deaths.	Mean. Temp.	1868. Deaths.	1868. Temp.
Forty-seventh ..	5	4	10	2	10	8	12	3	9	9	7·2	41·4	4	39·8
Forty-eighth ...	6	6	4	9	4	8	3	12	5	12	6·9	41·8	13	42·5
Forty-ninth	10	5	4	7	3	7	3	4	4	6	5·3	42·5	9	45·6
Fiftieth	5	6	2	5	4	6	3	8	6	6	5·1	40·5	12	47.6

EXPERIENCE IN PRIVATE PRACTICE.

I cannot pretend to offer an opinion as to the general increase or decrease of these complaints in private practice. There is in our profession very little interchange of notes and statistics, and no organized correspondence with any body or society, and I fancy no medical man could draw a sound deduction as to the greater or less prevalence of any particular disease from the state of his own practice. He who should believe and say disease was extravagantly rife in London because he individually happened to be much in vogue, would deliver himself of as notable a fallacy, I apprehend, as another who should declare it was totally extinct, because from being out of repute, out of date, out of the stream, or for some other of the thousand reasons which sway the British public, he never happened to see a patient at all.

Each one, however, may without difficulty contribute a little information to the common stock by analysing the mass of cases which are presented to him. I shall give here one or two opinions, resulting from my own experience, which may, perhaps, be hereafter of value to others wishing to compare the proportions of the various affections in 1879 with those prevailing in our day.

In the first place—the venereal affections now seen in private practice are slight. Patients come to the medical man early. The *mauvaise honte*, which formerly acted to their prejudice, is passing away, and the necessity for immediate treatment generally admitted. To this cause I attribute to a great extent the mildness of the disease, and the rapidity of cure in the majority of cases. No doubt can exist that improved treatment and a more correct diagnosis are operating in the same direction; science has been assisted by the almost complete abstinence of the upper classes generally from intoxication, though not from liquor, and the liberal ablutions now so much and so beneficially in fashion.

The loss of the virile organ is, now-a-days, a thing almost unheard of in private practice. A surgeon might practise in London for many years without gaining any experience of the affection of the bones of the nose which causes that organ to fall in. It is true that we occasionally meet with an obstinate case of this affection in highly strumous patients, but even these, under appropriate treatment, escape the sad deformity, and ultimately recover. I have, every now and then, cases of tertiary symptoms, which return again and again, and offer most rebellious instances of the virulence of the disease amongst the weak and debilitated; but still death from syphilis is almost unheard of in private practice. I did see one some time ago. It came on gradually from a want of rallying power in the system, and a few tubercles were found in the lungs. It is to be regretted that in the present day the indurated sore is not more rare, attended as it is with many sad sequelæ. Secondary symptoms are not severe, but, although slight, they linger on for months, now better, now worse, until the powers of the system, if well supported, get the better of the affections of the tongue or the eruption on the skin. Rarely, now, are the deeper structures affected, and patients generally, if not very injudiciously treated, completely recover within a reasonable time.

The results of private practice bear out the statistics from the public institutions, that gonorrhœa is the most frequent of the venereal affections. It no longer, however, takes the formidable shapes of bygone times, although it is often to the full as tiresome from assuming the chronic form.

I am often obliged to remind nervous patients who complain of tardy cures, that though they have to thank advancing science for such mild results as now form the penalty of their frailty, they must not expect a day when the complaint is to be divested of all pain or annoyance. Neither the disease nor our treatment are in general so much to be blamed for the worst phases which the former even now occasionally assumes, as the naturally bad constitution of the sufferer or the perverse industry he has applied to the debilitation of a sound one. He has oftentimes his own neglect to thank for doubled and trebled suffering —often his own folly in bringing to us only the reversion of a case complicated, and perhaps aggravated, by one or other of the villanous quacksalvers who are still permitted to flaunt their nostrums in the public face, to gull, to swindle, and to kill.

The observations I made in 1857 on the extortion of quacks, applies equally to the subject in 1869, and I allow the case which appeared in my last edition to remain as a beacon to warn the unwary. A gentleman who believed himself to be suffering from spermatorrhœa went to a noted quack and paid his usual fee. A specimen of his urine was immediately demanded, and on examination under a microscope, pronounced to be full of spermatozoa. The patient showed unmistakable signs of alarm, and the quack, finding he had the proper sort of customer, boldly predicted speedy death, to be averted only by the purchase of a cure for fifty pounds. The first call of nine pounds on account of this sum was paid on the spot, and the remainder within a few days. The patient was then, I am assured, presented with a large box of medicines, ready packed, and desired to keep in a room at the same temperature for twenty-eight weeks, or thereabouts, and not attempt to breathe the outer air. After some weeks of unrewarded perseverance in this *régime*, the unhappy patient again sought the presence of the wizard, and complained that he felt no better. He was asked, " How could he expect it ? Had he not disobeyed ? His presence there was proof enough of that !" He pleaded in vain, that to keep his room for twenty-eight weeks, if not impossible, would be his ruin, and was told that, having by his own act removed the responsibility from the learned doctor's shoulders, their contract was at an end, and he must now put up with the possible ill consequences, and the certain loss of his money. It was under these circumstances that he came to me, in a highly nervous state, and of course much annoyed at being bereft of fifty pounds by this " microscope dodge." In three weeks he recovered, and would not have rushed, as he did, into the courts of law but for the impudent plea set up for not returning the money after failure of the consideration. The recipient of the fifty pounds actually stated that the deluded one had been guilty of masturbation, and therefore could not show his face in court. The challenge was accepted, and the infamous imputation of course faded away. I cannot show the sequel better than by quoting the following passage from the judgment of the Court :—

" I have not the slightest doubt upon this case—that it is a case for damages, and that the plaintiff is entitled to recover the whole of the sum claimed. I think it is highly creditable to the plaintiff that he had the moral courage to come into court and expose this transaction ; and as to the agency,* the assistant, whoever he may be, has certainly committed a gross fraud, and one cannot help feeling warmly that this fraud was practised. At the same time one cannot help seeing as to —— —— not having been present at the interviews, that this is a mere stratagem to secure himself against the consequences of being brought into a court of justice ; and the whole of the case, I think, is very discreditable to the defendant, and the plaintiff is entitled to the judgment of the court for the whole of the amount sued for. One cannot help saying that the whole case is most discreditable and disgusting, and I shall allow the highest expenses to the witnesses."†

The editor of " The Lancet" observed, in conclusion of his remarks upon this case :—

" How long is this system to continue ? It is a disgrace to the laws, which falsely pretend to regulate practitioners of medicine and to protect the public, that such things are allowed. The case in question is

---

* It was alleged by the defendant's counsel that the offence had been committed by an assistant of the defendant.

† This case is reported in full in the Appendix of Author's " Treatise on the Reproductive Organs," which see.

simply an illustration of a system so ruinous, so devastating, so fatal to its victims, that it calls loudly for legislative interference. Laws, however framed, will probably be inadequate altogether to suppress those outrages upon humanity ; but legislation may do something to mitigate and arrest them. If we are to have laws for the protection of women and the suppression of obscene publications, why should we not have an Act of Parliament to suppress a traffic which, in its consequences, is equally detrimental to the health and happiness of a large portion of the public ?"

CHAPTER IV.

EXISTING PROVISION FOR THE CONTROL AND
RELIEF OF PROSTITUTES.

I HAVE now passed in review before the reader the leading features of prostitution, as exhibited in this country, and I have shown him the vast extent of the evil, by placing before him the numbers of the women who snatch a precarious living from this life of sin. Some, as we have seen, enjoy in their turn, for a brief season, a pre-eminence in guilt, on whom large sums are lavished, to be recklessly squandered on the adornment of their bodies, and indulgence in sensual excesses, without thought for the time of want and misery that surely overtakes the prostitute who prolongs the pursuit of her calling beyond her prime to that sad period when health, and youth, and beauty, and all that renders woman attractive, are no longer hers ; while others, and these the vast majority, are forced to give, in exchange for the bare means of keeping life, all that makes life worth having, and are oft-times sunk so low as to abandon their bodies for the poor return of a few paltry pence. The ruin wrought on these wretched women is bad enough, but, as we have seen, it is not all, or nearly all, the evil produced by the system. Vice does not hide itself, it throngs our streets, intrudes into our parks and theatres, and other places of resort, bringing to the foolish temptation, and knowledge of sin to the inno-cent ; it invades the very sanctuary of home, destroying conjugal hap-piness, and blighting the hopes of parents. Nor is it indirectly only that society is injured ; we have seen that prostitutes do not, as is generally supposed, die in harness ; but that, on the contrary, they for the most part become, sooner or later, with tarnished bodies and pol-luted minds, wives and mothers ; while among some classes of the people the moral sentiment is so depraved, that the woman who lives by the hire of her person is received on almost equal terms to social inter-course. It is clear, then, that though we may call these women outcasts and pariahs, they have a powerful influence for evil on all ranks of the community. The moral injury inflicted on society by prostitution is incalculable ; the physical injury is at least as great. Let us take the case of London : in this city, as the return shows, there are 6515 women known to the police to be prostitutes ; it is not too much to say that out of every four of these women one at least is diseased, so that we have among us more than 1500, at a moderate computation, human beings daily engaged in the occupation of spreading abroad a loathsome poison, the effects of which are not even confined to the partakers of their sin, but are too often transmitted to his issue, and bear their fruits in tottering limbs and tainted blood. Broken constitutions, sickly bodies, and feeble minds are times out of number the work of the prostitute. In a few words, then, prostitution consigns to a life of degradation thousands of our female population, ruining them utterly body and soul, who in their turn retaliate on society the wrong inflicted on themselves. It makes our streets unfit thoroughfares for the modest, and a reproach to us when compared with the decency observable in foreign cities. It exercises an evil influence on the nation at large, depraving the minds and lowering the moral tone. It is the cause of disease, premature decay, untimely death. Having thus become to a certain extent acquainted with the evil whose ravages we desire to mitigate, we may now shortly examine the actual state of the law with regard to it—that is, what pressure it is in the power of the authorities to exercise upon it, and how far that power is exerted.

The duties of the metropolitan police and their means of discharging them are limited and defined by the Act of Parliament of the 2nd and 3rd of Victoria, cap. 47, dated 17th August, 1839, and intituled " An Act for further Improving the Police in and near the Metropolis;" being an amendment of Sir Robert Peel's original Statute, the 10th George IV.

I have before me a copy of the 2nd and 3rd of Victoria, and on examination I find the clauses bearing upon prostitution to be the 44th, 52nd, 54th, 58th, and 63rd.

The 44th clause runs as follows :

" And whereas it is expedient that the provisions made by law for preventing disorderly conduct in the houses of licensed victuallers be extended to other houses of public resort; be it enacted, that every person who shall have or keep any house, shop, room, or place of public resort within the Metropolitan Police District, wherein provisions, liquors, or refreshments of any kind shall be sold or consumed (whether the same shall be kept or retailed therein, or procured elsewhere), and who shall wilfully or knowingly permit drunkenness or other disorderly conduct in such house, shop, room, or place, or knowingly suffer any unlawful games or any gaming whatsoever therein, or knowingly suffer or permit *prostitutes*, or persons of notoriously bad character, to meet together and remain therein, shall for every such offence be liable to a penalty of not more than five pounds."

It would appear that no more right of entry or power of action is given to the police by this clause, or any other in the Act before me, than they enjoy under the Licensed Victuallers' Act, the 9th of George IV., cap. 61, the governing statute in this case, by which they can only enter houses in case of disorder on request of the landlord, and can only proceed against him by summons or sworn information of one or more witnesses.*

* The power of entering licensed refreshment houses is, now, however, given to them by a later statute, as will be presently mentioned.

The 52nd clause of the same statute provides :

" That it shall be lawful for the Commissioners of Police from time to time, and as occasion may require, to make regulation for the route to be observed by all carts, carriages, horses, and persons, and for preventing obstructions of the streets and thoroughfares within the Metropolitan Police District, in all times of public processions, public rejoicings, or illuminations ; and also to give directions to the constables for keeping order, and for preventing any obstruction of the thoroughfares in the immediate neighbourhood of her Majesty's palaces and the public offices, the High Court of Parliament, the courts of law and equity, the police courts, the theatres, and other places of public resort, and in any case when the streets or thoroughfares may be thronged, or may be liable to be obstructed."

The 54th clause provides, in continuation :

" That every person who, after being made acquainted with the regulations or directions which the Commissioners of Police shall have made for regulating the route of horses, carts, carriages, and persons during the time of Divine Service, and for preventing obstructions during public processions, and on other occasions hereinbefore specified, shall wilfully disregard, or not conform himself thereto, shall be liable to a penalty of not more than forty shillings. And it shall be lawful for any constable belonging to the Metropolitan Police Force to take into custody, *without warrant*, any person who shall commit any such offence within view of any such constable."

The same 54th clause also provides :

" That every common prostitute or night-walker, loitering, or being in any thoroughfare or public place, for the purpose of prostitution or solicitation, *to the annoyance of the inhabitants or passengers*, shall be liable to a penalty of not more than forty shillings, and to be dealt with in the same manner."

And again, that "every person who shall use any profane, indecent, or obscene language, to the annoyance of the inhabitants or passengers;" and also "every person who shall use any threatening, abusive, or insulting words or behaviour, with intent to provoke a breach of the peace, or whereby a breach of the peace may be occasioned," may be also so dealt with.

The 58th clause enacts :

" That every person who shall be found drunk in any street or public thoroughfare within the said district, and who while drunk shall be guilty of any riotous or indecent behaviour, and also every person who shall be guilty of any violent or indecent behaviour in any police station-house, shall be liable to a penalty of not more than forty shillings for every such offence, or may be committed, if the magistrate by whom he shall be convicted shall think fit, instead of inflicting upon him any pecuniary fine, to the house of correction for any time not more than seven days."

The 63rd clause enacts :

" That it shall be lawful for any constable belonging to the Metropolitan Police District, and for all persons whom he shall call to his assistance, to take into custody, without a warrant, any person who, within view of any such constable, shall offend in any manner against this act, and whose name and residence shall be unknown to such constable, and cannot be ascertained by such constable."

Two other Acts, under the provisions of which the conduct of prostitutes admits of regulation may be here noticed ; they are 23 Vic. c. 27, and 25 George II. c. 36. The first of these is " An Act for granting to her Majesty certain duties on wine licences and refreshment houses, and for regulating the licensing of refreshment houses and the granting of wine licences." By the 7th section of this act, confectioners and eating-house keepers are entitled to take out licences to sell wine to be drunk on the premises; and by the 9th section a penalty of £20 is imposed upon any person keeping a refreshment house, for which a licence is required under the act, without having procured such licence. The licenses are, under the provisions of this act, to be granted by the persons having charge for the time being of the collection of the Excise revenue ; notice of the application for any such licence must be given to the Lord Mayor, or Aldermen, or Justices, by whom the granting of the licence may be prohibited. By the 18th section, constables and police officers are empowered to visit licensed refreshment houses ; and by the 27th section, no such house may be kept open for the sale of refreshments between the hours of one and four A.M., and by the 32nd section, every refreshment-house keeper, who shall suffer prostitutes to assemble at, or continue in or upon his premises shall, upon conviction, pay for the first offence a fine not exceeding forty shillings ; for the second offence, a fine not exceeding £5 ; and for every subsequent offence, a fine not exceeding £20, or be subject to a forfeiture of his licence, at the discretion of the justices before whom he shall be convicted.* The second Act above referred to provides, that any house, room, garden, or other place kept for public dancing, music, or other public entertainment, of the like kind in the cities of London and Westminster, or within twenty miles thereof, without a licence had for that purpose from the last preceding Michaelmas Quarter Sessions, shall be deemed a disorderly house or place. The police have power, under this statute, to enter any such unlicensed place, and seize every person who shall be found there, in order that they may be dealt with according to law ; and every person keeping such house is liable to a fine of £100, to be paid to the informer, and to be otherwise punished. The 5th section, in order to encourage prosecutions against persons keeping bawdy houses, and other disorderly houses, enacts, that if any two inhabitants of any parish, or place, paying scot and bearing lot therein, do give notice in writing to any constable of such parish or place, of any person keeping a bawdy house, or any other disorderly house in such parish or place, the constable shall forthwith go with such inhabitants to a justice of the peace, and enter into a recognizance in the penal

---

* It is much to be lamented that a recent decision, making it incumbent on the police to show that the prostitutes are assembled for purposes of prostitution, has rendered this important clause almost nugatory. I may here also mention another way by which the object of this act is frustrated, by the simple expedient of discontinuing their applications for licences, the night-house keepers cease to fall within its provisions, and consequently to liability to visits from the police.

sum of £30 to prosecute such person for such offence, such constable to be allowed the reasonable expenses of prosecution, and on conviction the sum of £10 to be paid to each of the two inhabitants ; and by the 8th section, it is enacted that any person who shall at any time thereafter appear, or behave him or herself as master or mistress, or as the person having the care, government, or management of any bawdy house, or other disorderly house, shall be deemed and taken to be the keeper thereof, and shall be liable to be prosecuted and punished as such, notwithstanding he or she shall not in fact be the real keeper or owner thereof. The punishment is fine or imprisonment, or both, and, by 3 George IV. c. 114, hard labour. I may here mention that the licensing of theatres, and other places for the exhibition of stage entertainments, is regulated by 10 George II. c. 28; and the licensing of public-houses by 9 George IV. c. 61, to which I have before alluded. The attitude assumed by the law towards prostitution may be briefly stated as follows :—

It requires the police to repress flagrant acts of indecency and disorder in the streets and places of public resort ;

It restrains the opening of theatres and places of amusement or refreshment without a licence, which must be applied for annually, and is continued only during good behaviour, thereby making it the interest of managers and proprietors to discountenance gross disorders, and to maintain so far as possible the outward forms of decorum in their establishments ;

It prohibits the opening of refreshment houses during certain hours of the night, a prohibition imposed, notwithstanding the hardship thereby inflicted on some classes of workmen, for the purpose of putting an end, if possible, to the shameless debauchery nightly exhibited in the Haymarket and its environs ;

It encourages the prosecution of keepers of brothels and other disorderly houses ;

But it ignores the existence of prostitution as a system, exerting its authority in those cases only which, by open contempt for order and decency, obtrude into notice and demand repression. Men and women are, in fact, left in this matter to their own consciences ; and so long as they respect public decency, their private conduct passes unchallenged, while the different parishes are left to decide for themselves whether or not they will permit known prostitutes to find shelter within their borders. How far this state of the law is wise and right will form the subject of consideration in a future chapter. One result of prostitution, with the evil and extent of which we dealt in the preceding chapter, has forced into action on behalf of certain classes and certain districts an unwilling legislature ; the result of that action we shall presently consider, but first of all we will glance at the means at present provided for alleviating disease.

LOCK HOSPITAL.

If we turn to London, a city of 3,000,000 souls, we find but ONE institution *specially* devoted to the treatment of venereal diseases—

the LOCK HOSPITAL,* formerly of Southwark, afterwards of Grosvenor Place, now of Westbourne Green and Dean Street, Soho, the existence of which for more than a century was one continued struggle. Formerly, both male and female patients were received at Westbourne Green; now females only are taken in there, the male patients having been transferred to the branch establishment in Dean Street, Soho, which contains 30 beds, though the funds of the institution only admit of 15 being occupied at present. Out-patients, both male and female, are attended to at Dean Street, and apply in large numbers. In 1868, 5052 males and 800 females were treated there as out-patients. In connexion with the Female Hospital at Westbourne, is the Asylum, containing an average of about 60 inmates, but capable of receiving 80, for the reformation of patients who have been cured in the hospital.

A new wing, called the Prince of Wales's Wing, has been recently added to the female division of this hospital. The cost of the erection for building alone was £9800, and when swelled by the sums expended on foundations, gas stoves, baths, fittings, furniture, and everything required for habitation, amounted to £12,000. It contains 75 beds, which would make the cost £160 per bed. But this would be an unfair estimate, because the new part contains all the kitchens, store-rooms, and other offices required for 150 patients, together with all the residents' rooms. The parts of the old building previously devoted to these purposes have now been either converted into wards, or given up to the use of the asylum. In 1867, 169 ordinary patients were admitted, with an average stay in hospital of 50 days each. The daily average, therefore, of ordinary patients present throughout the year was 23·15. During the first nine months of 1868, 160 ordinary patients were admitted, with an average stay of 39·3 days, making the daily average of patients 22·94. Nominally there are now 30 beds for ordinary patients, but as four of these are reserved as extras for special cases, the regular number may be considered to be 26. The contributions in 1867 amounted to £2282 13s. 10d., in addition to which a sum of £2116 17s. 6d. was raised by a special subscription, and devoted mainly to reducing the liabilities incurred by the erection of the new wing. There were, in 1867, 708 Government patients received under the provisions of the Contagious Diseases Act, to be presently noticed, with an average stay

---

* Mr. Cunningham, in his "Handbook of London," tells that "Lock is derived from the French word *loques*, signifying rags, bandages, lint; hence, also, locks of hair, wool, &c." But as the Lock Hospital in Southwark was founded, I believe, on the site of a house for lepers, who were formerly kept in restraint, I incline to prefer the obvious etymology to the more recondite one promoted by that ingenious author. The following passage is from Turner's work on Syphilis (p. 175), published in 1724 :— "As to your desire of knowing how many patients might be taken into the Lock Hospital, Southwark, I here send you an exact account of those that were admitted and discharged from that house in 1720, which was the last year they were under my direction.

"Admitted from January 17$\frac{19}{20}$ inclusive to January, 1720, exclusive 115
  Cured and discharged   108
  Died   7
                                                    "SAM. PALMER."

of 31 days, making their daily average 60·1, and when added to the ordinary patients, giving a total daily average of 83·25. During the first nine months of 1868, 853 Government patients were received with an average stay of 28·15 days, or a daily average of 84. The number of beds now paid for by Government is 120. In the beginning of 1867, only 40 beds were set apart for Government patients, the number was gradually increased till it reached 100 in September, and the present figure of 120 was attained in the spring of 1868. Additional wards are now in course of erection, and will shortly be opened, for the reception of 30 more Government patients, making 150 in all.

GUY'S HOSPITAL.

The registrar for this hospital, Dr. Steele, has kindly forwarded me some recent particulars relative to the accommodation for venereal patients at this institution. That gentleman states, that out of 700 beds the hospital devotes 28 to male venereal cases, and 30 to female. During the year 1868, there were treated in the hospital 422 cases of syphilis, of these 123 males and 124 females were cured ; 69 males were relieved and 87 females ; 8 males left unrelieved, and 5 females ; 1 male died, and 1 female, and the cause of the deaths was sloughing of the vulva, and laryingeal disease.

In a private communication, Dr. Steele adds :—"I don't think it likely that we will increase the accommodation for venereal cases, as the supply of this department has been more than equal to the demand for accommodation during the past year or two."

This account is very satisfactory, and bears out the statement made to me by Mr. Callender, at St. Bartholomew's, but forms a strong contrast with the fact noticed in the last edition of this book, in 1857, when I wrote :—"Dr. Steele has been good enough to inform me, since the date of the report, that only one-third of the female candidates eligible for beds can ever be taken into the house."

The proportion of venereal out-patients seen at this hospital are about 43 per cent.

ST. MARY'S HOSPITAL, PADDINGTON.

Venereal patients are not admitted.

The registrar, Mr. Moore, writes me :—"We have no accommodation for in-patients with venereal disease—indeed, we have a law especially forbidding their admission, but, nevertheless, in the course of the year, some 30 or 40 cases with the constitutional results of syphilis, do gain admission. With regard to the out-patients during 1868, 21,677 new cases were treated as out-patients and casualties. Of these I calculate that about 1500 only were cases of venereal disease."

UNIVERSITY COLLEGE HOSPITAL.

In answer to my enquiries, the clerk of the committee writes me word :—"There are no beds set apart in this hospital specially for venereal diseases, and further, that syphilitic prostitutes are not admissible. With regard to the out-patients, no special record of the numbers treated for venereal disease is kept."

KING'S COLLEGE HOSPITAL.

The secretary writes me word :—" I beg to inform you that there are not any beds in this hospital specially devoted to venereal diseases. A few such cases, however, are usually received during each year. About 32,000 out-patients were relieved in the past year, and of that number it is estimated some 4000 were treated for venereal diseases."

In 1857, I stated that this hospital devoted 6 of its 150 beds to venereal females, while males suffering from syphilis were occasionally admitted into the ordinary wards ; and that about 6000 out-patients were annually treated for venereal complaints.

ST. THOMAS'S HOSPITAL.

The authorities write me word :—"We have no beds given up specially to venereal diseases, and we can give you no reliable information of the number of out-patients suffering from venereal diseases."

In 1857, this hospital devoted 61 beds to venereal diseases, of which 25 were for females, and 36 for males.

CHARING-CROSS HOSPITAL

Appropriates no beds to venereal diseases, but special cases are admitted on the urgent request of the surgeon. A large number apply for advice and are relieved, but as very few of them obtain governors' letters, their cases are not registered, and therefore no accurate statistics can be procured. It was thus I wrote in 1857. I believe a similar state of things exists in 1869.

ST. GEORGE'S HOSPITAL

Appropriates no beds to venereal diseases.

THE ROYAL FREE HOSPITAL

Devotes twenty-six beds to female venereal patients, and none to males. On turning to page 56 it will be seen that a larger proportion of venereal out-patients are here prescribed for than at any other institution in London, forming, according to the average I have established, two out of every three out-patients who apply for surgical assistance.

MIDDLESEX HOSPITAL.

Some years ago, persons labouring under syphilis were not admitted in-patients to the Middlesex Hospital, except on pre-payment of two pounds, and this bye-law was printed on all the letters or petitions for admission. The reason assigned was, that persons who contracted syphilis ought not to partake of a charity, intended for more deserving objects than the vicious and licentious. I need not say that evasions became very common, and the regulation practically inoperative. The guardians of workhouses used to send their very bad cases to the hospital, paying the two pounds ; but such patients rarely recovered under many months, and the governors found that their cost greatly exceeded the amount received for their treatment. This, with the limited number of persons who could afford to pay, the protests of the surgeons, who were unable to teach pupils the treatment of syphilis, and, it is to be hoped, more philanthropic and correct sanitary views on the part of the governors, has erased the law in question from the statute book ; and this institution now devotes eight beds for women, and twelve for men, to the gratuitous treatment of venereal cases.

LONDON HOSPITAL.

The following bye-law formerly existed at the London Hospital :— " No person shall be admitted with the venereal distemper, except by the special order of the House Committee, subject to such regulations as they shall from time to time establish."

The secretary, Mr. Nixon (now, 1869,) writes me :—" We have a special ward for female venereal cases, with 15 beds. Into this ward, 44 patients were admitted during the six months ended 30th June last. Male venereal cases are received into all surgical wards. No separate register kept."

ST. BARTHOLOMEW'S HOSPITAL.

Having been educated at this hospital, I may be pardoned for re-joicing at the noble prominence my *Alma Mater* has been enabled to assume in alleviating the miseries of humanity. This present work of mine may probably be traceable to the unequalled opportunities this noble institution afforded me of seeing venereal affections in the com-mencement of my studies, and it still continues to devote more wards to the treatment of venereal cases than does any other general hospital.

I have already stated, page 50, that this institution contains 75 beds, given up to venereal cases. There are 25 devoted to males and 50 to females, 597 cases were treated in the hospital for syphilis and other specific complaints in the year 1868, and as we have seen at page 52, more than half the out-patients are sufferers from venereal affections.

Since the last edition of this book appeared, venereal diseases must have become much modified.

Mr. Callender, in charge of Mr. Paget's wards, has kindly furnished me with the following observations. He says " that at the present day the system of competition, (to which I alluded at page 138 of my former edition), for admission to the female venereal wards has ceased. It oftentimes happens that there are not enough applicants for the empty beds. The cases are comparatively slight. A warm bath, rest in bed, and a little lotion causes a complaint which looked very formidable on entering the hospital to become a relatively mild affection. Sloughing phagedæna in the female is now very rarely met with.

I regret to say that the indecent system of exposing females before the whole class of students is still pursued, and that the employment of the speculum is the exception, not the rule. It is with regret I mention the shortcomings of my *Alma Mater*. Before another edition of this book appears, I trust I may be able to chronicle that every woman entering the venereal wards is examined with the speculum ; that the examinations are made in a separate ward or behind a screen raised at the further extremity, and thus separated from the gaze of her fellow-sufferers, and that only a few pupils are allowed to be present at a time.

Having passed in review the existing provision for the control and relief of prostitutes in the metropolis, let me draw my readers' attention to what occurs in some of our principal towns in England. I have been unable, with the exception of Cambridge, to verify the condition of our county towns, and therefore quote the following data from the Report of the committee for the prevention of venereal diseases, appointed by the Harveian Society of London, and published in 1867 :—

"Very few towns have lock hospitals at all; and those which have such, have far too few beds for all patients requiring admission. Liverpool Southern, and other hospitals, send their venereal cases to the Lock Hospital, which has 50 beds, and an average of 45 inmates of these beds, male and female. The Dublin Lock Hospital only admits female patients, and has, on an average, 86 such cases, and no out-patients. Staffordshire General Infirmary has four male and four female lock beds, frequently empty. Chester Infirmary has, on an average, two female lock patients. In the Royal Infirmary of Edinburgh, according to Dr. Gillespie's report, there are 26 venereal beds; the Edinburgh Lock Hospital is only for females. The Royal Infirmary of Glasgow has no beds for venereal cases; and the Glasgow Lock Hospital has only 45 beds for these cases. Belfast General Hospital has six venereal inmates, and a small ward set apart for females. There is no Lock Hospital in that town.

"In Manchester it is stated that, in the years 1864-65-66, out of an average number of 75,000 patients seen in public practice, the average number of new venereal cases in Manchester and Salford did not fall far short of 3,500 cases annually, out of a population of about 390,000. The Manchester Lock Hospital has an average of 20 in-patients and 56 out-patients daily. The Southern Hospital of Manchester, the Ardwick and Ancoats Dispensary, the Chorlton-in-Medlock Dispensary, report that from one-third to one-eighth of their surgical patients are venereal cases. The Manchester Workhouse, Bridge Street, sees daily 91 venereal cases, or 1 in 8 of its surgical cases, and has 15 beds for male and 46 for female venereal cases. The Rumpsall Workhouse has a daily average of 8 male and 12 female venereal cases, but no special beds. The Salford Workhouse sees daily 9 male and 63 female venereal cases, in which 39 cases of infantile syphilis are included. It has 6 female venereal beds. The Chorlton Union Workhouse has 20 female venereal beds, and sees a daily number of 7 male and 14 female venereal cases. The New Borough Gaol, Manchester, sees daily 10 venereal cases, or 62 per cent. of its surgical cases are so affected. It has no special beds for such cases. The New Bailey has daily 11 male and 3 female venereal cases, or nearly 43 per cent. of its surgical cases arise from these diseases. The Salford Hospital and Dispensary, St. Mary's Hospital, the Clinical and Bridge Street Children's Hospitals, report that from 1 in 10 to 1 in 30 of their patients are venereal cases. The Eye Hospital, Manchester reports that 1 in 20 of its cases are venereal. Manchester Royal Infirmary has no beds for venereal cases, and has on an average 23 male and 22 female venereal cases daily. In a letter from Dr. Bradley, that gentleman remarks, "we are fully convinced that the quacks and chemists attend a large proportion of the entire number of venereal cases occurring in Manchester." He adds, "Our Committee feel assured, that the above statistics give the minimum number of cases of venereal disease existing in Manchester ; that, in all probability, the evil extends to a much greater degree than can possibly be ascertained by any public inquiry ; that it effects a positive injury on the national physique ; and that the steps which the Harveian Society are taking are urgently called for, and merit every legislative support." Dr. Bradley states, that 387 venereal cases are seen daily in Manchester in public practice, being a proportion of 1 in 7 of the whole daily patients seen, both medical and surgical.

CONTAGIOUS DISEASES ACT.

However much it may be the duty of the State to leave for settlement to the individual conscience all questions of morals and religion, it can hardly be seriously contended that it is right to abandon to the care of the improvident and profligate the restraining of contagious maladies, yet this, except in a few military and naval stations, is virtually the case in England. A woman who knows herself to be diseased, is free to invite all comers to the enjoyment of her person, and to spread among them deadly contagion. The total of venereal beds is, as we have seen, in St. Bartholomew's, 75; in Guy's, 58 ; in Middlesex, 20 ; in the Royal Free, 26 ; in the Lock, exclusive of those required by Government, 30. Thus, although the population of London numbers over 3,000,000, there are only 209 beds given up to females labouring under venereal affections, if we deduct the 120 beds at the Lock Hospital devoted to the Government patients sent there from Woolwich, Aldershot, and other garrison towns.

These figures speak for themselves, and when we remember the deadly character of the disease with which we have to contend, the strong temptations that lead to its contraction, and the vast numbers who yield to that temptation, and compare them with the means at our disposal for supplying an antidote to the poison, we may well marvel at the indifference of society and the supineness of Government. But if we can ill excuse the laws, which afford no protection to those who, after all, are comparatively free agents, what shall we say of them, if we find them placing thousands of men every year in the utmost jeopardy, compelling them almost, for the convenience of the State, to have recourse to the prostitution by which they are surrounded, and yet providing for them no means of safety or adequate relief ? It is hardly credible that, until a few years ago, this was the case in England. At length in 1864 the injury inflicted by this apathy on our soldiers and sailors, and the loss sustained by the public purse, seem to have touched the conscience or the cupidity of the legislature, and in that year an act was passed, the 27 & 28 Vic. c. 85, having for its object the remedy of the evils to which the army and navy are exposed ; its provisions, however, proved totally inadequate to meet the requirements of the case, and it,was followed in 1866 by a more comprehensive measure, the 28 & 29 Vic. c. 35, commonly called the Contagious Diseases Act.

This act now extends its operation to Canterbury, Dover, Gravesend,

Maidstone, Southampton, Winchester, Portsmouth, Plymouth and Devonport, Woolwich, Chatham, Sheerness, Aldershot, Windsor, Colchester, Shorncliffe, the Curragh, Cork, and Queenstown. By the 15th and 16th sections, a justice of the peace, on information being laid before him that a woman, living in any place to which the act extends, is a common prostitute, and on oath before him substantiating such information, may, if he thinks fit, order that the woman be subject to a periodical medical examination by the visiting surgeon appointed under the provisions of the act, for any period not exceeding one year, for the purpose of ascertaining at each such examination whether she is affected with a contagious disease ; and thereupon she shall be subject to such a periodical medical examination, and the order shall be a sufficient warrant for the visiting surgeon to conduct such examination accordingly ; and by the 17th section any woman, in any place to which the act applies, may, by a submission signed by her, in the presence of, and attested by the superintendent of police, subject herself to a periodical examination under this act for any period not exceeding one year. Any woman found on examination to be diseased, may either go herself, or will be apprehended and sent, to some hospital certified for the reception and detention of government patients. The reception of a woman in a certified hospital by the managers or persons having the management or control thereof shall be deemed to be an undertaking by them to provide for her care, treatment, lodging, clothing and food during her detention in hospital. This period of detention is limited to three months, or, on the certificate prescribed by the act that further detention is necessary, to a further period of six months, making nine months in the whole. If a woman considers herself detained in hospital too long, she may apply to a justice for an order of discharge. Prostitutes refusing to conform to the provisions of this act are liable to be punished by imprisonment, and any one permitting a woman who to his knowledge is suffering from a contagious disease, to use his house for the purpose of prostitution shall, in addition to the other consequences to which he may be liable for keeping a disorderly house, be liable to six months imprisonment with or without hard labour. The appointment of the necessary surgeons, inspectors of hospitals, and other officers, is intrusted to the Admiralty and War Offices, by whom also hospitals may be provided and certified for use, and all expenses incurred in the execution of the act must be defrayed. The carrying out of the act in the minor details is of course intrusted to the police. It is also provided that adequate provision must be made by the several hospitals for the moral and religious instruction of the women detained in them under this act. We have already seen that a considerable number of beds have been secured at the Lock Hospital for the use of Government patients. The most admirable arrangements have been adopted at this institution for the examination and treatment of the patients committed to its care, and as the possibility of carrying out an act having for its object the diminution of disease forms an important element in considering the advisability of further extending its sphere of usefulness, I shall offer no apology for relating pretty fully the method pursued in this instituton.

LOCK HOSPITAL.

I was anxious to see the working of the existing Government Lock Hospital, and Mr. J. Lane kindly allowed me to accompany him, and explained everything on my visit in October, 1868.

The patients (female) are lodged in a new wing; the wards are lofty, and kept scrupulously clean. Each inmate has a separate bed, provided with three blankets, and a hair mattress, an extra blanket being given in winter. Each patient has two pannikins, a half-pint and a pint tin can, with a pewter spoon and a steel knife and fork, and a little box in which she may keep her things, is placed near her bed. The patients are not allowed to go into other wards, but there is an open court in which they take exercise, and they have a sort of hospital dress in place of their own clothes, which are left under the care of the matron. At the head of the bed hangs a towel.

In a little room at the end of the ward water is laid on, and copper basins are hung by a chain to the wall; these basins are kept for the women to wash their faces. This arrangement is specially made to prevent any possible contagion. Fixed to the floor is a bidet, across which the female sits. There is here an admirable device for facilitating the cleansing of the private parts; by which means, a brass syringe, with a long pewter ball, and holding, say six ounces, she injects the lotion, and the waste fluid runs away on opening a plug fixed in the bottom of the bidet. The only improvement I could suggest was that each patient be furnished with two small napkins to dry the organs after injection. The patient always uses an injection before presenting herself to the surgeon, in order that the organs may be in a proper condition for examination, and I must say the cleanliness shown does great credit to the nurses who manage the wards.

The inspections are conducted in the following manner :—The women are introduced one at a time from the wards by one nurse into a special room, containing a properly-raised bed, with feet, similar to the one in use on the Continent. The patient ascends the steps placed by the side of the bed, lays down, places her feet in the slippers arranged for the purpose, and the house surgeon separates the labia to see if there are any sores. If no suspicion of these exists, and if the female is suffering from discharge, the speculum is at once employed. In this institution several sizes are used, and they are silvered and covered with India-rubber. The head nurse after each examination washes the speculum in a solution of permanganate of potash, then wipes it carefully, oils it ready for the next examination, so that the surgeon loses no time, and the examinations are conducted with great rapidity. In the course of one hour and three-quarters I assisted in the thorough examination of 58 women with the speculum.

In this institution the house surgeon examines the women; the surgeon superintending and prescribing the remedies.

Mr. J. Lane, in a recent paper, has so well described the method of treatment adopted by him, that I shall give an account of it in his own words :—

" Since the admission of patients into this hospital, under the Contagious Diseases Act, from Woolwich and other military districts, the treatment of uterine and vaginal discharges has constituted a large part of its practice. In fact, in 1867, as many as 58 per cent., and in 1868, 65 per cent. of the class of patients alluded to, were placed under treatment for this form of disease alone, uncomplicated by any symptom of a syphilitic character, either primary or secondary. These patients are, for the most part, strong, healthy girls, aged from 17 to 25, well fed, and in good condition. Their disease appears to be entirely local, both in its origin and character. It arises, as I believe, in the great majority of cases, simply from the continual irritation and excitement of the generative organs consequent upon their mode of life, though it may be caused, no doubt, occasionally by direct contagion from urethral discharges in the male. The secretion, when they first come under observation, is of an obviously purulent or muco-purulent character, and evidence of its contagiousness is afforded by the fact (as I am informed) that nearly all of them have been accused of communicating disease before being subjected to examination. It is remarkable how little pain or inconvenience is suffered by these patients; usually they make no complaint whatever, and many of them are unaware that any thing whatever is the matter with them, although, when examined with the speculum, a profuse discharge, derived chiefly from the uterus, is found lodged in the upper part of the vagina. Associated with this, especially in the more chronic cases, abrasions of the epithelium, excoriations, or superficial ulcerations on the vaginal portion of the cervix uteri are very frequently seen. Anything approaching to an inflammatory condition, to which the terms acute gonorrhœa or vaginitis might be applied, is uncommon, and when met with, it is usually in young girls, as yet unseasoned to a life of prostitution. Incidental complications, of a painful character, such as labial abscess, or inflammatory bubo, are occasionally seen, but are not of frequent occurrence.

" An external examination alone is quite insufficient for the discovery of these complaints. Purulent secretions from the vulva or lower part of the vagina are, of course, evident enough; but a profuse uterine discharge may be present, and no trace of it be visible until the speculum is employed. There is, however, a considerable difference in women in this respect; in some, the vagina appears to be equally contractile throughout its whole length, and therefore, any secretion formed in it, or entering it, speedily appears externally; while in others, and these are the majority, its contractility is much less at the upper than at the lower part, and discharges are consequently retained in the former situation.

" When these discharges are of purely local origin, and there is no constitutional fault, their cure may be speedily effected by local applications. The plan commonly pursued at the Lock Hospital is to make the patients use vaginal injections for themselves three or four times daily. The lotions employed are the diluted liquor plumbi subacetatis, or solutions of sulphate of zinc, alum, or tannin, in the proportion of five grains to the ounce of water. The syringes are large enough to hold six ounces of the lotion, and have a pipe long enough to reach the upper part of the vagina readily. Both these points are important, for the syringes commonly used will not contain sufficient fluid to wash out the canal effectually, and the pipe affixed to them will not admit of its reaching the upper part of the vagina at all. When the vaginal mucous membrane is inflamed and tender, the house-surgeon, when the speculum is used, which is at least twice a week in all these cases, inserts a strip of lint dipped in the lead-lotion, and this is allowed to remain for three or four hours. If the inflammation be acute, the application of the strip of lint is repeated daily through a small speculum. By these means, discharges proceeding from the *vagina* may usually be cured in a few days, but the injections should be continued as long as any abnormal uterine secretions are observed, for the latter, if not frequently washed away, will be likely to re-excite disease in the vaginal mucous membrane.

"But vaginal injections are of little or no use for the cure of discharges proceeding from the interior of the cervix uteri—a complication which is almost invariably present in these cases. In the treatment of this condition, success will depend mainly on the amount of personal care and attention afforded by the surgeon himself. At the Lock Hospital, the speculum is used twice a week in all, and three times a week in many of these cases ; and through it suitable applications are made to the os and cervix. The nitrate of silver, either solid or in solution, is the remedy most in favour, especially in the earlier stages of the treatment, and when the discharge is purulent ; later, simple astringents, such as tannin, alum, or perchloride of iron, are employed. Before using the caustic, all discharge should be wiped away from the os uteri with a piece of dry cotton-wool ; and the plug of tenacious matter, which usually fills the cervix, should also be removed, or it will prevent the remedy reaching the diseased surface. The application of a strong solution of alum coagulates this discharge, and renders its removal more easy. The stick of nitrate of silver is then inserted to the depth of about an inch into the canal of the cervix, and is also applied to any abraded or ulcerated surface which may be seen around the os ; or, instead of the stick, a solution of the nitrate (a drachm to an ounce of water) may be applied by means of a piece of sponge or cotton wool about the size of a pea, which is passed along the cervical canal with a suitable pair of forceps. I prefer to use the solid nitrate on the first one or two occasions, and afterwards the solution. By these means, the discharge speedily loses its yellow colour, and becomes white or semi-transparent. When this result is obtained, a stringent solution, such as the milder Liquor Ferri Perchloridi of the *British Pharmacopœia,* or solutions of alum or tannin (a drachm to an ounce of water), may be substituted with advantage for the nitrate of silver. The glycerinum acidi tannici, or acidi gallici, are also frequently used ; but they do not appear to possess any advantage over the watery solutions.

"Other methods of applying remedies to the interior of the cervix uteri have been tried, but the plan above described has been found most convenient and effectual. A very efficient mode is to inject the solutions into the cervix with a syringe ; but this has the disadvantage of being sometimes followed by abdominal pains—no doubt, from the fluid penetrating too far into the body of the uterus. I have also used suppositories containing nitrate of silver, sulphate of copper, or alum, incorporated with cocoa-butter, in the proportion, by weight, of one part to four or five, and made into pencils of appropriate size for introduction into the cervix uteri. These answer well enough ; but, on the whole, I am disposed to prefer aqueous to greasy applications. The essential point, whatever the substance or solution chosen, is to take care that it is effectually applied along the whole length of the canal of the cervix uteri. There is rarely any pain occasioned by the use of caustics or astringents to these parts. The patients are almost invariably quite unconscious that anything is being done.

" In 1867, the number of admissions for this form of disease was 414, and the average period occupied by the treatment was twenty-three days ; but 36 per cent. were cured in periods of from seven to fifteen days, 21 per cent. in from fifteen to twenty days, and 13 per cent. in from twenty to twenty-five days. The remaining 30 per cent. occupied periods exceeding twenty-five days, the longest being ninety-four days. Many of these latter, however, were suffering from some constitutional condition which may be held accountable for the delay, such as phthisis or some other form of strumous disease, or impairment of health from long continued habits of dissipation.

" Readmissions for a recurrence of this form of disease are unfortunately too frequent. The 414 *cases* alluded to do not, therefore, represent an equal number of patients ; for fifteen women were admitted twice, and four three times, during the year. In fact, as many as eighty-four had been in the hospital previously, some of them as often as six or seven times since October, 1866. When discharged, a large proportion return to habits of prostitution ; and, as might be expected, after a time relapse into the same condition. We seldom see them again, however, till after a lapse of several months ; so it may fairly be inferred that they remain in a sound state for a considerable period.

" The above remarks are founded upon, and refer especially to, cases of *simple* utero-vaginal discharge, in which, as far as can be discovered, no syphilitic taint is present. These, of course, are only capable of communicating a simple urethritis or gonorrhœa. Women suffering from constitutional syphilis are, however, very often affected with uterine discharges and ulcerations. Such cases are much less amenable to local treatment ; and appropriate constitutional remedies must, of course, be employed at the same time. In my opinion, the uterine ulceration so often concurrent with secondary syphilis is as much a secondary manifestation as mucous tubercles on the vulva, or the analogous condition so often met with on the mucous membrane of the mouth and throat ; and its secretion is equally capable of communicating true syphilitic infection."—*British Medical Journal*, Dec. 5, 1868.

The Hospital pays Mr. Marshall (the house surgeon) £150 a-year, and I may add my testimony to the able manner in which he examines his cases. I was surprised to hear that the visiting surgeons, Messrs. J. Lane and Gascoyen, receive nothing; their services are perfectly gratuitous, and the hospital benefiting by the grant from Government gives them nothing. This is not as it should be. They have to certify that every patient is sound before leaving the hospital, and their remuneration should be handsome for executing this monotonous, although highly important duty.

The medical officers told me, in reply to my enquiries, that there had been occasional disturbances among the patients. The nurse first tries to stop any outbreak of temper; if unsuccessful, the house surgeon is appealed to, and if he fails, the girl is conveyed to the police station by the hospital porter, who is empowered to act as a police constable in relation to these patients, who are then liable to two months' imprisonment.

I have little to say about the patients; in appearance they are not generally prepossessing; a few among those whom I saw were young, and looked middle-aged and plain. The primary syphilitic affections were few, but the diseases of the uterus numerous, similar to those I witness in private practice, and such as are to be seen in Paris, at the St. Lazare Hospital.

The following is the scale of dietary at the hospital :

DIETARY.

ORDINARY.

Breakfast	...	...	8 oz. Bread ; ½ pint Cocoa.
Dinner	...	...	Five days—½ lb. Meat ; ½ lb. Potatoes.
			Two days—1 pint Soup ; Soup Meat.
			1½ oz. Rice.
Tea ...	...	...	6 oz. Bread ; ½ pint Tea.
Supper	...	...	1 pint Gruel.

MEAT DIET.

Breakfast	...	...	As above.
Dinners	...	...	½ lb. Meat ; ½ lb. Potatoes, every day.
Tea ...	...	...	6 oz. Bread ; ½ pint Tea.
Supper	...	...	1 pint Gruel.

BEEF TEA AND PUDDING DIET.

Breakfast	...	...	As above, and 1 pint of Milk.
Dinner	...	...	1 pint Beef Tea ; 2 oz. Rice in a pudding.
Tea ...	...	...	As above.
Supper	...	...	1 pint Gruel.

Mutton Chop or Fish, when ordered, instead of Meat Diet or ordinary. Rice occasionally instead of Potatoes.

Extras.—Porter, Wine, Spirits and Milk.

ALDERSHOT HOSPITAL.

The Aldershot hospital is situate a short distance from the camp on a rising ground, and consists of a series of one-storied huts, made of galvanized iron. The day of my visit was a very cold one, but I found the interior warm and comfortable. It contains six wards, arranged for the accommodation of 90 patients. Three of these wards are fitted up with 14 beds each ; two with 20 ; the other, a smaller one, with eight only—giving 90 beds in all. Each patient has a folding bed to herself, which is kept scrupulously clean, and done up as a hammock during the day, the patients having to take their meals and pass the day in the wards.

Dr. Barr writes me word that now (September, 1869) "the new wards and day-room are finished, they are built of brick with slate roofs, and are larger and more healthily constructed than the smaller ones." The following table will show that there are now 70 beds for this district, instead of 50 as heretofore.

Return showing the Number of Prostitutes brought under the Provisions of the Contagious Diseases Act, for the Four Quarters under mentioned.

	13 Weeks ended 1 April, 1869.	31 December, 1868	10 September, 1868	30 June, 1868	QUARTER ENDED	
70	70	70	70	70	Number of Beds in Lock-wards of Hospitals.	
796	185	208	228	175	Number Admitted to Hospital on Certificates of Visiting Surgeon.	
2,504	943	761	502	298	Number Examined and found free from Disease.	
3,294	1,128	969	730	467	Number who submitted Voluntarily under Section 17.	
6	—	—	—	6	Number against whom it was necessary to proceed by Informations before Magistrates.	
3,300	1,128	969	730	473	Total Number brought under Provisions of the Act.	
757	185	201	211	140	Number Discharged free from Disease, who still follow their former Pursuits.	Number Discharged from Hospitals.
18	3	4	6	5	Number who have entered Homes, &c.	
20	4	3	8	5	Number who have Returned to their Friends.	
8	4	—	3	1	Number Discharged as Incurable.	
783	196	208	228	151	Total Number Discharged.	

So admirable are the arrangements at this institution, that one thing only came under my notice that could possibly operate as a drawback to the health and comfort of the inmates. The view from the windows, which are kept constantly closed, is interrupted by means of blinds and whitened glass, and a certain amount of light and air thereby excluded.

This is to be regretted, but seems absolutely necessary, as, in consequence of the close proximity of the hospital to a much frequented road, great difficulty was experienced previously to the adoption of this course, in keeping the inmates from presenting themselves at the windows, and holding conversations with soldiers and others outside the building. The lavatory appliances are similar to those adopted in the London Lock Hospital, already described, and appear to answer admirably. There is a large syringe connected with a pump, the use of which is superintended by the nurse to whom the duty is entrusted of seeing that the women keep themselves scrupulously clean. I observed that the practice was in vogue of placing on a shelf, at a height of six feet from the ground, a funnel-shaped vessel filled with water, with which an india-rubber tube is connected, and a strong stream of injection can thus be applied to a woman placing herself in a bath beneath. Every patient received into the hospital is required to take a bath immediately on her admittance; her clothes also are taken from her, and well fumigated and washed; they are then made up into neat packages, and are not returned until her time for leaving the hospital has arrived. For her use in the meantime a good supply of warm clothing is provided by the Government. The patients in each ward that I inspected seemed to be in good health, and were comely looking girls, appearing to great advantage in the hospital uniform. The demeanour of these women, as we passed along, was most respectful; there was no noise, no bad language, no sullenness, no levity. The patients are employed when convalescent in laundry and kitchen work, under the superintendence of a paid laundress and cook. In addition to this they make their own clothes, and keep them in proper repair. At the time of my visit they were engaged in making 40 sets of clothing for the use of the Lock Hospital then about to be opened at Cork. Many of the women, on admission, are found totally ignorant of ordinary domestic duties; but great pains in this respect are taken with them during the period of their detention, so that on leaving they are generally found to have become decent needle and washerwomen, and to have acquired sufficient knowledge of cooking to enable them to dress plain joints and vegetables. The good done by this means has been shown in more than one instance, where a woman so benefited by instruction, has taken service, almost directly after receiving her discharge from the hospital. The patients are permitted to take a walk daily in an exercising ground behind the hospital. I understand that perfect order is maintained among the older residents without much interference on the part of the surgeon, who has unbounded authority, though it requires great tact and determination on his part to reduce new comers to a proper state of submission and obedience. Doubtless, also, the dread of not being cured rapidly, and thus having their stay in hospital prolonged, helps materially in the task of controlling these, at other times, lawless women; they are also overlooked by a superior class of nurse, and the police in uniform are always to be found at the hospital gate, which is closed to the public. When the patient is discharged she is free, if she pleases, to return to her old haunts; but, if she desires it, she can be placed in an asylum, or if she has friends willing to receive her, and to whom she is willing to go, she is sent to them at the expense of the Government. The good effect of the system inaugurated in this country by the Contagious Diseases Act is apparent even in those women who return to their abandoned ways. They no longer come to the periodical inspections in rags and dirt, but present on these occasions quite an altered appearance; some, as I am informed, even staying at home previously to presenting themselves, to wash the little linen they possesss, and put their dresses otherwise into a decent state. Thus are these miserable women being humanised little by little, and the Government is doing at Aldershot a very efficient work by very efficient men. I cannot do better than conclude this notice of the Aldershot Lock Hospital with an extract from the report made by Dr. Barr on the 1st of January, 1869 :—

" *Periodical examinations* of the prostitutes living within the Aldershot district were established in April last (1868), and as anticipated, at first with only partial success. It seems the attendance on appointed days of the whole number of women known to come within the meaning of the act was a matter of great labour and difficulty to those engaged in carrying it out. A few months since every effort was made by at least half the women, and often with success, to evade these inspections. Aided by their companions, they were hidden during the daytime in various places, the movements of the police being watched; or, on hearing of the approach of the latter, they would leave the district for a few days, secretly returning at night. Others procured shelter in private houses, the occupiers denying their presence; and thus in various ways they screened themselves from the notice of the officers in search of them. It is no little credit to Inspector Smith, of the Metropolitan Police, that he has surmounted these obstacles, and that during the last three months there has been, with small exception, the orderly attendance of the known prostitutes of the district. The number of registered persons belonging to this class has been, during the term mentioned, from 270 to 300. Of this number, an average of 60 have been in hospitals, while the attendances for periodical examination have been 1,147.

"It would be difficult to over-estimate the importance of these examinations. Without a firm persistence in their regular occurrence, with every exertion to discover and include all loose women known and suspected in the district, it will be absolutely impossible to detect a third part even of the worst sources of disease in these localities. As I shall state presently, many women who have for years resided in the neighbourhood, married and single, have been brought to me strenuously denying both prostitution and disease. Nevertheless, these patients have been found so badly affected as to require long detention for medical treatment; while subsequent information has proved that secretly, and in some cases abetted by husband or paramour, they have long received the visits of soldiers and others, and must have been frequent causes of disease among them. Again, as I also mention further on, various individuals, tramps, persons seeking employment in the hay and corn fields, and during the hop-keeping season, hovering about the camp every evening for immoral purposes, have been found at their examinations needing active treatment, and very dangerous acquaintance for the troops.

" I do not believe that in a single instance has a woman been compelled to attend these examinations without sufficient ground for her appearance. During the last three months, I have been applied to at the hospital's examination room to inspect women who voluntarily attended, in order to check false reports which had been circulated concerning them. My decision as to their freedom from disease was considered a satisfactory refutation of the statement complained of.

" At the present time the majority of the ordinary prostitutes raise few objections to these frequent examinations. They are reminded of the day and hour of attendance by the police, and accordingly most of them are present. With few exceptions, they make a point of appearing in as cleanly a state as, under their peculiar circumstances, they are enabled ; and on the day of attendance the morning is spent in washing, ironing, drying, and preparing what is often the only suit of clothes possessed by the owner. As a rule, they also come in a state of sobriety ; the few exceptions I invariably find diseased. On one occasion only during the last eight months have I received an insolent remark at these inspections, it being from a notorious gaol-bird who had come from London, and who was influenced by drink at the time. I detained her in hospital, and in a few days she was so completely subdued as to rank among the most quiet inmates of the wards. On her discharge she immediately left the neighbourhood.

" With the object of lessening the chances of contagion, I have for some time strongly impressed upon those attending these examinations, as well as those discharged from hospital, the necessity of using every day some simple injection, particularly before and after intercourse. This is attended to by many of the women regularly—more seldom by the majority, a number of whom I find only use the injection for some hours previous to attending these examinations. Certainly, since the more strict attention to these inspections, the wards have been constantly filled, but diseased women who had hitherto escaped, have been discovered in the search, as well as those new comers who are so frequently suffering from venereal affections."

The following summary appeared in the " British Medical Journal" of the 12th of December, 1868 :—

" Dr. Barr, the surgeon in charge of the Female Lock Hospital at Aldershot, sends us a very encouraging account of the effect of the preventive measures in that district. We may congratulate the Government on having so zealous an officer to carry out the Contagious Diseases Act, and to superintend the only hospital which Government controls itself. Periodical examination of all liable to be in a contagious state, which is indispensable to render the Act effectual, was begun at Aldershot in April, 1868. The success at first was only partial, but has steadily increased, and now all the known prostitutes are included ; and, in a place like Aldershot, very few likely to spread disease escape the observation of the police. During the week ending November 21st, 105 persons were examined ; of these, only fourteen were detained, and

seven of the fourteen were recent arrivals in Aldershot. The average detention in hospital was, during the third quarter of 1868, 22·5 days, against 36 days in the corresponding quarter of 1867. This shows that the women suffer less severely; and the average would be even lower than it is, but for the number of severely diseased women who come into the district from a distance with new regiments, or simply in order to get admittance to the hospital. This improvement in the character of the disease enables the surgeon to keep the patients in until they have no symptom of the disease left about them. This was at first rendered impossible by the heavy pressure on the beds, and patients were discharged often before they were assuredly well, to make room for others far worse, waiting to fill their places. The number of beds, at present seventy, is still inadequate to keep vacancies ready for all the diseased women at Aldershot. This evil results from the afflux of strangers from beyond the limits of the district. But for this, the accommodation provided at Aldershot would suffice. Twelve months' experience of the Act, while proving its extreme value most incontestably, has shown some defects to be remedied before the object of the legislature can be secured. The greatest inconvenience arises from the practice of not receiving pregnant women into hospital, because there is no provision in the wards of an ordinary hospital for their reception. Still they do not desist from propagating disease on account of their condition; and Dr. Barr urges that the examining surgeon should have the power of ordering their detention in the parish infirmary while liable to communicate disease to others. Nor would this be putting a burden on the ratepayers, for the charges on the parish have been much relieved by the establishment of the Lock Hospital at Aldershot. Dr. Barr gives a terrible account of the necessity for reformatories into which young girls may be received. An anecdote we must insert:—
'One morning recently, three sisters, the eldest only nineteen, were among those to be examined. The youngest, a mere child, cried to go home to her mother, *so like a child*, that I sent for that parent before examining the daughter. The mother told me, in a flood of tears, that her husband was out of work, and the two elder daughters dragged the youngest away with them to the camp during her absence.' Dr. Barr adds that two of the sisters were retained for being infected with disease. He also most wisely insists on the good compulsory detention of thése young girls in reformatories would do. Compulsory detention of young vagabond children and young thieves has done much good; and there can be no reason why its beneficent action should not be extended to young girls who have been led astray by want or thoughtlessness."

We may now briefly notice the working of this Act in two other places to which its operations are extended, and I am indebted to Dr. Stuart for the following particulars:—

WOOLWICH AND CHATHAM.

"Under its provisions periodical examinations have been established since August, 1868, at Woolwich and Chatham. Before that time the women were brought up for examination on suspicion or information. They are ordered to be held on alternate days at each place, so that three separate examinations may be held weekly, if required; and it is also ordered that all the prostitutes, varying in number from 200 to 300 in each town, be inspected not less than once a fortnight, and oftener if it is thought necessary in any case.

"As, however, a considerable number of these women are not stationary, but remove from one garrison town to another, new and fresh women are also examined every week.

"Among the prostitutes *resident* in the districts under the Contagious Diseases Act, the character of the disease has wonderfully changed : genital syphilis is comparatively rare; when it occurs it is soon detected, and sent for treatment, so that the frightful ravages formerly so common, and still in many women showing evidences of its former malignity in the scars and loss of texture still visible in their sexual organs, are now rarely, if ever, found. Most of the severe cases of primary syphilis now sent to the certified hospitals are not those of *resident* women, but of women coming in from neighbouring places, and remaining in the garrison towns a night or two to allow themselves to be brought in by the police and sent to hospital.

"I have had cases of badly diseased women who have occupied two or three days in walking in the greatest misery from Dover to Chatham, in order to obtain assistance; and from Maidstone, Gravesend, Sittingbourne, Faversham, and other places, the applications are far from uncommon.

"Acute gonorrhœa is also, I think, not so common as it was, although as severe as ever when it does occur.

"At the hospital at Chatham, I believe that whereas in the first quarter of the present year 56 days was the average duration of treatment for syphilis, in the third quarter, ending 1st October, it was only 33 days, and would no doubt have been still less, but for the severe cases sent from *other places*.

"My instructions to select cases for detention, having respect to the number of vacant beds, are—firstly, to send cases of primary syphilis; secondly, acute gonorrhœa; and then thirdly, all these cases having been detained, vaginal discharge, either complicated with secondary disease, or suspected to be contagious from information derived from infected parties.

"There are about 110 to 115 beds available for the women in Woolwich and Chatham. No doubt a few more would be desirable, as doubtful cases are sometimes necessarily deferred admission.

"I think the police, who have shown marvellous tact and judgment in carrying out their duties, have no real difficulty in applying the Act to all *known* prostitutes. The great difficulty consists in bringing under medical inspection a very large number of women who exercise their calling in a clandestine manner, not entirely trusting to it for their support; not residing at brothels, but with friends or parents, and following some other occupation. There is great reason to believe these equal or exceed in number the regular resident prostitutes, and are frequently diseased.

"The great defect in the present Act is in its partial application.

" The condition of the women among the resident prostitutes is very decidedly improved in the last two years, so far as personal care and cleanliness are concerned; and also as to their language and conduct while under my notice at the examining house. As to any real improvement in their morals or character, I do not believe in it. Few of those who are induced to go to the Homes or Refuges are permanently reformed; a large proportion, after remaining from a few weeks to a year or year and a half, sooner or later relapse.

" At Woolwich, on each examining day, a female missionary from one of the London societies for reforming these women, attends and converses with them; and she has told me that out of more than fifty she had induced to enter the Homes during the last ten years, she could not select five that had become permanently reformed.

" Out of 219 cases examined at Woolwich at the commencement of the periodic examination, 48, or from one-fourth to one-fifth, were cases of relapse after admission to Homes; and I have every reason to believe the proportion still larger, inasmuch as these women are often reluctant and ashamed to admit they have been in Refuges, and afterwards relapsed.

" The adoption of periodical examination has, I think, given unmixed satisfaction among the prostitutes, as they do not now think any favour or partiality is shown to one more than another."

CHATHAM.

Average time occupied in curing patients (prostitutes) in St. Bartholomew's Hospital.

Time.	Disease.	Number of days under treatment.
January quarter ending 31st March, 1868	Syphilis	56
	Gonorrhœa	30
Ditto from 1st April to 30th June, 1868	Syphilis	41
	Gonorrhœa	29
Ditto from July to 1st October, 1868	Syphilis	33
	Gonorrhœa	28

Number of prostitutes examined from 1st January to 31st December, 1867.

		Sores.	Gonorrhœa and Vaginal discharge.	Total diseased.
At Woolwich	656; of these	119 ...	222 ...	341
Ditto from 1st January to 29th August, 1868	}683	98 ...	228 ...	326
Periodic ditto from 29th Aug. to 26th Nov., 1868... ...	}492	57 ...	101 ...	158

Number of prostitutes examined from 1st July to 31st December, 1867.

		Sores.	Gonorrhœa and Vaginal discharge.	Total diseased.
At Chatham	607	93 ...	262 ...	355
Ditto from 1st January to 21st August, 1868	}849	128 ...	331 ...	459
Periodic from 21st August to 27th Nov., 1868	}639	59 ...	114 ...	173

The benefits derived by the troops from the operation of the Contagious Diseases Act, will be more easily appreciated by an examination of the tables on the health of the army during the last few years, and a comparison of the returns made since the passing of the Act, with those of the previous years,* but it cannot fail to be satisfactory to the reader to find that the different officers to whom the carrying out of this Act has been intrusted, are able to speak with so much confidence as to the physical and moral improvement of the women subjected to its provisions. Great need was there for the passing of this act of justice and mercy. It has accomplished much, but much remains to do, and I shall in a future chapter point out different particulars in which, as it seems to me, improvements may still be effected.

In further confirmation of the views above set forth, I may append the following letters that appeared, the one in the " British Medical Journal," the other in the " Lancet" of 19th December, 1868 :—

" The Prevention of Contagious Diseases.

"Mr. John W. Trotter, Assistant-Surgeon Coldstream Guards, Windsor, writes to us :—' It may interest some of your readers to have the opportunity of making a comparison between the amount of enthetic diseases arising among an equal number of men in two stations, in one of which the Contagious Diseases Act is applied, and the other where it is not. The period of comparison comprises three months in London, where the Act is not in operation ; and three months at Windsor, where it has been lately introduced. The larger number of admissions in November arose from an influx of strangers during the Windsor Fair—a fact also observed by the superintendent officer, who informed me that, during the three months noted, eighty-eight women had been examined, of whom twenty-five had been sent to hospital suffering from gonorrhœa, and nine from syphilitic sores. In the table for August, ten of primary sores, and four of gonorrhœa, were admitted on September 2nd, on an inspection of the men after arrival at Windsor, and before they were allowed to leave barracks :—

| | LONDON. | | | WINDSOR. | |
	Primary Sores.	Gonorrhœa.		Primary Sores.	Gonorrhœa.
June	13	9	September	3	4
July	19	8	October	4	3
August	33	19	November	9	0
Total	65	36	Total	16	7

" ' These figures speak for themselves.' "

" Comparison of the Operation of the Contagious Diseases Act upon a Regiment of Guards.

"To the Editor of the ' Lancet.'

" SIR,—The extensive benefits which have been conferred upon the soldier when quartered in garrison towns where the Contagious Diseases Act is in full operation has been frequently alluded to in a general way,

* See page 59.

but perhaps the few statistical details which I have ventured to append may prove an additional stimulus towards convincing sanitary reformers of the necessity of extending the Act to the civil population also.

" The town and district of Windsor are placed under effectual super-vision, and the 1st Battalion of Coldstream Guards was stationed there during the months of June, July, and August, when the number of admissions for specific contagious diseases during that period was 64. On the 1st September this battalion marched to London, and has been stationed at Chelsea Barracks, in which locality the admissions for the same classes of disease have increased to 90 during a similar period of three months, the character of the diseases being also much more severe and damaging to the constitution of the men.

" The 2nd Battalion of the same Regiment relieved the 1st Battalion at Windsor early in September, having had a total contagious disease sick-list during the latter three months' occupation of Chelsea Barracks of 110; but since their occupation of the Windsor station there has been a reduction to 69 admissions for a similar period.

" I think the foregoing statistical facts are conclusive; and if the liberty of the subject still interferes with the more general application of the Act to the Metropolis for the benefit of the civil population, surely the interest of the soldier demands that protection should be afforded him in the districts of the London barracks similar to that which he now obtains in every principal garrison town of the kingdom; but the great increase of admissions from this class of diseases among the same number of otherwise healthy men must be conclusive of the injury which is liable to be disseminated among the civil population who reside in the non-protected localities.

"Your obedient servant,

" JOHN WYATT.

" December, 1868."

CHAPTER V.

PROSTITUTION ABROAD.

THE reader who has thus far accompanied me, will, I think, be of opinion that I have called his attention to a state of things demanding serious notice, and the speedy adoption of remedial measures. A move in the right direction has, as we have seen, been made at Aldershott and some other similar places, but the great bulk of prostitution throughout the country presents to us a formidable evil, with which hitherto the legislature has not even attempted to cope. A great difficulty meets us at the very outset of our endeavours to deal satisfactorily with this subject. Any scheme of legislation, having for its object the regulation of prostitution, must have for its starting point the recognition of it as a system, requiring not repression, but direction. This position appears repugnant to the moral and religious sense of a large and influential portion of the community. They consider that a system which openly sets at defiance the laws of God, and exists only because men wantonly gratify those desires which they ought to control, should, if it can not be repressed, at least be left to itself, to work out in its own evil way its evil course, and to link inseparably with lawless indulgence the natural penalties attached thereto. We shall better appreciate the full force of this position, if we contemplate the attitude adopted by the state towards prostitution in other countries. We start with the conviction that the present state of things in our own land is intolerable, an insult to our civilization, at least as great as to our Christianity. The question has received a consideration abroad, which has been denied to it at home; experiments have been tried on the continent which we in England have hitherto declined to make. If on full examination of the means adopted in other countries for grappling with this evil, and of the results obtained by them, we refuse to follow their example, we may at least profit by their experience. To whatever conclusion our research may lead us, of one thing we may feel assured, that honest and laborious consideration of a difficult problem must inevitably obtain the reward denied to indolent or prejudiced indifference. We shall meet in the course of our inquiry with much that is strange, and it may be repugnant to our feelings. Our true wisdom is to shake off national prejudices, and to extend to institutions found among others the like patient and impartial examination that we would demand for our own; but we must at the same time be careful not to accept rashly things merely because they are new, or to reject things because they are old. Above all, we must pay to the religious and moral instinct the liveliest deference, being convinced that whatever is really repugnant to this has within it the seeds of evil. If we come to the conclusion that this condemnation must, in fact, be passed upon the foreign systems, we may still find some principle underlying their practice that we may with advantage adopt. At all events, the examination to which I now invite the reader cannot fail to be useful in this respect, that the comparison of other systems with our own will bring home more clearly to us our defects, and even in learning what to avoid in others, we may discover something to borrow from their systems, something to avoid in our own. I propose, then, in this chapter to examine in detail the systems adopted in the leading European states, commencing with France, both as our nearest neighbour, and as the country that has always led the way in the advance of modern civilization and the growth of modern ideas, and I will only ask the reader to bear in mind that the object of our inquiry is no less how we may elevate the prostitute, than how we may protect the public, for we may lay it down as a golden rule that to benefit society at the expense of the prostitute is as unrighteous and injurious as it is to benefit the prostitute at the expense of society.

SYNOPSIS OF FRENCH REGULATIONS FOR WOMEN.

The great object of the system adopted in France is to repress private or secret, and to encourage public or avowed prostitution.

I may, however, as well premise by observing that the authorities of Paris by no means pretend to have established a control over the whole prostitution of that city. The *concubinaires* they cannot reach. The large sections of superior professional prostitutes, whom the French term *femmes galantes* and *lorettes*, evade them, as do also vast hordes of the lowest class of strumpets who throng the low quarters and the villages of the Banlieu. M. Antin, an official of the Assistance-Publique, estimated in 1856 that there were 20,000 females* in Paris having no other ostensible means of subsistence, on whom a tax in aid of retreats from prostitution might be levied. He assumed that 10,000 of this number could be rated at an annual contribution of fifty francs; 5000

---

* Mr. Tait, a writer on prostitution in Edinburgh, whose estimates I receive with every respect, but at the same time with considerable reserve, informs us that in that city they number about 800, or nearly 1 to every 80 of the adult male population. In London he considers they are as 1 to 60; in Paris, as 1 to 15; and in New York, as 1 to 15. The manner of these calculations is as follows:—One-half of the population of each place is supposed to be males, of whom one-third are thrown aside as too young or too old for the exercise of the generative functions. The remainder is then divided by the alleged number of public women in each community—namely, in Edinburgh, 800; in London, 8000; in Paris, 18,000; and in New York, 10,000. It appears that the above estimate for London is not far short of the mark, the number of recognised women being about 8600; but the number of males, of twenty years of age and upwards, being close upon 700,000 (632,545 in 1851), we should arrive at the proportion, for London, of one prostitute-overt to every 81 (not every 60) adult males.

at eighty francs ; 3500 at 100 francs ; 1500 at 200 francs—yielding in all 1,550,000 francs.

It appears that, in 1778, the then existing statutes being too cumbrous to check the flagrancy of prostitution, the following simple and expeditious police decree was devised to strengthen the hands of the authorities. Although partially repealed, it is the last operative enactment on the subject, and is, as will be seen, the basis of the existing regulations :—

ART. I.—No debauched women and girls to solicit in the streets, on the quays, squares and public walks, and boulevards of this city of Paris, even from windows, under pain of being shaven and locked up, and in case of a second offence, of corporal punishment, as provided in previous ordinances, decrees, and regulations.

ART. II.—No owners and occupiers of houses to underlet to, or harbour in their houses, persons of other than good conduct, morals, and repute, or to permit within the same any cover for debauchery, under penalty of 400 francs.

ART. III.—All such owners and occupiers of houses as aforesaid, whereinto loose women have been introduced, to make a declaration within twenty-four hours before the commissary of the quarter, against him or her who has so imposed upon them, to the end that, on report of the fact by the said commissary, the delinquents may be fined 400 francs, or even specially proceeded against.

ART. IV.—No person, of whatsoever calling or condition, to underlet, by the day, week, fortnight, month, or other term, any chamber or furnished place, to debauched women or girls, or directly or indirectly to take part in any such hiring, under penalty of 400 francs.

ART. V.—All persons letting hotels, furnished houses, and lodgings, by the month, fortnight, week, day, &c., to inscribe forthwith, day by day, and without blanks, the name, surname, quality, birth-place, and ordinary domicile of each lodger, upon a police register which they shall keep for the purpose, to be checked by the commissaries of their respective quarters ; not to harbour in such hotels, houses, or lodgings, any persons without ostensible description, or women or girls who have recourse to prostitution ; to keep separate apartments for men and women ; not to permit men to occupy private rooms with women calling themselves married, except after exhibition by them of their marriage certificate, or their written identification by known and respectable persons, under penalty of 200 francs.

Signed by the Lieutenant of Police,

16th November, 1778.   LENOIR.

It will be observed, also, that in attributing 8000 public women to London and 18,000 to Paris, this writer has not allowed for the enormous clandestinity of our own capital, while he has more than quadrupled the French official returns, I presume, on that account.

In Paris, in 1854, among a population numbering 1,500,000 persons, there were 4206 registered "filles publiques," that is to say, one overt prostitute to 356 inhabitants, over and above the unnumbered clandestine ones, who are variously estimated ta 20,000, 40,000, 50,000, and 60,000.

This ordinance, which was soon found to be too strong for itself, amounting as it did, in fact, to a prohibition of illicit intercourse, was set at nought by the public and all concerned, who boldly faced the crusades of zealous officials, and were regarded as martyrs when convicted. It was subsequently swept off at the Revolution, and prostitution became rampant.

It is true that a law was passed in July, 1791, which addressed itself to the suppression of procuration ; but its framers, doubtless mindful of the spirit of the times, prudently avoided the subject of prostitution, and this one, therefore, among other vices of Paris, being relieved from all the restraints which anterior ordinances had imposed upon it, very shortly achieved the frightful eminence which is a matter of history, and to check which the Directory and the Council of Five Hundred were loudly called on by the voice of public opinion to interpose. The President of the Directory, Rewbell, drew up a powerful appeal to the latter body, inviting them to legislate for the suppression of the disorder which menaced public morality. The embarrassing nature of the subject, however, imported into the document a proposition of so singular a nature, considering its source, as to be worth extraction. It may also, if my view be correct that it is a suggestion of a secret police, form an additional aid to the reflections of the advocates of strong measures in our own country.

" It is our duty to submit one observation more. It appears to us essential that your treatment should prescribe a form of process which shall exempt police inspectors and agents from the inconvenience of being called as witnesses against such of the accused, or their vagabond hangers-on, whom they may happen to know ; the result of which would be to neutralize the action of zealous agents of police, through the persecution and insult they would undergo when charges were dismissed for want of sufficient evidence, and the personal danger they would incur in the course of their investigations."

Nothing was done until 1796, when the newly-instituted prefecture of police took the matter in hand, and *projet de loi* was prepared, but fell through. The same thing occurred again and again. Napoleon the First, who had private reasons for moving in the matter, was compelled to act arbitrarily. Since his time the law of July, 1791, has remained the only authority and cover for the proceedings of the Executive in this regard ; and an opinion has always prevailed in certain quarters that these were more sanctioned by expediency and the *force majeure* of bureaucracy than by legality.

The Prefect Pasquier, towards the close of the first Empire, actively engaged in a code of regulations, which never came to the foot of the throne. In 1816, when, after the occupation of Paris, the morality of the city was at a low ebb, and venereal diseases at their maximum, some plans for regulating prostitution were entertained by men in office ; but it being ruled, at the instance of the Minister of Police, that the 484th article of the penal code gave the administrators of justice powers amply sufficient for the restraint of excess, the agitation dropped. The words of this clause (and I have preserved in my translation the ambiguity of the original) are as follows :

" With regard to subjects not touched by the present code, to which special laws and regulations apply, the courts and tribunals will continue to observe them."

It is argued by some French jurisconsults that the only ancient enactment bearing upon the question, and capable of being revived by this article, that of 1788, having been abrogated at the period of the Revolution, and the penal code being otherwise silent upon the subject, is that of 1791 above cited. But this being in fact directed only against private debauchery of minors, &c., and not against public prostitution, the latter form of vice is absolutely unprovided for, and the present system pretending to be based upon the statute and buttressed by the penal code, is in point of fact an illegal excrescence. Eighteen months afterwards, on receipt of applications for some model regulations for provincial cities, the prefect of police, Anglès, drew up a paper on the whole subject, which he wound up as follows :—

" Sooner or later the principle of individual liberty must triumph, and prostitution must become, under the shadow of general principles, as unrestricted as any other commerce ; or, legislation explicitly admitting distinctions and exceptions, must place under the eye of the magistracy charged with the protection of morality and order, such characters as, by their attitude and the depravity of their sentiments, are in continual opposition to religion, morals, good order, and the interest of society."

In 1819, the Government commissioned the advocates, Mason and Billecoq, to draw a Bill for the Chambers, which had no result. In 1822, again, a new law was contemplated, but no more ; and to the present day the question has not been again mooted. The police administration has pursued its way in perfect conviction of rectitude, and of course without questioning the legality or illegality of its own proceedings.

The official registration of common prostitutes was first loosely set on foot in 1765, and re-organized in 1796, under the Convention. Through neglect it was inoperative until 1801 ; then, after reorganization, it fell gradually into desuetude until 1816, when the present mechanism was adopted, and has undergone slight change, except in 1828, when exhibition of her *acte de naissance* was first demanded of each person presenting herself for inscription, and the poll-tax was abolished.

The keepers of licensed houses acted formerly also as agents in collecting women into the grasp of the authorities ; but this has been suppressed on obvious grounds, that if it were permitted they would become purveyors.* The registration is now either on the voluntary demand of the female, or by requisition of the *Bureau des Mœurs*. On appearing before this tribunal, the candidate, after declaring her name, age, quality, birth-place, occupation, and domicile, is submitted to a searching examination, as follows. Is she married or single ? Has she father and mother living, and what are their pursuits ? Does she reside with them ; if not, why not, and when did she leave them ? Has she children ? How long has she inhabited Paris, and can she be owned

---

* The *maisons de tolérance* are nevertheless recruited, in fact, through the exertions, and at the cost of their keepers, from hospitals and other sources in the capital, and by agency and correspondence from the departments and Belgium.

there? Has she ever been arrested, and if so, the particulars? Has she previously been a prostitute; if so, the details? Has she had any, and what, education? Has she had any venereal affection? Her motives for the step?

She next proceeds to the *Bureau Sanitaire,* is medically examined, and enrolled in that department. If found diseased, she is consigned to the Saint-Lazare Hospital forthwith. Steps are meanwhile taken to verify her replies at the *Bureau des Mœurs,* and formal communications are now made to the mayor of her native commune, with an appeal for the woman's redemption to her parents. I present a copy of the latter, which is of course slightly varied if a female has voluntarily presented herself for examination —

" Monsieur—

" Votre fille   âgée de   , a été arrêtée le pour fait de débauche" (*if diseased,* " et placée à l'infirmerie de Saint-Lazare afin d'y recevoir les soins que sa santé exige.)

" On l'a invitée à retourner près de vous, mais elle s'y est refusée bien qu'il lui ait été offert passeport gratuit avec secours de route.

" Je vous prie, en conséquence, de me faire connaître quels moyens vous comptez employer pour assurer son retour (en cas de maladie après guérison) au cas où vous ne pourriez venir la chercher vous même ou charger une personne sûre du soin de vous la renvoyer."

Should the relatives of the girl be willing to receive her, she is remitted to them at the public cost. She, however, frequently refuses to disclose them, or is ignorant of their existence, and it rarely occurs that they reclaim her. If, as has happened, she be a virgin or a minor, she is consigned to a religious establishment. Should spleen or despair cause the step, and she show symptoms of good qualities, immediate attempts are made to change her intention, and she is often sent home, or placed in a reformatory at the public cost. If her parents reside in Paris they are communicated with. All, in fact, that the *Bureau des Mœurs* can do, I should in justice say, I believe to be done, to warn and restrain the female about to enrol herself in the ranks of public prostitution, and only when all has failed is the formality complied with. This formality, which takes the form of a colourable contract or covenant between the prostitute and the authorities, would seem to argue a sort of consciousness on the part of the latter of the entire illegality of the proceedings throughout. It runs as follows :—

" L'an   , pardevant nous, commissaire de police,
            bureau   , s'est presentée pour être inscrite comme fille publique, la nommée   , native de   , département d   , demeurant à Paris,   No.   , enregistrée d'après décision du   , laquelle, instruite par nous des règlements sanitaires établis par la prefecture, pour les filles de cette classe, nous déclare s'y soumettre, et s'engage, en conséquence, à subir les visites periodiques de MM. les médecins du dispensaire de salu-

brité, promettant de se conformer strictement à toutes les règles prescrites pour la surveillance.

"Le Commissaire de Police,

"D——.

"En foi de quoi elle a signé."

This over, the individual is presumed at liberty to select the category of prostitution in which she will be comprehended. If she is totally destitute, or any arrangement to this effect had been previously entered into, she is registered to a certain licensed house, to whose licensed proprietress she becomes a marked and numbered serf or chattel, to be used or abused, within certain limitations, at discretion. If she has command of capital enough to furnish a lodging of her own, she is provided with a ticket, or *carte*, of which I append a translation :

185 }	*Here are entered her name, age, general appearance, residence, &c.*			
18—.	First fortnight.	Signature of medical officer.	Second fortnight.	Signature of medical officer.
January				
February ...				
March				
April				
May				
June				
July				
August				
September...				
October				
November ...				
December ...				

On the reverse of which are printed the following

Obligations and Restrictions imposed on Public Women.

"Public women, *en carte*, are called upon to present themselves at the dispensary for examination, once at least every fifteen days.

"They are called upon to exhibit this card on every request of police officers and agents.

"They are forbidden to practise the calling during daylight, or to walk in the thoroughfares until at least half-an-hour after the public lamps are lighted, or at any season of the year before seven o'clock, or after eleven P.M.

"They must be simply and decently clad, so as not to attract attention by the richness, striking colours, or extravagant fashion of their dress.

"They must wear some sort of cap or bonnet, and not present themselves bareheaded.

"They are strictly forbidden to address men accompanied by females or children, or to address loud or anxious solicitations to any person.

"They may not, under any pretext whatever, exhibit themselves at their windows, which must be kept constantly closed and provided with curtains.

"They are strictly forbidden to take up a station on the foot-pavement, to form, or walk together, in groups, or to and fro in a narrow space, or to allow themselves to be attended or followed by men.

"The neighbourhood of churches and chapels, within a radius of twenty-five yards, the arcades and approaches of the Palais Royal, the Tuileries, the Luxembourg, and the Jardin des Plantes, are interdicted.

"The Champs Elysées, the Terrace of the Invalides, the exterior of the Boulevards, the quays, the bridges, and the more unfrequented and obscure localities are alike forbidden.

"They are especially forbidden to frequent public establishments or private houses where clandestine prostitution might be facilitated, or to attend *tables-d'hôte*, reside in boarding-houses, or exercise the calling beyond the quarter of the town they reside in.

"They are likewise strictly prohibited from sharing lodgings with a kept woman, or other girl, or to reside in furnished lodgings at all without a permit.

"Public women must abstain when at home from anything which can give ground for complaints by their neighbours, or the passers-by.

"Those who may infringe the above regulations, resist the agents of authority, or give false names or addresses, will incur penalties proportioned to the gravity of the case."

To recapitulate, then; the public women called *filles soumises*, *inscrites*, or *enregistrées*, over whom the *Bureau des Mœurs* of the prefecture of police has cast its net, are divided into two categories :—

1. Domiciled in, and registered to certain licensed houses, for whom the keepers of those houses are responsible.

2. Free prostitutes, who are responsible to the authorities direct.

The first, or *filles des maisons*, are known at the Bureaux by their number, and that of the house to which they are *inscrites*, and are termed by themselves *filles à numero*. Their health is inspected by the official medical staff, at the house of their inscription, once in every week. The second form two sub-classes—viz., women who have their own apartment and furniture, and others who, by special permit, live in furnished lodgings, &c. To all of these, who are termed *filles à carte*, or by the police *isolées*, a *carte*, or bill of health, from time to time is supplied, to which the *visa* of the medical officer of the *Bureau Sanitaire* is affixed at the health inspections for which they present themselves once every fifteen days, in compliance with obligation 1.

This sanitary department was placed upon its present footing in 1828. The medical staff consists of ten superior and ten assistant surgeons, and the number of inspections in 1854 was :—

At the dispensary	97,626
At the registered houses	53,404
At the depôt of the prefecture (which answers to a first-class police station here) ...	4,777
	155,807

The inspection, for which the speculum is very frequently used, is performed with all the delicacy consistent with accuracy, and great despatch ; the average time occupied being three minutes, which includes filling up the papers. The total number inscribed upon the register of the *Administration des Mœurs* at the close of the year 1854, was 4260, showing an increase of 515 only over 3745, the number registered in December, 1833. Of these, 1502 were *numérotées*, or attached to the houses, and the other 2758 were free, or *isolées*.

The same policy which considers the registration of the prostitute indispensable to public order, dictates the exercise of considerable caution in liberating her from supervision. The formalities which attend what is termed the authorized " radiation," are numerous and strict. The petition must invariably be in writing, and supported by evidence of an intention really and truly to abandon the mode of life. The corroborative demand of an intending husband ; of parents or relatives who will be responsible for future conduct ; in certain well-authenticated cases, that of one who will secure her as a mistress against future want ; or a medical certificate of inability to continue prostitution, all command respect and action, more or less immediate. But the mere profession of changed sentiments is treated with suspicion, and a probation of two or three months under private surveillance is insisted upon. The prayer is granted only on its being made clear that it results from something more than an *intention passagère*, or disgust at the inspection —that means of honest support are more than probably forthcoming, and that public order and salubrity will not be jeopardized by the reappearance of the petitioner as an *insoumise* upon the public streets.

The authorised annual radiation during the ten years ending 1854, averaged 258, of whom 24 per annum became wives. The unauthorised averaged 725, and the recaptures 450 per annum, respectively.

The Parisian *maisons de tolérance*, formerly called *bordels* (hence the English word brothel), in which prostitutes are lodged gregariously, are, generally speaking, under the most complete supervision of the police. Numerous formalities must be gone through before a licence is granted by the *Bureau des Mœurs*, and stringent regulations must be complied with under inexorable penalties. The houses must be confined to the one purpose, excepting in the Banlieu, where, from the impossibility of exercising perfect control, and other considerations, a dispensation is granted to deal, during pleasure, in liquor and tobacco. They may not exist near places of worship, public buildings, schools, furnished hotels, or important factories. They may not be on a common staircase. They are not allowed to be near one another, within the walls, but in the banlieu their concentration is imposed. They must be distinguished from other houses by the size of the figures of their number, which must be two feet in length.* Their total number in January,

---

* This public way of calling attention to the nature of the house does not seem to be confined to modern times. I am told by those who have visited the remains of Pompei, that stone phalli are to be seen over the doors of some of the excavated houses, and one gentleman has assured me that he has seen the inscription written up —" Hic habitat Felicitas." It would thus appear as if the sign over the door was a very ancient device to denote the nature of the calling carried on within.

1854, was 144 within, and 68 without, the town, against corresponding numbers of 193 and 36 in 1842. The number of women registered to these houses in 1854, were 1009 and 493 respectively.

Among the regulations applicable to the *maîtresses*, or *dames de maison*, are the following :—

They must lodge no more inmates than they have distinct rooms.

They may keep no child above four years old upon the premises.

They must report, within twenty-four hours, every application made to them for lodgings, and every change of lodgers, and also keep accurate registers for the inspection of the police. Their windows must be kept constantly closed, and be either of ground glass or provided with blinds and curtains.

They may place no person at their door as a sign of their business, before seven or after eleven, P.M.

They must enforce upon the women under their authority the observance of the provisions of the *carte*.

They may not receive minors, or students in uniform ; and

They must report immediately all cases of disease, and generally keep record of all that passes in their houses, or transpires with regard to their inmates.

Those of the Banlieu must conduct their lodgers once in every week to the central sanitary office for examination ; must demand the permits of the military at night, and make return of all cases of excessive expenditure on their premises, or residence by strangers for more than twenty-four hours.

They may not send abroad more than one woman each at one time, the effect of which provision is that there being (for the sake of example) 204 houses and 1504 *femmes numérotées* on the register, the streets may be said to be permanently secured against the presence of 1298 individuals of the class.

The *dames de maison* are of course a vicious and, as a general rule, ferocious mercenary band, tyrannising over the unfortunate helots who form their stock-in-trade, and abjectly crouching before the inspector, the surgeon, and the mouchard. The possession of a house of this kind is the highest aspiration of the prostitute. Such a woman sometimes succeeds in attaining to this pernicious eminence, but it is more frequently in the hands of families in whom houses and goodwill descend as heritable property. The recent editors of Parent's work instance that as much as £2400 has been given for such an establishment, and £8 has been offered as fine to avoid suspension for three days of one of the lowest. Large as these sums may seem, especially when reduced into francs, they will by no means surprise persons cognizant of the property amassed by those who minister, for ready money only, to the lower gratifications of even our more thrifty countrymen.

The gains of the mistresses of these houses in the better part of

Paris are enormous. A medical friend told me that he once, while attending a woman of this class, said he supposed she gained a great deal?—"Yes, my income is considerable," she replied, "more than the pay of a French maréchal!"*

I have above alluded to the external signs by which these houses may be recognised; they are not unfrequently pointed out to the stranger by the *Laquais de place*, who think that all foreigners are anxious to see them. And certainly the visitor discovers on entering them scenes of sensual extravagance, to which his eyes are unaccustomed in England. Here vice finds a retreat of voluptuous splendour, to which in soberer climes she is a stranger. The visitor is received by the mistress of the house, and ushered into a sumptuous ante-room; on a curtain being drawn aside, a door is revealed to him, containing a circular piece of glass about the size of a crown piece, through which he can reconnoitre at his ease a small, but well-lighted and elegantly-furnished, drawing-room, occupied by the women of the establishment. They are usually to be seen seated on sofa chairs, elegantly attired in different-coloured silks, with low bodies, and having their hair dressed in the extreme of fashion; the whole group being arranged artistically, as in a *tableau vivant*, and the individuals who comprise it representing the poses of different celebrated statues, selected apparently with the object of showing off to the best advantage the peculiar attractions of the different women. From the room of observation the visitor can, if he pleases, select his victim, in the same way as the traveller in Galway, on his arrival at a certain hotel, can choose from a number of fish swimming about in the tank the particular salmon on which he would prefer to dine. If this somewhat cold-blooded process of selection is distasteful to him, and he desires to become acquainted with the women in a less summary manner—or if the object of his visit is merely amusement, or the satisfaction of curiosity, without any ulterior aim, he can enter the room, and enjoy the society of its occupants, and will find that the terms of the invitation addressed by the old women at the street door to passers-by are strictly carried out—"Si vous montez voir les jolies filles cela vous engagé a rien," all that is expected from him being to stand a reasonable amount of champagne, or other refreshment, and make himself generally agreeable. It is almost unnecessary to add that to indulge such curiosity is an act of extreme rashness, for in such places all that is possible is done to rob vice of its hideousness, and the visitor is surrounded by an atmosphere of luxury, and by all accessories calculated to captivate the senses and arouse desire. In some of these houses scenes may be witnessed which can only be enacted by women utterly dead to every sense of shame, in whom every vestige of decency has been trampled out, leaving them merely animated machines, for stimulating and gratifying the basest passions. The life of these women must be monotonous enough. They rise about ten, breakfast at eleven (*a la fourchette*), dine at half-

* Some of these mistresses are said to gain as much as from £20 to £30 a-day, and if, as is often the case, the same individual owns two or three houses, she may retire on a fortune in about five years.

past five, and sup about two; they seldom go out walking, and when they do it is in the company of the mistress or sub-mistress.* They pay great and minute attention to their persons, taking baths very frequently, and spending the greater part of the day between breakfast and dinner in preparing their toilette, gossiping together, and smoking cigarettes; some few can play the piano (an instrument usually to be found in these houses), but, as a rule, they are, as might be expected, totally devoid of accomplishments. They have no rooms to themselves, but live *en pension*, taking their meals together; the mistress of the house, or her husband, or lover, as the case may be, presides, and the women take precedence at table among themselves, according to the time that they have been in the establishment. After dinner, commences the operation of dressing, and otherwise preparing themselves for the public, who chiefly frequent these houses in the evening, and after midnight. By half-past seven or eight o'clock they are ready to make their appearance immediately on the bell being rung.

They are generally dressed in accordance with the latest fashion in vogue at balls and *soirées*, and leave untried no device of art for improving or supplementing nature, spending large sums of money on cosmetics and perfumery, often dyeing their hair and darkening their eyebrows and eyelashes, and in some cases having sores painted over to conceal them from their medical attendant.

These women are undoubtedly, as a rule, well-fed and well-dressed. There is usually a debtor and creditor account between them and the mistress of the house, with whom it is always an object to keep her lodgers in her debt, this being the only hold she can have upon them. They are supposed, by a pleasing fiction, to pay nothing for their lodging, firing, and light, and there is certainly no actual charge made on this account; but, as a makeweight, one-half of what they earn is considered to be the mistress's portion, while the other half is paid over to these avaricious duennas, and goes towards defraying the boarding and other expenses. Such a bargain can only be struck by utterly improvident and reckless persons, and goes far towards proving them incapable of regulating their expenses for themselves; it is believed in France that, if they were not cared for by their mistresses, they would sink at once into the extreme of poverty, and this affords, to my mind, one of the few excuses that can be made for the toleration of such houses. I have read in a French work upon prostitution some horrid paragraphs that I do not care to extract, showing the fearful depth of infamy to which these miserable women are sunk, it being even hinted that their mistresses compel them to practise unnatural crimes by threats of expulsion, to which also they are encouraged by extra *douceurs* from the debauched *habitués*. So long as a woman is much sought after, the mistress proves obsequious and kind, taking her occasionally to the theatre, and permitting her other indulgences; but so soon as the public desert the waning prostitute, a cause of quarrel is found, and she is brutally turned out of doors, often with no better covering than an old petticoat or worn-out dress. Thus is it that the public prostitutes step at once from luxurious *salons* to dirty

* These houses are usually managed by a mistress and sub-mistress.

hovels. A man servant is rarely met with in these houses, the domestics being generally prostitutes.

Parent-Duchâtelet, in speaking of the inmates of these houses, says : " These unfortunates are obliged to abandon themselves to the first comer who calls for them, if even he is covered with the most disgusting sores ; there is no drawing back, if they would avoid blows and the very worst treatment. Their mistresses give them no repose ; for, to make use of a comparison that has often been employed by the inspectors, the most brutal carter takes greater care of the horses under his charge than these women do of the girls whom they employ to make a fortune out of.

The downward course of a prostitute is thus described by Alphonse Esquiros :—" The young, pretty, and pleasant-looking girl commences her career in the better class of houses ; but each year, each month robs her of a charm, and produces a wrinkle. The thermometer descends thus in a very short time as low as *ugliness.* The girl accompanies this rapid movement, stepping down from one house to another, from affronts to affronts, from one quarter of the town to another, from St. James' to St. Giles'. To those who have been unable to shelter themselves from the reverses of their calling, either by putting aside a little money or by providing themselves a home, the autumn of the year brings with it dreadful suffering ; they must wait at the end of an alley with the best grace they can. The girl must quit the boudoir to walk the streets, must walk them in the rain and in the cold ; yes, and must do so half clothed, seeking that universal and lost husband, who pushes her aside with his elbow. She must submit to the jeers and taunts of her younger companions in misfortune, till further feebleness overtakes her. Many of them have become old women before they have reached their thirty-second year. Let a girl once enter these houses, she must necessarily bid adieu to heaven, to liberty, to honour, and to the world. I would write over the door of such a house those celebrated words of the Italian poet—' All hope abandon, ye who enter here.' "*

The houses appropriated in Paris to the temporary accommodation of prostitutes and their frequenters, termed *maisons de passe,* have been always considered more dangerous to public morality than the mere lodging-houses. They have been consequently the objects of much anxious vigilance by the authorities, who, nevertheless, proceeding on the principle that anything is preferable to uncontrolled clandestine prostitution, have taken them under their supervision so far as possible. Their numbers are, however, unknown. The only record given by Parent, and we may therefore safely assume the only one to be got, is, that in 1825 there were 150 of them recognised. To facilitate the operation of the police, every such establishment is compelled to bear on its books two registered women, and is therefore to all intents and purposes subject to the general dispositions with regard to the *maisons publiques.* The proprietors are subject to heavy penalties for receiving, *en passe,* girls under fifteen years of age, public women not known to them, or verified as such by production of the *carte,* or students of the public schools.

* Alphonse Esquiros, " Les Vierges folles."

The *fille en carte* of Paris obtains, of course, what she can for her services, but the usual fee is from two to five francs.   In the tolerated
houses, the sum charged by the establishment varies from five to twenty,
in addition to which the generosity of the visitor usually dictates a
trifling present to the victim, *pour ses gants,* as it is called.   At the
Barriers, artisans pay by custom one franc, soldiers fifty centimes, or
a fivepenny silver piece.   Excited to drink (for, as I have mentioned, the sale of liquor at the lowest class of houses is winked at by
the police) by their visitors and the *dames de maison,* each from different
motives, these *filles numérotées* of the Banlieu are from habitual intoxication so incapable of sanitary precautions or observance of decorum, that
in their case, at least, the regulations of the *Bureau des Mœurs* may be
esteemed rather a blessing than a curse.

Similar systems, more or less improved upon the Parisian type, prevail at Toulon, Lyons, Strasburg, Brest, and other large French garrison
towns ; but as they appear unlikely to furnish the reader with any
useful information, I will spare myself and him any further reference
to them, until I have to speak of French hospital arrangements.

This sketch of French prostitution would be incomplete if I did not
compare the condition of the streets of Paris with that of our own.   The
prostitutes in Paris are not spread over all the streets, as in London ;
they are only to be found in certain localities prescribed by the police.
The *fille de maison* may be met gaudily dressed, quickly walking back-
wards and forwards, in certain back streets ; but even there she is not
allowed to actually solicit, though, as may be supposed, she does not fail
to attract the attention of passers-by.

The *fille à carte* is the prostitute whom the stranger is most likely to
meet with, and she is generally less gaudily dressed than the *fille de
maison,* and is allowed by the police to walk up and down in certain
less frequented streets, but not to go beyond them. She likewise is not
allowed to solicit.

The Clandestine Prostitute, notwithstanding all the precautions of the
police to register every woman gaining her livelihood by prostitution,
is frequently to be met with in the streets of Paris.   Work girls, servants, and girls serving in shops, who wish to increase their small
earnings, and yet are not registered by the police, come under the head
of clandestine prostitutes.   These last of course are not more subject to
control than ordinary persons, but the police in Paris strictly supervise
all women known by them to be prostitutes, and render the streets
passable at all hours of the evening or night to respectable females, and
solicitation is strictly forbidden.   Moreover, Frenchmen do not, as a
rule, go into the streets of Paris after dinner to meet with adventures ;
they rather frequent the casinos or houses of accommodation.   And
even if some women are to be seen in certain streets in Paris in the
early part of the evening, after half-past eleven the streets are
quite deserted, as the police oblige every woman to retire to her room
at that hour.   How different is the condition of the streets of London ;
and we might well follow in this respect the example of the French.
In London a man has prostitution thrust upon him ; in Paris he has
to go out of his way to look for it ; so that external decency, so out-

raged in England, is there maintained. We may now turn from the social to the sanitary aspect of the question.

It would be vain and unsafe to attempt any estimate of the proportion of diseased prostitutes, who are following their calling in the streets of London. But the French authorities are at least enabled to show the exact proportion of disease among the limited number who are under police control, and the editors of the third edition of Parent-Duchâtelet's work have added the following interesting table :—

Annual Average of Syphilis among Registered Prostitutes in Paris in the Suburbs, as well as the Unregistered.

Year.	Registered prostitutes attached to brothels within the walls.	Ditto, in the suburbs.	Registered prostitutes living at large.	Unregistered women captured being prostitutes.
	Diseased.	Diseased.	Diseased.	Diseased.
1845	1 in 142	1 in 59	1 in 261	1 in 6
1846	1 in 151	1 in 53	1 in 183	1 in 6
1847	1 in 154	1 in 51	1 in 350	1 in 6
1848	1 in 125	1 in 37	1 in 181	1 in 5
1849	1 in 128	1 in 44	1 in 200	1 in 5
1850	1 in 148	1 in 47	1 in 142	1 in 5
1851	1 in 198	1 in 60	1 in 180	1 in 5
1852	1 in 184	1 in 75	1 in 349	1 in 5
1853	1 in 183	1 in 122	1 in 402	1 in 5
1854	1 in 176	1 in 102	1 in 376	1 in 4

The greater proportion of disease affecting prostitutes attached to brothels is explained by the girls being compelled (particularly in the lower description of house) to prostitute themselves to all comers, no matter how numerous, be they covered with rags or not, who can satisfy the demands of the *dame de maison*. But the woman living at large has a choice left her whether or not she will tolerate a man she may think diseased.

Among the registered females there were, in 1854, 358 cases of uterine disorder, and among the unregistered 282—total, 640.

Certain razzias made lately upon the clandestine prostitutes frequented by the soldiers have proved that two and sometimes three out of five of them were diseased.

PARIS CIVIL HOSPITAL EXPERIENCE FOR FEMALES.

The earliest official recognition of syphilis by the French was in 1497 and 1498, when an hospital for the "protection" of poor destitute males from infection—for contagion was not then imagined to be a cause—was decreed by the Parliament of Paris. The necessity of *curing* was first acknowledged in 1505, but the malady was unchecked until the compulsory establishment of the parochial dispensary of St. Eustache, in 1536. This, like many succeeding experiments, was abortive, and it was only in 1614 that, by joint action of the Hôtel Dieu Committee and the Bureau des Pauvres, a service was organized for male patients ; but as corporal chastisement was exhibited with the medicaments of the period, the institution for cure of " la gross vérole," as it was called, made but little progress.

The first Parisian female hospital was in a corner of the prison of La Salpêtrière, established in 1657, for the punishment of disorderly women. Its patients, and those of the above-mentioned male hospital, were subsequently moved to the Hospice de Bicêtre, where in 1730 there were 400 patients, all in the direst wretchedness and neglect. The horrors of Bicêtre were atrocious,—in spite of all attempts to remedy them by Maréschal, the Court Physician ; the minister Breteuil, who was shocked on an inspection in 1784 ; and other reformers—until great improvements were introduced by Michel Cullerier, appointed surgeon in 1787. This able and virtuous man persuaded the Constituent Assembly, in 1792, to remove his charges to the then new Hôpital du Midi.

In 1812, sixty beds for venereal patients were organized at the Hôpital St. Louis ; and in 1815, when the invasion brought a frightful amount of disease into the city, additional accommodation became again necessary. La Petite Force prison was made a subsidiary hospital, and subsequently a part of the Hôpital la Pitiè being also called into similar use, the municipal authorities, who had theretofore not flinched, sought assistance from the public treasury. The Minister of the Interior demurred. The Prefect Anglès insisted that this was not a local but a public question ; but without avail. No material progress was made. The dispute as to the expense entirely prevented it ; and when Parent-Duchâtelet wrote, he lamented that no special hospital for diseased women existed, as well as a special prison for the criminal and disorderly; these institutions being at the time of his death still amalgamated. In 1835, however, the body whom we might here denominate the Board of Hospital Commissioners, recognised the propriety of the separation, and the *regime* which now prevails was set on foot.

The venereal hospitals of Paris are Saint-Lazare, for police female patients, say 200 beds ; Lourcine, female, 270 beds. There are also a limited number of beds for peculiar cases in the General Hospital, St. Louis, and about 15 or 20 reserved for paying patients at the Maison Dubois, or Municipal Infirmary, in the Rue du Faubourg St. Denis.

The Saint-Lazare Hospital, in the Faubourg St. Denis, combines an infirmary for females with what we should here term a bridewell. It is under the control of the prefect of police, whose department consigns to it all the regularly enrolled females reported unsound by the medical branch, and the captured *insoumises* who are found diseased upon examination at the dépôts. The infirmary department is under the direction of two physicians, two house surgeons, an apothecary, twenty-two wardswomen, and eight Sisters of Charity of the order of Marie Joseph. The patients are very carefully classed with a view to the separation of the old from the young, and the hardened from those whose reclamation is not hopeless. Such as manifest a disposition to return to their parents are sedulously kept apart.　The total of beds is about 300, of which 200 occupy the venereal wards.

The following table of admissions is furnished by Messrs. Trebuchet and Poirat-Dâuval, who have together superintended the last edition of Parent-Duchâtelet's work.　I have every reliance upon the accuracy of any figures relative to the French hospitals furnished by these gentlemen, as they are both of them connected with the Prefecture of Police :—

				1853.	1854.
Filles de Maison de Paris.　Syphilis	.	.	.	307	313
„　　　„　　Banlieu.　„	.	.	.	214	263
„　　　„　　Isolées　„	.	.	.	120	124
Non-specific and Uterine Affections	.	.	.	350	358
Insoumises.　Syphilis	.	.	.	313	460
„　　　Non-specific and Uterine Affections			.	212	282
				1516	1800

The mortality from all causes was, in 1853... 16
„　　　　　„　　　　　„ 1854... 17

The LOURCINE HOSPITAL was, after long and anxious consideration, established by the Hospital Board, in 1836, as a free receptacle for unregistered (officially *du civil*) syphilitic females.　Of its 276 beds, there are 36, in a distinct ward, appropriated to mothers suckling infected infants, and 13 to girls under fifteen years of age.*　The "service" comprises three superior and seven subordinate medical officers, 12 Sisters of Charity of the order of La Compassion, and 13 wardswomen, besides other female servants ; and its expenses amounted in 1855 to 181,543 francs, or £7261.

	Adults.	Girls under sixteen.	Total.
The admissions were, in 1854	1358	 127	 1485
„　　　„　in 1855	1384	 82	 1466
The average of eleven years being ...	1398	 80	 1478

No less than 85 of the children in 1854, and 60 in 1855, were born syphilized within the walls, or introduced under two years of age with their mothers—a frightful proof of suffering entailed upon innocents by the depravity of their parents.　The numerical disproportion of their deaths to those of adults has been already noticed at page 35, and other interesting figures with regard to the statistics of this hospital will be found in the following pages.

On application, the patients are examined with the speculum, and as often, subsequently to admission, as may be considered necessary.　A part of each ward is partitioned off, and thus the woman is secured from the observation of all other inmates, while undergoing the examination.

* M. Battel observes with profound regret the number of young girls from twelve to fifteen years of age infected with syphilis, and sometimes exhibiting traces of violence.　This he ascribes partly to the prevalence among the lowest class of an execrable superstition, to the effect that connexion with a child is a cure for syphilis in the male.

It has been found, in practice, that the few who object are females of the most shameless and abandoned description, who cling to the idea of being cured without revealing even to the medical staff the entire extent of their disease. Friends of patients are, under ordinary circumstances, admitted on two days in the week. The interviews usually take place through a grating, and in presence of a Sister; but when the visitors are relatives, these precautions (which are enforced to control, so far as possible, the recruiting operations of the *dames de maison*) are dispensed with. Threatened suspension of the privilege in case of disorderly or indecorous behaviour is found generally sufficient to ensure the quiet and propriety of the hospital. It is an interesting fact, well worthy of observation, that though at neither Lourcine nor Saint-Lazare is attendance at religious worship made compulsory, the ceremonial is for the most part eagerly and devoutly observed by all who are not bedridden, and the chaplains produce pleasing evidence of the value of their reformatory counsels.

The inmates of the Lourcine are employed—for employment is the mainstay of morality as idleness is the handmaid of evil—under the direction of the lady visitors and at certain very trifling wages, about the entire household service, washing, and needlework of the institution. They may quit the establishment at their own pleasure, even before being cured. In the latter case, urgent remonstrances are offered, and every kind of official delay is interposed; but should this, as indeed rarely happens, fail to restrain them, they are of course placed under the surveillance of the sanitary police as pestiferous, and therefore dangerous to public health.

There are, I believe, thirty detectives employed in Paris to watch and trace clandestine prostitutes. If they see a suspicious-looking woman in the streets or at the public balls, they follow and arrest her, and unless she can give a satisfactory account of herself, she is examined, and if found diseased, sent to the St. Lazare Hospital, three francs being the premium paid for her discovery. These mouchards, as they are called, become as well known to the women as a hawk is to small birds. I was present on one occasion when some captured women arrived at the hospital. They were brought like prisoners in an omnibus, which was driven into the courtyard. I was given to understand they were fair representatives of their class; if so, they are very plain. The women whom I saw on this occasion were short and thick-set, but not altogether unprepossessing; although generally stout, they did not look as if they drank freely, nor were they sensuous-looking, but all the police authorities agree that they would rather gain their subsistence by prostitution than work. Idleness is their besetting sin. On the occasion I refer to, they appeared to consider their calling like any other occupation, and to regard one another with an *esprit de corps*, as if they were so many postmen or policemen—prudery and impudence were equally absent. They seemed only anxious to escape from captivity, which they could not do without the signature of the medical man, certifying that they were sound. They appeared to treat the contagious diseases with which they were infected as so many evils incidental to their business. Every profession has its drawbacks! I was told that it is mostly the young girls who are diseased; the older prostitutes avoid contagion by examining every man who desires to have relations with them, previously to permitting intercourse; but these even are not exempt from uterine affections, and suffer seriously from the complaints peculiar to their sex, quite independently of venereal disease.

The object of the wary, old prostitute is to exercise her calling with the least expenditure of self, and to gain as much money as possible. In reply to my question, why do so many old, deformed, and worn-out women carry on the *métier* and not retire, I was told that to live required food, and to gain the wherewithal to appease their appetites for luxuries entailed labour—now these women prefer prostituting their persons to gaining a livelihood by honest labour, and seem to think that they are not humiliated thereby, but regard themselves as a class useful to the state and recognised by the police. And notwithstanding what the public may think, they do not despise themselves till they are worn out, when they gradually pass into some other calling. Those whom I saw did not look vicious, but seemed well to do in the world, and so far as I could judge, were not much troubled with aught else than how to live from hand to mouth. In only one instance at this examination at which I assisted was any feeling of modesty evinced, one woman objecting to the presence of any one but the regular medical attendant; however, when told that I was a foreign doctor, she seemed quite satisfied. All the others entered, and were examined as if it formed part of the day's duty.

The service at St. Lazare is superintended by Sisters of Charity, who attend the surgeon and carry out his instructions. Dr. Clerc first goes into the wards to visit patients who are unable to leave their beds. In proof of the mildness of syphilis in his wards, I may state that out of 150 patients, not more than two or three were confined to their beds. About 50 are examined each day, and thus the whole pass under the inspection of the surgeon twice a week. I should mention that special permission is required for any visitor to attend this hospital in company with the surgeon. My medical readers may like to know the character of the disease exhibited by the cases (33) which I witnessed in one morning at St. Lazare. In after years it may be important to draw comparisons between the state of things existing *now* and *then*, as it is now to compare the phases of disease of 1868 with those of 1857. I append a table :—

Chancre..	3
Erosion of vulva	2
Chancre of vulva	1
Affection of womb	2
Mucous tubercles of lips	2
Epithelial affection of the urethra	3
Enlargement of the glands of the vulva	2
Vegitations	4
Urethritis	3
Lupus of the vulva	1
Erosion of the womb	2
Enlargement of the womb	1
Vaginitis	1
Vulvitis with follicular chancre	1

Itch	...	...	...	...	...	...	...	I
Fissure of the anus	...	...	...	...	...	...	I
Ulceration of the vulval glands		...	...	...	...	I
Bubo and chancre	...	...	...	...	...	...	I
Abscess of the vulval glands ...		...	...	...	...	I

$$\overline{33}$$

It has seldom been my lot to witness a more interesting series of cases than those noted above, but my readers must understand that each case was complicated by the presence of more than one affection. I have grouped them according to the most prominent symptom. I find in my note book the following comments, written down at the time of my visit :—In England, I have rarely in hospital practice found chancre in anomalous positions. In Paris these affections may be found on all parts of the body, and the sufferer evinces no shame at the discovery. The treatment of mucous tubercles adopted at the St. Lazare was to touch them with the acid nitrate of mercury, and then to cover the parts with bismuth, in order to keep them dry. It is believed almost impracticable to administer mercurial pills to French prostitutes as there is a popular prejudice against the drug, and they subsequently spit out the pills, although taken in the presence of the sisters. The opinions I have enunciated elsewhere were corroborated at the St. Lazare Hospital, viz., that women rarely suffer under secondary symptoms, as, fortunately for the sex, constitutional syphilis shows itself only by the occurrence of a few mucous tubercles on the throat or vulva.

The *epithelial affection of the urethra* is a very obstinate complaint. It had been treated locally with iodine ; recovery was slowly occurring, but it would be impossible for the patient to gain her future living by prostitution.

Affections of the glands of the vulva is a much more common complaint in Paris than in London. On either side of the vulva one or more ducts may be noticed, large enough to admit a quill. Similar appearances are seen on the tonsils. On squeezing these, pus may be seen exuding in considerable quantities. The treatment consists in injecting them with a small syringe containing a solution of nitrate of silver.

Vegitations are removed with scissors or by the application of lime or potash in little sticks kept in dry powder to prevent their deliquescence.

Urethritis is a common affection. To discover it the finger must be passed into the vagina, and the urethra be pressed from behind forwards. Ulceration will not produce urethritis in the same female, but it will produce it in the male, and then the male may contaminate the female. Urethritis in the female is then generally produced from contact with the male. Dr. Clerc treats urethritis in the female by cauterizing the passage with Lallemand's instrument. No ill consequences follow, the woman having no prostrate ; nor need we fear inflammation of the bladder. I noticed several cases of excessive dryness of the vagina ; the organs seemed to be bereft of secretion, and Dr. Clerc thinks that excoriation in the male may follow from this cause.

In addition to the experience I here gained as to the measures adopted for the detection and restraint of clandestine prostitutes, I was anxious to investigate personally the plan pursued by the French police in procuring the examination of the public women ; I am indebted to the kindness of my confrère, Dr. Dennis, for the opportunity afforded me of doing so. The women living in the brothels are brought on the days appointed for examining them under the charge of their respective submistresses to a central depôt. The doctor holds his sittings in a private room ; each woman being introduced separately, and the examination made privately. On the occasion of my visit no one was present except the doctor, the patient, and myself. I have never seen a more complete and satisfactory method of examination. As soon as it is finished the girl passes out to have her *carte viséd* by the police authorities.

Dr. Dennis told me that he makes 174,000 examinations per annum. Of these, two-thirds are with the speculum. The women whom I saw were very cleanly,* and although at the examination at which I assisted there were at least fifty of them brought promiscuously from different parts of Paris, it was not found necessary to send one to the hospital. Few of these women were good-looking, and most of them appeared to be middle-aged, and one who, I should think was sixty years of age, was, to my surprise, still on the register. I had some suspicion as to the cause of her appearance in such company, as she could hardly have been carrying on the trade on her own account ; she was probably an agent in the pay of one of the houses—half spy, half procuress. I asked one crooked-eyed woman who came from the suburbs of Paris, how many men she was accustomed to receive per day ; she replied, ten or twelve. The fee paid her by soldiers was usually half a franc, other men paying a franc. On being further questioned, this woman admitted that she sometimes received as many as forty men in twenty-four hours. Notwithstanding such excesses as these, the generative organs presented no unusual appearances. I, however, pass by the other questions I put to these women, to describe a circumstance unprecedented in the whole of my previous or subsequent inquiries on this painful subject. A girl about seventeen, possessing a good figure, and very intelligent, was introduced, looking frightened and abashed. "Doctor," said she, "I am truly in distress ; I have nothing to eat ; see the rags which cover me. I have received a fair education, but have been turned out of house and home. I have, I acknowledge, an inherited impetuous temper, and poverty compels me to come here. I am about to enter on a life of infamy, but no other course is open to me. I hope you will find me sound. I know I am not diseased, for I have never known man. Wicked as I am, I have done all in my power to be again received at home, and I desire to enter Madame ——'s house." The police, before inscribing such a girl on the public register, and introducing her to prostitution, would write to her parents. She

---

* I was informed that on the day after these inspections the houses are specially frequented by the public, in the belief that there is then less chance of contracting disease. It is, therefore, reasonable to suppose that under the French system many yield to indulgence whom the fear of the natural penalty would otherwise deter. In considering the advisability of introducing health inspectors among the civil population in England this should not be lost sight of.

underwent the examination, was declared sound, and existence, at least, was thus assured to her for a time.

I am not aware that any system in any civilized country exists which could prevent such a girl taking such a course. She passed from my sight, but has left on my mind an indelible impression, and I insert the sad story here, believing that its recital may bring home to the reader, in the most forcible manner possible, the full horrors of prostitution.

Do many prostitutes, we may well ask, enter upon their career in this way? Is their name legion? who shall say? I cannot in the present chapter pursue this subject further; I shall revert to it hereafter, when, having considered the causes of prostitution, I pass on to the discussion of the means that can best be adopted for grappling with it.

During a recent visit to Paris, I asked M. Ricord, who has had a thirty years' experience of hospital direction, and is thoroughly superior to the prejudices in favour of the *viæ antiquæ*, which are not seldom contemporary with such length of service, whether he had any idea as to improving the system of venereal management in Paris. He was of opinion that no change could be advantageously introduced beyond rendering the sanitary police examination of registered women yet more accurate, and permitting the unregistered to enter all the hospitals indiscriminately. The obligation now imposed upon this class of repairing to the Lourcine only, thereby making public the nature of their ailments, and setting a stamp upon their pursuits, acts, he thinks, prejudicially, by causing concealment, neglect, and aggravation of disease.

FRENCH CIVIL HOSPITAL EXPERIENCE FOR MALES.

The male venereal hospital for Paris is called Du Midi. It is established for the gratuitous treatment of males only. It contains 336 beds for in-patients; 22 of these, however, are reserved for patients who can pay 1s. 3d. per diem. At the period when I had the privilege of attending this hospital, in addition to the in-patients, the students had the advantage of seeing not less than 140 or 150 out-patients daily, under the management of my masters, M. Ricord, M. Cullerier, and M. Puche, aided by a staff of seven other medical officers of various grades, and forty attendants. Its expenses for the year 1855 were 203,123 francs, or £8125. As, unfortunately, there is not the same opportunity of employing the patients as in the female hospitals, their sufferings from want of occupation, have been considerably abridged by the formation of a lending library of 700 volumes. The devotion by the hospital board of 22 beds to persons who can pay a franc and a-half per diem in consideration of seclusion, has proved, as may readily be imagined, a boon to many an unfortunate sufferer, disqualified by his antecedents for the very mixed society in the free wards, but too poor, or perhaps too proud, to secure in private such advice as is open at the Midi to all comers.

The number of admissions for half a century, by periods of ten years, and also during the years 1854 and 1855, with the mean stay in hospital and mortality, appear in the following tables, which offer some facilities for comparing the male and female venereal statistics, as returned by the male hospitals and the Lourcine :—

	MALE HOSPITALS.			LOURCINE.			
Decennial Period.	Annual Average Number of Adult Men Admitted.	Mean stay during period. Days.	Deaths.	Annual Average Number of Adult Females.	Mean stay during period. Days.	Deaths.	Children under 16, of both sexes, Admitted.
1805 to 1814	1392	57	1 in 56	1294	65	1 in 67	—
1815 to 1824	1196	61	1 in 62	1248	71	1 in 57	—
1825 to 1834	1438	45	1 in 80	1743	50	1 in 88	—
1835 to 1844	3246*	32	1 in 126	1633	47	1 in 97	1698
1845 to 1855 (eleven years)	3120	33	1 in 168	1398	57	1 in 72	1435

	MALES (HÔPITAL DU MIDI).		FEMALES (LOURCINE).	
Years.	Admissions.	Mean stay during year. Days.	Admissions.	Mean stay during year. Days.
1845	2931	36·18	1419	56·65
1846	2789	38·22	1574	49·84
1847	2837	37·21	1384	61·73
1848	2747	36·12	2149	45·70
1849	2772	36·06	1381	49·86
1850	3159	32·94	1247	58·78
1851	3019	33·47	1102	66·51
1852	3367	30·23	1114	64·38
1853	3660	30·00	1274	56·21
1854	3425	31·06	1358	62·75
1855	3632	29·72	1384	59·89
Total ...	34,338	... ...	15,386	... ...
Mean ...	3121	33·46	1399	57·20

Adult Males at Hôpital du Midi.

					1854.	1855.
Admissions ...	...	...	...	...	3425	3632
Mean stay ...	...	...	...	...	31·06	29·72
Venereal mortality ...	...	...	...		15	34

* This increase was due to the concentration in 1835, at the Midi, of venereal males who had previously been treated elsewhere.

Adult Females at Lourcine.

						1854.	1855.
Admissions	...	...	...	...	...	1358	1384
Mean stay	...	...	...	...	...	62·75	59·89
Venereal mortality	...	...	...	...		0	1

Population of Paris, 1,337,153.

The preceding tables call for a few remarks.

1. The extraordinary rise in the number of patients at the Midi in the ten years following 1835 was due to the concentration there during those years of patients previously treated elsewhere. The male returns, therefore, since 1835 may be taken to refer to that hospital alone.

2. Mortality of infants and children under sixteen has been given in previous pages.

3. Out-patient returns are not included.

4. The actual admissions of males into hospital during 1855 exceeded by 25 per cent. those of 1845, and have an upward tendency. Their mean stay has been gradually shortened to the extent of 16 per cent. during the same period, while the corresponding admission of females shows the very slight decrease of 2·40 per cent., and their mean stay a prolongation of 5·70 per cent.

Although the average of males under treatment during the period from 1845 exceeded by 55 per cent. that of the period ending 1814, their average stay in hospital had diminished from 57 days to 33, or 42 per cent. The variation in the female averages during the half century appears not quite so trifling as during the last decennial period. The admissions have on the whole increased 8 per cent.; the length of illness has shortened 12 per cent.; and mortality has decreased 8 per cent.

An enormous increase of female sickness followed the Revolution of 1848, and that among the males after the troubles of 1850 is still more marked. The St. Lazare Hospital received at the latter period 150 patients in excess of its proper accommodation. The duration of female sickness during the term of eleven years ending 1855 was to that of the male as 57·20 to 33·46—*i. e.*, it was 40 per cent. longer. It is alleged by the officials that the mean duration of the disease among the *soumises* at St. Lazare—in whose persons it is supposed to be arrested at an early period by the visiting surgeons before having made great ravages—is as much as forty-five days.

As my present readers and future investigators into the various phases of venereal diseases at different periods of time, may be interested in hearing what were the forms seen in the Parisian Venereal Hospital, I subjoin a summary of cases extracted from the former edition of this book, which I made up while going round M. Ricord's wards at the Hôpital du Midi, on the 14th of October, 1855. I may premise that he saw out-patients twice a week, and selected from them the most urgent and surgically interesting cases for immediate admission into the house. On the day of my visit the following forms of disease presented themselves among the in-patients :—

Balanitis	1
Paraphymosis	2
Circumcision	3
Gonorrhœa	8
Varicocele	2
Tubercle on penis	1
Warts	2
Swelled testicle	5
Fistula, urinary	1
Infecting chancre	12
Chancre on gum	1
Urethral chancre	1
Inoculated chancre	1
Serpiginous chancre	1
Indurated ditto	14
Phagedænic ditto	5
Bubo	17
Strumous ditto	5
Secondary symptoms, papular	1
Syphilitic herpes	1
Condylomata	1
Secondary symptoms	3
Iritis	2
Tertiary symptoms	2
Doubtful	2
Disease of foot	1
Itch	1
Syphilitic affections of the skin	1
Convalescent	2
TOTAL	99

On Easter Monday, the 2nd of April, 1850, when I also visited the same wards, there were a few beds vacant, but the following is the *resumé* of the cases—I append it for comparison sake :—

Indurated chancre	33
Secondary symptoms	21
Bubo	8
Vesical catarrh	4
Phagedænic chancre	2
Epididymitis	7
Urinary fistula	1
Vegitations	2
Tertiary symptoms	8
Iritis	1
Simple chancre, non-indurated	11
Gonorrhœa præputialis	3
Scrofulous affection of the testis	1
Blennorrhagia	3
Stricture	1
Chancre of the anus	3
Gonorrhœal rheumatism	1
Albuminuria	1
Hæmorrhoids	1
TOTAL	112

The first thing that will strike the most casual observer, who looks over the cases, is the large proportion of indurated chancres—thirty-three being in the wards at one time.* Here the student may study

* It appears that the French army quartered in Rome in 1850 suffered under most

induration in all its forms. The frequency of this symptom in the wards depends upon M. Ricord's admission by preference, of those patients who present it.

We may reasonably expect that in a country where the health of the civil population is the object of so great solicitude, that the sanitary condition of the army and navy will not be neglected. Accordingly, we find the men enrolled in these services, and other *employés* of the Government, subject to strict regulations in this respect.

FRENCH MILITARY AND NAVAL EXPERIENCE.

I regret to say that I have been unable as yet to obtain, through the Foreign Office, the recent official statistics of the French army and navy, and consequently I am obliged to fall back upon statements regarding the French troops that are not so recent as those of other foreign countries.

It would appear, from the following statement in the *Statistique Médicale de l'Armée Française pendant l'année* 1865, that the effective force of the French army consisted of 348,968 men. During that year, 31,918 soldiers suffered from venereal diseases; hence it follows that 92 per 1,000 men only are affected, instead of 325, the average number among English troops, as is shown at page 58. We must admit that venereal diseases are nearly four times more common among our troops than they are among the French. Dr. Jeannel says the treatment of venereal patients in the French forces, both by land and sea, costs annually £60,000; the treatment of venereal patients costs the civil hospitals of Paris alone more than £24,000.* This sum must be quadrupled if we wish to appreciate the expense required by the treatment of civil venereal patients in the whole of France.†

It may then be affirmed that in France venereal diseases cause hospital annual expenses to amount to £156,000 at the least.

If, as seen in previous pages, the authorities in France have found it desirable to legislate for the prostitute, the army has not been forgotten, and precautions have been taken to protect the French soldier from the consequences of prostitution, and the regulations are very strictly carried out in France.

Every French soldier or sailor attacked with syphilis is bound to report himself to the surgeon-major of the service to which he belongs, and should he do so spontaneously, receives no punishment. If he

---

severe forms of primary syphilis. In a few days after infection gangrene of the prepuce took place, and severe forms of buboes were very common. Constitutional symptoms came on more quickly than in France, and showed themselves in two-thirds of the cases; whereas in French military hospitals secondary symptoms are exceptional. Yet the same treatment (mercurial) was employed. It was likewise remarked that iodide of potash was more useful in primary and secondary symptoms in Italy than in France.—M. Chalon, Chirurgien sous-aide: "Annales des Maladies de la Peau," vol. iv., pp. 161, 162.

* 812 beds at £28 each amounts to £22,736; but there is always a certain number of venereal patients in the ordinary hospitals.

† Lyons has 282 beds for venereal patients; Marseilles, 160; Bordeaux, 85; Strasbourg, 60; Brest, 60; and all the large towns have a certain number according to the amount of their population.

should not do so, he is treated *à la salle des consignes*, and punished with a month *de consigne* on his leaving hospital. He is called npon to point out the woman that has infected him; but this regulation is hard to enforce, as, rather than inform, the men take punishment. In many cases it would be an impossibility, as they frequent a plurality of women, and are occasionally too far gone in liquor at the time of the act to establish an identity.

Every soldier, sailor, or workman in the arsenals is, moreover, subjected, on his arrival at his station, to a special examination; and if any traces of syphilis, however slight, are detected, he is immediately sent to hospital. The more trifling venereal affections are, however, treated at the barracks, a circumstance deserving, I think, the attention of the home authorities in England, who send every case, however slight, to hospital. The penalties which formerly were in vogue when a man was found diseased, are now never inflicted, unless the culprit has attempted to evade the ordinary examination. No one is granted leave of absence without previously undergoing an examination, whereby his freedom from contagious disease may be ascertained. Dr. Jeannel has, in his recent work, given several statistical tables, showing that the proportion of men affected with venereal diseases considerably varies in the various garrison towns.

Proportion of Venereal Diseases in the Garrison at Paris.

YEARS 1858, 1859, 1860.

Average number of men	50,311
Average number of venereal patients entering the hospital ...	2,036
Average number per 1,000 men suffering from venereal disease...	40

Proportion of Venereal Diseases in the Garrison of Lyons.

YEARS.	1860.	1861.	1862.	1863.	1864.
Average annual force of the garrison	29,158	19,782	20,858	18,515	17,824
Number of venereal patients entering hospital	2,448	2,046	1,793	1,392	1,179
Proportion per 1,000 men affected with venereal disease ...	121	103	85	69	66

Proportion of Venereal Diseases in the Garrison at Marseilles.

YEARS.	1862.	1863.	1864.	1865.
Average annual force of the garrison ...	3,431	4,362	3,786	3,172
Number of venereal patients entering hospital	267	258	203	1,227
Proportion per 1,000 men affected with venereal disease...	77	59	53	71

Proportion of Venereal Diseases in the Garrison at Bordeaux.

Years.	1862.	1863.	1864.	1865.	1866.
Average annual force of the garrison	1,800	1,922	1,900	1,875	1,806
Number of venereal patients entering hospital	105	157	103	71	78
Proportion per 1,000 men affected with venereal disease ...	58	81	54	37	43

According to the comparative statistics of venereal diseases in several garrison towns published in 1863, the general average of 27 garrisons gave in 1858 the proportion of 74 venereal patients per 1,000 entering the military hospitals ; whereas in Paris the proportion was reduced to 34 per 1,000 during the same year. In 1860, the average of 27 garrisons gave 71 per 1,000 ; the garrison of Paris contributed only 33 per 1,000. These statistics did not comprehend slight bleunorrhagic affections, which did not require hospital attendance, and were treated at the Regimental Infirmary (Jeannel, p. 258).

In the English report on the causes of reduced mortality in the French army serving in Algeria, for 1867, it is stated—

" We had frequent opportunities of discussing the measures in operation for the prevention of syphilitic diseases in the army in Algeria. These consist of monthly inspections of the troops, and the usual police measures of inspecting public women, and treating those found to be affected. These police measures have no more special reference to the army than they have to the population generally.

" There are dispensaries for the purpose in the principal towns, and the colonial medical officers are also charged with similar duties. Syphilis and its consequences are very prevalent among the Arab population, and are the result of their degraded morals. This disease is often hereditary among them, and leads to frightful results from neglect.

" The opinion was universally expressed by medical officers that the frequency and severity of the disease among the troops in Algeria had been diminished by police measures.[*]

" The subject is one of great importance, and while stating the opinions given to us, it is necessary at the same time to give the comparative admissions from syphilitic diseases in the army serving in Algeria, as compared with those of the French army serving in Italy, as these are contained in the *Statistique Medicale de l'Armée*, given us officially for 1862-63, the two years for which these statistics had been hitherto published. During these years the admissions from primary syphilis in the army in Algeria amounted to 50·0 per 1,000 'mean present,' while in Italy the admissions were 36·1 per 1,000 'mean present.' The admissions from primary and constitutional syphilis together were in Algeria 59·8 per 1,000, while in Italy they

[*] The greater frequency of this disease among French troops in the Roman States, where there is no such police regulation, was cited in proof of this.

were 41·1 per 1,000. During 1864 the admissions from primary syphilis were 20 per 1,000 'mean present' more in Algeria than in Italy."

EXPERIENCE IN THE FRENCH NAVY.

When a ship comes into port, the patients labouring under syphilis are confined to the ship, and can only leave to go to hospital.

When disease is detected, the patient is questioned as to who infected him, but the answers are not to be depended on, and often wrong persons, out of revenge or other motives, are designated.

In consequence of these regulations, the frequency of venereal disease has very much diminished, so much is this the case that some sea-port towns formerly requiring 300 beds, now demand only 100.

Government has not always been supported as it should be; prejudice still survives; and there are people who, thinking that the syphilitic patient should be punished when he has sinned, have refused to allow venereal patients to enter an hospital, even when Government has offered to advance money towards the support of the patients. In other cases the patients have been put away in some odd corners of the institution; and in other instances the treatment of the patients have been neglected for weeks.

The following is a statistical table of the venereal patients, and the number of days sailors stayed in hospital in the five military ports of the French empire in the year 1865 :—

	Number of Venereal Patients.	Days in Hospital.
Cherbourg	517	21,569
Toulon	873	35,824
Lorient	246	10,086
Brest	1500	61,500
Rochfort	541	22,181
TOTAL	3677	151,160

Dr. Jeannel, p. 369.

EXPERIENCE IN THE FRENCH MERCHANT SERVICE.

According to Monsieur Rochard, more than a fourth of the sailors and soldiers are infected annually; venereal patients are a fifth among the number of diseases admitted into the hospital at Brest, and figure for about a third as regards stay in hospital. These positive data enable us to form some idea of the mischief which syphilis produces in the other portions of the population, and of the ravages which it makes among prostitutes of all kinds, the majority of whom are not subjected to any regular treatment.

Dr. Jeannel, p. 368.

The French merchant service is not under very strict surveillance at present, hence the frequency of the venereal affections in seaport towns.
See " *Gazette de Hôpitaux*," *August* 31, 1867, p. 403.

SYNOPSIS OF BELGIAN REGULATIONS.

I am indebted to Dr. J. R. Marinus, Joint-Secretary of the Belgian Royal Academy of Medicine, for a view of prostitution in Brussels. That city owes to the exertions of M. Charles de Brouckére, her chief magistrate, and of her Commercial Council, a very stringent code of regulations, passed in virtue of their general power to make bye-laws, and based, to a great extent, upon the abortive suggestions for legislation prepared by the Hygienic Conference in 1832, the Academy of Medicine in 1842. and the Central Public Health Committee in 1838 ; and upon the experience of the Parisian system, which, as has been seen, is the growth of long study and practice.

All prostitutes are by these edicts divided into two classes—

1. *Filles de maisons-tolerées,* called *numérotées.*
2. *Filles éparses,* corresponding to the French *fille en carte.*

As the regulations as to admission, enrolment, radiation, tickets, houses, &c., are so similar to those in force at Paris that their recital would be tedious, I shall content myself with giving statistics, and particularising a few of the more characteristic features of the Belgian *régime.*

Thus, for instance, " every girl or woman who shall be pointed out as giving herself up clandestinely to a life of prostitution, shall be summoned to the police office, to make her statement and produce any justification of her conduct she may wish. The accusation and report, with her justification, shall be brought before the council, and her registration as a public prostitute will take place, if approved of by the council. In this case the decision shall be announced to the girl within twenty-four hours, through the officer of police charged with this duty.

"Every girl not registered, who shall be detected furtively practising prostitution, shall be immediately arrested and brought before the police officer, there to be interrogated. From thence she is to be sent to the dispensary, to be examined by the surgeon. The next step is for the police to draw up a report on the circumstances giving rise to the arrest, which report comes before the council.

"Each room, according to the police instructions, is to contain a bottle, holding a solution of caustic soda, say one ounce of liquoris soda to one pint of distilled water ; also a bottle containing sweet oil ; both bottles to be legibly labelled."

I am indebted to the courtesy of the Earl of Clarendon for the following statistical table received from H.M. Minister at Brussels, and forwarded through the Foreign Office.

TABLE No. I.

Movement of Prostitution in the City of Brussels from the 1st of January to 1st December, 1868.

	OBSERVATIONS.		Schaerbeek	St. Fosse-ten roode	Total
Number of Beds given up for Treatment.	Clandestine Prostitutes.	37			37
	Registered Women.	43			43
Approximative Number of Clandestine Prostitutes.	Arrested as Prostitutes since the 1st January.	170			170
	Residing in Lodgings.	150			150
	Residing in Cafés and Public-houses reputed to harbour Prostitutes.	100	40	40	180
Women sent to Hospital as Venereal since the 1st January.	Clandestine.	226 (makes 54% in 11 months.)	...	2	228
	Registered.	149	3	1	153
Registered Prostitutes present 1st December, 1868.	Total.	275	...	...	316
	Isolated.	192	...	...	192
	In Houses.	83	18	23	124

(Schaerbeek and St. Fosse-ten roode: These are the suburbs of Brussels.)

9

The main difference between the Belgian and French systems appears to me to be, that the circulation of prostitutes in the streets after sundown is prohibited under the former; women under twenty-one may not be inscribed; and the medical visitation, *au speculum*, takes place twice a week by the divisional surgeons, and whenever else he may please by the superintending officer.

All the *éparses* and third-class *filles de maisons* are seen at the dispensary, and the first and second classes of the latter order at their domiciles. The *éparses* may secure this privilege by payment of an extra franc per visit.

The tariff of duties payable by houses and women is as follows:

Every 1st class *maison de passe* pays 1 pound per month.
„ 2nd „ „ 10 shillings „
„ 3rd „ „ 4 „ „

Every first-class *maison de débauche* pays 48s. to three pounds monthly, according to the number of its authorised occupants—from 6 to 10; and two shillings extra for each such additional person.

Every such second-class house pays 16s. to 26s. for from 3 to 7 women, and one shilling extra for each additional female.

Every such third-class house pays 6s. to 13s. for from 2 to 7 women, and one shilling extra for each additional inmate.

Every 1st class *fille éparse* pays on each inspection 4 pence.
„ 2nd „ „ „ „ 3 „
„ 3rd „ „ „ „ 1½ „

Upon punctuality for four successive visits these payments are returned; for inexactitude they are doubled.

All women who, on examination, are discovered to be diseased or to present any suspicious appearance, are sent to hospital, and medical men are strictly enjoined not to treat diseased prostitutes at their own houses. The consequence of these regulations is, that syphilis has almost disappeared from the Brussels hospitals; to such an extent is this the case, that so far back as 1856 Mons. Decortu, an assistant-surgeon at the Saint Pierre Hospital (the Brussels St. Lazare), was able to write in the following terms:—" Sur 98 femmes atteintes de chancre la terminaison par l'induration spécifique n'a été observée que 6 fois, ces 6 femmes seules ont subi un traitement mercuriel avec un succès complet. Toutes les autres femmes soit 92 n'ont été soumises qu'à un traitement local; les chancres ont tous été gueris sur place par cicatrice nette; beaucoup de ces femmes nous ont ensuite été renvoyées à l'hôpital pour de nouvelles maladies contractées dans l'exercice de leur profession, et jamais leur guérison radicale ne s'est démentie et la santé brillante dont elles jouissent toutes aujourd'hui, prouve de la manière la plus saisissante que la chancre n'est qu'une affection contagieuse locale qui ne peut produire par lui-même la syphilis et que l'induration seule est la source fatale de cette terrible cachexie."

From the returns of this hospital, to which are consigned pauper males and the women (*soumises* and *insoumises*) found diseased upon examination at the police dispensary, Dr. Marinus, to whom I have before been indebted, has extracted materials from which I compile the following table. I have incorporated with it the return for five years of the Garrison Hospital :—

Year.	Public women entered.	Free women entered.	Males.	Total civil return.	Military hospital return.
1846	323	58	—	—	—
1847	519	125	—	—	—
1848	532	157	—	—	—
1849	498	113	—	—	—
1850	365	98	—	—	—
1851	327	56	—	—	—
1852	298	76	261	635	361
1853	280	89	206	575	360
1854	297	57	235	589	357
1855	228	53	233	514	216
1856	137	50	212	399	413

The success of the Brussels system I can personally testify to. In a paper I read before the Royal Medical and Chirurgical Society, in July, 1860, after a recent visit to the Belgian capital, I stated that at the time I visited the hospital, only 11 men out of a garrison of 3,500 soldiers were laid up ; 6 of these affections were merely slight cases of gonorrhœa. To show that this was not an accidental immunity, a table was given of the whole of the diseases under which the Brussels troops suffered during 1859, and the following remarkable deductions were drawn : First, the extraordinary rarity of venereal disease, 1 out of 10 men only suffering from the affection ; and secondly, the singular mildness of the complaint. The almost total exemption from syphilis is a no less remarkable phenomenon. Only 62 cases of chancre occurred during the 12 months in the garrison ; in other words, 1 only in 56 men fell ill during that period. Secondary symptoms were almost unknown, as only 10 men came into hospital with this serious complaint.

To show that this immunity was not confined to the military hospitals, I gave a table, showing that in the wards of the civil hospital only 42 cases were under treatment out of a population of 260,000. I met the question, " How do you show that this immunity is a consequence of the sanitary regulations to which you ascribe it ?—may it not have existed before the regulations ?" by giving M. Thiry's reply : " In the wards, where we now have 42 cases, we formerly (i.e., before the present system had been set on foot) had from 150 to 160 venereal patients."

I further stated that on the morning I was present eighty registered women were examined with the speculum, yet I could discover no trace of disease in any of them. Their certificates were signed, and the thorough examination concluded in an hour and a half.

I further stated my belief that if the suburbs of Brussels were placed under the same surveillance, syphilis would be stamped out.

Neither the *maisons des filles* nor the casinos of Brussels present any peculiar characteristics. Of the public thoroughfares, I may remark, that a young man may pass through the streets of Brussels without danger of being solicited ; the mechanic might reel home half drunk without any woman addressing him, and the police authorities themselves seem hardly aware how thoroughly their regulations are carried out.

The preventive measures taken in the Belgian army against venereal diseases are no less stringent than those by which the health of the capital is sought to be secured. I need make no apology, considering the importance of the subject, for inserting a translation of the following statistics of venereal disease and prostitution as received from Her Majesty's Minister at Brussels, and forwarded through the Foreign Office by the kindness of the Earl of Clarendon :—

" Venereal affections may be considered amongst those most frequently found in the Belgian army.

" We give in the annexed table the number of these diseases treated in the military Belgian hospitals during the years 1858 to 1867. The effective average of each garrison is likewise indicated.

" With regard to what particularly concerns the city of Brussels, we give particulars and more details on the venereal affections treated there during a period of ten years in the military hospital of that city. The following are the precautionary measures put in practice at Brussels to prevent the development of these affections. Every Saturday the surgeon (in presence of the officers of the week) examines the sub-officers (sous officiers), corporals, and soldiers.

" Every diseased sub-officer or soldier who shall have spontaneously acknowledged to the surgeon of his regiment at once the first traces and symptoms of disease, and shall have pointed out to the surgeon the house where he has been infected and the woman who has communicated the disease to him shall be called on the hospital carte *vénérien déclaré*.

" Every sub-officer or soldier found suffering from venereal affection, the severity of which shows that the disease must have existed more than four days without the possibility of mistake on the part of the patient shall be written down on the hospital carte as *non-déclaré*. In the second case the soldiers are deprived of their pay during their sojourn in hospital, and on their joining their regiment after their cure, a punishment, varying according to the severity of the case, may be inflicted upon them for having concealed and voluntarily aggravated their condition.

" The surgeons forward to the chief commanding officer an account indicating the houses where the patients have been infected, as well as the women who have been pointed out by the soldiers as having communicated to them the disease. The commander-in-chief of the regiment transmits these statements to the civil medical police, who immediately subject the woman implicated to a medical examination.

" Every soldier who joins his regiment, or who quits it by permission for some days, or goes on furlough, is examined in the way mentioned above.

" Surgeons use all their influence with the soldier to obtain from him by persuasion any information which may contribute in a manner very efficacious to diminish the severity of venereal disease.

" It is very necessary that the soldier should have the conviction that these inquiries have the special object of preserving him as much as possible from new attacks and the amelioration of public health, and that they are not merely for the purpose of taking stringent measures against any one.

"No venereal patient can be treated in barracks however slight the affection may be.

TABLE No. I.

Number of Venereal Patients treated in the Belgian Military Hospitals during the Years 1858 to 1867, inclusive.

		1858.	1859.	1860.	1861.	1862.	1863.	1864.	1865.	1866.	1867.
ANTWERP.		283	380	321	513	762	550	468	430	370	608
	Average effective of the Garrison ...	...	...	...	...	8240	7590	8040	8850	5850	6500
ARLON.		34	14	22	35	35	29	26	16	26	24
	Average effective of the Garrison ...	420	438	438	346	370	362	360	350	470	460
BEVERLOO.		248	509	342	366	242	191	241	217	267	304
	Average effective of the Garrison ...	2359	4316	3221	3139	2958	2914	3852	2814	3218	2905
BRUGES.		100	130	113	72	98	106	106	107	94	93
	Average effective of the Garrison ...	1363	1187	1214	1020	1052	1262	1243	1198	1133	1367
BRUSSELS.		467	301	345	340	385	454	378	336	359	286
	Average effective of the Garrison ...	...	...	...	...	3277	3517	3262	2371	3313	3488
CHARLEROY.		27	52	40	30	78	56	80	64	91	77
	Average effective of the Garrison ...	693	894	861	627	568	715	657	530	879	956
DIEST.		37	50	42	42	30	14	25	35	29	51
	Average effective of the Garrison ...	488	510	454	368	336	352	383	327	401	483
GHENT.		349	308	296	323	282	392	406	416	328	360
	Average effective of the Garrison ...	3079	2634	2633	2420	2420	2572	2618	2784	2996	2730

TABLE No. 1—*continued*.

		1858.	1859.	1860.	1861.	1862.	1863.	1864.	1865.	1866.	1867.
LIEGE.	Average effective of the Garrison ...	344	261	193	202	227	225	240	245	241	296
		2500	2300	2200	2000	1800	1700	1700	1600	1700	1900
LOUVAIN.	Average effective of the Garrison ...	119	131	120	108	167	112	126	109	165	97
		900	900	900	900	900	900	900	900	900	900
MALINES.	Average effective of the Garrison ...	170	184	120	169	99	113	88	99	140	170
		1220	1136	1055	978	1021	1070	1034	1132	1135	1129
MONS.	Average effective of the Garrison ...	142	145	128	124	98	122	124	141	125	90
		3224	2774	2758	2169	1639	1612	1512	1154	1251	1256
NAMUR.	Average effective of the Garrison ...	122	168	91	73	143	186	115	126	141	141
		1877	2035	1768	1292	1222	1351	1300	1250	1278	1357
YPRES.	Average effective of the Garrison ...	102	98	63	57	78	92	73	100	80	87
		982	834	779	510	753	857	872	886	897	954
OSTEND.	Average effective of the Garrison ...	75	45	31	37	60	58	61	68	37	62
		951	815	484	455	626	722	638	668	744	724
TOURNAY.	Average effective of the Garrison ...	220	177	153	137	177	206	203	163	175	185
		324	324	324	324	324	324	324	324	324	324
TERMONDE.	—	33	50	50	54	56	36	59	42	34	67
		...	...	...	...	...	725	747	687	732	869

TABLE No. II.

Number of Venereal Patients treated in the Military Hospital of Brussels during the Years 1858 to 1867, inclusive.

Nature of the Affection.	1858.	1859.	1860.	1861.	1862.	1863.	1864.	1865.	1866.	1867.
Urethritis	268	211	148	182	237	276	216	191	187	173
Balano Posthitis ...	35	...	17	35	11	31	28	32	30	17
Orchitis...	28	27	37	33	27	27	17	26	32	27
Paraphymosis ...	3	...	1	5	4	4	5	3	12	3
Chancres	97	46	59	60	91	91	69	51	62	42
Bubo	2	3	12	5	1	7	4	8	12	9
Vegetations	14	3	14	12	8	8	15	18	3	3
Mucous Tubercles .	11	2	3	5	2	5	15	5	8	4
Syphilis...	9	9	14	3	4	5	9	2	13	8
Total	467	301	305	340	385	454	378	336	359	286
Years.	1858.	1859.	1860.	1861.	1862.	1863.	1864.	1865.	1866.	1867.
Average effective of the Garrison	3287	3315	3278	3290	3277	3517	3262	3371	3313	3488

Efficient Average of the Belgian Army during the Seven last Years.

Years.	1863.	1864.	1865.	1866.	1867.	1868.
Number of men	32,349	32,060	33,343	31,732	31,504	32,092

"In the year 1868, 16,608 patients entered the hospitals, and 2,908 venereal patients, in an effective of 32,092 men, were treated in the hospitals and military infirmaries; that is to say, 90 venereal patients per 1,000 men   (See Table No. 1 for more ample details.)

"The mean effective for the garrison of Brussels in 1868 was 3,488 men.   Patients in the hospitals at Brussels in 1868 : 2,063 men.   Proportion of venereal diseases treated in 1868, in the same hospital : entered, 333 venereal; 9%.   (See the Table No. 2.)"

The following correspondence has been established between the medical men of the military hospitals and those of the police office, which is stated to have had an excellent effect upon the health of this garrison.

The hospital staff forward day by day to the medical department of the police minute and exact particulars of each military venereal patient taken into hospital, with his account of the place, house, and woman who he has reason to think infected him. The women thus named to the police are soon brought up, and if upon examination any of them should prove to be diseased—yet neither on the police surgeon's list nor in hospital—they are speedily introduced to both, and restrained for a time from further operations against the public health.

Truth compels me to avow my opinion, that however much the virulence of syphilis may have abated, and the health of the Brussels garrison been improved within twenty years, there is no marked improvement in the general tone of morals there.

For the fact appears to be, that while the regulations of the central police are remarkably stringent upon a few hundred women who reside within the walls, their application in the suburban communes is at the discretion of the local magistracy.

SYNOPSIS OF THE HAMBURG REGULATIONS.

The flourishing city of Hamburg proper began as early as A.D. 1292 to provide in its municipal code for the toleration and control of fornication. The system at present in force was initiated by the town itself in 1807, improved upon under the French occupation in 1811, and finally settled in 1834. It is of great length, and minute, as might be expected, in the extreme ; but though of great value as a check upon the most fruitful sources of venereal disease, is, like its doubles in other cited instances, a painfully weak experiment as regards public morality.

I subjoin a summary of the police regulations now in force in this city :—

" All brothel-keepers, male and female, and registered girls, should bear in mind that their profession is only *tolerated*, but not ALLOWED, OR EVEN AUTHORISED OR APPROVED OF. Still less have they reason to believe that their profession is to be put on a par with other authorised professions because a tax is levied upon them, or to brave on that account other honest citizens. They must always remember that this tax is levied only to defray the necessary expenses of their police supervision and the cure of the diseases which public girls bring upon themselves by their blameable way of living, and therefore they must on all occasions be neither impudent nor overbearing, but MODEST, and especially must behave themselves in a docile manner towards the police officers and their regulations.

" Places, other than authorised brothels, where meetings between men and women take place for purposes of cohabitation (so called absteigequartiere), will not in future be tolerated, if—

" 1. The keepers, male or female, have not been duly registered.

" 2. At least one registered girl does not live there.

" 3. Any but registered girls are admitted.

" No keeper, either of this or another sort, to allow other girls or women to meet men at his house, under penalty of heavy punishment, or withdrawal of the concession (license). It is ordered that the girls may claim (calculate) for one visit in an extra room, which visit does not last over half-an-hour.

" 1st Class, no more than $1=4s. 7d.—and for every hour further also $1 per hour.

" 2nd Class, one half.

" No consideration is hereby taken of any further claims in consequence of demands (requests) made to them by their visitors.

" Girls are strictly forbidden to undress in the guest-room.

" This tariff to be posted in all rooms, also where girls live, and is to be shown (produced) at the request of each guest.

" A public girl who gives herself (abandons herself) in an unnatural manner to men, will be punished with the heaviest (severest) punishments promulgated in these regulations."

POLICE REGULATIONS AT HAMBURG.

" SEC. 9.—Girls from the country (foreign parts) who allow themselves to be kept by single men, must apply for a permission from the police for residing here, and are besides to be requested (obliged) to pay the tax, at all events according to their means, without, however, being subjected to the medical inspection. They have, in return, on due payment of the tax, the right of free cure in the general hospital. If it were proved that such a girl has connection with many men, or even if suffering herself from venereal disease she has infected men, she will be treated as any other public girl.

" SEC. 9.—In order to facilitate the departure (sending away) of registered girls, a ' travelling fund' has been established since 1st January, 1860, to which every foreign registered girl is to contribute 2 ' schillings' (2¾d. English) each week. Every girl leaving the city receives from this fund, on her departure, the money necessary to enable her to return to her native country.

" SEC. 17.—All dance music is forbidden in brothels, as well as cards and other games, under penalty of $10 (£1 12s. 9d.), and if the offence is repeated, proportionate imprisonment.

" SEC. 19.—It is strictly forbidden to the keepers and public girls to give credit (trust) to guests (visitors), and they must observe that they are not allowed the right to bring an action before the civil authorities (court) for such a claim.

" If it comes to be known that they have given credit, they will be, according to circumstances, severely punished, besides losing their claim. No keeper or registered girl is to extort money from or offer violence to a visitor, or to take from him (receive) any articles in pledge. In return, they have the right to cause to be arrested (taken into custody) visitors who will not or cannot pay anything, or with whom they cannot agree as to payment.

" Swindles or thefts in brothels shall be always severely punished, and shall always involve the withdrawal of the license from the keeper, if he has had any share in them, or in extortions. The presumption will always be against him, and he will be punished with the others, unless he can perfectly (entirely) prove his innocence.

" SEC. 25.—Public girls must submit themselves twice a week to the medical visit (inspection), which, whenever practicable, is to take place at their residence, and in the morning. No girl who feels herself un-well (ill) in the genital parts, or who has her courses, may allow cohabita-tion to take place. No more is the same to be allowed to a venereally affected man, or to one suspected of such infection.

" The violation of these regulations entails at least one week's (8 days) imprisonment, to begin after the cure, if the girl is found ill, and under aggravating circumstances, a more severe imprisonment (punish-ment.)

" SEC. 31.—The tax upon girls consists of 8, 6, and 4 marks (12s. 3d., 9s. 2d., 6s. 1d.) per month, according to the class of the keeper or girls. To girls who have to suckle children, this tax may be remitted, accord-ing to circumstances.

" If the tax is not paid, and cannot be collected, the license will be withdrawn from the keeper, or from the girl, or if a foreigner, she will be sent away from the town.

" SEC. 32.—The following tariff for drinks must be posted in all the rooms of a brothel, and shown to each visitor, if requested :—

	m.	sch.	s.	d.
Champagne, 1st quality, per bottle . . .	10	0 —	15	3
,, 2nd ,, ,, . . .	7	8 —	11	6
White Wine and Red Wine per bottle . .	3	0 —	4	7
Rhine, Port, and Madeira wine ,, . .	5	0 —	7	7
Porter beer ,, . .	1	8 —	2	4
,, half bottle	0	12 —	1	2
Ale, per bottle	1	8 —	2	4
,, half ,, ...	0	12 —	1	2
Punch and grog	0	6 —	0	7

With the exception of the provision common to this town and Berlin, that the keeper of a licensed house must defray the cost of curing any person whose contamination by venereal disease in his house can be esta-blished, I think there are no other features peculiarly worthy of notice in the Hamburg *régime*, either with respect to the *maisons de passe* or the *maisons tolérées*. But I may not conclude this necessarily brief notice without offering, as additional material for thought, the statement, which I extract for what it is worth, from Dr. Lippert's communication to the last edition of Parent-Duchâtelet :—

" Marriage seems to be on the decline in Hamburg much as in other more populous communities, for it is remarked that—

In   1709   there was 1 marriage to 45 souls.
From 1826 to 1835 ,,   1   ,,   97 ,,
,, 1840   ,,   1   ,,   100 ,,
And in 1825 and 1826, according to the registers of the latter year,

accouchements three or four months after marriage took place in about one case in two."

Our countrymen who have visited Hamburg are no doubt familiar with the fine bold countenances of the females of the second class, who, flashily, yet not inelegantly dressed, habitually pose themselves at their open windows, by twos and threes, talking loudly together, but without more than furtive recognition of, or allurement to, the passer-by beyond this mere display.

I am again indebted to the courtesy of Lord Clarendon for the following official particulars obtained for me through the Foreign Office. The importance of the data cannot be too highly estimated in making our comparisons as to what proportion of accommodation ought to exist in London.

"The population of this city and its suburbs was, according to the census taken in December, 1867, 225,074 souls, including 1311 military. The average number of soldiers maintained in it as a garrison is 1060, consisting of 2 infantry battalions of 530 each; of this body there are generally about 30 men in the hospitals, the proportion of sufferers from venereal disease being 10 in every 1000.

"No estimate can be formed of the extent of clandestine prostitution existing in this city, it is doubtless considerable, the number of registered prostitutes is, as we have seen, according to the last estimate, 1076, of whom about 120 are usually in hospital. No fixed number of beds are set apart at the hospitals, for diseased women, but the supply is always equal to the demand."

SYNOPSIS OF REGULATIONS IN BERLIN.

The regulation of the prostitution of Berlin, a city of 702,000 inhabitants, has long been the cause of contention between the severe puritanism of the religious public and the police administration of the place. It has been warmly argued by the former that, inasmuch as marriage is a desirable state, it can be fostered by uprooting the vices peculiar to celibacy, and therefore, when this party has been in the ascendant, vigorous crusades have been carried on against prostitution. The town has been repeatedly purged of prostitutes since the Reformation, but has as often immediately fallen a prey to desertion of infants, adultery, abortions, and clandestine prostitution. Hence the public recognition of that which they could neither suppress nor ignore with public advantage, has been forced upon the authorities.

It appeared to a Commission of Inquiry, in 1717, when repression was in vogue, that clandestinity had attained such magnitude that the Bridewells were inadequate for the reception of the arrested women. The tolerated houses which had been previously shut up were therefore again opened. The monthly contribution by prostitutes to a sick fund was instituted in 1791, and in 1795 the houses were classified. In 1796 a strong and successful attempt at suppression by the religious party induced the old result of increased disease and secret vice. After a return to toleration, the same thing again occurred in 1845, when the licensed houses (twenty-six) were closed, despite the remonstrances of the police department, and their 300 inhabitants banished, as well as all other females without ostensible means of support. But unnatural offences, self-abuse, secret prostitution, and illegitimate births, became so common, and syphilis so much more than ever severe and frequent, that even General von Wrangel was induced to make a forcible appeal, on behalf of the army's health, against the *quasi* improved order of things. The number of females who entered the public hospital had risen from 627 and 761 to 835, and that of the males from 711 in the year 1845 to 979 in the year 1848.

In the year 1850, a Commission of Public Morals was founded to act with the police department in framing and enforcing regulations, and in 1853 a code was promulgated in the hope of assisting—

1. Public health, by checking contagious disease.

2. Public morality, by preventing seduction and the corruption of morals generally.

3. Public safety, by denying refuge in the haunts of prostitution to thieves and other dangerous characters.

The provisions of this code have become, to a great extent, obsolete, as the opinion both of the government and of the public generally has, since its promulgation, declared strongly against the brothel system, and such places were finally abolished in 1855. I am enabled, by the courtesy of Lord Clarendon, to insert the following copy of a dispatch from Mr. Petre to Lord A. Loftus, showing the course now (since December, 1868) adopted by the police authorities in respect to prostitutes.

" Women notoriously addicted to prostitution who have either been judicially condemned for professional whoredom, [or who confessedly lead a life of clandestine prostitution, or who have been seen several times walking in the streets in company with other known prostitutes, or who have been in the 'Charité' hospital here under treatment for syphilis, are placed under the control of the sanitary police, and are obliged to present themselves regularly once a week to be medically examined. They receive directions as to their outward behaviour, and are subjected to the restrictions suited to the particular requirements of the place. Women who are found on medical examination to be infected with syphilitic disease are immediately received into the 'Charité' hospital. Prostitutes transgressing the regulations, unless the case is one which falls within reach of the ordinary laws, and therefore one for judicial cognizance, are examined on the charge as reported by the executive officer, and are either dismissed with a warning, or, on a repetition of the offence, a committal briefly stating the reasons is made out, and they are sent to the prison by an exercise of executive authority for a period not exceeding four weeks.

" These measures have been established with a view to maintaining public decency in the streets and places of public amusements on the one hand, and on the other to preventing the spread of syphilitic disease.

" Attention is specially directed to the proceedings of pimps and persons who, contrary to law, with a view to profit give credit to minors— in the present instance to prostitutes under age—and by lending them ornaments and dress, supply them with aids to prostitution. The passages in the law applicable to the proceedings above mentioned are the Government Instruction of October 23rd, 1817 (Collection of Laws, page 254). The ordinance of December 26th, 1808 S. 48 (Collection of Laws, page 265) and chap. 146 of the State Law Book, which contains a summary of the ordinances directed against prostitutes.

"The staff of the Sitten Polizei ('Morals' Police) consists of one director, one assessor ('decernent'), five clerks, five inspectors, and ten police officers. The ordinary district police is likewise at the disposal of the Sitten Polizei.

"The work of medical inspection is performed by four doctors, who receive salaries, according to the number of hours during which they are employed, of 1000, 200, and 150 dollars. The name of every woman who has ever come into contact in any way with the Sitten Polizei is inserted in the list of 'suspected' persons alluded to in the accompanying copy of report. This list, alphabetically arranged, is of material importance in guiding the proceedings of the police in regard to women who are not sufficiently well known in the town to justify open interference, but who are suspected of prostitution, as it cites the particular document in which the name of the woman in question is mentioned, together with the circumstances under which the attention of the police was previously directed to her.

"Report for the month of August, 1868, *of Prostitution in Berlin.*

Number of females inscribed on the books as suspected of prostitution on the 1st of August, 1868	13,168
Addition during the month	138
	13,306
Number placed under medical control in August, leaving 1st September	21
	13,285
Number of women subjected to regular medical examination on the 1st August	1,621
Additions during the month	87
	1,708
Number released from medical examination during the month :—	
(a) On account of work and service ...	48
(b) Death	0
(c) Pregnancy	2
(d) Illness	2
(e) Departure	4
(f) Consigned to care of parents	2
(g) Marriage	3
(h) Payment of release fines (Freiheits strafen) ...	61
	1,647

Number of women who withdrew from prostitution during August 971

Arrests during the month :—

1. Unauthorized residence	206
2. Neglecting to present themselves for medical examination	247
3. Accosting men in the streets	256
4. Indecent proceeding	990
5. Clandestine prostitution carried to excess	21
6. Attendance required by police report ...	38
7. Residing with pimps	—
8. For proof of their sanitary condition ...	—
9. Violation of public decorum	—
Total ...	1,758

Admission to the venereal hospital of females under arrest or under medical caution during August :—

(a) Itch	3
(b) Syphilis and itch	11
(c) Recent syphilis	134
(d) Secondary syphilis	12
(e) Suspicious eruptions	9
	169

Police return of the number of soldiers of the Garrison infected with syphilitic disease during August 24

Royal Presidency of Police, ' Sitten Polizei.'
  Berlin, September 4, 1868.

"The subjoined police form shows the method of dealing with women who, though not actually enrolled in the police lists of prostitutes, behave in such a manner as to subject themselves to grave suspicion :—

           " Berlin, 18th August, 1868.

"This day appeared, known by nobody, * * * from * * * age * * * residing at * * *

"She was informed, that as she was strongly suspected of an immoral way of living, she was forbidden :—

  I. To entice male persons to her lodgings through words, winks, signs, or any other announcement (for instance, showing a lamp or light), either from the window or from the door.

  II. To make herself conspicuous, or to entice men through words, speech, or signs in public places, in the street, in squares, in the theatre, or any other public buildings.

  III. To enter the lodgings of people suspected of being procurers or who have been already punished for this misdemeanour.

IV. To go about in the neighbourhood of barracks, military buildings, the park of invalids, and any other places much frequented by soldiers.

V. To take lodgings in the neighbourhood of churches, schools, and royal buildings, as well as to enter ground floor habitations.

VI. To go into the boxes of the first range in any theatre, except the pit of the royal theatre, and the 'Krollsche Local' (a kind of Vauxhall).

"This ordinance will be enforced by a punishment of up to four weeks police imprisonment, pronounced according to the Instructions of the Government, dated the 23rd of October, 1807, and the Ordinance of 26th December, 1808.

"The population of Berlin on the 3rd of December, 1867, was 702,000.

"The number of registered prostitutes subjected to regular sanitary control is at this time 1639. Of these an average of 225 present themselves daily for medical examination, and the reports prove that $2\frac{1}{4}$ per cent. of these are found to be infected with syphilis.

"The number of females strongly suspected of prostitution, and who are, therefore, under the censorship of the police, was, at the end of last month (July, 1869), 13,538. But there are besides a great number of females who, by their outward appearance and mode of living, excite a reasonable suspicion that they are addicted to prostitution, but who carry on the business with such circumspection that the police have no cause for interference. Amongst these are to be reckoned the greater number of dressmakers, milliners, and actresses, deserted wives, and bar-maids, &c. Their number may be computed at 12,000.

"The prostitutes infected with syphilis are here received into the Charité Hospital, which has up to the present time always had sufficient accommodation for the reception of all prostitutes affected with syphilis. There are, therefore, no particular number of beds set apart for this purpose. As a rule, there are generally from 100 to 140 cases of this description under treatment."

"Prussian Army.

"The average actual strength of the Prussian army in 1867 was 240,000. The average of men treated in hospital in 1867 was 50·9 per 1000. The average of venereal cases, 62 per 1000."

I may here add a series of remarks, extracted from an interesting work by "M. Senkke's, Royal Police Assessor at Berlin," on the subject of prostitution, which appear to me to be valuable, both as affording a fair illustration of the tone of thought upon this subject prevalent at Berlin at the present day, and as containing some judicious hints that may prove useful in considering the course that legislation should take at home :—

M. Senkke says "that in Berlin, as in England now, there is less distinction than formerly between the prostitute and the modest female.

"Prostitution has the effect of amalgamating classes.

"Prostitutes now creep in wherever the acquisition of money has obtained them a position.

"Men are becoming more fastidious in their sexual requirements. Formerly they were satisfied with brothels, now they require something less public and more refined ; and hence brothels are not so numerous as formerly.

"Modesty in prostitutes is appreciated more than it was formerly.

"Prostitution is a misdemeanour, not punished by society, but by the diseases it produces and inflicts on its votaries.

"Private persons and individuals will not undertake to prosecute prostitutes, or appear as witnesses against the frail sisterhood. Prosecutions must be undertaken by the police, and to remedy the evils of prostitution the police must interfere.

"*Axiom:* 'Prostitution will always find its level, according to the views society takes of it.'

"No experiments will succeed in eradicating, or sensibly diminishing an evil which is inherent in human nature, and which owes its intensity (intensities) to the times.

"In Berlin it is found objectionable to bring prostitutes before the usual law courts ; it is better to punish them or judge them by the police, not allowing counsel to appear or make speeches in their defence.

"The trial of such cases should not be postponed, but instant sentences pronounced ; otherwise the witnesses will not be forthcoming.

"The object should be to withdraw the punishments prostitutes undergo from publicity." (This is the case with the present Contagious Diseases Act in our own country.) "The privacy of trials then leaves no stigma on the girl if she subsequently reforms, or changes her mode of life.

"In Berlin, infractions of the police regulations (see p. 140) are first met by a caution, which may be repeated. Then comes the arrest of the girl ; then incarceration from four days to four weeks."

M. Senkke goes on to say that in England, Bavaria, and Austria there is no special inspection of prostitutes.

"At Berlin, in 1864 there were 1 in 1000 persons
      in 1866   „   1 in 1100

affected with venereal disease, as appears from returns from the Trades Union and Military Hospitals, and the cases were slight. Thus two objects are gained by the regulations :—

     1. Maintenance of Public Order.
     2. Diminution of Syphilis.

"In the regulation of prostitution, we must set our faces against landladies giving credit to prostitutes. To establish confidence, the girl must see that the procuress is looked after, as well as the prostitute.

"Thus the prostitute, as well as her surroundings, should form a consideration in treating of prostitution.

"Discretion must be given to the police.

"We must not only punish the prostitute ; we must try what home and religious instruction, example, medical advice, and justice will do."

The Charity Hospital above referred to, specially devoted to the treatment of venereal diseases, is supported to a great extent by public funds, and partly, as has been seen, by contributions exacted from prostitutes. It must, however, be noted, that owing to the strict sanitary regulations enforced, these probably furnish but few of the cases whose length of stay in the hospital appears to indicate a marked degree of severity. The majority of the latter are, I think, traceable to clandestinity.

The following return of in-patients, and the duration of their cases, is compiled from the registers of the establishment, and cannot fail to be interesting :—

Year.	Admissions. Males.	Days in hospital.	Admissions. Females.	Days in hospital.
1844	741	21	657	31
1845	711	26	514	42
1846	813	30	627	51
1847	894	34	761	43
1848	979	33	835	53

The report made in May, 1853, to the Berlin Board of Public Morals, by Dr. Stumpf, chief medical officer of the King's Guard, upon the health of the garrison, then numbering 19,030 men, is worth consideration. It is to be regretted that the Doctor did not append the strength of the forces in question at the earlier dates to which his report refers. Supposing it to have been equal at the various periods, there must have been the surprising reduction in the number of syphilitic cases of 50 per cent. in two years, and 64 per cent. during the three years following the reintroduction of toleration and increased activity of the inspection.

He says :—" In answer to the letter of the Board, dated April 30, 1853, I have to report that, among other things, we have observed, during the last few years, a remarkable diminution of syphilis among the garrison. While in the year 1849 there were 1423 cases,

in 1850 ,, 526 ,,
1851 ,, 526 ,,
in the first quarter of 1853 ,, 59 ,,

Also, in respect of intensity, the disease forms a most favourable contrast with that of former years. In my opinion, the above numerical proportion furnishes the most sufficient proof of the utility of the existing sanitary regulations."

SYNOPSIS OF THE REGULATIONS IN VIENNA.

I am again indebted to the kindness of Lord Clarendon for permission to insert the following translation of a dispatch relating to prostitution in Vienna. It is dated March 19th, 1869, and is as follows :—

" With reference to Mr. Bonar's note of the 23rd of November of last year, asking for certain information respecting prostitution in

Austria, and respecting venereal diseases in the army, and the measures adopted for checking the spread of them, the Imperial and Royal Ministry for Foreign Affairs has the honour to make the following replies, which have been derived in part from the Ministry of the Interior.

" The rules in force in the army for prevention of syphilis are contained in various ordinances, and can be shortly summed up as follows :—

" 1. All the men, from the sergeants downwards, inclusive of officers' servants, are examined once a week by a medical officer, for the purpose of ascertaining whether they are affected by syphilis or itch. Moreover, the soldier is taught to consider it his duty to report at once any illness of this nature. All men found suffering from syphilis are sent to hospital, and are moreover asked whether they are disposed to state the name of the person whom they believe to have given them the disease, and in case they consent notice is given to the proper authority, in order that further official steps may be taken.

" 2. In the same way, all soldiers going on or returning from leave of absence, as well as those who return from having been some time on detachment duty, are examined by a medical officer.

" 3. All sick soldiers sent to hospital are examined as regards syphilis, both on their arrival and on their dismissal from hospital.

" As regards the frequency of syphilis in the army, the following data afford information :—

" 1. The average strength of the army is 237,000 men.

" 2. In the twelve months of the last year (1868) there was a total of 172,752 sick in the military hospitals, of which 26,722 were syphilitic cases. The proportion, therefore, is 1 in 6·83.

" 3. The proportion of syphilitic cases per 1000 men is 112. The proportion is in reality not quite so high, as 237,000 men represents the actual strength of the army, whilst amongst the cases of syphilis (26,722) all soldiers are included who, during their leave of absence, sickened of syphilis, and sought refuge in the military hospitals. As this latter class find no especial mention in the actual reports of sickness, it is not possible to give the actual proportion of sufferers from syphilis per 1000 men.

" No registry of prostitution is kept in Vienna, as allurement (anzucht) as a profession, pimping and fraud in allurement, are forbidden by the laws of March 27, 1852 (Regulation No. 117), (§ 509,515).

" To prevent as much as possible the spread of syphilis by public women in the large towns, and especially in Vienna, the organs of the police occasionally make visits, and have the public women they have seized medically examined, and if found to be ill of syphilis, given over to the public hospitals to be cured.

" In these establishments no separate beds are kept for the treatment of prostitutes suffering from syphilis ; as a rule, they come together with the rest of the syphilitic women in the same hospital.

" The average number of beds for syphilitic patients in the three large public hospitals of Vienna is in round numbers 600, of which 200 are for male, and 400 for female patients.

" According to the census of 1864, the male population of Vienna is

269,189; and the female, 276,979; total, 546,168 inhabitants. **A** tabular statement is annexed.

Population of Vienna—according to Census of 1864.

AGE.	MALE.				FEMALE.			
	Single.	Married.	Widowers.	Separated.	Single.	Married.	Widows.	Separated.
Up to 15.	65,495	...	...	...	62,198	2	...	...
From 16 to 50	109,643	56,101	2,294	399	102,036	62,644	7,552	630
Over 50 Years	4,839	24,727	5,348	353	8,100	16,569	16,919	329

"For information concerning prostitution in Hungary, the Ministry of Foreign Affairs has addressed itself to the Hungarian Ministry of the Interior.

"It will not fail to inform His Excellency of the result of its inquiries as soon as possible, and the undersigned avails himself, &c., &c.

"Vienna, March 19, 1869.

"To the Minister for Foreign Affairs.

"H. E. LORD BLOOMFIELD."   "BIEGELEBEN.

I extract the following interesting observations, bearing upon the prostitution of Vienna, from Mr. Wilde's work upon the institutions of Austria :—

"Public brothels are not tolerated by the police, and public women are sent into the houses of correction ; this, however, is but the letter of the law, not the practice ; for though it has been stated that, owing to the present condition of morality, such persons *are not required* in that country, yet the lowest calculation allows the number of public females in the capital to be 15,000. It is, however, much to be admired that the same disgusting exhibitions which are witnessed in the capitals of Great Britain are not permitted by the Austrian police ; all persons considered of an improper character, when found in the streets after a certain hour, being conducted to the police office, and if on examination found to be diseased, being at once sent into hospital. Public women are not licensed in Austria, but the police have the power of entering their dwellings, accompanied by one of the police physicians, and if they are diseased compelling them to go into hospital. Notwithstanding the apparent moral condition of the city after nightfall, which must at once strike a foreigner, I am much inclined to think that the public exhibition of vice is often a test of private morality ; as instances pro and con I might adduce the cities of Rome and Vienna on the one hand, and Dublin on the other."*

In the same work, if we turn to p. 212, we find, as if corroborative of the writer's opinion as to Austrian immorality, that in the city of Vienna almost one in every two children is illegitimate ; this, he adds, is only surpassed by Munich, where it is recorded in 1838 the number

* Wilde, pp. 313, 314.

of illegitimate exceeded the legitimate by 270, and yet in that goodly city public women as well as tobacco-smokers are not allowed to appear in the streets; or in other words, during the last seven years, ending 1837, the proportion of illegitimate to legitimate births have been as ten to twelve in Vienna.*

Mr. Wilde goes on to observe, at p. 213, " It may be asked are there any political reasons for encouraging such a condition of morals, for by thus permitting, it encourages? Yes, the Austrian State, whose political web extends not only into the paths of literature and science, but sends its far-stretching fibres into every domestic circle in the land, has, I have been credibly informed, and I believe it to be true, an object in thus countenancing illegitimacy—it is that of checking over-population, as those who are informed upon the subject of population well know it has the power to do, by decreasing the number of births and increasing the infantile mortality."

At pp. 209 and 210, he says—" Startling as it may appear, it (the law) has offered a *premium for illegitimacy*. Let us see how this is brought about : 1st. The laws, both civil and ecclesiastical, relating to marriages in Austria, are so strict that few of the lower orders are able to avail themselves of that rite ; 2nd. A female, even of the better class, does not (at least to the same extent as in other countries) lose caste on becoming illegitimately with child ; 3rd. In the seventh month of her pregnancy (and many of them are enabled to get in sooner) she applies to the Lying-in Hospital, states her poverty, and is asked two questions—Are you legitimately or illegitimately with child? If she answers the latter she is received *sans cérémonie ;* she is given a suit of clothes provided by the State (an imperial livery) to wear, and her own are carefully preserved till the period of her departure. After delivery she has to nurse her own, and perhaps another child, and on her departure she gets a bonus of five shillings. During the first two months the child is committed to her own care ; it is then sent into the country

* "LICENTIOUSNESS IN STOCKHOLM.—It has been called the most licentious city in Europe, and, I have no doubt, with the most perfect justice. Vienna may surpass it in the amount of conjugal infidelity, but certainly not in general incontinence. Very nearly half the registered births are illegitimate, to say nothing of the illegitimate children born *in* wedlock. Of the servant girls, shop girls, and seamstresses in the city, it is very safe to say that scarcely ten out of a hundred are chaste ; while, as rakish young Swedes have coolly informed me, many girls of respectable parentage, belonging to the middle-class, are not much better. The men, of course, are much worse than the women, and even in Paris one sees fewer physical signs of excessive debauchery. Here the number of broken-down young men, and blear-eyed, hoary sinners, is astonishing. I have never been in any place where licentiousness was so open and avowed—and yet, where the slang of a sham morality was so prevalent. There are no houses of prostitution in Stockholm, and the city would be scandalized at the idea of allowing such a thing. A few years ago two were established, and the fact was no sooner known than a virtuous mob arose and violently pulled them down. At the restaurants, young blades order their dinners of the female waiters with an arm around their waists, while the old men place their hands unblushingly upon their bosoms. All the baths in Stockholm are attended by women (generally middle-aged and hideous, I must confess), who perform the usual scrubbing and shampooing with the greatest nonchalance. One does not wonder when he is told of young men who have passed safely through the ordeals of Berlin and Paris, and have come at last to Stockholm to be ruined."--Northern Travels. By Bayard Taylor. Sampson Low and Co., Ludgate Hill.

at the public expense, and if a male it is always a welcome visitor in the family of an Austrian peasant, for if it can be reared to eighteen years of age it is rendered up to the conscription instead of the eldest son of its adopted father."

PROSTITUTION IN ITALY.

Rome.—In the holy capital of sunny, passionate Italy, prostitution is in no shape recognised by either Church or State, on the ground, I believe, that the Pontiff's secular and religious functions are one and indivisible ; and that the admission, much more the toleration, by Christ's Vicar, of unhallowed connexion is an utter impossibility. But even the traditional sanctity of the centre of Christendom, the presence of St. Peter's Chair, and the partial training to self-mortification, which might be supposed to combine with ardent faith and blind obedience to the Church in strengthening virtue, are insufficient to counterbalance the instincts of men and the influence of climate. The mere aspirations of the religious, and the example of the virtuous world, are in Rome, as elsewhere, very feeble against the common promptings of nature, especially when backed, as they are in Italy, by temperament, idleness, and beauty. In the Pontifical States, of all civilized communities—where, over and above other considerations, the fearfully rapid development of syphilis by the climate, and the disproportionate amount of female celibacy entailed by monastic institutions among the males, might be alleged as excuses for its extended toleration and regulation—prostitution is nominally prohibited. Its resorts are proscribed, and so continually hunted from point to point, in compliance with no written law, by arbitrary authority, that scarce a dozen houses can contrive to lurk within the limits of the Roman police jurisdiction, and then only through the bribed connivance of the lower officials.

But the reverse of this pleasing show of external propriety shows clandestine prostitution, with its inevitable concomitants, depravation of morals and wide diffusion of intense disease, has invaded domesticity itself.

We are informed by Dr. Jacquot, a physician of the French army of occupation—and with regard to the last and most deplorable of them there is abundance of prior corroborative testimony—that there prevail in Rome five shapes of clandestinity.

1. *Les Pierreuses*, whom he describes to be a horde of creatures grown formidable since the military occupation, and plying their trade by night, with troops of men, in the angles of walls, ruins, colonnades and porticoes. "When in charge of venereal soldiers in Rome," he says, "I have traced as many as five cases of syphilis to one night's operations of a woman of this description."

2 and 3. Prostitution-covert in accommodation-houses, sometimes kept by procuresses, and frequented by women of all classes.

4. *Femmes galantes*, who are mistresses of both residents and visitors from generation to generation.

5. Prostitution in private life.

With reference to the second, third, and fourth categories, no remark is necessary; but the last source of supply requires, I think, some brief observations, beginning with a recital of Dr. Jacquot's impressions.

"As a consequence of this disastrous rule (viz., suppression), prostitution in Rome is more or less all-pervading. It is carried on, alas! too often in families, under the parental eye, almost as though it were an admissible calling. A mother will introduce you to her daughter; the young girl, whose turn is yet to come, to her elder sister; and the little brother will light you up the stair—a degree of turpitude and degradation which, by the way, exists also at Naples, where prostitution is tolerated. If the customs of the Cicisbei have left the mansions of the rich and noble, where they were nurtured by idleness and immorality, necessity has imported acquiescence nearly as degrading into the less opulent houses of the middle rank."

Ladies of this caste submit themselves occasionally to sheer prostitution by visiting the *maisons de passe*, or strangers who gain access to them through the intervention of procuresses. This demoralization is, I conceive, less traceable to vicious propensities than to impatience of restricted means—less to absolute penury than to the attrition of factitious wants engendered by the passion for display and luxury, which leads the smaller proprietors, the lackland nobility, and the underpaid official gentility of the south, into expenses totally unwarranted by their incomes. The carriage and pair is so imperious a necessity with the Roman lady, who can by no means brook the humble one-horse vehicle, that the Milanese have an old saying—"The Romans put their stomachs into harness;" and sometimes the observer of to-day might add, "their honour too."

I have a holy horror of travellers' facts; so I will leave to others the most easy labour of collecting a farrago of semi-incredible tales of Italian frailty, and conclude by saying, that the women who will thus set virtue at no higher price than wardrobe or equipage, are oftener than not excellent mothers, and (though many an English reader would here exclaim, *Credat Judæus*, &c.) truly affectionate wives—at least, so say men who pretend thoroughly to understand Italian society. In judging of prostitution, as of the other immoralities of one people, we shall do well not to gauge them inexorably by our own manners and customs. The ladies of ancient Rome bore, as protecting amulets, carved golden images that we should now consider emblems of indecency; and the pair of monster horns that deck the chamber of a married pair in modern Italy, as a charm against witchcraft, is a " word of fear distasteful to the wedded ear" among the nations of the north.

Among the lower orders—save, perhaps, among the Transteverini, where virtue is the rule—misery operates as elsewhere. So little work is there to be found in a country with neither manufactures nor agriculture—so potent is the love of the *far niente* among the modern Romans —that the poor man's wife is too often welcome to his bed if she only bring the spoil of the travelling or the native *debauché* for which she has bartered her adulterous embraces. This deplorable state of morals, although it has not attained the colossal proportions attributed to it by hostile malice, is nevertheless no secret; and persons who have long withheld credence from it become in time convinced that there are grounds for believing in its existence.

But monstrous though it be, and deplorable—no less remarkable are the gigantic provisions made, in this poverty-stricken, police-ridden capital of 150,000 souls, for the poor and needy, and the sick and sorry. A community, not more extensive than some London parishes, lodges, feeds, and keeps entirely, more than 4000 aged and infirm persons, orphans, and foundlings, besides giving general out-door relief, and caring specially for more than 1000 superannuated artisans. It maintains the surgical hospital of St. James, of 384 beds, of which a number are allotted to venereal patients ; and those of the Good Shepherd and Santa Maria Transteverina. Besides these foundations, there are the refuges of Santa Croce and Loretto for repentant females ; a vast pilgrim hospital ; and "homes" out of number for the houseless poor, and for destitute females. The objects of public Christian charity in Rome number in all somewhere about 22,000 annually, and the sums drawn from the Roman public for the noble work would astonish even the rich and open-handed municipality of Paris, still more so the sometimes short-sighted guardians of parochial purses in our own plethoric metropolis.

The following interesting letter on Roman prostitutes appeared in the *Medical Times* of the 27th July, 1861 :—

" *Rome, July* 3.

"In this city we have no authorised 'houses of tolerance' (to use the expression of our polished neighbours on the other side of the Alps), as it would be contradictory to the spirit of priestly rule to legitimise by temporal authority a thing daily condemned by the clergy in their spiritual exhortations. It is true that our rulers are less scrupulous in other respects ; and in the lotto, the stage, and the ballet, make certain concessions to the public which are not in accordance with the strict laws of morality ; but there always remains a difference between allowing the worship of Mercury and Terpsichore, and erecting temples to Venus Vulgivaga. Nevertheless, the private calling of prostitutes is, generally speaking, not impeded, and they have more liberty accorded to them here than is the case in other large towns. The police have no control over them, and the superintendence of these unfortunates is in the hands of the guardians of public morality generally, viz., the priests of the fifty-four parishes into which the Eternal City is divided. These are, again, under the immediate control of the Cardinal-Vicar, that is, the Bishop who represents the head of the State in its Episcopal functions. This dignitary now and then finds it necessary to interfere, whenever he thinks the scandal too great, and believes it to be his duty to protect an individual or a whole family from moral decadence. In such cases, the individual in question is carried away from her residence at any time of the day or night, and brought to the Hospice of St. Michele, a large institution for educating and sheltering a great variety of refractory and other individuals. One part of it is reserved as a prison and house of correction for prostitutes. The drawback to this system is, that a sanitary control of prostitutes is very difficult, and is not even attempted; if the State acts thus, from a moral point of view, with the intention of leaving profligacy to be punished by its natural consequences, it certainly attains this end; and the diseases consequent upon this vice are, therefore, very general in town and country. A progressive spreading of syphilis from Rome, in a centri-fugal direction, to the neighbouring places has occurred, and the small towns in our proximity, such as Tivoli, Frascati, Albano, and others, which a number of years ago were very slightly tainted by venereal disease, are now considerably affected by it; and the once celebrated beauty of their men and women, which was formerly of a truly magni-ficent character, is fast disappearing. These places are, therefore, no longer that apparently inexhaustible mine of strong and healthy wet-nurses, which they were once considered to be, when almost every young woman was capable of filling that position. In fact, many an old Albanese has nursed a dozen little Romans at her breasts. The places mentioned are, therefore, no longer resorted to by those in want of wet-nurses, and we have to go further if we wish to find incorrupt manners and uninfected constitutions.

" Scrofulosis, tuberculosis, and rickets have greatly increased in Rome and its neighbourhood within the last decennia. This may be the effect of the spreading of syphilis, although we cannot at present give evident proofs for such a supposition; but we ought certainly to recol-lect that a great many syphilidologists consider the diseases just named to be hereditary consequences of syphilis. M. Diday, for instance, in his work on the 'Syphilis of Newly-born Infants,' expresses his convic-tion, that in children of syphilitic parents, rickets and the morbid dis-position inherent to that disease, are found as the only residuum and offspring of the syphilitic dyscrasia, which contaminated the blood of the parents.

" It is impossible to give numeric statements regarding prostitution, as it exists in Rome now-a-days, with any degree of accuracy. It cannot be denied, however, that public decency is less violated here than per-haps in any other capital of Europe; and this ought to be thankfully acknowledged.

" The Surgical Hospital of S. Giacomo, in the Corso, contains wards for syphilitic patients. The men are in one common room, which is somewhat separated from the rest; and the women in another special ward, which is quite apart from any other. The numbers of patients received there is small, when compared to the number of inhabitants, which amounts at present to 160,000; but it is still smaller, when compared to the frequent occurrence of the disease. There is certainly no want of useful benevolent institutions of every kind in this city; but the administration, and the use made, of these numerous, liberally-endowed and well-planned institutions, is in every way deficient. With regard to the wards for syphilitic patients, it seems a great mistake, that only such persons are received as inmates who are obliged to keep their beds; all others are treated as out-patients, and they, of course, propa-gate the disease further among the public. Besides, the persons received as in-patients, are frequently discharged before they are thoroughly cured. This is not only dangerous to the individual concerned, but also to the public health. The treatment of the disease is based upon those antediluvian and long-exploded notions, according to which gonorrhœa is an equally virulent disorder with chancre, and capable of giving origin to secondary syphilis. Both distempers are, therefore, treated with mercury ; no regard is had whether a primary ulcer is indurated or not, no attempts are made to destroy gonorrhœa or the primary ulcer as soon as possible, but in both cases the secretion is, according to the doctrines of humoral pathology, allowed to exist for any length of time, in order that the system may thus be purified from the poison, which has been introduced into it. The speculum is not properly used. The wards containing females are inaccessible to the young surgeons, who have to make a two years' practical study in the S. Giacomo Hospital. The consequence is, that stricture, incomplete recoveries, and useless mercurialism, are of every-day occurrence. Generally speaking, however, the climate is favourable to the course of these diseases, and severe forms of gonorrhœa with cystitis and peri-urethral abscess, gangrenous primary ulcers, virulent bubos, &c., are, on the whole, rare. The relative proportion of secondary affections to the primary disease does not offer anything unusual. The series of secondary symptoms appears in the same succession as elsewhere, viz., swelling of the glands, eruptions of the skin, ulcers of the throat, &c. They generally commence in the second month ; of the exanthemata the papulous, and also psoriasis, are very common. Tertiary forms are not rare, but in spite of gross negligence, they are not of a destructive character.

"I have seen very favourable curative effects of the climate on foreigners who suffered from old residuums of syphilis, which had been long under treatment, but never been entirely eradicated, not even by iodide of potassium and sarsaparilla, and which it is often very difficult to distinguish from traces of a mercurial cachexy ; such as superficial little ulcers of the mucous membrane of the mouth and pharynx, with constant redness and loosening of the parts ; a continuous desquamation of the epidermis at the angles of the mouth, with now and then a superficial ulcer there ; dark spots on the chest and arms, &c. In such cases a journey to Italy from the North, a winter's stay in a mild climate, with daily exercise in the open air, and all the other changes in the mode of life connected with it, have often effected a great improvement, which was no doubt due to a favourable change being brought about in the nutrition and reproduction ; or the remedies mentioned before, together with bitter medicines and iron, have had a beneficial effect.

"As sulphur-baths are very useful in cases of this kind, I will mention that there are three such mineral springs in the neighbourhood of Rome, the use of which, in cases of long-standing syphilis, is very highly thought of by doctors as well as by patients. These are, 1st, the baths of Tivoli. Every one who has travelled from Rome to Tivoli has seen the aqua albula, and, through his olfactory nerves, has been made acquainted with the fact that it contains sulphuretted hydrogen. The water rises in the Campagna, a little below Tivoli, from two lakes, which once were craters, and where hot and cold springs mix. This mixture has, at the outlet of the second lake, a temperature of 77° F., is rich in sulphur and alkalies, and what is more rare in sulphur springs, it also contains a large amount of carbonic acid gas. The bathing season lasts from the end of May until the end of July (at most). The patient either drives there every morning from Rome (which can be done in two hours) and returns the same day, or he may live in Tivoli, and take the omnibus or a donkey every morning down to the baths, which are at one hour's distance. The water is also carried to Tivoli in tubs.

"2. The waters of Stigliano (aquæ Stygianæ,) are more important than the aqua albula, as they contain a very large amount of sulphur, besides iodine, and have a very high temperature. They are a short day's journey from Rome, in a north-westerly direction. The temperature of these springs amounts to from 103° to 122° F., and as they have a very powerful influence upon the system, they are especially suitable for torpid cases of disease.

"3. Finally, the mineral waters of Viterbo are very celebrated and much used. A spring containing iron and carbonic acid rises there, close to a warm sulphur spring. These waters have escaped the fate of seeing their celebrity for centuries covered with grass, and their ancient contrivances for bathing overgrown with ivy. On the contrary, they have always been greatly esteemed, while those of Tivoli and Stigliano were for a long time given up to archæology, and have only within the last decennium been restored to balneology.

"On these and a few other mineral waters I shall give you some more information in a future letter. To-day I confine myself to mentioning their effects in venereal disorders. To return to the subject from which I started, I will only express my opinion that the authorities here might, while avoiding giving unnecessary trouble and annoyance, and without legitimising houses of ill-fame, still establish a hygienic control over prostitutes; for even if it were their intention to leave the individual sinner to his natural punishment, they still owe it to the State and the progeny of such persons, to do all in their power to prevent this disease from being transmitted and spread by those infected. In order to effect this end it would be desirable that a number of medical men should be especially instructed in the diagnosis and treatment of syphilitic disorders. They should study the subject practically in Paris for at least six months, and several wards should be opened in different parts of the town for facilitating the cure of the infected. Quite recently a comprehensive *règlement* for prostitutes has been established in Turin; and several points of it might well be applied to Rome; but as no great love exists here for anything that comes from Turin, I do not expect that any change for the better will take place for some time to come."

Naples.—The stews or *bordelle* of this capital are fully recognised, if not licensed, by the police, and undergo inspection at intervals by underpaid Government officials, who derive additions to their income from the contributions of the class whom it is their supposed duty to supervise. There are also in Naples great numbers of *quasi* clandestine prostitutes, chiefly Sicilians, who are supported through the activity of the *ruffiani*, or pimps, who operate in the frequented quarters of the town, and pester Englishmen especially with their offers of service. The low prostitution of the town, ministering for the most part to the desires of the military and marine, is gathered together in the suburb outside the Porta Capuana. Report says, there is a certain fixed tariff for the enjoyment of these women ; and the entrance to and exit from their quarter are under the charge of military posts, which, every other route being carefully blockaded, all visitors must pass. A drive through this "inferno" was, and perhaps is, one of the great sights for strangers at Naples. Its shameless denizens would expose themselves most fully to *the curious* in the open street. They were supposed to number some thousands, but I am afraid to say how many ; and also have reason to think, although I repeat it with reserve, that residence in the quarter is imposed upon some of them as a punishment for private erotic delinquencies, attended by more than usually notorious scandal.

I am inclined to think this system of suburban prostitution may have obtained in the days of the dramatist Ford. In *Love's Sacrifice,* (Act iv., Scene 1), D'Avolos is made to say :—"Your only course, I can advise you, is, to pass to Naples, and set up a house of casualty ; there are many fair and frequent suburbs, and you need not fear the contagion of any pestilent disease, for the very worst is very proper to the place."

The English cemetery is close to the prostitutes' quarter, and until the latter was hemmed in, the chaplain, on the road to the scene of his labours, was obliged, unless he made a long *détour*, to pass through some of its streets.

CLANDESTINE PROSTITUTION ON THE CONTINENT.

I have now performed that part of my task which consisted of exhibiting to the contemplation of the reader the various methods adopted in foreign lands of dealing with prostitution. It will have been noticed that a division unknown to us at home is made abroad between public or registered and clandestine or unregistered prostitutes. We are thus brought face to face with two rival systems, the one private prostitution as practised in England, the other public prostitution, the system under which it is the object of continental nations to place all abandoned women who live by the hire of their persons. Clandestine prostitutes, as we have seen, are those who elude the state regulations, and carry on their trade in defiance of the law. Dr. Jeannel describes the clandestine prostitute as follows ; he says (page 214) :—"We may call a woman a clandestine prostitute who lives by her person, and has the address to withdraw herself from special police supervision and periodical examinations." Also at page 213 he says :— "The characteristic fact of the business of the clandestine prostitute as of the registered prostitute giving rise to the intervention of the police, and which it is important clearly to define, consists in going to seek or in sending to seek in a public place strange men in order to exercise with them lewd acts for a money consideration."—JEANNEL, p. 213.

Registered women present diseases of a trifling character compared with the severity of the affections which clandestine prostitutes present when infected. As these unhappy women gain but a few pence by each act of intercourse, and the distress that surrounds them often obliges them to hire themselves out for a morsel of bread, they daily receive by the dozen soldiers, vagrants, and others whom they meet in their day's journey; it is easy to judge of the mischief these unfortunate women produce wherever they go.

"At Paris, from 1826 to 1828, the clandestine prostitutes arrested by the police were found diseased in the proportion of 26 per 100 ; and from 1845 to 1854 in the proportion of 19 per 100. This proportion of 19 per 100 diseased recurs again in 1866 among the clandestine prostitutes arrested at Paris. Under divers circumstances the clandestine prostitutes assembled at St. Cloud, at Boulogne, at Sevres, and in the neighbourhood of the barracks of Paris, have been found diseased in the proportion of 40 to 50 per 100. At Strasbourg, the proportion of clandestine prostitutes found diseased at first rose to 83 per 100. This proportion was still 73 per 100 in 1854, 50 per 100 in 1855, and 32 per 100 in 1856.

" At Bordeaux the proportion of diseases among clandestine prostitutes which had been 49 per 100 in 1859 was still 25 per 100 in 1865."—DR. JEANNEL, page 370.

Number of Unregistered Prostitutes Arrested and found Diseased in Paris during ten years.

YEARS.	Number of Unregistered Women.	Number of Syphilitic Women.	Women affected with Ulcerations or Itch.
1857 ...	1405	434	152
1858 ...	1158	314	142
1859 ...	1528	358	144
1860 ...	1650	432	132
1861 ...	2323	542	153
1862 ...	2986	585	214
1863 ...	2124	425	177
1864 ...	2143	380	213
1865 ...	2255	468	204
1866 ...	1988	432	169
Total ...	19,560	4370	1700

Table, showing the Results of the Sanitary Examinations made at Bordeaux, on the Registered and Clandestine Prostitutes, during Nine Years, from the Year 1858 to 1866.

YEARS.	1858.	1859.	1860.	1861.	1862.	1863.	1864.	1865.	1866.
REGISTERED PROSTITUTES:—									
Number of examinations	15,292	28,240	26,780	25,647	24,052	25,175	26,368	26,965	26,888
Number of women found diseased	346	482	322	247	312	446	381	406	439
Proportion of women diseased per 100 examinations	2.26	1.70	1.20	0.96	1.29	1.77	1.55	1.50	1.63
CLANDESTINE PROSTITUTES:—									
Number of examinations	406	569	749	580	815	872	1025	629	646
Number of women found diseased	200	238	184	126	188	206	209	162	177
Proportion of women diseased per 100 examinations	49.26	41.82	24.56	21.72	23.0	23.06	20.39	25.61	27.24

"In 1859, 21,652 women were examined at the dispensary at Bordeaux with the speculum. The number of cases discovered by this instrument was reduced to 33. In 1860, the number examined were 20,397 ; the number of cases of disease discovered was 49, but if we confine ourselves to ulcerations which are severe, the number of diseased cases discovered in 42,000 women is reduced to 30—that is to say, 0.71 cases of disease per 1000.

" Thus, the proportion of registered prostitutes found diseased has never exceeded the proportion of 2.26 per 100 or 22 per 1000, whereas among clandestine prostitutes in 1858 (the year which preceded the re-organization of the service) 49.26 per 100, or 492 per 1000, were found diseased. This proportion remained at 418 per 1000 in 1859, and in the following years, notwithstanding the search made after them, from 203 to 272 per 1000 were found diseased. According to a summary of these documents we may set it down as an established fact that in the city of London, in the other towns of England, as well as in the principal naval stations beyond Europe where prostitutes are not submitted to any special examination, the proportion of infected women will exceed 50 per 100. Thus, the maritime towns of England and the United States frequented by an immense population of sailors belonging to all nations must be considered as very active centres of venereal contagion."—JEANNEL, page 223.

At Rotterdam, H. Van Oordt has given the following statistical account of the cases of infection found among the prostitutes of Rotterdam :—

1. Registered women in houses ... ... 1 in 7.
2. Women registered strangers ... ... 1 in 5.
3. Clandestine prostitutes ... ... 1 in 2 or 3.

" These statistics are far from being encouraging as to the health of these women. We have already seen, that at Bordeaux the proportion of registered women found diseased has never exceeded 18 per 1000 during the last eight years. As regards clandestine prostitutes who are only examined accidentally when surprised in *flagrante delictu*, we find them diseased in the proportion of a third, or even a half, both at Bordeaux and Rotterdam. What proof more striking than this can be given of the necessity of submitting prostitutes to these periodical sanitary examinations."—JEANNEL, page 268.

Such are a few of the statistics bearing upon this point. We may also profitably allow French opinion to express itself in support of the proposition that the great object to achieve in legislating for prostitution is publicity.

" Registration, it may be necessary to remark, gives to the prostitute who has submitted to it a certain liberty, narrowly limited, it is true, by the regulation, but still a real liberty in the exercise of her infamous business, but it is this liberty which is called toleration. The clandestine prostitute, on the other hand, who withdraws herself from being registered, does not enjoy this toleration ; it follows, then, that she is constantly fearing the police, and she is hampered (*entravée*) in her business, and that the registered prostitute competes with her in such a way, that in the long run she is unable to resist. Toleration is, then, an efficient remedy against the dangers of clandestine prostitution.

" Another fact demonstrated by experience is, that clandestine prostitution appears each day, and extends with an extreme rapidity immediately that the police supervision is relaxed, and this is what we should expect. Young girls who have recourse all at once to the resources of public prostitution are few; most of those found at the bottom of this slough have slipped into it little by little. They are in the majority of cases servants or workwomen, who have gradually brought themselves to prefer the easy and sometimes voluptuous wages of prostitution — the seductions of coquetry, gluttony, and dancing, and the attractions of a lazy and dissipated life, to small wages and the interminable privations of an honest and laborious existence. Thus, registered prostitution is recruited from clandestine prostitution, just as the latter has its source in idleness, indisposition for work, gluttony, coquetry, improvidence, and debauchery. Clandestine prostitution is then immoderate vice, producing without measure moral and physical deterioration. Registered prostitution is vice restrained within the possible—it is public health protected.

" Let us add that the soldiers' trulls, tramps, and such like, in short all those wretched creatures who pass and repass from the empty arches and dark recesses of old buildings to prisons and refuges, often escape from police supervision, and are almost always the subjects of venereal affections. Thus, at Lyons, for example, one may say that nine times out of ten, infected soldiers are unable or unwilling to point out the real source of their disease, which they have contracted from clandestine prostitutes of the lowest grade, or with vagrant women whom they pick up in strange places, far from all police supervision. At Bordeaux, in 1864, a girl of this sort horribly infected with syphilis had fixed her domicile on the quay under the first arch of the bridge, and there had received during two months every night the company of 12 soldiers, varying them each day from the guard established on the bridge.

" Thus, as we examine more closely the social question of prostitution, we become the more convinced that toleration—that repugnant thing— is the lesser of two inevitable evils.

" There are few girls who pass through the first years of their career of vice without becoming infected, and there are some so susceptible to contagion, that hardly are they out of hospital cured of one complaint than they become susceptible to another attack. Among 307 clandestine prostitutes registered at Bordeaux from the year 1863 to 1866, 241 or 78 per 100 had been infected with venereal disease once at least before registration."—JEANNEL, p. 214.

From the discoveries made with regard to clandestine prostitution in France and other continental countries, we learn the evils to which the prostitutes in this country must, of necessity, be exposed, and which they must as surely entail on the community. They are in a few words at once the victims and the vehicles of loathsome disease, and are exposed to the most cruel and abject misery. The public prostitutes on the Continent are, as we have seen, free to a great extent from the disease, and present it when existing in a mitigated form. The advocates of public prostitution are not necessarily seeking to introduce the terrible *maisons de filles*. We see from the example of Berlin that brothels are not necessary adjuncts to the public system. To create and maintain a class of harlots for the benefit of the public health is, doubtless, repugnant to English feelings, and to preserve public decency by licensing vice, seems to us an intolerable outrage on religion. Such a system appears better suited to heathen times, and to grate harshly on Christian civilization ; it has, however, at least, the merit of being logical, and is, apart from its cruelty, in accordance with common sense. It sees an evil, and, therefore, seeks a remedy—a dire disease, and, therefore, withstands its progress and limits its sphere of action— a vice incurable, irrepressible, and, therefore, seeks to regulate it; unfortunately the method adopted has, at least, the appearance of sanctioning vice, and undoubtedly tends to harden the heart and to blunt the conscience. While remembering the injury it inflicts on individuals, we cannot but admire the benefits that it bestows on the public, and from a material point of view, even on its victims. Nor must we shut our eyes to the plentiful provision that French charity, with which its cruelty is so strangely discordant, makes for the relief of the suffering. We are wont to be proud of the exuberance of English bounty ; in this instance, at all events, our neighbours put us to the blush. The French system, though fairly obnoxious to the charge of sacrificing the individual to the public, is careful, so far as it can, to provide relief for the sufferings that it creates or finds, and with all its inherent mischief may compare favourably with the dull stupidity that shuts its eyes to well-known evils, and by refusing to recognize accomplished facts and actual circumstances, endows them with a tenfold power of mischief, and which, while it justifies its inertness by religious theories, forgets the first practical duty of the Christian, which is, to " love his neighbour as himself," or, in other words, never to be made aware of the miseries of others without attempting, if he has the power, to provide a remedy, and thus starting from false premises, though with the best intention, Christian England persistently neglects to heal the sick, to raise the fallen, or to elevate the morals of the people, and not only provides a plentiful supply of evil for the present, but lays up for the future still more abundant mischief. We may be assured that all the evils found on the continent to be inseparably linked with clandestine prostitution, are present with ourselves in at least an equal degree. Would we know what is English prostitution, we may find it if we will not search at home reflected accurately in clandestine prostitution abroad. From what has been done in foreign lands, we may learn what might be done at home, and the evils into which others have fallen in the honest effort from which we shrink at home to provide a remedy for the worst form of human misery should be regarded not so much as rocks on which we must inevitably strike and sink, as beacons to warn us of the dangers into which others have fallen, and to enable us to avoid them.

CHAPTER VI.

CAUSES OF PROSTITUTION.

I HAVE to the best of my ability called attention to prostitution as existing among us in the present day, by laying before the reader such facts as I have been able to gather concerning it both in this and other countries. We may now, informed as to the nature of the evil with which we have to deal, and guided by the experience gained in foreign lands, consider what measures we can best adopt for alleviating the evils incident to it, and for checking, so far as possible, the system itself. It seems not inconvenient at the outset of such a discussion to consider the causes that produce, or tend to perpetuate, the evil state of things with which we have in the previous chapters become acquainted. Such an inquiry may at first appear superfluous, for unhappily these causes are neither few nor far to seek, and only too apparent to the most careless observer. It will, however, become evident on reflection, that a mere indistinct appreciation of them is not sufficient for our purpose, which requires a distinct and methodical statement, setting the different causes under their appropriate heads, and thus enabling us to separate those inherent to human life, and ineradicable, from those dependent on accident and circumstance, and capable of diminution, if not of removal. Practical legislation on a difficult and intricate subject, which requires careful and delicate handling, is the object before us—the more plain, simple, and unambitious the legislation, the greater chance will there be of its proving successful. Sentimental and utopian schemes must be avoided, the line between the possible and the impossible clearly drawn, existing facts and the conclusions fairly deducible from them, however painful, must be recognised, to enable us to do this, and to produce a plain, straightforward, and practical remedy, for the very serious evils depicted in my earlier chapters, we must clearly appreciate not only the effect, but the cause. I may first of all broadly state the somewhat self-evident proposition that prostitution exists, and flourishes, because there is a demand for the article supplied by its agency.

Supply, as we all know, is regulated by demand, and demand is the practical expression of an ascertained want. Want and demand may be either natural or artificial. Articles necessary for the support, or protection of life, such as meat, and drink, fire, clothes, and lodging, are the objects of natural demand. In these the extent of the demand is measured entirely by the want, and this latter will neither be increased by an abundance of supply, nor diminished by a scarcity. Articles of luxury are the objects of artificial demand, which depends not merely on the want, but is actually increased by the supply; that is to say, the desire for these articles grows with the possession and enjoyment of them. This feature is peculiarly noticeable in prostitution, though in strictness, perhaps, it cannot be placed in the category of artificial wants. The want of prostitutes grows with the use of them. We may also observe that in other cases the demand is active, and the supply passive, in this the supply is active, so that we may almost say the supply rather than the want creates the demand. We must not here lose sight of the fact that the desire for sexual intercourse is strongly felt by the male on attaining puberty, and continues through his life an ever-present, sensible want; it is most necessary to keep this in view, for, true though it be, it is constantly lost sight of, and erroneous theories, producing on the one hand coercive legislation, on the other neglect of obvious evils, are the result. This desire of the male is the want that produces the demand, of which prostitution is a result, and which is, in fact, the artificial supply of a natural demand, taking the place of the natural supply through the failure of the latter, or the vitiated character of the demand. It is impossible to exaggerate the force of sexual desire; we must, however, bear in mind that man is not a mere material existence; his nature includes also mind and spirit, and he is endowed with conscience to admonish, reason to regulate, and will to control his desires and actions. Woman was created to be the companion of man, and her nature presents the exact counterpart of his. It is evident, that if so composite a being permits any of the different constituent parts of his nature to attain to undue proportions, he thereby impoverishes and weakens the others, and in proportion as he does this, and accords indulgence to one set of qualities and inclinations at the expense of the rest, he deteriorates from his real nature. He is, in truth, an unmanly man, who devotes all his time and care to athletic and physical pursuits and enjoyments, so is the man who forgets or despises his body, and gives all his care to the mind and intellect, and so also is the man who withdraws from life its enjoyments and duties, and devotes himself exclusively to meditation and spiritual exercise. Men in proportion as the different elements in their being receive fair play and produce their desires, may be considered to approach more or less nearly the standard of human perfection. The intercourse, therefore, of man or woman ought to appeal to their threefold organization of body, mind, and spirit. If the first predominates over and excludes the others, sexual desire degenerates into lust; when all are present, it is elevated into love, which appeals to each of the component parts of man's nature. The men who seek gratification for, and the women who bestow it on, one part of their being only are in an unnatural state. And here we may distinguish the indulgence of unlawful love from commerce with prostitutes, the one is the ill-regulated but complete gratification of the entire human being, the other affords gratification to one part only of his nature.

One other distinction also we must carefully notice, and that is that in the one case the enjoyment is mutual, and that in the other the enjoyment is one-sided, and granted not as the expression and reward of love, but as a matter of commerce. But if it be derogatory to their being, and unnatural to bestow gratification on one part of their nature only, what shall we say of the condition of those unfortunate women to whom sexual indulgence affords no pleasure, and who pass their lives in, and gain their living by, affording enjoyments which they do not share, and feigning a passion which has ceased to move them. The woman who abandons herself for gain, instead of in obedience to the promptings of desire—

> " Who while her lover pants upon her breast,
> Can count the figures on an Indian chest,"

is in an unnatural state, and so is the man who uses her, and obtains for a mere money consideration that enjoyment of the person which should be yielded only as the result and crowning expression of mutual passion. We may further observe that commerce with a prostitute is an ephemeral transaction, which (though it may be followed by serious consequences) yet entails no obligations. Illicit attachments are more lasting, though usually transitory, and entail limited obligations. Both conditions are substitutes for, or imitations of the relationship resulting from love, and known as the married state, which, arising from mutual desire, and granting the highest privileges, imposes corresponding obligations, and is usually as lasting as life itself, and proves at once the mainspring and chief safeguard of society.

We may now consider a little more in detail the want, the demand, and the supply. The want is, in its inception, a natural want, and is simply the perversion of the natural desire of every male for female companionship ; it is asserted by some writers that indulgence in sexual intercourse is necessary for the male as soon as he has attained puberty, and they present us with pitiable pictures of the unhappy condition to which many are reduced, who from timidity or religious or moral influences refrain from giving free scope to their desires, and who deduce from this the somewhat startling proposition that freer sexual intercourse than is at present countenanced by the conscience and practice of society, should be accorded. No doubt the cases cited by the supporters of this theory are very pitiable ; they will, however, scarcely have the hardihood to assert that marriage immediately on attaining puberty would tend to the proper development of the man, or be otherwise than injurious : rather than marriage or sexual gratification, we would suggest, as the true remedy, that morbid excitement should be corrected by healthy bodily exercise and mental application. If the young permit themselves to dwell unduly on sexual ideas a demoralized condition of mind and body must result. For helpless sufferers, if such there are, and their existence be not simply due to the imagination of prejudiced advocates of immorality and wickedness, the cure is to be found in the cricket-field, the river, or the racquet-court, and the different athletic sports and intellectual studies suitable to their age. I confidently assert that marriage or sexual indulgence, before maturity is attained, is most prejudicial.

To show that abstinence is not in itself injurious, the case of the ancient Germans may be cited, to whom the company of the other sex was strictly prohibited until their age had exceeded twenty years; their stalwart frames and reckless valour were the admiration and terror of the more dissolute Romans, to whose well-armed and disciplined legions their naked prowess opposed a long, doubtful conflict; their vigorous bodies, martial countenances, and intrepid conduct, proved that abstinence from sexual indulgence had neither tamed their spirit nor weakened their *physique*. It may be objected that the times with which we have to do are more artificial, and that it is impossible for the boy to emerge into youth and manhood without having sexual ideas presented to his mind; the difference is one only of degree, let him eschew sexual thoughts and obscene conversation, and give himself to healthy exercise and vigorous study, and sexual abstinence, far from proving injurious, will scarcely seem a hardship.

This position is further strengthened by the analogy of the lower creation. Stallions are not put too early to the stud. The rams reserved till two years old produce a better progeny than those employed for this purpose at one year old. Bulls may be used at nine months, but those destined to perpetuate the short-horn and other valuable breeds are permitted first to attain the age of two years.* So much for the natural want. The want that finds relief in prostitutes, is the unbridled desire of precocious youths and vicious men. In like manner, the demand is occasioned by the indulgence of the vicious, and therefore, unnatural want. It arises from men forgetting that they are not placed in this world merely to gratify their appetites. Life has its lawful pleasures; it has also its duties and obligations. Idleness is easier than industry, but the rewards of life are given to the diligent.

> " Labor improbus omnia vincit."

To steal is easier than to work, self-indulgence than self-restraint. Because legal penalties and social infamy are the portion of the thief, only the abandoned have recourse to this means of living; but the circumstance that legal penalties are not attached to immorality affords no justification for self-indulgence; it should be rather an argument for restraint, as this depends on a good conscience and upright will; just as a debt of honour is often considered more obligatory than a trade debt, so ought men to be more careful to follow the path of virtue than simply the common rules to which the law compels them. Man's plain duty is to seek in honourable love the gratification of manly desire, and to wait for enjoyment till he has earned the right to it. " Be fruitful and multiply, and replenish the earth," is the Divine reason for the presence of the sexual instinct. " Flee youthful lusts " the Divine rule of life. There is a right and wrong way of gratifying natural desires; it is, as we have seen, not only possible to choose the right, but more beneficial both to mind and body. The period during which the Roman arms were most terrible and triumphant was the time when female honour was most revered and the domestic virtues most esteemed and

---

* I would refer those wishing to pursue this subject further to my work on the reproductive organs, pages 27 and 53, " Continence and Incontinence."

practised; while the Capuan winter proved more disastrous to the Punic conquerors than Cannæ to their vanquished enemies. An answer to the theory propounded by Malthus and adopted by Mill—an answer which, in our opinion, will be a good one for many generations to come at all events—is, that, while vast tracts of the earth are uninhabited and untilled, and even unexplored, it is too soon to raise the bugbear of over-population resulting from obedience to the laws of our being, and to advocate the adoption of preventives, which, whatever may be thought of them in other countries, are thoroughly repugnant to Englishmen.

The demand for prostitution arises, then, from ill-regulated and un-controlled desire, and may be referred to the following heads :—

The natural instinct of man.

His sinful nature.

The artificial state of society rendering early marriages difficult if not impossible.

The unwillingness of many, who can afford marriage, to submit to its restraint, and incur its obligations.

To a man's calling preventing him from marrying, or debarring him when married from conjugal intercourse.

The unrestrained want and lawless demand, call for the infamous supply; but want and demand are insufficient of themselves to create supply; they are strong provoking causes, but not creative. We must go a step further to discover the sources of supply. It is derived from the vice of women, which is occasioned by

Natural desire.

Natural sinfulness.

The preferment of indolent ease to labour.

Vicious inclinations strengthened and ingrained by early neglect, or evil training, bad associates, and an indecent mode of life.

Necessity, imbued by

The inability to obtain a living by honest means consequent on a fall from virtue.

Extreme poverty.

To this black list may be added love of drink, love of dress, love of amusement, while the fall from virtue may result either from a woman's love being bestowed on an unworthy object, who fulfils his professions of attachment by deliberately accomplishing her ruin, or from the woman's calling peculiarly exposing her to temptation.

I have now called attention to the principal causes of the impure desire and the supply attendant on it.

I shall presently examine them more in detail, but will first of all notice one or two other points connected with this subject that seem not unworthy of consideration. And first I may remark that this demand and supply may either be left to themselves or artificially stimulated—that is, men may be left to find the means of gratifying their impure desires; women to find for themselves the market for their persons, or there may be third parties directly interested in stimulating the demand and increasing the supply. I allude, of course, to procurers and brothel-keepers, who, though it is hardly accurate to include them among the causes of prostitution, as they are themselves rather results of it, undoubtedly cause its continuance and increase.

I may further observe that prostitution is at once a result produced by and a cause producing immorality. Every unchaste woman is not a prostitute. By unchastity a woman becomes liable to lose character, position, and the means of living; and when these are lost is too often reduced to prostitution for support, which, therefore, may be described as the trade adopted by all women who have abandoned or are precluded from an honest course of life, or who lack the power or the inclination to obtain a livelihood from other sources. What is a prostitute? She is a woman who gives for money that which she ought to give only for love; who ministers to passion and lust alone, to the exclusion and extinction of all the higher qualities, and nobler sources of enjoyment which combine with desire, to produce the happiness derived from the intercourse of the sexes. She is a woman with half the woman gone, and that half containing all that elevates her nature, leaving her a mere instrument of impurity; degraded and fallen she extracts from the sin of others the means of living, corrupt and dependent on corruption, and therefore interested directly in the increase of immorality — a social pest, carrying contamination and foulness to every quarter to which she has access, who—

> "like a disease,
> Creeps, no precaution used, among the crowd,
> Makes wicked lightnings of her eyes,"
> ——————"and stirs the pulse,
> With devil's leaps, and poisons half the young."

Such women, ministers of evil passions, not only gratify desire, but also arouse it. Compelled by necessity to seek for customers, they throng our streets and public places, and suggest evil thoughts and desires which might otherwise remain undeveloped. Confirmed profligates will seek out the means of gratifying their desires; the young from a craving to discover unknown mysteries may approach the haunts of sin, but thousands would remain uncontaminated if temptation did not seek them out. Prostitutes have the power of soliciting and tempting. Gunpowder remains harmless till the spark falls upon it; the match, until struck, retains the hidden fire, so lust remains dormant till called into being by an exciting cause.

The sexual passion is strong in every man, but it is strong in proportion as it is encouraged or restrained; and every act of indulgence only makes future abstinence more hard, and in time almost impossible. Some consider that prostitution is the safety valve of society, and that any serious diminution of the number of prostitutes would be attended with an increase of clandestine immodesty. Such a consequence is not one that I think need be apprehended; the insinuation that virtuous women, to be made to yield, require only to be assaulted, is a base and unworthy calumny; nor is it to be supposed that the man who will use a harlot is prepared to insult or injure a modest woman. But intercourse with depraved women debases the mind, and gradually hardens the heart, and each act of gratification stimulates desire and necessitates fresh indulgence; and when grown into a habit, not only breeds distaste for virtuous society, but causes the mind to form a degraded estimate of the sex, until all women seem mere objects of desire and vehicles of indulgence. The prostitute is a sad burlesque of woman, presenting herself as an object of lust instead of an object of honourable love—a source of base gratification, instead of a reason for self-restraint; familiarising man with this aspect of women till he can see no other, and his indulged body and debased mind lead him to seek in them only sensual gratification, and to make, if possible, of every woman the thing that he desires—a toy, a plaything, an animated doll; a thing to wear like a glove, and fling away; to use like a horse, and send to the knackers when worn out; the mere object of his fancy and servant of his appetite, instead of an immortal being, composed, like himself, of body, soul and spirit—his associate and consort, endowed with memory and hope and strong affections, with a heart to love, to feel, to suffer; man's highest prize and surest safeguard; the inspirer of honest love and manly exertion, powerful

> "Not only to keep down the base in man,
> But teach high thought and amiable words,
> And courtliness, and the desire of fame,
> And love of truth, and all that makes a man."

It thus appears that prostitution depends not only on demand and supply, and external causes, but is itself a cause of its own existence, because the possibility of indulgence weakens the force of self-restraint, by creating the idea in the mind of unlawfully and basely gratifying the natural instinct, to which indulgence adds force and intensity, and thus in a measure creates the want, producing from a desire capable of restraint a habit impossible to shake off; while the supply being active, and itself desiring exercise, does not wait for the demand, but goes about to seek it, suggesting, arousing, stimulating evil thoughts and unhallowed passions.

I may now consider more in detail the different causes of prostitution to which I have alluded above. They may, I think, be divided into Primary or Universal, and Secondary or Special. The Primary, comprising mainly the natural instinct, the sinful nature, to which may be added idleness, vanity, and love of pleasure; the Secondary, comprising the remainder of the causes already referred to, may be conveniently grouped under the headings—Artificial, Local, Individual. The existence of the natural instinct I have already referred to as necessarily and inseparably accompanying the divine command, "Be fruitful, and multiply and replenish the earth." This is the law of our being, and our instincts accord with the law. It is impossible, therefore, that the sexual passion can ever die out, nor is it to be desired that it should; so long as it continues, however, prostitution is at least possible.

The children of Adam not only possess this instinct—they have also a sinful nature, which is as much a part of their being as the natural instinct: the one is as ineradicable as the other, and so long as this natural instinct remains allied with a sinful nature, human beings will be liable to be dragged into impurity and unlawful indulgence, and so long as they remain in this condition prostitution is inevitable. Religion will to the end of time enable those who yield to its influence to resist their sinful nature, and to restrain within due limits the natural instinct. The moral sanction, less sacred than the religious, is still a strong one, and induces avoidance of the base and degrading, and choice of the true and good and decent; while prudence preserves some who are deaf to the voice of religion and blind to the beauties of a moral life. It is impossible to suppose that the majority of the human race have at any time submitted themselves entirely to the following out of either a religious or a moral code, nor is it likely that they ever will; so that we cannot expect that religion, morality, or prudence will ever succeed in banishing sin from society as at present constituted: and the primary and universal causes must be held to come within those that are inherent in human nature, and ineradicable. My other chief division, the secondary or special, may, as we have seen above, be subdivided into artificial, local, and individual causes. Artificial causes comprise those arising from the habits and laws of society for the time being, or from any special circumstances into which any class of men may be brought by their relation towards the State. Local causes comprise those peculiar to particular places, or rather which make some places specially haunts of prostitution. While the individual comprise that large and various group of causes which, though they may perhaps fall under one or both of the other subdivisions, are so clearly referable to individual cases as to require separate notice. It may be said, indeed, that the primary causes and the first two subdivisions of the secondary—namely, the artificial and local—are causes tending to produce prostitution as a system, of which we may predicate that it always must exist in a greater or less degree of intensity; while the individual causes are those which enable us to account for the presence in the class of unfortunates of the different individuals, of which the following are the principal—seduction, poverty, *idleness*, *love of dress*, *love of pleasure*, vicious training and associations, and evil habits. Idleness, vanity, and love of pleasure are, from one point of view, characteristics that will always be found existing in human beings as a part of human nature, independently of the accidents of birth, fortune, and education, and in that sense I have included them among the primary causes. Regarding them from another point of view, they are individual characteristics, and unlike the natural instinct and evil inclination, which are both essential parts of human nature and of every human being, and so true both in the universal and the particular; though true in the former, they are often untrue as regards the latter, and I have included them in this last sense among the secondary causes. I have made these observations to explain the apparent carelessness of including the same causes under the two headings. It has seemed advisable to be guilty of this seeming inaccuracy, to enable the mind to place before it at once all the universal and all the special causes, I may now notice briefly the artificial causes.

I consider it would be alike ungenerous to attempt to paraphrase, and impossible to express better than himself, the ideas of "Theophrastus," upon the anti-matrimonial tendencies of modern middle-class society, in his communication entitled, "The Other Side of the Picture," to the editor of "The Times," May 7, 1857:

"The laws which society imposes in the present day in respect of marriage upon young men belonging to the middle class are, in the highest degree, unnatural, and are the real cause of most of our social corruptions. The father of a family has, in many instances, risen from a comparatively humble origin to a position of easy competence. His wife has her carriage ; he associates with men of wealth greater than his own. His sons reach the age when, in the natural course of things, they ought to marry and establish a home for themselves. It would seem no great hardship that a young couple should begin on the same level as their parents began, and be content for the first few years with the mere necessaries of life ; and there are thousands who, were it not for society, would gladly marry on such terms. But here the tyrant world interposes ; the son must not marry until he can maintain an establishment on much the same footing as his father's. If he dare to set the law at defiance, his family lose *caste*, and he and his wife are quietly dropt out of the circle in which they have hitherto moved. All that society will allow is an engagement, and then we have the sad but familiar sight of two young lovers wearing out their best years with hearts sickened with hope long deferred ; often, after all, ending in disappointment, or in the shattered health of the poor girl, unable to bear up against the harassing anxiety. Or even when a long engagement does finally end in marriage, how diminished are the chances of happiness. The union, which, if allowed at first, would have proved happy under worldly difficulty, has lost its brightness when postponed until middle life, even with competence and a carriage. Perhaps the early struggles would have only strengthened the bonds of affection ; but here I feel that I am on dangerous ground. Already I hear society loudly exclaiming that I am advocating improvident marriages, that I would flood the country with genteel paupers, that I am advising what is contrary to the best interests of society.

" But stay awhile, society. Your picture of marriages at thirty-five, with a Belgravian house for the happy couple, a footman in splendid uniform, and at least a brougham, is very pleasing ; but there is a reverse to the canvas, and that a very dark one. How has the bridegroom been living since he attained his manhood ? I believe that there are very many young men who are keeping themselves pure amid all the temptations of London life. God's blessing be with them, for they are the salt of our corrupt city. But I know that there are thousands who are living in sin, chiefly in consequence of the impossibility (as the world says) of their marrying. Some go quietly with the stream, and do as others do around them, almost without a thought of the misery they are causing, and the curse they are laying up for themselves. But many, perhaps most of them, are wretched under the convictions of their conscience. Living in the midst of temptation, they have not sufficient principle to resist its fascination, and although they know where God intends that they shall find their safety, yet they dare not offend their family, alienate their friends, and lose their social position by making what the world calls an imprudent marriage. The very feeling which Heaven has given as a chief purifier of man's nature is darkening their conscience and hardening their heart, because the law of society contradicts the law of God. I might touch upon even a more terrible result of the present state of things—medical men and clergymen will understand what I mean—but I dare not, and I have said enough.

" I must in sadness confess that in the face of the powerful tyranny of social law in this country, it is difficult to suggest any general remedy for this evil. But the mischief is on the increase with our increasing worship of money, and public attention ought to be appealed to on the subject. If our American eulogist be right in commending ' pluck' as one of our distinctive characteristics, it is not our young men who should lack the quality. If they will shake off the affectations of club life, and claim a position in society for themselves and for their wives, because they are qualified for it by education and character, and not merely because they represent so much money, they will soon force the world to give way, and strike down one of the greatest hindrances to their own happiness, both temporal and eternal. It will not in general be difficult to bring the daughters over to the same opinion. Mothers and sisters are seldom very hard-hearted in such cases, and by united efforts the stern father may be induced to give his blessing, even though the happy couple (ay, happy, let the world sneer as it will) have to begin on little more than the proverbial bread and cheese.

" The recognition of this principle would do much to check some of our most deadly social evils. It would make many a girl whom the tyranny of the world now dooms to a joyless celibacy a happy wife and mother. It would raise the tone of character of our young men, bringing out into healthful exercise the home affections, which are now denied them, at the very time of life when their influence is most beneficial. It would drive away all frivolity and effeminacy before the realities of steady work, which early marriage would oblige them to face. It would purify our streets, and check many a bitter pang of conscience, and save many a soul. We are experiencing the bitter fruits of man's law—let us see whether God's law will not work better."

The upper ten thousand too often, I fear, forget that the outside million—among whom, it has been quaintly said, they " condescend to live"—cannot be relied on to travel for ever in the grooves cut out for them by their betters, and assume that if no overt and organized resistance to the Medo-Persian ukases of society and fashion appears on the surface, those edicts are immutable—that tyranny permanent. But the fact is—and they should be reminded of it—that with regard to some things, and among them marriage, there is a numerous and increasing class, by no means the waifs and strays of the community, who are disposed, not to question or propose any change in the law, but simply to ignore it, and to " put up," as they say, " with the consequences."

The numberless cases of *mésalliance* daily occurring, whereof the majority entail, beside the paltry consequence of " Coventry," the very serious ones of unfruitfulness and domestic infelicity, seem to me to point the finger of warning to the guardians of our social code. That finger indicates a blot upon the table of the law,—cause of a nascent canker, which—not, perhaps, for many a long day, but certainly some day—if left untreated, will corrupt the fabric.

I extract the following passages from the admirable editorial remarks upon the foregoing letter of Theophrastus :—

" Do we not make difficulties for ourselves here, even where nature makes none, and create by our system a huge mass of artificial temptation which need never have existed ? . . . . A great law of Providence cannot be neglected with impunity, and this undue, artificial, and unnatural postponement of marriage ends in a great blot upon our social system. Vice is the result, and vice creates a class of victims to indulge it. If Providence has ordained that man should not live alone, and if conventional maxims or mere empty fashion and the artificial attractions of society lead to overlooking, or superseding, or tampering with this law, the neglect of a Providential law will surely avenge itself in social disease and corruption in one or other part of the system. It is not, then, because we wish for a moment to encourage improvident marriages, but because we feel convinced that our modern caution here has outstepped all reasonable limits, has become extravagant, has from being a dictate of natural common sense become a mere conventional and artificial rule, the voice of empty fashion, and a gratuitous hindrance to social happiness and the designs of Providence, that we call serious attention to this subject. The fear of poverty has become morbid, and men cry out not only before they are hurt, but before there is any reasonable prospect of it. They must see in married life a perfectly guaranteed and undisturbed vista of the amplest pecuniary resources before they will enter upon it. They forget that married men can *work*, and that marriage is a stimulus to work, and again and again elicits those latent activities of mind which produce not only competency, but affluence."[*]

But, from present signs, so sadly do I, with " Theophrastus," despair of any contraction, by the lawgivers of fashion, of the ample line of *chevaux de frise* they have skilfully disposed round lawful wedlock ; so ferocious, on the contrary, is the struggle for " position," so terrible an Ægis lurks in the bitter sound of " genteel beggary," that I am more inclined to look for the sanction by society of self-immolation by superfluous virgins, the revival of convents, or the Malthusian modes of checking population which prevail elsewhere, than for the rich, still less the poor genteel, to permit their unfeesimpled or undowered offspring to increase and multiply young, so called " paupers," of still less estate, without the fear of mammon's law before their eyes, and in obedience to the will of Him who feeds the young ravens.[†]

[*] " The Times," May 9th, 1857.
[†] As illustrating this portion of my subject, I may here insert the following letters which attracted considerable attention at the time of their publication, and are perhaps still in the recollection of many of my readers :—

WHY WOMEN CANNOT MARRY.

" *A Belgravian Lament.*

" To the Editor of *The Times.*

" Sir,—We, seven Belgravian mothers, appeal to you, the Editor of *The Times* newspaper, to permit us to make known our present distressing condition. It is known that you allowed seven labouring men to appeal to the public on some question of tea and paper, which concerned their interest. We have just heard that seven clergymen have, by writing something somewhere, compelled their brother clergymen to ask the

The foregoing remarks apply, of course, almost exclusively to the upper sections of society, but hindrances to marriage are not confined

---

bishops for a 'synodical judgment ;' we don't know what it is, but we take the fact as a proof that seven of a class can make a stir in their own interest by uniting to print opinions.

"We are mothers—with one exception, noblewomen ; and in this one case of exception, wealth, tact, beauty, and great worldly success have given a position not the less exalted because the name is new among us, and yet connected with one of the largest of our national princely commercial firms. We have all without exception daughters at our disposal, of whom we have now for several seasons, industriously and in all propriety, endeavoured to dispose. To make them eligible as wives of high rank we spared no pains, no cost, no amount of careful study. They were carefully reared at our country seats in every principle that we, and religious governesses at high salaries, esteemed to be good. They have had the fullest advantages the best masters could afford to perfect their accomplishment in all which 'society' expects in young ladies of this advanced day. We can in all truth declare how carefully and patiently we guided their steps when they first came 'out' into our 'world.' It was for us to see that they acquired that happy, graceful tact which does not at once permit the simplicity of the school-room age to develope into a seeming precocious knowledge of the world, but rather makes the first 'season' a cautious training in that knowledge of evil which the good must cease to regard with surprise, but must not cease altogether to regret.

"We have taken every advantage, some of us, of at least seven seasons, and yet our dear girls are still at home. We cannot accuse ourselves of any neglect of our duty, as mothers with one purpose at heart — their establishment as wives ; we have ever diligently sought their attachment, as far as Providence permitted us, to the 'heirs' of the day. Pray understand, we do not complain that we have been denied ample field and opportunity to work thus for our children, to introduce them to the notice of those for whom we have reared and educated them. Balls, bazaars, breakfasts, concerts, scientific *conversazioni ;* the churches and chapels, where music, art, or eloquence attract the young men of the day ; the Opera, Epsom, Ascot, Volunteer reviews, even the Crystal Palace—all these gave us opportunities. No one can say we ever neglected or misused them ; our coachmen and ladies'-maids we can boldly appeal to, to say how, from day to night, night to day, we have worked for our daughters ; but all has been in vain.

"We seven have at this moment twenty-four daughters, actually what our sons call 'in running,' not one of them has had an offer that any one of us mothers for a moment could have seriously entertained.

"Now, we pray again not to be misunderstood. We utterly deny what is said at the clubs, that our girls are all just alike ; in fact, these ill-natured men say they are automatons put together for one object, dressed after one model, having only the same ideas, and very few of them. This, sir, is a wicked calumny. In our twenty-four there are several decidedly fast in conversation, loud in dress, who in the ball-room, or in the 'Row,' are ever as the very soul of that circle of young men who at the clubs use this scandalous language. We have two, if not three, of decidedly religious views, who really did enjoy the Spurgeon season, who like Sims Reeves best in an oratorio, and in real truth only continue to go 'out' in accordance with that sense of duty which makes them leave it to us to still seek homes of their own for them, fitting their position. The majority are really amiable, can fairly be considered as attractive, are in heart, in intellect, and appearance all we, their mothers could reasonably desire for our purpose of getting them well established. All is in vain. The House of Commons is so stupid, the Court is so quiet ; fishing and yachting, Norway and Cowes so attractive to the men. Palmerston tells us we must really hurry any matters we have on hand, for the days of the Session and the season are numbered. We, alas ! have nothing to hurry. Only one day last week the marriages in your pages were so numerous that they jostled the 'deaths' into another column ; but what a list it was !— hardly a name we knew !

"Now, sir, do view this matter seriously. We offer a supply of that which ought to be to the nobility of our day, what cotton is to Manchester, but all demand has

to the upper classes. I am, however, only concerned with this fact, that by the unwritten custom of society, persons must not marry unless

---

ceased. Milliners press us. Jewellers are rather more pressing than becomes them. Our husbands are irritable. Marriage in our world seems to be repudiated. We cannot lay it to the American difficulty; Cavour had nothing to do with it; neither Louis Napoleon's iron ships, Gladstone's Budget, last year's harvest, the Volunteer movement, nor the Revivals, can have affected our interest, though these subjects seem to have infected the whole nature of our husbands, for they forget the girls to talk of these. *We* know, alas! our evil has no political or simply commercial origin. However unpleasant, indelicate the truth, all dreadful as it is to us to write, marriage in our set is voted a bore—is repudiated.

"It is all very well for our married relatives to talk of this or that event in life taking our friends and acquaintances to Cresswell; but, sir, how sad is it to see that there is in existence a rule of life which won't even hear of marriage, even with all the facilities for its after-dissolution which that eminent man so blandly affords. With all pain, and some shame, we declare it,—an openly recognized anti-matrimonial element pervades good society. The just privileges of our daughters are set aside; the 'heirs' dance with them, flirt with them, dine with us, shoot our game, drink our claret, but they will not marry. And why? Because what our simple-minded daughters call 'the pretty horsebreakers' occupy naughtily and temporarily where we should occupy *en permanence*.

"Go where we will, the mother's eye has this social cruel pest intruded upon it; these bad rivals of our children are no longer kept in the background, as things we know, but, knowing, are to seem not to know. Neither Row nor ring, church nor chapel, opera nor concert are wanting in their evident, recognized presence. Our husbands have been at their 'balls'—the best dancing, they say, and perfect decorum. In short, 'establishments' reign; our children seem condemned to live and die either unestablished, or to be given away at last as wives to people of limited means and no position. Time was, Sir, when a Lawrence, and then a Grant, placed on the walls of the Royal Exhibition lovely pictures each season of daughters now first offered to the attention of England's fashionable world,—pretty advertisements of our pretty chaste wares. That day seems for ever gone. The picture of the year is a 'Pretty Horsebreaker'—but too well known—by Sir E. Seaview, R.A.

"Now, sir, do tell us, are we to blame? Is this our fault? It is hinted that we have connived at and fostered this evil until it has caused famine to our hopes —that we have made such a poor affectation of blindness that it was accepted as proof that we condoned, and hence it is that those whom too late we have learnt to hate have been intruded on our society, and ride side by side with our daughters. It is said we made our desire to settle our girls vulgarly obtrusive, and drove away by boring those we most desired to attract; that, by making heavy settlements so imperative, we drove younger sons to the evil life which was comparatively cheap, seeing that they never could hope to support the expensive life of married propriety; that we, by encouraging the 'heirs' whose 'horsebreakers' were notorious, sanctioned the sin that we might catch the sinners, and thus confirmed them in their non-marriage life. Pray help us, Sir. Shall we go to the Bishops who are in town— to Convocation? Is not ours a *gravamen?* What will become of special licences? Who will care for the Sponsor question? Our churches and Prayer-book, they will become mere symbols to us. The whole girl-life of our order is in danger; the pretty confirmations at the Chapel Royal, the prettier ceremonies of St. George's—alas! alas! And then the sin of it all!

"A Sorrowing Mother for Seven of them.

REPLY WHY MEN WILL NOT MARRY.
"*Horsebreakers and Heartbreakers.*"
"To the Editor of *The Times*."

"Sir,—It may seem, and it probably is, a rash thing for a single 'unprotected male' to break a lance, even in sport, with the seven redoubtable champions of Belgravia.

they be in possession of a certain income. We may be thankful that the ecclesiastical law forbidding the clergy to marry, and thereby letting

---

"Be that, however, as it may, I venture reverently to pick up the dainty gauntlets they have thrown down, and in all courtesy approach a subject that is evidently causing no little dismay in many a noble matron's heart.

"The first and greatest subject of their lament is that the present is not a marrying age, in token whereof they adduce their aggregate of one score and four maidens, some of whom have run through the somewhat questionable ordeal of seven trying seasons, and yet are still 'on hand,' with every prospect of remaining indefinitely in that humiliating position.

"We are told how judiciously these fair damsels have been educated, with what skill they have been prepared for the great 'mart,' how sedulously and yet how vainly they have been exhibited at bazaars, breakfasts, concerts, churches, operas. We are further assured that the interesting beings in question are of every denomination, some being decidedly 'fast,' others what in ordinary parlance is termed 'strictly religious.'

"There is no doubt either that each of the twenty-four has been anxiously and laudably exerting herself to present her mamma with a son-in-law, and yet, after years of unremitting toil, after the sedulous exercise of every fascination on their part, and a lavish expenditure on dresses and dinners by their beloved parents, no fish worthy of being landed has risen to the tempting baits.

"It may well be asked, what is the cause of this unnatural and undesirable condition of things?

"The matrons of Belgravia point angrily to those whom they designate as 'the pretty horsebreakers,' who cluster amid the shady retreats of Brompton, or dwell among the calm groves of the Evangelist.

"Those frail young beings are, however, not the cause, but rather the result, of the circumstances so feelingly described and so deeply deplored.

"The cause must be sought nearer home, in 'ye manners and ye customs of ye nineteenth century,' in the absurd, artificial, hypocritical atmosphere in which we live —in the 'shams' that surround us—in the follies, the frivolities, and the vices we connive at and yet abuse. The true blame rests in the thorough hollowness, worldliness, and insincerity of the age—in that morbid but almost universal craving on the part of every one to appear something that he is not.

"The present topic is one that has been constantly ventilated in the clubs and in society, so that there need be no hesitation in speaking upon it boldly and confidently.

"I know perfectly the reason why no inconsiderable number of my acquaintance prefer braving the miseries and solitude of celibacy to encountering the expenditure and anxieties, together with the fearful risks, of matrimony.

"Years ago, when contemplating a certain important step, I sounded my then 'soul's idol' as to her expectation of the style in which we were to live. She intimated blandly enough that her aspirations were of the humblest order—'Just a brougham and pair, a saddle-horse (necessarily implying two), a house in a quiet part of Belgravia, a cottage in the Isle of Wight, an occasional box at the opera.' Her fortune was under £2000, my income being at the time £500!

"On testing subsequently the views of other damsels, I found that the discrepancy between them was slight. What wonder, then, that I, for one, should bid adieu to all hopes of matrimony?

"In the room at this club where I am now writing there are fifteen men similarly engaged. With several of these I am well acquainted, and I happen to know that they have been compelled reluctantly to follow my example. The fact shortly stated is this. Girls, no matter how portionless, are now so expensively, so thoughtlessly, brought up—are led to expect so lavish an outlay on the part of a husband, that, unless his means are unlimited, he must, to comply with the wishes of a modern wife, soon bring himself to beggary.

"Hence it is that hundreds have been forced to abandon all notion of a connubial alliance, taking up instead with a simpler and more economical arrangement, temporary or permanent as the case may be.

"I dined yesterday with a friend thus domiciled, and a more comfortable, a more elegant *ménage* I never beheld. The partner of his joys and cares was as perfectly well conducted as any lady, however highly born. Well educated, she converses with

loose on the community thousands of men in danger and adding to the numbers of the tempters and tempted, is no longer in force in this

---

ease in three languages, sings, plays, and draws really well, converses readily on the topics of the day, and displays no ordinary quickness in ready and witty repartee. In addition to this, she superintends admirably all the details of his small establishment, looking after his cuisine, and managing his cellar perfectly. He assures me that at the end of the year he has actually (out of an income of £600), a larger balance left than he had when dwelling alone in the Albany.

"Had he in an hour of weakness yielded to the wiles of a genuine 'heartbreaker,' allowing himself to be captivated by her pure but syren arts, I need not say how different would his pecuniary position have been at this moment.

"'Respectability'—in the opinion of many young men—as Diogenes observed with regard to repentance, may be too dearly purchased. I do not pretend for a moment to defend these matters, I simply state how they have originated.

"The matrons of Belgravia who think all such things too shocking to be endured, have at least the remedy in their own hands.

"Discard at once and for ever the foolish, unreasonable anticipations you have hitherto inculcated into the minds of your daughters, instead of 'flying' them at young bankers or wealthy lordlings, and, by education, fitting them only to squander fortunes they have not yet secured; teach them habits of economy, and let them prove to the rising generation that virtue may be rendered less costly than vice. Above all, let young ladies be made to divest themselves of the notion that a husband is only a victim created to supply them with the means of prodigality. Thus, and thus only, can Lais and Aspasia, Blondelle and Loribelle, with all the pretty sister-hood, so well indoctrinated in the *propria quæ maribus*, be effectually disarmed.

"Far be it from me to deny that extravagance enough is to be encountered even among the ranks of the 'horsebreakers;' but it is a mistake to suppose that there are not many among them who possess tact and art enough to retain permanently in their possession young hearts that would have fondly beaten responsively to a far holier attachment had not the cold frown of a too zealous matchmaker sternly forbidden the bans, thus excluding the unfortunate victim for ever from a higher and more ennobling career.

"Yours, &c.,

"Queen of Clubs, June 27." "BEAU JOLAIS.

THE MODERN GIRL'S WAYS OF PASSING THE SEASON.

In "The Times" of July 1, 1861, appeared the following statement:—

"In London they ride in the crowded park from 12 to 2, then home to luncheon; probably some friends drop in at that hour; then a short drive—a visit or two; then the 5 o'clock tea, the sort of little assembly so happily called 'kettledrum;' then home to dress for dinner or the Opera, to be followed perhaps by a rout. The 'whole to conclude,' as the play-bill says, with a ball, and perhaps a cotillon at 3 o'clock in the morning. Why, Sir, it puts me out of breath even to write it. Their life in the country is nearly as hard. They are always going from one country-house to another, where they dress four times a day. Rustling silks for breakfast, a habit or linsey petti-coat and Balmorals for the mid-day ride or walk, a pretty dressing-gown for the 5 o'clock tea, a London ball dress for dinner, and the subsequent romp of 'whip up Smouchy' on 'Pont.'

"In London I never was 'at home' in the morning. Mothers now tell me that young men are running in and out of the house all day as long as the girls are at home. And then the conversation; when people talk for 15 hours a day there must be much folly, if not worse, spoken. Spirits must flag when there is so much straining, and topics more exciting than proper will be introduced.

"I should like to have seen the young man in my daughter days that would have dared to allude to Mrs. Brittle's hat, Miss Rarey's palfrey, or Madame Lacon's 'ram-pagious' ponies. My girls really knew very little of these things, and what they did know they were told to keep to themselves.

"Mothers,—If your daughters do not obtain what I admit is the laudable and natural object of female life—married happiness—you are somewhat to blame. You are

country ; still we have some among us whose calling virtually prohibits them from marrying—I allude, of course, to soldiers.

The married establishment of the non-commissioned officers and rank and file of the regiments and corps serving at home and abroad (India excepted), is not permitted to exceed the following proportions :—

Our Regimental Staff Sergeants.

3 out of 4 or 5 ⎤
4　　″　6　″　7　⎟ Serjeants of each troop, battery,
5　　″　8　″　9　⎟　　　or company.
6　　″　10　″　upwards ⎦

Seven per cent. of trumpeters, drummers, and rank and file calculated upon the establishment.

A soldier must have completed seven years' service, and be in possession of at least one good-conduct badge, in order to be eligible to have his name placed on the roll (of married men). Thus we find that 93 out of every 100 soldiers are of necessity unmarried men, and this brings me naturally to my second subdivision, namely, local causes. Considering that the men subject to the above restrictions, are for the most part in the prime of life, in vigorous health, and exposed to circumstances peculiarly calculated to develope animal instincts, we may reasonably expect to find a large demand for prostitutes in all garrison towns, and may feel sure that there is always a supply in proportion to the demand. Our principal seaport towns are, of course, exposed to the same evil, from a similar cause.

But prostitution abounds not only in places where large numbers of unmarried men are collected together, but also where in the course of their daily work the sexes are brought into close and intimate relations. Factory towns, therefore, must be included in the list of places peculiarly liable to the presence of prostitution, though perhaps in this case the prevailing mischief may be more accurately termed general immorality, or depravity, than prostitution proper ; the difference, however,

---

the true leaders of society. You belong to a class—the class of British matrons—the noblest, and I believe the purest, that ever distinguished your sex.

"Take courage and speak out. Many of you know the evils which afflict society. You, and you only, can check them. If you can't put them down, you can at least drive them from the surface.

"Let your daughters lead such a life that some hours a day may be given to thought, or at least repose. Let pleasure be only a secondary object in their existence. Take them not to the places where the creatures you call the 'pretty horsebreakers,' but what I call 'poor degraded unfortunates,' ply their wretched trade.

"Teach the young men, most of whom are more thoughtless than vicious, that they must subject themselves to those restrictions that society has long imposed upon its members—that they cannot worship Vice in Virtue's presence. Close your doors against those who transgress rules that every boy in London knows perfectly well. Respect not persons, but adhere to duty ; and, as long as there is chivalry and manliness left in British youth, your beautiful and high-spirited daughters need not fear the rivalry of the 'pretty horsebreakers,' and your sons will soon feel that the supremest blessing of a man's existence is to be found in need

"'Life's darling divinities,
Time-honoured children and wife.'

"Your obedient servant,
"GRANDMAMMA."

is not very great, and, for the purposes of this work, immaterial. I must not forget to include among local causes the serious mischief incidental to the gang system in various agricultural districts. Public attention has on several recent occasions been prominently called to the evils thus arising, and it is not unreasonable to hope that adequate steps will be taken for improving the moral condition of the agricultural poor. Where women and men, and girls and boys are working together indiscriminately in the fields, with, in many cases, long distances to traverse in going to and returning from the scenes of their labours, it is obvious that opportunity cannot be wanting, and that temptations must not unfrequently be yielded to, and that the morals and habits of the people will be of a very low order. We may, however, expect to find large cities contribute in a greater degree than other places to the manufacture and employment of prostitutes. Here always abound idle and wealthy men, with vicious tastes, which they spare neither pains nor expense to gratify. Here also are the needy, the improvident, and the ill-instructed, from whose ranks the victims of sensuality may be readily recruited. The close proximity of luxury and indigence cannot fail to produce a demoralizing effect upon the latter. Garrison, seaport, and factory towns, and large cities, are all places peculiarly liable to the presence of prostitution, containing, as they do, within themselves in an eminent degree the seeds and causes of vice. Some places, such as London, combine within themselves all these qualities, and are therefore notably and exceptionally exposed to this evil. It is impossible to suppose that in such localities prostitution can ever become extinct. Wherever men are peculiarly exposed to temptation by the state, it seems only just that the state should take care that the evil condition that it imposes should be rendered as little injurious as possible. This position has of late years, as we have seen, received a tardy recognition ; it is reasonable, I think, to extend this principle a little further, and to adopt a similar course in all cases where we know that the existence of vice is inevitable ; it is useless to shut our eyes to a fact ; it is better to recognise it—to regulate the system, and ameliorate, if possible, the condition of its victims.

We see, then, that the primary causes are absolutely ineradicable, and that the artificial and local causes are of a nature scarcely more yielding. Although the primary causes are ineradicable, they are, as we have seen, capable of being modified or intensified, that is to say, they grow by indulgence and diminish by restraint. A weakening of the primary causes will, of course, have a corresponding beneficial effect upon the artificial and local causes. The primary causes, though really the source and strength of all the others, are in a certain sense latent —that is to say, though always present, they depend on accident and circumstance to bring them actively forth in all their vigour ; these in turn depend upon individual causes, and thus though the primary are ineradicable, and the artificial and local almost equally enduring, they are capable of being modified by the reduction of the individual causes, the nature of which we will now consider.

Inability to marry, unwillingness to accept the obligations imposed by married life, vicious habits, idleness, and love of pleasure, are all causes which operate on individual men, and induce them to have recourse to the society of prostitutes; these, however, are all included in one or other of the different heads which we have already noticed, and it will be more convenient to consider individual causes as wholly relating to female frailty, the previous divisions accounting sufficiently for the demand. The causes of the supply have now to be examined; and first we may consider how far seduction operates in bringing women into the ranks of prostitution. It appears to be pretty generally admitted that uncontrollable sexual desires of her own play but a little part in inducing profligacy of the female. Strong passions, save in exceptional cases, at certain times, and in advanced stages of dissipation, as little disturb the economy of the human as they do that of the brute female. How delicately is this alluded to in the following passage from the *Westminster Review* :—

" We believe we shall be borne out by the observation of all who have inquired much into the antecedents of this unfortunate class of women—those, at least, who have not sprung from the *very* low, or the actually vicious sections of the community—in stating that a vast proportion of those who, after passing through the career of kept mistresses, ultimately come upon the town, fall in the first instance from a mere exaggeration and perversion of one of the best qualities of a woman's heart. They yield to desires in which they do not share, from a weak generosity which cannot refuse anything to the passionate entreaties of the man they love. There is in the warm fond heart of woman a strange and sublime unselfishness, which men too commonly discover only to profit by,—a positive love of self-sacrifice,—an active, so to speak, an *aggressive* desire to show their affection, by giving up to those who have won it something they hold very dear. It is an unreasoning and dangerous yearning of the spirit, precisely analogous to that which prompts the surrenders and self-tortures of the religious devotee. Both seek to prove their devotion to the idol they have enshrined, by casting down before his altar their richest and most cherished treasures. This is no romantic or over-coloured picture; those who deem it so have not known the better portion of the sex, or do not deserve to have known them."*

Again, the same writer observes :—

" Many—and these are commonly the most innocent and the most wronged of all—are deceived by unreal marriages; and in these cases their culpability consists in the folly which confided in their lover to the extent of concealing their intention from their friends—in all cases a weak, and in most cases a blameable, concealment; but surely not one worthy of the fearful punishment which overtakes it. Many—far more than would generally be believed—fall from pure unknowingness. Their affections are engaged, their confidence secured; thinking no evil themselves, they permit caresses which in themselves, and to them, indicate no wrong, and are led on ignorantly and thoughtlessly from one familiarity to another, not conscious where those familiarities must inevitably end, till ultimate resistance becomes almost impossible; and

* July, 1850.

they learn, when it is too late—what women can never learn too early, or impress too strongly on their minds—that a lover's encroachments, to be repelled successfully, must be repelled and negatived at the very outset."

That seduction in the proper meaning of the word can be charged with causing the unhappy condition of many of these unfortunate women is, I think, extremely doubtful; that numbers fall victims to the arts of professional and mercenary seducers is, I fear, equally true.

While visiting the Lock Hospital at Aldershot, the resident medical officer, Dr. Barr, drew my attention to an interesting-looking girl, aged fifteen. As her case is one illustrating the fall from virtue of many another female, I may insert the story here, and can do no better than give it in Dr. Barr's own words :—

" A few months since, E. P——, a pleasing-looking young girl, aged fifteen, was brought by the police to the examining room. I found it necessary, as she was painfully diseased, to detain her for treatment, and a few days since, being recovered, she was sent home to her parents. Her story is shortly, that for some months previously she had been nursemaid in a respectable family, but having quarrelled with her mistress, who was too exacting, and being very unhappy, she resolved to leave her situation. While on an errand one evening she met with a girl not much older than herself to whom she imparted her intention. This young person, who had lately been seduced by a soldier, and had heard a glowing account of Aldershot from him, told E. P—— of her intention to visit this place, and spoke of advantages they might both gain by travelling together. Unfortunately this girl's tale was too readily listened to, and that evening the subject of my narrative called on her parents, who are honest tradespeople in —— Street, Borough, and receiving from them some clothes, &c., without informing them of her intention, left London with her adviser on September 12th last. Between London and this locality she was persuaded to yield to the solicitation of a man known by the girl with whom she travelled, but on arriving at the station and tiring of her companion, she separated from the latter, who remained in Aldershot. Afraid to return to her home she determined with imperfect ideas of distance to proceed to Yeovil, Somerset, where she believed some relative lived. The few shillings she possessed being soon spent she was forced to sell her bundle of clothes to procure food ; and being by this time truly miserable, she resolved to go back to her friends, and retracing her steps again passed through a part of this district on her road to London. Without a penny remaining, weak for want of food, footsore and exhausted by travel, this poor young creature was accosted by the fellow alluded to above, who, quickly detecting her condition, commiserated her, and offered to supply her with food, clothing, and lodging if she would consent to meet a soldier or two who were friends of his. Alternate persuasion and threats overcame her resistance. She was taken by her rascally protector to places where the soldiers congregate. A new and pretty face was sufficient attraction, and she became a toy for them during the evening ; sleeping afterwards with ' Ginger,' to whom, according to agreement, she handed the money received for her prostitution. This course lasted from the Friday of her arrival until the following Tuesday, her protector hiding her from the police in the day time, but on the last-named day they took hold of her and brought her to me for examination. The girl's evidence having been heard, the parents were written to by Inspector Smith, and almost immediately the mother and sister came to see her. Accustomed as I have been to witness meetings between those lost and their friends, and to listen to the heartrending details of sin and grief, I shall not easily forget the scene that occurred on this occasion. The mother, a well-conducted woman, told me that the family had been almost heartbroken by the sad event. As soon as it was known that the girl had left her situation without notice of her intention, they put an advertisement in the *Times*, and had numerous handbills printed and circulated, imploring her return. A whole month having passed without hearing anything of her, their misery can hardly be described, and to add to their unhappiness, the husband, a hard-working, industrious man sustained a fracture of the leg, and was removed to a hospital. The poor mother, in the midst of her misfortune, fearing the worst results, whenever she heard of a body being found in the river or elsewhere, rushed to make inquiries, fully expecting to recognise her lost child in the inanimate form before her. Thus, until hearing from the police inspector, she was ignorant of the fate of her daughter during the period named. She finished by saying the girl had always been a good, engaging child at home ; had, with the rest of the family, regularly attended Sunday school, and though poor, until this unfortunate occurrence, they had been a happy family. To make this sad story still more painful, and to add to the great affliction of this poor family, the girl is pregnant. The Association for the Protection of Women have taken up this case against the man referred to. A detective has been employed to search into the affair, and in the interests of humanity I trust he and similar scoundrels will receive their just punishment."

We have seen that many women stray from the paths of virtue, and ultimately swell the ranks of prostitution through being by their position peculiarly exposed to temptation. The women to whom this remark applies are chiefly actresses, milliners, shop girls, domestic servants, and women employed in factories or working in agricultural gangs. Of these many, no doubt, fall through vanity and idleness, love of dress, love of excitement, love of drink, but by far the larger proportion are driven to evil courses by cruel biting poverty. It is a shameful fact, but no less true, that the lowness of the wages paid to workwomen in various trades is a fruitful source of prostitution ; unable to obtain by their labour the means of procuring the bare necessaries of life, they gain, by surrendering their bodies to evil uses, food to sustain and clothes to cover them. Many thousand young women in the metropolis are unable by drudgery that lasts from early morning till late into the night to earn more than from 3s. to 5s. weekly. Many have to eke out their living as best they may on a miserable pittance for less than the least of the sums above-mentioned. What wonder if, urged on by want and toil, encouraged by evil advisers, and exposed to selfish tempters, a large proportion of these poor girls fall from the path of virtue? Is it not a greater wonder that any of them are found abiding in it? Instances innumerable might be adduced in support of this statement. I have said enough to acquaint the reader with the miserable condition of these children of want; it is not my purpose to pain and horrify or to distract the attention from the main purpose of my book; those who desire a narrative of facts fully supporting this statement, I would refer to Mr. Mayhew's work on London Labour and London Poor. Misplaced love, then, inordinate vanity, and sheer destitution are the causes that lead to woman's fall and that help to fill the ranks of prostitution. But love should not lead to the forfeiture of self-respect. Vanity may be restrained; want may be relieved from other sources. A still more frightful cause remains behind—more frightful because here the sinner has had no choice, so far as man can see, except to sin. Neither love nor vanity nor want have induced the surrender of virtue, for in this case virtue never existed, not even the negative form of virtue, the not-sinning state, the children of the very poor or very vile, what is their lot? It is a picture from which one recoils with horror, and the reality of which in this Christian country it is hard to believe. The cause to which I now allude is found in the promiscuous herding of the sexes (no other word is applicable through the want of sufficient house accommodation). I cannot better convey an adequate notion of the miserable dwellings of the very poor and the indecent mode of life resulting therefrom than by inserting the following extract from a letter written by Mr. Mayhew to the *Morning Chronicle* some years since. If any doubt its accuracy, let them visit for themselves these wretched hovels, and see what barriers they form against decency and virtue. He says:—

" Let us consider, for a moment, the progress of a family amongst them. A man and woman intermarry, and take a cottage. In eight cases out of ten it is a cottage with but two rooms. For a time, so far as room at least is concerned, this answers their purpose; but they take it, not because it is at the time sufficiently spacious for them, but because they could not procure a more roomy dwelling, even did they desire it. In this they pass with tolerable comfort, considering their notions of what comfort is, the first period of married life. But, by-and-by they have children, and the family increases until, in the course of a few years, they number perhaps from eight to ten individuals. But all this time there has been no increase to their household accommodation. As at first, so to the very last, there is but the one sleeping room. As the family increases additional beds are crammed into this apartment, until at last it is so filled with them that there is scarcely room left to move between them. As already mentioned, I have known instances in which they had to crawl over each other to get to their beds. So long as the children are very young, the only evil connected with this is the physical one arising from crowding so many people together in what is generally a dingy, frequently a damp, and invariably an ill-ventilated apartment. But years steal on, and the family continues thus bedded together. Some of its members may yet be in their infancy, but other of both sexes have crossed the line of puberty. But there they are, still together in the same room—the father and mother, the sons and the daughters—young men, young women, and children. Cousins, too, of both sexes, are often thrown together into the same room, and not unfrequently into the same bed. I have also known of cases in which uncles slept in the same room with their grown-up nieces, and newly-married couples occupied the same chamber with those long married, and with those marriageable but unmarried. A case also came to my notice—already alluded to in connexion with another branch of the subject—in which two sisters, who were married on the same day, occupied adjoining rooms, in the same hut, with nothing but a thin board partition, which did not reach the ceiling, between the two rooms, and a door in the partition which only partly filled up the doorway. For years back, in these same two rooms, have slept twelve people, of both sexes and all ages. Sometimes, when there is but one room, a praiseworthy effort is made for the conservation of decency. But the hanging up of a piece of tattered cloth between the beds—which is generally all that is done in this respect, and even that but seldom—is but a poor set-off to the fact that a family, which, in common decency, should, as regards sleeping accommodations, be separated at least into three divisions, occupy, night after night, but one and the same chamber. This is a frightful position for them to be in when an infectious or epidemic disease enters their abode. But this, important though it be, is the least important consideration connected with their circumstances. That which is most so is the effect produced by them upon their habits and morals. In the illicit intercourse to which such a position frequently gives rise, it is not always that the tie of blood is respected. Certain it is that, when the relationship is even but one degree removed from that of brother and sister, that tie is frequently overlooked. And when the circumstances do not lead to such horrible consequences, the mind, particularly of the female, is wholly divested of that sense of delicacy and shame which, so long as they are preserved, are the chief safeguards of her chastity. She therefore falls an early and an easy prey to the temptations which beset her beyond the immediate circle of her family. People in the other spheres of life are but little aware of the extent to which this precocious demoralization of the female amongst the lower orders in the country has proceeded. But how could it be otherwise? The philanthropist may exert himself in their behalf, the moralist may inculcate even the worldly advantages of a better course of life, and the minister of religion may warn them of the eternal penalties which they are incurring; but there is an instructor constantly at work more potent than them all, an instructor in mischief, of which they must get rid ere they make any real progress in their laudable efforts—and that is, *the single bed-chamber in the two-roomed cottage.*"

Bad as are these pauper dens, nurseries of vice more fearful still abound in our Christian capital. In the former some effort after decency may be made, but in the latter, not only is there no such effort, but the smallest remnant of modesty is scouted and trampled down as an insult and reproach. I allude to the low lodging-houses which afford to the homeless poor a refuge still more cruel than the pitiless streets from which they fly. In these detestable haunts of vice men, women, and children are received indiscriminately, and pass the night huddled together, without distinction of age or sex, not merely in one common room, but often one common bed; even if privacy is desired, it is impossible of attainment; no accommodation is made for decency, and the practices of the inmates are on a par with the accommodation. It is fearful to contemplate human beings so utterly abandoned, reduced below the level of the brute creation. By constant practice, vice has become a second nature; with such associates, children of tender years soon become old in vice. This is no fancy sketch, or highly-coloured picture. In this manner thousands pass from childhood to youth, from youth to age, with every good feeling trampled out and every evil instinct cherished and matured; trained to no useful art, and yet dependent for a living on their own exertions, what wonder if all the males are thieves and all the females prostitutes. The crowding together of the sexes, and consequent indecency, is not entirely confined to the large towns.

My readers may recollect the effect produced by the letter of a brickmaker's daughter, when published in "The Times" for Feb. 24, 1858. I subjoin portions of it bearing on the present subject :—

"My parents did not give me any education; they did not instil into my mind virtuous precepts nor set me a good example. All my experiences in early life were gleaned among associates who knew nothing of the laws of God but by dim tradition and faint report, and whose chiefest triumphs of wisdom consisted in picking their way through the paths of destitution in which they were cast by cunning evasion or in open defiance of the laws of man.

"I do not think of my parents (long in their graves) with any such compunctions as your correspondent describes. They gave me in their lifetime, according to their means and knowledge, and as they had probably received from their parents, shelter and protection, mixed with curses and caresses. I received all as a matter of course, and, knowing nothing better, was content in that kind of contentedness which springs from insensibility; I returned their affection in like kind as they gave it to me. As long as they lived I looked up to them as my parents. I assisted them in their poverty, and made them comfortable. They looked on me and I on them with pride, for I was proud to be able to minister to their wants; and as for shame, although they knew perfectly well the means by which I obtained money, I do assure you, Sir, that by them, as by myself, my success was regarded as the reward of a proper ambition, and was a source of real pleasure and gratification.

"Let me tell you something of my parents. My father's most profitable occupation was brickmaking. When not employed at this, he did anything he could get to do. My mother worked with him in the brickfield, and so did I and a progeny of brothers and sisters; for, somehow or other, although my parents occupied a very unimportant space in the world, it pleased God to make them fruitful. We all slept in the same room. There were few privacies, few family secrets in our house.

"Father and mother both loved drink. In the household expenses, had accounts been kept, gin and beer would have been the heaviest items. We, the children, were indulged occasionally with a drop, but my honoured parents reserved to themselves the exclusive privilege of getting drunk, 'and they were the same as their parents had been.' I give you a chapter of the history of common life which may be stereotyped as the history of generation upon generation.

"We knew not anything of religion. Sometimes when a neighbour died we went to the burial, and thus got within a few steps of the church. If a grand funeral chanced to fall in our way we went to see that, too—the fine black horses and nodding plumes—as we went to see the soldiers when we could for a lark. No parson ever came near us. The place where we lived was too dirty for nicely-shod gentlemen. 'The Publicans and Sinners' of our circumscribed, but thickly-populated locality had no 'friend' among them.

"Our neighbourhood furnished many subjects to the treadmill, the hulks, and the colonies, and some to the gallows. We lived with the fear of these things, and not with the fear of God before our eyes.

"I was a very pretty child, and had a sweet voice; of course I used to sing. Most London boys and girls of the lower classes sing. 'My face is my fortune, kind sir, she said,' was the ditty on which I bestowed most pains, and my father and mother would wink knowingly as I sang it. The latter would also tell me how pretty she was when young, and how she sang, and what a fool she had been, and how well she might have done had she been wise.

"Frequently we had quite a stir in our colony. Some young lady who had quitted the paternal restraints, or perhaps, been started off, none knew whither or how, to seek her fortune, would reappear among us with a profusion of ribands, fine clothes, and lots of cash. Visiting the neighbours, treating indiscriminately, was the order of the day on such occasions, without any more definite information of the means by which the dazzling transformation had been effected than could be conveyed by knowing winks and the words 'luck' and 'friends.' Then she would disappear and leave us in our dirt, penury, and obscurity. You cannot conceive, Sir, how our young ambition was stirred by these visitations.

"Now commences an important era in my life. I was a fine, robust, healthy girl, 13 years of age. I had larked with the boys of my own age. I had huddled with them, boys and girls together, all night long in our common haunts. I had seen much and heard abundantly of the mysteries of the sexes. To me such things had been matters of common sight and common talk. For some time I had trembled and coquetted on the verge of a strong curiosity, and a natural desire, and without a particle of affection, scarce a partiality, I lost—what? not my virtue, for I never had any. That which is commonly, but untruly called virtue, I gave away. You reverend Mr. Philanthropist—what call you virtue? Is it not the principle, the essence, which keeps watch and ward over the conduct, over the substance, the materiality? No such principle ever kept watch and ward over me, and I repeat that I never lost that which I never had—my virtue.

"According to my own ideas at the time I only extended my rightful enjoyments. Opportunity was not long wanting to put my newly-acquired knowledge to profitable use. In the commencement of my fifteenth year one of our be-ribanded visitors took me off, and introduced me to the great world, and thus commenced my career as what you better classes call a prostitute. I cannot say that I felt any other shame than the bashfulness of a noviciate introduced to strange society. Remarkable for good looks, and no less so for good temper, I gained money, dressed gaily, and soon agreeably astonished my parents and old neighbours by making a descent upon them.

"Passing over the vicissitudes of my course, alternating between reckless gaiety and extreme destitution, I improved myself greatly; and at the age of 18 was living partly under the protection of one who thought he discovered that I had talent, and some good qualities as well as beauty, who treated me more kindly and considerately than I had ever before been treated, and thus drew from me something like a feeling of regard, but not sufficiently strong to lift me to that sense of my position which the so-called virtuous and respectable members of society seem to entertain. Under the protection of this gentleman, and encouraged by him, I commenced the work of my education ; that portion of education which is comprised in some knowledge of my own language and the ordinary accomplishments of my sex ;—moral science, as I believe it is called, has always been an enigma to me, and is so to this day. I suppose it is because I am one of those who, as Rousseau says, are 'born to be prostitutes.' Common honesty I believe in rigidly. I have always paid my debts, and, though I say it, have always been charitable to my fellow-creatures. I have not neglected my duty to my family. I supported my parents while they lived, and buried them decently when they died. I paid a celebrated lawyer heavily for defending unsuccessfully my eldest brother, who had the folly to be caught in the commission of a robbery. I forgave him the offence against the law in the theft, and the offence against discretion in being caught. This cost me some effort, for I always abhorred stealing. I apprenticed my younger brother to a good trade, and helped him into a little business. Drink frustrated my efforts in his behalf. Through the influence of a very influential gentleman, a very particular *friend* of mine, he is now a well-conducted member of the police. My sisters, whose early life was in all respects the counterpart of my own, I brought out, and started in the world. The elder of the two is kept by a nobleman, the next by an officer in the army ; the third has not yet come to years of discretion, and is 'having her fling' before she settles down."

The extreme youth of the junior portion of the "street-walkers" is a remarkable feature of London prostitution, and has been the subject of much comment by foreign travellers who have published their impressions of social London. Certain quarters of the town are positively infested by juvenile offenders, whose effrontery is more intolerably disgusting than that of their elder sisters. It is true, these young things spring from the lowest dregs of the population ; and, from what I can learn of their habits, their seduction—if seduction it can be called —has been effected, with their own consent, by boys no older than themselves, and is an all but natural consequence of promiscuous herding, that mainspring of corruption among our lower orders. That such as these are generally the victims of panders and old *débauchées* is as untrue as many of the wretched fallacies set about by some who write fictions about social matters in the guise of facts ; but whatever the prime cause of their appearance in the streets as prostitutes, it is none the less strange and sad—none the less worth amending, that the London poor should furnish, and London immorality should maintain, so many of these half-fledged nurselings, who take to prostitution, as do their brothers of the same age to thieving and other evil courses, for a bare subsistence.

Although a large number of women fall victims as above, it cannot be denied that others early evince a natural indisposition to do work when they might obtain it, and may thus be said to court admission into the ranks of prostitution. That idleness and vanity are almost inevitable bequests from parent to child, is proved by the fact that the children of the numerous diseased prostitutes, consigned by the police to the St. Lazare Hospital in Paris, notwithstanding all the religious teachings of the Sisters of Charity, and the excellent secular education given them within the walls of that institution, where they are received as old as seven or eight years, almost invariably become prostitutes. The foundlings, or deserted children, oftentimes illegitimate, who crowd our workhouses, are in like manner a very fruitful source for the recruitment of the metropolitan pavé.

With the absolute neglect of children by parents, and the interminable scheming of lustful men, I may end the roll of causes which have operated in this direction since the dawn of civilization, and, singly or combined, will so continue, I presume, to operate for all time.

CHAPTER VII.

RECOGNITION AND REGULATION OF PROSTITUTION IN THE ARMY AND NAVY.

We have now reached that stage of our inquiry, which enables us to consider how far the existence of prostitution should be taken cognizance of by the law, and what means, if any, should be adopted towards controlling or repressing it, and remedying or alleviating the evils attendant on it. It is a well known maxim that the law cannot remedy every wrong, or insist upon the fulfilment of every obligation. To do this, would be simply to instal itself in the place of conscience, to whose influence, however impotent in many cases, the carrying out of the moral law must in a great measure be remitted. In like manner the legislature is compelled to leave to the individual conscience questions of morals and of honour. If it strays from this rule it can scarcely avoid falling into tyranny. We have already had occasion to notice the fact that serious evils result from the attempt to suppress immorality by legislative enactments, and that the law which attempts to arrogate to itself too great an influence, ends in making itself ridiculous, while undue efforts to restrain, provoke resistance and thereby actually increase the mischief that they attempt to repress. It is important to check public excesses ; it is essential to respect private liberty. The truth of this position is now recognised in most civilized countries ; but the principal European states refuse to shut their eyes to the existence of an evil that threatens if left to itself to assume the proportions of an overwhelming public calamity, and therefore seek to regulate its action and alleviate its mischief. The question has arisen in England, whether our know-nothing and do nothing system is not somewhat wanting in common sense and worldly wisdom, and whether measures analogous to, though not identical with, the foreign systems should not be introduced into this country. It is reasonable to expect the existence of great variety of opinion on this question. We may, I think, in considering it, divide the great mass of the community into free agents and persons under disability. It is obviously unreasonable to deal with both classes in a manner precisely identical, and whatever opinion we may entertain as to the impolicy of state intervention in the former case, we must, I think, admit the possibility at least of benefit accruing from it in the latter. May we not in fact go a step further, and lay down this principle, that wherever the state places men under disability, it lays itself to a like extent under obligations to them, and that in all cases where the causes of evil can be clearly traced to the public necessities, it is bound, if it can not remove them, to alleviate and mitigate, so far as possible, the corresponding evil results.* In other words, wherever prostitution is by the state made a necessity, it is bound to regulate it; and those who are exposed by the state to its influence, must so far as possible be shielded by the state from the mischiefs arising from it.

This position has been virtually accepted by the legislature, in passing the Contagious Diseases Act of 1866. It is my intention in this chapter to contemplate the advantages conferred by a system of inspection, and to consider how far the provisions of the act can be extended or improved, and what further steps may be taken to provide more effectually for the health of the troops. The Contagious Diseases Act provides, as we have already seen, for the inspection and detention, if diseased, of all prostitutes pursuing their calling in certain places named in the act.

We have already noticed the advantages accruing in foreign countries from the regular inspection of women : in Paris, the large proportion of *filles clandestines* found diseased compares in a marked manner with the small proportion of *filles inscrites* similarly affected. The health of Continental armies is in this respect far better than the health of the English and American, while in Belgium, the diminution of syphilis effected by police supervision has almost reached extinction. We may cite the case of Malta, as a further proof of the advantages accruing from a judicious system of inspection :—

"Sir Patrick Grant, the Governor of Malta, gives most valuable information respecting the effect of sanitary restrictions in that island, in an official letter to the Home Government. His Excellency reports that, up to 1861, much contagious disease prevailed among the troops in Malta. An ordinance was passed in that year to check it, which occasioned 'an immediate diminution of these diseases to almost an unprecedented extent, and it has continued so up to the present time' (July, 1868). Sir P. Grant is convinced 'that large or small bodies of men should be personally examined before being granted access to an isolated community, and he will enforce a strict adherence to this well advised prin-

---

* Since the above paragraph was written Government has, through one of its public officers, given utterance to the principle which I have long contended it should advocate. I therefore subjoin it.

In the recent report from the Select Committee on Contagious Diseases Act, 1866, Mr. J. Simon, the Medical Officer of Health to the Privy Council, is asked questions by Sir John Trelawny :—

1306. Is it your opinion that the restrictions upon marriage, in the case of soldiers, have any tendency to create a class such as those who practise clandestine prostitution? —Undoubtedly.

1307. Then the State is responsible in some degree for that condition of things; would it not therefore follow that it is peculiarly the duty of the State to protect the population from that disastrous state of things?—The sense in which I understand the Contagious Diseases Act is, that the State acknowledges that obligation; that is my interpretation of the Act.

See also page 11 of the Eleventh Report of the Medical Officer of the Privy Council, 1868, in which similar opinions are expressed.

ciple.' The essential conditions of the ordinance of 1861 are : 1, regular examination twice monthly, with the power of examining any person complained of ; 2, the detention of the diseased while liable to communicate their disorder. The yearly average examined in Malta has been about 100, and the examining physicians have remarked that some women are repeatedly sent to hospital, while others remain constantly healthy. The number of cases of disease, not individuals—for, as before said, oftentimes the same woman is admitted over and over again —has steadily decreased ; in 1861 it was 85, in 1867 it was only 32. Corresponding diminution has attended the admissions for contagious disease among the troops. Mr. Inspector-General Paynter says that, in 1860, before the regulations were enforced, 916 men were sent to hospital ; in 1861, the number dropped to 689 ; and in 1862, when the regulations had been enforced a year, the number fell to 340. To the present time, the annual number has been constantly under 300 ; this includes, also, an average of 50 men who are diseased before they land from England. The average strength of the garrison is over 5000 men; and many strangers call at the island in the course of the year. A few English camp-women who follow the regiments manage to evade the regulations, from whom much of the disease which still remains is spread. In the navy, the results of sanitary restrictions are still more complete, the sailors, being comparative strangers, cannot evade the regulations in the way the soldiers do. The average naval force in port at Malta is 3800 ; and the number of men who land in the year reaches 8000 ; but Dr. Domville reports that, during the last two years, only six cases of disease contracted in the island have been admitted into the naval hospital."*

The following evidence given by Sir H. Storks before the Lords' Committee, shows that at the time (1861) referred to by Sir P. Grant, no system of examining women was in force. He says :—

" Up to the year 1859 the prostitutes were inspected under a law, or a presumed law from the time of the knights ; but in the year 1859 they found that there was no law which compelled them to submit to the inspection. I will just read to the committee a part of a report which was made by the Comptroller of Charitable Institutions at Malta: ' Females leading a life of prostitution were, from the time of the knights, I believe, subjected to certain police regulations, and to periodical personal inspection ; but in the beginning of 1859 it was found that the " personal inspection " was not ordained by law, but was a traditional abuse of power which may be put at defiance by the slightest resistance. The fact was artfully communicated to the peculiar class of persons concerned, and a general resistance was soon made to the practice.' The consequence was that a law was introduced and passed through the Council."

The law, he told the committee, " was carried out very strictly, as regards the examination of prostitutes, and with very great success. As an example of the actual state of Malta in the year 1865, as compared with stations where the women of the town are not inspected, I would refer to the condition of the garrison with regard to the venereal

* The British Medical Journal, 14th Nov. 1868.

disease during the spring and summer of that year.   On the 12th April the 84th regiment disembarked at Malta, and on that day the cases under treatment in the hospital, including the whole garrison of the fortress, amounting to 6,192 men, were five.   The 84th regiment reported 19 cases on arrival, and a week after their disembarkation there were 38 cases in the regimental hospital, the increase arising from un-detected cases during the voyage.   The 29th regiment disembarked on the 1st of July, and reported 16 cases of venereal.   The day previous there were only 23 men under treatment for this disease in the garrison, and the majority of those cases were in the 84th regiment.   After the 29th regiment had been a week in the command, 23 cases were under treatment in the regimental hospital.   Both regiments came from Dublin to Malta ; and on the 21st of October, the day on which I wrote my report, there were only eight cases of venereal disease reported in the garrison, and the force may be reckoned at something above 6,000 men. In the Ionian Islands the law was applied with great care and vigour with regard to the registration and inspection of prostitutes ; all the women of the town were registered by the police, and periodically inspected by the police physician.   They were periodically inspected at Malta also.   The careful and periodical inspection was attended with the happiest results in the Ionian Islands.   The disease might be said to have almost disappeared in the Islands of Corfu, Zante, Zephalonia."

The following question and answer deserve attention, bringing out as they do very strongly the contrast exhibited in the two places referred to, in one of which the examination system was carried out, and not in the other :—

" 493. Duke of *Somerset*.]   Are you aware whether or not in any foreign countries, in foreign ports for instance, at New York or anywhere else, precautions of a like nature have been more adopted since the Act has been in force in this country ?"

" No ; there have been several applications from the colonies for Government assistance for that purpose.   At Hong Kong a similar Act has been carried, and there have been applications from Jamaica and other places for Government assistance.   But to show how completely the operation of the Act may succeed, I should like to mention the case of the ' Calypso ;' she went to Honolulo, in the Sandwich Islands, and out of a crew of 153, 33 officers and men were sick with the disease ; there there is no restriction of any kind ; but she afterwards went to Tahiti, where the French have control, and have all the women looked up and regularly examined, and in the four months that they were there, with all the men nearly living on shore, there were only three cases of disease.   And at Malta, I think the Committee have very likely been informed, as it is well known, the disease completely came to an end, entirely owing to the regulations that were established."

We thus see what happy results may be obtained from judicious supervision.   A marked improvement is already observable at home in those places to which the Act of 1866 extends.

At the Aldershot hospital the number of men per 1,000 upon the strength of the troops who were admitted into the hospital for venereal disease in 1865, were 302, and in the last return that we had for the March quarter of 1868, the ratio for the year was 207 only.

At Woolwich the percentage to strength was in

1867.

Gonorrhea	12·3
Syphilis	9·3

In 1868, to 27th November.

Gonorrhea	9·5
Syphilis	4·4

In Windsor, although we do not find any great difference numerically, the character of the disease has been greatly mitigated, and must be further very considerably diminished as soon as the 15 mile area now sanctioned by Government has been put in force, as well as the health inspections of the troops have been carried out—regulations which, as we shall see in subsequent chapters, are most important for the efficient working of the Contagious Diseases Act. All doubt on this question has, however, ceased to exist. The Committee of the House of Commons, in the last report, July, 1869, reports to the House :—

" I.—The Operation of the Act.

4. "Although the Act has only been in operation two years and a half, and at some stations only seven months, strong testimony is borne to the benefits, both in a moral and sanitary point of view, which have already resulted from it.

5. "Prostitution appears to have diminished, its worst features to have been softened, and its physical evils abated."

So far as my opinion is of any value, I should say that everything that can be done under the powers vested in them, in the cause of sanitary reform, by the medical officers and the inspector at Aldershot charged with the duty of discovering and examining the women of that district, has been achieved. Dr. Barr and Inspector Smith seem to have their hearts in the work, and carry out the Government instructions with temper and energy. I have no reason to doubt that equal zeal and ability are displayed in the other districts. Additional precautions there are, however, not provided for by the Act, which should be taken ; and if they are not introduced, I fear the result will be that much of the good effected by its provisions will be undoubtedly virtually nullified. For instance, it is not sufficient to detect, cure, and discharge diseased women ; steps should be taken to make their career after leaving the hospital less dangerous. With this end in view, they should have strongly impressed upon them the necessity of cleanliness, and be made to understand how greatly it lessens the chances of receiving infection. They should also be instructed to have frequent recourse to ablutions and injections ; and it might, I think, be useful to supply them, on receiving their discharge, with syringes and lotion, either free of expense or at a price that would induce them to purchase these instruments, and yet entail no loss on the Government, who should supply requisite lotions and instruments at cost price.

PRECAUTIONS TO BE TAKEN BY SOLDIERS.

Careful supervision of the health of the men is scarcely less important than weekly examinations of the women, but the precautions must be of a practicable nature, and such as can be carried out without harassing the men.

To fit myself (a civil surgeon) for recommending what may in my opinion be desirable, I have taken some trouble in visiting barracks, and conversing with many military friends, and I think the following suggestions will be found of value to the service. I may further add that the recent report of the Contagious Diseases Act (July, 1869), has furnished me with most valuable corroborative evidence, from which I have made free extracts.

It is now many years since I first called public attention to the want of washing conveniences for soldiers; they were provided with baths and basins for cleaning their faces, but lavatories were unknown, and I attributed, and I regret to say it, still attribute a great proportion of the venereal diseases under which soldiers suffer to this deficiency of proper accommodation for washing their persons after having exposed themselves to infection. The importance of this is now becoming recognised, and I am glad to read the evidence of Dr. Balfour, who says, in reply to question 1115 :—

" I should recommend the introduction of some clause into the Act by which all brothels, beershops, or public-houses, where the women congregate for the purpose of prostitution, should be compelled to have a lavatory, so that the men might use it at the time; and I believe that the practical effect of ablution would be very much greater if performed immediately after the act, than if it were performed some hours afterwards; and I think it probable that the men would be more disposed to use it at the moment than they would on coming into barracks two or three hours afterwards, when they had perhaps taken more beer than they could well carry; and their great anxiety in that case is to pass the sergeant of the guard without being detected as being in liquor."

I would strongly urge the military authorities to take the necesssry measures for inducing men exposed to the chances of venereal contagion to take the most ordinary precautions of washing the parts exposed immediately on their return to barracks. In order to carry out these purposes of cleanliness, I would suggest the Government building proper lavatories at some convenient place near the entrance of the barracks.

Lavatories and bath-rooms are provided at Chelsea, but there are, I believe, many barracks existing where such accommodation is quite inadequate, if not altogether wanting, and I have looked in vain for any special lavatories enabling the men to wash themselves privately after encountering the risk of infection. There appears to be a very general impression among military authorities that, if provided, they would not be used; it is even asserted that they have been tried in some places, and discontinued on account of the difficulty of enforcing their use. To make an order that cannot be enforced is a great mistake, and to enforce any such order would no doubt be attended with the greatest difficulty. It is a matter that must be left entirely to each man's discretion and good sense ; no order should be made ; but it does not follow that because the practice cannot be insisted upon as a matter of discipline, that facilities should not be offered to those who may be inclined to follow the dictates of their own prudence, or the advice of the surgeons. There can be no doubt that the best results would attend their employment, and I would therefore suggest that lavatories for this purpose should be built near the entrance of the barracks, so that the sergeant on guard might induce every soldier on returning from a carouse to make use of them. These lavatories might be made with little divisions similar to those seen in railway urinals, the number varying according to the requirements of the force. Each separate compartment should have water laid on, with a little tap, and small zinc basin, and chain, in which the soldier could wash the infected organs. I further propose that carbolic acid be previously mixed with this water, in the proportion of half-an-ounce to the pint.

The great advantage to be derived from the use of other lotions might also be pointed out, and authority might be given to the surgeons to issue them at their discretion.

Various lotions have been recommended as preservatives against syphilis. The following is the hygienic liquid recommended for the use of prostitutes at Brussels :—Take of solution of caustic soda (liq. sodæ), or solution of caustic potash (liq. potass), 1 oz. ; water, 1 pint.

Jeannel thinks that decomposition takes place by the absorption of carbonic acid when exposed to the air ; that it destroys the epitheleum ; may produce excoriations, and debilitates the mucous membrane. He prefers the following hygienic water which he has employed at Bordeaux :—Take of alum, half an ounce; sulphate of protoxide of iron, 15 grs. ; sulphate of copper, 15 grs. ; compound aromatic alcohol, 1½ drs. ; water, 32 oz. Mix.

The compound aromatic alcohol consists of a strong solution of essential oil of lemons, mint, lavender, &c., in alcohol, at 85 c.

This hygienic water, prepared in large quantities, is sold to the prostitutes at the price of a penny a quart at the dispensary. The consumption among the prostitutes at Bordeaux during the last six years has risen to 90 gallons per month. This liquid coagulates the albumen. As it is but slightly charged with ferruginous salts, it does not stain the linen, and its agreeable smell engages the patient to use it as a cosmetique. Its green colour, its metallic taste, and its very aromatic smell prevent any one mistaking it for water, or running the risk of drinking it. Mons. Rodet, of Lyons, recommends the following preservative :—Take of distilled water, 1 oz. ; perchloride of iron, citric acid, hydrochloric acid, of each 1 dr. Mix. And he further considers that it possesses a destructive action on virulent liquids. Supposing this solution to be efficacious, it presents certain caustic properties, and cannot be used at the discretion of women, although it might be employed by a physician. Moreover, it stains linen. Mons. Worbe has proposed a lotion made with the solution of bichloride of mercury, with the addition of laudanum, acetate of ammonia, and alcohol.

I should myself prefer to any of the above, a lotion composed of from sixty to eighty parts of water to one of carbolic acid ; and, if expense were no object, a little glycerine could be added with advantage. This, also, would be an excellent lotion for the men to use on re-entering barracks.

It is, I fear, too much to expect that all diseased women will be detected by any possible system of examination. It is also right that temptation should not be permitted to thrust itself, so to speak, upon the soldier. I wish, therefore, to make one further suggestion, which is, that measures should be taken for clearing the streets of the disreputable females who hang about the entrance of barracks after nightfall, and entice the soldiers as they enter their barracks. The picquets which are sent out of an evening to bring in soldiers, clear public-houses, and prevent disorders, have no power to apprehend these dangerous women.

In making the above suggestions, I, of course, assume that the present restrictions on the marriage of soldiers are indispensable, and that nothing can be done to enable a larger proportion to marry, or to alleviate the condition of the women so unfortunate or so improvident as to contract marriage with soldiers without the necessary licence being first obtained. The next most necessary precaution is the recon-stitution and the remodelling of the regular weekly health inspectors for every regiment.

The late (1869) Report of the Committee on the Contagious Diseases Act has recommended it in the following words :—

" Whilst it would be unadvisable to subject non-commissioned officers and married men of good character to such examination, it appears not unreasonable that, for the general good of the service, other soldiers should be periodically examined ; and your Committee have reason to suppose that such a system, properly conducted, would not prejudice the service."

As, then, the health inspection will, doubtless, be strictly carried out by the army authorities, I shall in this edition leave out the reasons I had prepared for its recommendation, but I think public attention should be called to the dangers run if the examination is not carried out in a decorous and decent manner. That these health inspections have been unpopular and inefficient is not surprising, when we read the following description given by no enemy to the service but by Inspector-General Dartnell, as reported in the " British Medical Journal," April 28, 1860 :—

" I shall now make a few remarks on the periodical health inspections of our troops. These take place regularly once a week throughout the whole army, under the surgeons and assistant-surgeons of the different regiments, and have always been strictly insisted on (and in general pretty strictly carried out), as a chief means for the detection and pre-vention of disease. The regulation is, therefore, a very valuable one, and has been in force for a great number of years. As regards its bearing, however, on the detection of venereal disease in its earlier stages, I believe it to fall far short of the desired object. That part of the inspection which requires the special examination of the genitals (performed as it usually is) is disgusting, offensive, demoralising, and degrading, alike to the soldier who submits to it, and the medical officer who performs it. Is it, therefore, to be wondered at that it should be frequently evaded by the soldier, and often loosely and imperfectly performed by the officer? The former finds excuses whenever he can for shirking the inspection altogether; and, if he be affected with a recent chancre or sore of small size, it is not a difficult matter, and in the hurry of inspecting perhaps several hundred men, to conceal it even from the most lynx-eyed examiner.

"The health inspection is differently performed in different regiments, according to the custom in the corps, or the views or convenience of the surgeon. In some regiments the men are marched in a body to the hospital, and passed into or through a room, one by one, for individual examination. This is the surest and least offensive mode of performing it; but it necessarily occupies a great deal of time, is wearisome to all parties, and often inconvenient in keeping the men long from their other duties. The more usual plan is to inspect them in their several barrack rooms, the men being drawn up in line, and called to 'attention' as the medical officer enters the room. In some cases, they stand in their ordinary fatigue dress, each man unbuttoning the front of his trousers, and parading the genitals for the inspecting surgeon; this operation generally giving rise to suppressed manifestations of mirth, shame, or indignation, according to the character and temper of individuals; but at all times, to say the least of it, humiliating and disgusting to the surgeon. Sometimes the soldiers are partially or even entirely undressed, or with the shirt on only, the front tail of which is lifted up as the surgeon passes down the line."

Can it be matter of surprise that inspections so conducted have produced disgust, and resulted in a general abandonment of the practice?

During a late visit to Woolwich, I stated to a very intelligent serjeant of the artillery my views on this subject. He affirmed that when he first joined the service, the above method of health inspection was in vogue, and was a very unpleasant ordeal to undergo, but he said that he would not object to be weekly examined if a private inspection were held in the manner I proposed. I may here advert to the method adopted by Inspector-General Dartnell, which I may as well give in his own words, as reported in the "British Medical Journal" of 28th April, 1860 :—

"'My plan,' I replied, 'is, that you give stringent orders for every man to report himself at the hospital the moment he perceives that he is affected with a venereal complaint, however apparently trivial. Should I feel satisfied, on examination, that he has had the disease above three days, I will report him to you, on his discharge from hospital, for having concealed his complaint, and you shall punish him, as severely as you think proper, for disobedience of orders.' 'But,' said the colonel, 'there is already a standing order of the regiment that the men shall report themselves at once for every complaint with which they may become affected.' 'I am aware of that,' I replied, 'but I wish you to make the order more stringent, and with a special bearing on venereal complaints, and if carried out to the letter, I promise you a result of which you will highly approve.' The order was given. The soldiers were, naturally enough, distrustful and shy of it at first; but soldiers are not slower to see advantage to themselves than their brethren in civil life, and soon they flocked to the hospital so promptly and readily as sometimes to incur the charge from their comrades of being malingerers for going into hospital with such trifling ailments; but this was a fault on the right side. Simple excoriations were quickly got rid of; and chancres, being in their very first stage, rapidly healed under the local application of caustic and water dressing. The men were discharged to barracks in a few days; they had no extra duty to bring up, if they had not concealed their complaints; and their constitutions were saved from the poisoning of the syphilitic virus, or of mercury given for its cure. After some time, the old cases of secondary syphilis, and sloughing buboes and chancres, were got rid of; and by the end of three months we had scarcely a case of syphilitic disease in the hospital.

"The health inspections took place, as usual, once a week. The men were paraded in their several barrack-rooms, each man, in cold weather, standing *on* his stockings; legs and feet bare; sleeves and trousers turned up; jacket and shirt-collar thrown open, to expose the throat and chest; hands, face, feet, and legs, washed clean. In passing down the line, it could be seen at a glance if the men had the appearance of health, and were free from ophthalmia, itch, ulcers of the legs, etc.; but no examination was made for venereal disease, because I felt satisfied that such cases would be honestly reported. I therefore left it to the soldiers' own honour and sense of duty, as well as self-interest, to come forward themselves; and I must do them the justice to say, I seldom— I believe I may safely add, never—had reason to regret the confidence I placed in them; while I know that they considered the exemption from personal examination in public too great a boon and indulgence to be lightly thrown away."

Fortnightly inspections of the troops also seem to be sufficient, and undoubtedly they should be made as seldom as is consistent with the attainment of the desired object, so as to make them as little harassing as possible to the troops. As regards the time occupied, let us listen to what Surgeon-Major Wyatt says in answer to question

"1374. How much time is spent in the examination of your battalion of 800 men?—It depends very much upon the nature of the light, whether it is a bright day or a dark day, and also upon the nature of the disease and the way the men behave. Sometimes they attempt to elude the examination by concealment at the time. It is impossible to say how long an examination would last altogether. Sometimes it would take three-quarters of an hour or half-an-hour; it depends upon circumstances."

Dr. Bostock considers that a surgeon may thoroughly examine 600 men in an hour; and doubtless the examination of men can be more rapidly made than that of women. I think, however, that the number is placed far too high, and that in considering the proportion of surgeons to troops, a far smaller one should be taken. Dr. Jeannel, to whom I have already frequently referred, and who is no mean authority on these matters, considers that one surgeon may easily examine 50 women

an hour, but that his attention cannot be given up to the subject satisfactorily for more than an hour and a half, so that he should not be
called upon to examine more than 75 in a day, and there ought to be
one surgeon to every 175 women.

At PARIS there are 13 surgeons for 3,862 prostitutes—that is to say,
one surgeon for every 297 women. It must, however, be remarked
that the houses are visited weekly, and the isolated women twice a
month. The number of sanitary visits made by the surgeons of the
dispensary amount annually to an average of 144,000, that is to say,
213 visits are made weekly by each surgeon.

At LYONS there are six surgeons for 550 women, that is to say, one
surgeon for every 91 prostitutes. These women are examined each
week; the proportion is, then, one surgeon for 83 visits each week.

At BORDEAUX there are four surgeons for 550 women, that is to say,
a surgeon for 137 women. The visits are weekly.

At MARSEILLES there are six surgeons for 816 women, that is to say,
a surgeon for every 136 women. The visits are weekly.

If, then, it be determined that the examinations of both women and
men be thoroughly and effectually made, a question arises, how often
shall the medical officers be called on to do their duty?

Dr. Jeannel seems to think that a weekly examination of women is
the best, and considers himself supported in this view by the opinion
of the Lyons Commission. If the examinations are more frequent,
they on the one hand tire the surgeons, who do not give sufficient
attention, and so public health gains nothing by it. On the other hand,
as M. Garin has judiciously remarked, the too great frequency of visits,
and their constant moving to and fro, become insupportable to the
prostitutes, who absent themselves, and thus the clandestine exercise of
their trade is encouraged, independently of the administrative difficulties which such a plan produces.*

Surgeon-Major Wyatt thinks, and has found by experience, that
weekly examinations of soldiers need not take place, if properly done.
He says, in answer to question

"1332. I think you say these examinations are conducted once a
week?—About once in 10 days, or a fortnight now. They used to take
place once a week; but, in consequence of the disease having so much
diminished in intensity, I recommended that the examination should be
twice a month on trial, unless there were special circumstances, such as
the occasion of a battalion going to a camp, and their being at Aldershot, where they would be necessarily inspected, owing to the application of the Act to Aldershot."

I would urge on those in authority, the necessity of preliminary education for this special service, and I would also venture to propose that the
medical men should not be overworked. We must neither exhaust their
energies nor fail to attract to the service competent men.

It is best to leave, if possible, in the hands of the military authorities the promulgation and carrying out of military regulations. I trust
that they will see the importance of health inspections, and establish

* Jeannel, p. 254.

them on a basis as little disagreeable as may be, both to the medical officers and the men. I would, however, venture to suggest another alteration—so long as the system continues of sending men to hospital for the slightest ailments, so long will soldiers be unwilling to report themselves on the first appearance of signs of disease ; they will, on the contrary, either neglect early symptoms altogether, or seek for remedies either from their more experienced comrades, or civilian sources. It is worth considering whether it would not be desirable to establish a system similar to the French plan, of treating slight cases out of hospital, instead of as at present sending to hospital, even the earliest detected case of gonorrhœa.

MARRIED SOLDIERS.

Marriage has been recommended as a remedy for many of the evils of prostitution in the army, and as the marriage of soldiers has of late years occupied much public attention, I took the opportunity when last at Aldershot of investigating the subject on the spot.

I am sorry to say that no one whom I conversed with had a very high opinion of soldiers' wives. I need scarcely say that but a few of the best-conducted men are permitted to marry, and this only with the permission of the Colonel. To such the privilege of having quarters and rations in barracks is given. The fact, however, remains, that in spite of this refusal, considerable numbers of soldiers marry, and what becomes of their wives I will at once attempt to show. The pay that remains after Government deductions are made, is fourpence a day. No married couple can live on such a pittance, so that if the woman has no independent income, she must sooner or later depend upon prostitution. Dr. Barr showed me a decent, middle-aged woman, in the hospital, as an instance in point. She had been taken up as a common prostitute, found diseased and sent to the hospital. I questioned her on her antecedents ; her history probably is that of many another woman. In good service at ———, she made the acquaintance of ——— in the 97th Regiment ; he assured her that his Colonel had given him permission to marry, and that she should wash for the officers ; she believing him, "the banns was put up regular," as she expressed it, "and we were married ; since that time he has only contributed four shillings to my maintenance." The expense of moving about with her husband's regiment is considerable, the temptation to earn a livelihood by prostitution great, other means of gaining a subsistence improbable, and the fall of such women into the ways of prostitution, unfortunately, too probably imminent. The impression is likewise very strong among the authorities that soldiers marry strumpets.

I could get no direct answer to my question, "But why do strumpets marry soldiers?" In civil life it may be expected fortune, or position, or to get away out of fast life ; the soldier's trull can have no such inducements, and the mystery remains a mystery still.

Another question I could not get answered is the following :—Who is the clergyman at Aldershot that will, knowing the results likely to accrue, repeatedly and knowingly join in holy matrimony these people? I am well aware there are lay as well as clerical persons who think that marriage is the panacea for all ills ; but surely some one in authority should interfere in this matter, to prevent the desecration of the holy rite. I cannot suggest whether it should be the Bishop or the Commander-in-Chief, but I hope those who have the power, and read this, will interfere. I was told lately of an instance of a marriage à la mode d'Aldershot having been witnessed by my informant, who saw the bridal party leaving a Wesleyan chapel, consisting of three young soldiers and three girls, all of whom had but recently left the hospital cured. I asked had all three been married ? " No," replied my informant, " one only had been spliced, the other two girls were bridesmaids. The three men were the bridegroom, the best man, and the party giving the bride away."

Thus is the holy ceremony travestied.

PRECAUTIONS TO BE TAKEN BY SAILORS.

If precautions have been found necessary for the army, how much more necessary is it that they should be introduced into the navy, may be judged of by the statistics given at page 63.

I would suggest that every man going on shore, should, on his return to his ship, be invited to wash himself in the lavatories appointed for the purpose. If there is no permanent lavatory below, I would have a temporary zinc or wooden structure erected on deck, that could be folded up and removed at will when the ship was ready for sea, and re-erected on the most convenient part of the vessel on the ship entering a port. I would further suggest the distribution of lotions similar to those recommended for soldiers at page 194.

I would moreover propose that weekly health inspections be made in all vessels in the Home Service, and where sailors are allowed permission to go on shore. This inspection should be made by the medical officer seated behind a screen, so that each sailor should be privately examined, and thus his feelings would be respected. I have reason to believe that some such plan as this would materially tend to the diminution of venereal complaints. Modifications of this plan have been tried in China, and it has been found that sailors do not object to the examination. I am credibly informed that some naval medical officers have objected to the annoyance of inspecting the men, but I hope this disinclination to take sanitary precautions is not general. Surely, if the surgeon to a London hospital does not object, in the discharge of his usual duties, to the trouble of inspecting 50 or 100 males, the naval medical officer cannot complain if he is called upon by the Admiralty to make these examinations for the benefit of the Service. If there be in future any medical man who will object to these inspections, let his attention be called to the answer of Surgeon-Major Wyatt, of the Guards, in reply before the Committee of the House of Commons to question

" 1335. Do you believe that it would be disagreeable to the military medical profession to conduct these examinations ?—I look upon it as a most important duty of a medical officer. I do not recognise the idea of the thing being disagreeable as an objection. I think if a medical man comes into the army, and it is necessary for the well-being of the soldier that these examinations should take place, like many other things, for instance, like attending the corporal punishment of soldiers when it existed, it would form a necessary part of his duty. I have never recognised any feeling of that kind."

I would leave it for more competent persons than myself to decide whether it be necessary for the whole ship's crew to undergo a personal examination ; might it not suffice, for all sanitary purposes, to examine only the two or three hundred men on board each ship who have already or are likely to contract venereal diseases ?

Before closing these observations on health inspections for the army and navy, I would call public attention to the remuneration which medical men receive for performing these very monotonous, and often disagreeable duties, and I would urge on the public authorities the advisability of remunerating the profession more handsomely than has been hitherto done.

No doubt can exist that my professional brethren have it in their power (now that the system is getting into working order) to almost banish venereal diseases from the public Services ; but to do this a thorough and conscientious examination is necessary, which, moreover, cannot be effectual, unless both the men and women are inspected, and the service not slurred over. If any carelessness is allowed, the extension of the disease must take place. To encourage particular attention, the pay should be increased. If better remuneration was offered, the unpopularity of the duties above spoken of would to a great extent vanish. In the various Lock Hospitals, the present officers, who have to a certain extent founded and carried out the intentions of the legislature, would remain, and not be induced (as soon as they had gained some experience) to seek other and more agreeable employment. Economy is here a very short-sighted policy, and I conscientiously believe that the medical officers attached to our Lock Hospitals are very much underpaid, as the following instances will prove.

In a conversation I lately had with Dr. Johnstone, who is a Surgeon-Major retired on half-pay, and who has recently been appointed to the newly opened Lock Hospital at Cork, he stated that he was to receive 5s. a day for his services. He holds the office of surgeon to the prison, but it becomes a serious question, in my opinion, whether such a small sum as £91 5s. per annum is sufficient remuneration for the performance of the onerous, delicate, and responsible duties imposed by the act of 1866, and the efficient carrying out of the treatment of contagious diseases in the Hospital at Cork. It is proposed, I believe, to pay the Civil surgeon who examines the women 5s. for each case, but Dr. Johnstone has the entire responsibility of the cases as soon as they are admitted into hospital, and their efficient treatment and the general arrangement of the Institution necessarily occupies several hours daily. I maintain, therefore, that £91 5s. cannot offer any inducement to an able man to accept, or to a conscientious one to retain, the office of surgeon to these new hospitals.

Mr. Lane, surgeon to the Lock Hospital in London, told me that he received no emolument from Government for making and superintending the weekly examinations, treating the patients, giving them certificates, and certifying that they are sound and fit to leave the hospital. I feel confident that Government cannot be aware that the medical officers receive no remuneration for these onerous duties, and that it will only be necessary to call official attention to the subject to remedy this very important omission, and I should propose a sum per case be paid on the patient leaving the hospital. The house surgeon at the London Lock had, until lately, only £100 a-year. Dr. Barr, at the Lock Hospital at Aldershot, receives £300 a-year from Government, and is forbidden to take any private practice. Considering the efficient way in which he carries out his duties, he is not over remunerated. I feel confident that no man will long continue to efficiently examine the women except he be fairly remunerated for his services. I would venture even to go a step further (considering the interest I have all my life taken in this cause), and suggest that no medical man be appointed to these duties who has not passed some time in one of the above-named training institutions, where the regulations for prostitutes are thoroughly carried out. I am fully convinced that special training is required, and that neither the ordinary civil surgeon nor the superannuated army man is adapted, without previous special instruction, to fully carry out this important act. From evidence given in the last report (1869) on the Contagious Diseases Act, Government seems fully alive to this fact, and I hope future administrations will carry out the same intentions.

I subjoin, for the information of my readers, a summary of the salaries paid to the medical men for performing these duties in France; but truly, it must be said, that unless a man is heartily devoted to his profession, he would not accept the inadequate remuneration there paid.

At Paris.

One Surgeon-in-Chief ...	...	...	...	£144
One Assistant-Surgeon	...	...	...	112
One Medical Secretary	...	...	...	112
Six Ordinary Surgeons	...	...	...	96
Three Supplementary Surgeons	...	...	64

At Bordeaux.

One Surgeon-in-Chief ...	...	...	...	£120
Three Surgeons	...	...	...	100

At Marseilles.

One Surgeon-in-Chief ...	...	...	...	£72
One Surgeon ...	...	..	...	56
Four Surgeons ...	...	...	...	...	40

Dr. Jeannel adds, " There are several cities where the honorarium does not exceed £48. We may state this salary is too moderate to attract or retain men capable of raising, by their instruction or their talents, duties which are too often looked down upon, and often very injurious to practise."[*]

* Jeannel, p. 307.

CHAPTER VIII.

REGULATION OF PROSTITUTION.

I CANNOT venture to hope that the sexual passion will in our time cease to operate or diminish very materially. I have no idea that the preventives of prostitution hereafter suggested, will, if adopted at all, operate otherwise than tardily and incompletely. It becomes us, then, to consider what curatives or palliatives are at our disposal. Having already attempted to depict, not extravagantly, the present external aspect of the vice, and the interest of society in its being well ordered, I will now consider the possibility of our regulating it by law, or mitigating its attendant evils.

We may here at once discard from our calculation the class of females who live in a state of concubinage. Their ill effect upon society, so long as they remain in that category, is moral, not physical. They do not, or according to my theory previously illustrated, they very rarely descend into the grade of public supply, but are, even on the Continent, and still more in this country, utterly beyond the reach of medical or public police supervision. The depravation of public health and the national power are more traceable to the young clandestine prostitute, and the promiscuous class who practise from year's end to year's end, for five, ten, fifteen, or twenty years of their lives in a chronic or intermittent state of unsoundness. The hardened common prostitute when overtaken by disease, pursues her trade as a general rule, uninterruptedly, spreading contagion among men in spite of her own pain, that she may live and avoid debt, until positively obliged to lay up for medical treatment, in lodgings or in an hospital. It is from her class that society may be prepared for, if not expect contempt of, and danger to public order and decency; and over it the police of foreign countries have established the partial control already described.

In Chapter IV. I considered the working of the Contagious Diseases Act at Aldershot and other places, and approved the objects that it has in view, and the means adopted under its provisions, for lessening the evil results of the system against which it is directed. I showed that whatever opinion might be held by myself, or others, as to the advisability of interference on behalf of the general mass of the community, it was plainly the duty of the legislature to afford relief and help to those who through its action, rather than their own vice, are exposed to contaminating and hurtful influences. We have seen that its results, from a sanitary point of view, have proved most beneficial, and I earnestly advocate that every place in which there are barracks for soldiers, and all sea-port towns, should be brought within its healing influence. The further question now arises whether its benefits should be confined to the present objects of its care, or be extended to the civil population.

On the propriety of adopting this latter course there is naturally great divergence of opinion, and some confusion of ideas. It is of the first importance that all who take part in the discussion should clearly understand their opponents' ideas and their own. It is happily a question far removed by its nature from the arena of party warfare, and the highest and most sacred interests of society demand imperatively that it shall not be made for party purposes the sport of rival politicians. It is, however, peculiarly susceptible to the influences of *prejudice and ignorance,* and we who desire by our labours to benefit the human race, must jealously guard against allowing our opinions to be warped by these twin enemies of truth. Some approach this question with selfish views, and desire to obtain by legal enactments immunity from danger in the gratification of base desires, while others, regarding prostitution as the safety-valve of society, wish to preserve, at the expense of others, their own wives and daughters from contamination. For such cold-blooded reasoners I have only the most unmitigated abhorrence and contempt ; their maladies and pain deserve no sympathy, and as for their wives and daughters, I can only join in the indignant remonstrance, " who are they that they should be considered while others are left to perish ?" Surely, in the eye of their Maker, the noblest lady in the land is no more precious than the poorest outcast, and the fair fame of the one is too dearly purchased if the price be the other's virtue. For the credit of humanity, I trust that such views are not widely held, and that few desire the perpetuation of this loathsome system. A life of prostitution is a life of sin, replete with evils both for those who follow it as a calling and for those who reap advantage from their shame. As such it can receive from Christian men neither countenance nor toleration. This negative statement is too cold, it is their plain duty to do all in their power to discourage and repress it.

I have already shown that the evil is in its nature highly complex, its causes are various, and of divers degrees of endurance and intensity ; of some of them, it may be fairly said that they are ineradicable and coextensive with human nature. So long as society has existed, its hideous counterfeit has been seen side by side and intermingled with it ; and so long as society endures we may safely predict that it also will remain a foul reproach to Christianity and civilization, a puzzle to philanthropists, statesmen, and divines. Two propositions must be clearly kept in view : the one, that it is a sinful system, highly displeasing to Almighty God, and offensive to all right-minded men ; the other, that until the world is purified from sin its extinction cannot be expected, and as a corollary to this last, I may add that it is an unextinguishable source of serious mischief.

The question then arises, what is to be done with this system, at once injurious, imperishable, utterly sinful and abominable. There are, as we have seen, two methods of dealing with it, diametrically opposed to each other, in vogue in the civilized world. The one is adopted on the Continent, and the other is adopted in England, and also in the United States. The former is the licensing, the latter the voluntary. They are of course based on entirely opposite principles. The LICENSING SYSTEM takes for its basis the indestructible nature of the evil and the terrible mischiefs which arise both socially and physically from its uncontrolled and misdirected energy ; it is argued that it is better to recognize what we cannot prevent, and to regulate it rather than leave it to itself, and since we cannot suppress, to define the conditions subject to which it shall exist. The VOLUNTARY SYSTEM is based on the proposition that prostitution exists in defiance of the laws of God, that the only recognition which the State may lawfully take of sin is to suppress it, and that if this is inexpedient or impossible, the only alternative is to leave it to itself to find its own level and its own remedy—to remit to the individual conscience the abstaining from or partaking in the sin, and to private philanthropy the alleviation of its attendant evils. The State, in fact, ignores its existence, taking cognizance only of it indirectly, when gross acts of public indecency and disorder enforce attention and demand repression. It is objected to the licensing system, that it is in fact licensing sin, and that permitting indulgence under certain restrictions is in truth lending the sanction of the law to evil practices ; it is also objected that it is practically useless, as the large majority of prostitutes contrive to evade its provisions. This is, however, not so much an objection against the system as an observation upon the method of carrying it out, and even if it be taken as an objection against the system, it seems to be one of little weight, because the facts are clear that several thousand women are thereby rendered physically harmless, that is to say, not merely a small, but a very large amount of good is done. Surely the refusal to reap a considerable benefit because we cannot reap all the benefit we desire is not wise. We should always bear in mind that half a loaf is better than no bread. It may however be said that the argument is not quite fairly represented, and that what is really meant is that the benefits derived from the licensing system are insignificant when compared with the evils introduced by it. The licensing system legalises vice by distinctly permitting it under certain given conditions, the result of which is to lend to prostitution the appearance, at least, of a lawful calling, and to diminish sensibly both in men and women the sense of shame. Such a lowering of the public morals is too dear a price to pay for partial security to the public health. Another argument is, that it is degrading to the woman to be forced to publicly admit herself a harlot, and that English prostitutes would never submit to any law compelling them to do so.

It is a somewhat curious style of arguing, to tell us in one breath that the system is bad, because it takes away from the shame naturally attaching to the life of a prostitute, and in the next that it is bad because it increases her degradation, and takes away, if submitted to, the last remnant of self-respect—that it is bad because it accords a certain recognised position to prostitution, and exalts it almost to the dignity of a profession, thereby diminishing or destroying the sense of shame at their calling felt, or supposed to be felt, by prostitutes, and making them consider themselves, at the worst, "martyrs to sensuality," to use the words of a celebrated *fille de joie*, and at the same time bad because it adds to the woman's sense of degradation, by compelling her to enrol herself publicly in the ranks of a shameful calling. If the calling have ceased, by the operation of the law, to be a shameful one, there is no degradation in admitting publicly connexion with it; if there is degradation in making this announcement, then has the trade not ceased to be shameful. These propositions cannot both be true at once; objectors to the licensing system must choose between them, and probably if they take their stand upon the first, their position will prove impregnable.

It is further objected that the licensing system encourages the trade of the brothel-keeper, and that to increase the security against disease is to diminish the sanction against indulgence, and thereby directly promote vice; it is asserted, in support of this view, that the tone of morals at Aldershot has visibly deteriorated since, and in consequence of the passing of the Contagious Act; this last assertion must be strictly proved before its truth can be admitted, or its value, as an argument, acknowledged. And of the virtue, which is only preserved from fear of pain, we may fairly observe that it is a sufficiently cheap and poor possession, hardly worth protecting; while with regard to the first of these objections, the present state of Berlin (see p. 139), already alluded to, may be cited as a sufficient refutation of it.

Whatever may be the failings of the licensing system, the demerits of the voluntary seem not inconsiderable. This latter is a systematic refusal to admit certain facts and their consequences, whose existence no sane person would attempt to dispute, or even casual spectators fail to observe, a perverse determination to ignore the presence of a vast mass of evil, because the best way to deal with it, is difficult to discover; the result is that disease carries on its ravages unchecked, private charity being unequal to the task of combating an enemy so gigantic. Our streets are a standing disgrace, the police being unable, with the limited authority intrusted to them, to cope with the disorderly characters that throng them. The great mischief of the licensing system is, that it tends to blunt the moral sense; of the voluntary system, that it leaves an evil state of things unchecked; this latter, out of regard for private liberty, neglects the public good, the former, for the supposed benefit of the state, remits to and confirms in a life of degradation individual members of the nation. It is difficult to choose between two evils, but happily for us the question is asked, and should be fairly answered, is there not some middle path that may be safely followed? Cannot prostitution be checked and regulated without being licensed? The Contagious Diseases Act exhibits an attempt to steer between these two extremes. It may be that some of its provisions are open to criticism; but critics should not confound two systems utterly different in principle. Though to a certain extent analogous in

their working, both involve the recognition of prostitution—both enforce the examination and detection, if diseased, of the prostitute ; the
one, however, licenses the plying of a shameful trade on certain conditions fixed by law—in fact, legalises the system ; the other proceeds
on the theory that it is useless to deny or ignore the fact that prostitution exists, and that worse evils even than those which now
oppress us might be apprehended from any attempts to repress it,
and that to strive to put it down is therefore worse than useless ;
but at the same time, that it is a thing to be kept within certain bounds, and subjected to certain restraints and surveillance.
By the Contagious Act we virtually say to the women, " You cannot be prevented from following this sad career which you have chosen ;
we cannot force you to abstain from vice ; but we can, and will take
care that your shameful lives shall no longer work injury to the health
of others, or outrage public decency." Some assailants of the Contagious
Act seem to confound it with the licensing system, and adduce arguments against it, to which, though the latter is plainly obnoxious, it
most certainly is not. I hope that I have said sufficient to show how
entirely different the two methods really are. We must not confound
recognition with license ; to license prostitution is to license sin, and in
a measure to countenance it. Recognition is not license, and has neither
the appearance nor the effect of encouraging vice. We are told that it
is unchristian to recognise and make provision concerning fornication.
Is fornication, it may well be asked, a greater sin than adultery ? Yet the
law recognises and provides for this. Can it be said by the establishment
of a Divorce Court to encourage adultery ? Does it, in providing for the
separation of faithless spouses, countenance their unchastity ? Does it
legalise adultery ? Such a contention is absurd ; it merely recognises
the fact that some people are untrue to their marriage vows, and provides the relief demanded by their unhappy cases. In the same way
the law, in recognising and legislating concerning prostitution and its
attendant evils, neither encourages, countenances, or legalises it.

Recognition is the first step necessary to be made by those who
would oppose any effectual barrier to the advance of prostitution. In
vain do we build lock hospitals and penitentiaries to heal or reform
those who by accident, as it were, have fallen into sin and reaped its
bitter fruits. Wilfully assuming, in spite of well-known facts, that the
unfortunates relieved by our charity are mere waifs and strays of
society, instead of being integral parts of a wide-spread system, poor
stragglers that have fallen into a ditch, and been bruised and soiled in
their fall, whom it is sufficient to extricate if possible, leaving the ditch
untouched, in the hope, perhaps, that it will in time be cleansed by
some accidental stream of purity, or choked up, it may be, by its own
filth ; whereas these saved ones are mere units out of thousands who
have fallen into a deep and wide-spreading morass, which claims fresh
victims yearly, and yearly encroaches on the honest soil around, who
may for a brief space struggle to regain their footing when first made
alive to the full horror of their position, but who unseen, or unpitied
and uncared for by the passers-by, soon cease to struggle, and, helpless
and hopeless, fall little by little, till they finally sink overwhelmed in

the black depths of the treacherous swamp. To what good general end do we rescue a few of these poor sufferers from time to time, as chance may favour, leaving the multitudes to perish, and, worst and most fatal folly, leaving the morass untouched, to extend as it pleases, and engulph all it can. To leave an open stinking ditch unclosed is bad enough—to leave the morass untouched is fatal. To know of its presence and its power, to feel it close to us and round about us, and to think that we can free ourselves from its fatal influence by gazing on fertile plains around, or admiring the secure ground on which we ourselves are standing, is to act no better than the stupid ostrich, who hopes to elude her pursuers by shutting her eyes to their approach. To take no steps to control its power, while we build far from its brink a few poor refuge houses, insufficient to contain one thousandth part of the fallen ones, into which they may struggle if they can, unhelped by us—nay, rather pushed further in—by way of dealing sufficiently with the mischief, is simply to reproduce Dame Partington's experiment with the Atlantic Ocean. What if the folly pleases and gratifies us? then let us at least remember that its result is the ruin of human souls—the pollution of the social fabric. What we have to do is to close the approaches to this deadly swamp—to drain it, and to fill it up, and at the same time to disinfect its foul malaria streams, and prevent them from overflowing into purer soil—to diminish its power for mischief—to stop aggregations to it—to withstand its extension. To do all this, we must take its measure, probe its depths, and accurately experience and understand its nature. We must look at it ourselves, and call the attention of others to it; we must discard euphemisms, and call it by its true name; we must prescribe the method of treatment, appoint its limits, and subject it to rule. What is this but recognition? The public are, I am happy to believe, at length awakening to a consciousness of the truth of this position, and the principle has received by the passing of the Contagious Diseases Act the sanction of the legislature, so that accomplished facts have to a certain extent closed the mouths of religious objectors.

It is still, however, unhappily true that the difficulties the philanthropist and surgeon have to meet in dealing with this subject are raised mainly on its moral and religious side.* Those who would ameliorate the physical condition of prostitutes on behalf of society are at once met by the objection—" Disease is a punishment for sin;" " syphilis the penalty paid by society for indulgence in fornication;" and many worthy persons are so deeply impressed with these convictions, as to say, " We will have none of your sanitary or preventive measures, in this respect at least." And again, " The present chances of contracting

* As this sheet is passing through the press, I have received the lately published 11th Report of the Medical Officer of the Privy Council for 1868. It is with the deepest regret I read the following official language :—" *Whether the civil fornicant may reasonably look to constituted authorities to protect him in his commerce with prostitutes, is the principle which I conceive to be at stake*" (page 18).

Again, at page 20, the same authority speaks of "*hospitals for diseased prostitutes as elements in a machinery proposed to be constituted by law for giving an artificial security to promiscuous fornication.*"

disease is the strongest means of deterring men from being unchaste This risk is the most potent barrier against vice. Remove it, and you put a premium on fornication, discourage matrimony, and upset society."

It must be my endeavour to show the real value of this kind of objection, and further, to advance views which I trust may not be deemed incompatible with Christianity and good morals. I admit, without hesitation, that the fear of contracting contagious diseases operates with many a gentleman of education and refinement as a deterrent from fornication, and that such afflictions, involving, as they in general do, both bodily suffering and financial loss, exert a major force upon the unlimited recurrence to debauchery of the poor, coarse, incontinent rake; I allow that, without this pressure, men's sexual passion is so strong, and the training to continence has been so neglected, that a life of sensual indulgence would, in the present state of society, be more a rule than an exception ; and I know that it exercises some little influence even when religion is unheeded, especially among the bulk of the better educated youth, whose minds are so little made up upon the sinfulness of fornication, that I believe the fear of suffering on earth operates more as a curb upon its licentious practice than the more remote contingency of punishment hereafter.

But, conceding this certain amount of deterrent power to the liability to disease, we shall look in vain for proof that it has had any effect towards extirpating the calling of the harlot, or the traffic in female virtue, which has of late years forced itself upon the attention of our legislature. For every thousand upon whom it operates there are ten thousand thoughtless, passionate, habitually licentious men, on whom all lessons are thrown away, and as many defiant scoffers at religion and morality, who will point out some grey-haired offender, permitted by Providence to "go on still in the way of his wickedness," for every "frightful example" that can be adduced on the other side.

As I am writing this, a very remarkable case, showing how little deterring a cause is syphilis from vice, occurred to me.

In the early part of my practice, a gentleman of position was brought to me by his medical attendant suffering from severe affection of the bones of the nose, following several attacks of syphilis. Under our care the patient recovered, but lately the disease has returned, and just now this patient is under my care, not only on account of a piece of bone that I have removed from the nose, but he has come to me with two new chancres, contracted recently when taking his holiday. I may mention that my patient has a wife and family. He confided to me that his sexual passions were very strong, and when he takes wine, as he freely and habitually does, he is very liable to expose himself in spite of the danger, the importance of which he is fully aware of.

The following characteristics of prostitution are worthy of observation : First, that it must be co-existent with human society, a social plague that cannot be got rid of. That women who have abandoned themselves to this course of life are, nevertheless, susceptible of good influences, and capable of improvement and reformation ; and, moreover, eventually return for the most part to a more regular mode of life.

That many enter upon this life owing to evil rearing, or driven by want. The first seems to point to the necessity of regulation, the second to amelioration, the third to prevention. I propose in this and the succeeding chapters to consider the subject under these three heads; and first regulation, as, having arrived at the conclusion that prostitution must always exist, it seems reasonable to consider how far it admits of regulation, before turning our attention to plans that may be adopted for amelioration or prevention. Prostitution cannot be put down, though its extent may be diminished and its attendant evils mitigated. It seems to admit of regulation in three particulars—viz., the health of the women, their places of resort, their appearance and demeanour in the streets. I have already sufficiently shown the great mischief that arises to the community from the presence in our midst of vast numbers of diseased prostitutes. We have seen that the voluntary system encourages the existence and spread of infectious disorders, evils which are, on the continent, sought to be obviated by the licensing system, which however is open to the serious objection that it is in fact licensing sin, that it makes the State an accomplice in wickedness, and results, as might be expected, in hardening the consciences of men and completing the degradation and ruin of the prostitute. Any change to it, therefore, from the voluntary system, notwithstanding all the mischiefs to which the latter exposes us, is out of the question. We have also seen that a measure has been recently adopted in parts of this empire for dealing with disease fairly obnoxious to none of the defects chargeable upon the licensing system, although it has been attacked with more zeal than wisdom on similar grounds. It is not my purpose to merely force opinions of my own upon the reader. I have set before him the evils to which we are exposed, and the methods of dealing with prostitution adopted in this and other countries. I am deeply conscious of the difficulties that beset our efforts to bring about a better state of things, and that it becomes a reformer to be tentative rather than dogmatic in his speech. I will therefore, instead of attempting to form any system of my own, call the attention of the reader to the evidence of Captain Harris, one of the Commissioners of Police, before the Committee of the House of Lords in June, 1868, as to the advisability of extending to the civil population the provisions of the Contagious Diseases Act. I cannot do better than give the evidence *in extenso*, with the addition of a few remarks of my own upon it :—

"742. Can you give us any ideas as to how far it is practicable to extend the Act to London?—I consider it very feasible. Knowing the object of the committee, I have prepared a paper upon the subject of this inquiry, which, if you will allow me, I will read : ' The prevention of contagious diseases being an object of primary importance, I beg to suggest that the operation of the Contagious Diseases Act, 1866, might, with advantage, be extended to the civil population of the metropolis. I would recommend that a special department of police be formed, similar to the common lodging-house branch, now in operation. That this department should consist of two divisions, administrative and active. That the administrative should be 1 chief inspector, 1 registering inspector, 1 serjeant clerk ; and that the active should be 4 visiting inspectors, 20 visiting serjeants.' I name a very small staff in the first instance, because it is easier to extend than to reduce the number. ' That this department be entrusted, (1) With the surveillance of houses of ill-fame, to enforce cleanliness and good order; (2) To maintain decency in the streets with regard to public morality; (3) To suppress the sale of indecent prints, photographs, &c.; (4) Repress, as far as possible, clandestine prostitution; (5) Apprehend procuresses; (6) Apprehend persons who procure abortion; (7) Search for women who fail to attend medical inspections. That to this department be entrusted the registry of prostitutes within the district. That no prostitute be registered unless, (1) There be proof of former offences; (2) Public notoriety, such as attendance at places of public resort, or where prostitutes assemble, or other form of conclusive evidence. That each registered woman be required to carry a card, on which shall be entered, (1) Name; (2) Address; (3) Date of last medical inspection. The following regulations should be printed on the back of this card: (1) To show card when demanded by officers of police specially employed in this department; (2) To present themselves every fortnight for medical inspection; (3) Not to stop or form groups in the public thoroughfares. I recommend that there should be a compulsory periodical medical examination of all females known to be prostitutes, and of all unmarried soldiers and sailors; more particularly previous to the former going on or returning from furlough; or when the latter are on board a harbour ship. As the early treatment of the disease is indispensable, examination, when persons are supposed to be diseased only, is insufficient; besides irregular examinations are objected to by the females themselves. The absence of regular and frequent examinations allows the disease to be communicated before discovered. It is necessary that ample hospital accommodation be provided; that the patients may be detained in hospital as often as found diseased, and as long as they continue so; and that when discharged from hospital, the discharge ticket be handed to the police to prevent its improper use. Under the present system there is a constant influx of diseased women into towns where the Act is in operation, showing the necessity of applying preventive measures to all places. Should the Act become general, it would be necessary to provide hospital accommodation in all unions of parishes.' (I presume half a dozen beds, in country districts, would be sufficient.) 'Some difficulty might be experienced at first from the want of sufficient hospital accommodation; I would recommend the establishment of hospital ships under the charge of naval surgeons; these vessels might be dispensed with as the disease lessened. I recommend that there should be a weekly medical examination of all women living in brothels; and that all drunken prostitutes charged before a magistrate should be medically examined before being discharged. It is found, where the Act has been in operation, that the more serious forms of disease are of rare occurrence; that the social condition of the prostitutes has been raised; that their homes and habits are improved, and that they are more cleanly in their persons. No objections would be raised on the part of these unfortunate women to the surveillance of the police of this special department; the common lodging-house serjeants are much respected by the lower orders, and considered in the light of friends ; and I feel assured that these unfortunate women would at all times look to the police for protection.'

" 743. You have used the phrase, to suppress 'clandestine prostitution :' how would you propose to do that ?—The examination that these women would be subjected to, would cause a great many to abstain from prostitution.

" 744. It has been proved that that has been the result of the Act, in places where the Act has been carried out ?—Yes, it has.

" 745. Is that the only mode by which you would suppress clandestine prostitution ?—The fact of women being subjected to medical examination would, in a great measure, prevent their entering into that course of life.

" 746. Then the simple carrying out of the extension of the Act, as it now stands, would effect that object ?—I think so.

" 747. Then you would simply propose a special police, to carry out the Act as it now stands, with the addition, as I understood your paper, of Lord Campbell's Act, against immoral prints ?—The police carry out the provisions of Lord Campbell's Act, at the present moment ; but I would suggest that directions be given to this special branch of police to carry out the provisions of this Act.

" 748. Then, as far as I can make out, you would make no change in the Act, except extending it, and supplying the police to work it ?—Yes, and making the medical examination compulsory.

" 749. It is compulsory already, is it not ?—Yes ; but from a want of sufficient hospital accommodation, the provisions of the Act are not enforced. I strongly advocate the registering of women, because I think that you cannot reach the whole of them unless they are registered.

" 750. That is the mode by which you would get hold of them, namely, by registering ?—Yes.

" 751. You think that the Act, as it now stands, requiring an information before a magistrate, is insufficient for getting hold of all the common prostitutes ?—Yes. I think that there might be other clauses introduced into the Act.

" 752. To what effect ?—I think that, if the Act were properly carried out by the police, houses of ill-fame might come under the control of the police. At the present moment the police do not interfere with these houses; for instance, in Portsmouth they have no control over them.

" 753. But as I read the Act, if a woman has got the disease in a brothel, the brothel-keeper is liable to punishment ?—Yes, if he does not give information of the existence of the disease. (*The Act is handed to the Witness.*) He is liable to a penalty, I see, for harbouring. 'If any person, being the owner or occupier of any house, room, or place within the limits of any place to which this Act applies, or being a manager or assistant in the management thereof, having reasonable cause to believe any woman to be a common prostitute, and to be affected with a contagious disease, induces or suffers her to resort to or be in that house, room, or place for the purpose of prostitution, he shall be guilty of an offence.'

"754. Earl *De Grey*.] I think your attention has been drawn to clause 15 and 16 of the present Act?—Yes.

"755. Do you not hold that under the 16th clause there is the power in justices to order the periodical inspection of any woman who may be represented to them, upon the oath of a superintendent of police, as being a common prostitute?—Yes.

"756. Whether she be diseased or not at the time when that statement is made to the magistrate?—Yes.

"757. Therefore, those clauses give the power in that respect which you think it would be desirable to extend?—Yes.

"758. But I understood you to say that power was not universally acted upon even in the districts to which the Act now applies, in consequence of insufficient hospital accommodation?—Yes, from the want of sufficient hospital accommodation, the provisions of the Act are not enforced.

"759. Then the defect in that respect arises not from the fault of the Act, but from the want of hospital accommodation?—Yes.

"760. You spoke of the keeping of a register of these women. The police at present exercise a certain control over common prostitutes; do they keep any register now of those people in London?—No, they do not.

"761. But your suggestion that a register of these women should be kept, would not, I suppose, involve the granting to them of any license as prostitutes?—No; certainly not.

"762. Would you approve of a licensing system?—No; I do not think that it would be desirable.

"763. You think that it would be repugnant to the general feeling of the country, I suppose?—I do.

"764. What distinction do you draw between a license of that kind, and the certificate which you suggested should be given?—That certificate would be simply a card to be produced to the special branch of police (provided one was established), to enable them to see where the woman resided, and whether she had undergone the periodical medical examination.

"765. That card, then, would simply be to show that she had complied with the provisions of the Act?—Yes.

"766. At present, I think, in all the places in which the Act is now in force, whether at dockyards or at military stations, the carrying it out is entirely entrusted to the metropolitan police?—It is.

"767. If the Act were to be extended to other districts of the country, not containing naval or military establishments, it might be difficult to extend the power of the metropolitan police there, might it not?—I think that great difficulty would be found in that respect.

"768. Do you think that the ordinary county constabulary could carry out the Act?—I think that the county constabulary might, but I should be sorry to entrust it to the hands of the borough police, except in such towns as Liverpool, Manchester, Bristol, &c.

"769. In the larger towns, you think, where there is an efficient police, the Act might be carried out by the local constabularies?—Yes.

"770. But that would be difficult in the case of smaller towns?—Yes.

" 771. Earl of *Devon*.] You select picked men for this purpose now, do you not ?—Yes.

" 772. Do you select men of a certain age ?—No.

" 773. Are they married ?—Two-thirds of our men are married ; so that, in all probability, married men would be selected to carry out the Act.

" 774. Viscount *Sidmouth*.] In places like Devonport and Portsmouth, I suppose the police are tolerably well acquainted with the women of the town ?—Yes, they are well known to them.

" 775. Are there occasions of a great influx of fresh women ?—Yes.

" 776. These would be immediately known to the police, I suppose ? —Yes.

" 777. Would it not be easy for the police to have authority to see that in any case of an influx of fresh women, they should be subjected to examination, because the police would know the parties to pitch upon, would they not ?—Yes, they would know the parties ; but at the present moment, with the very limited hospital accommodation at our command, it is useless to have them examined, as you cannot send them into hospital, even if found to be diseased.

" 778. What I mean is this, that it would be possible for the police to have power to compel these women to be examined, and not to exercise their vocation until they had passed this examination, and that, in the case of their doing so, they should be liable to some penalty ?—That would be quite possible ; but I do not think that power exists at the present moment.

" 779. Will you state whether you have known many cases where penalties have been inflicted under the 36th clause, for it seems to me that there would be some difficulty in getting a conviction for a person harbouring a prostitute, and ' having reasonable cause' to suspect that she has the disease ?—I do not think that there has been a single conviction under that clause.

" 780. Or a conviction for keeping brothels ?—No, there has been no conviction under this Act for keeping a brothel.

" 781. The conviction can only take place where the keeper of that house has ' reasonable cause to believe any woman to be a common prostitute, and to be affected with a contagious disease ?'—Yes ; that is to say, for carrying on her calling, she being in a diseased state.

" 782. But you have not known cases of conviction at present ?— No, I do not think that there has been a single conviction.

" 783. Earl *De Grey*.] You suggest now that any prostitute brought before a magistrate for being drunk and disorderly should be inspected before being discharged ; and I suppose that you would add, should be sent to the hospital if found to be diseased ?—Yes.

" 784. Is the number of prostitutes who appear before magistrates on charges of that kind a large number ?—There must be a very large number in the course of the year.

" 785. Would they form a large proportion of women of that character ?—Yes, of the very low prostitutes round about Wapping and Shadwell, and in that neighbourhood.

" 786. Lord *Penrhyn*.] You spoke of insufficiency of hospital accommodation just now : have you ever known any instances at Portsmouth or Aldershot of women being taken into the workhouse when suffering from the disease, in consequence of the deficiency of hospital accommodation ?—No, I do not myself know any case of the kind.

" 787. You are aware that there is a clause in the Poor Law Amendment Act enabling the guardians to retain any person in the workhouse suffering under contagious diseases ?—Yes.

" 788. You do not know whether it is acted upon or not ?—No.

" 789. Earl of *Devon.*] Do you know cases where the guardians have refused admission into workhouses to women suffering under this disease ?—No, I do not know of any such case.

" 790. Viscount *Templetown.*] Is the attention of the policemen selected for this particular duty strictly confined to that, or do they exercise all the other functions that belong to the police ?—I think that they exercise their ordinary functions ; if they saw any case of felony committed, or assault demanding their interference, they would interfere.

" 791. You are, I suppose, aware of what occurs among the police at Chatham and Sheerness, and Devonport and elsewhere ?—Yes.

" 792. Have you ever heard of any violence being shown towards them on the part of these women ?—No.

" 793. The police perform their duties with ease ?—Yes ; there is no difficulty whatever.

" 794. Lord *Penrhyn.*] Do not you think that it would be difficult to frame any Act by which a line could be drawn as to women above the class of common prostitutes ?—I do not myself think that there is the slightest difficulty whatever in that.

" 795. In what way would you propose that it should be drawn ; I am speaking of the class of woman who is above solicitation in the street, who comes above the class of common prostitutes, and yet is known to carry on this intercourse with men ; where would you draw the line ?—Speaking of London, I should propose that any woman who goes to places of public resort, and is known to go with different men, although not a common street walker, should be served with a notice to register.

" 796. Is there anything that you could take notice of beyond that fact of a woman going to public places and going with men from those public places ; you could not draw the line, so as to inquire into people's character, to know whether they had connexion with men or not, could you ?—It would be soon known to the police ; every woman has a place of resort, and I think the police could find out any woman's history in London, if they chose.

" 797. Do not you think that it would be difficult to draw the line in an Act ?—I do not consider that necessary ; I think that every common prostitute should be registered, and a day named for medical examination. It would be desirable to classify, as far as possible, the women for this purpose, a certain day in the week being set apart upon which medical examinations would be made by payment ; this would enable the better class of women to classify themselves, and would partly defray the expenses of putting an Act in operation. Great discretion, however, is necessary in carrying out an Act such as that contemplated.

" 798. Viscount *Templetown*.] Do you know whether the police employed in carrying out this Act obtain their information from the prostitutes themselves, or from the men?—I think they obtain information from the men ; but I do not consider that you can in every case rely upon it ; it is difficult for a man to say that he got the disease from any particular woman.

" 799. Do you think it would be difficult, from the information they possess, for policemen to find out from prostitutes whether any prostitute among them is diseased?—I think they might readily find it out from the women ; the women would tell upon one another.

" 800. Do you see any reason why it should not be an indictable offence when a woman, knowing herself to be diseased, gives disease to a man?—No, I see no reason why it should not be made so."

We learn from the above evidence of Captain Harris, that he considers the idea of extending the act to London very feasible. He has from his position ample opportunity of judging, and his experience and ability lend great weight to his opinion. There is one strong reason for extending the act to the Metropolis, which is, that in certain districts of it, if the conclusions arrived at in my last chapter (as to the necessity of bringing within it all places where troops are quartered,) are sound, must be included in its provisions. There is a two-fold disadvantage in placing some districts under surveillance and restriction, from which adjoining districts are free. In the one case, prostitutes plying their trade in the former are enabled to baffle the vigilance of the police, to defy the law, and spread disease, by living in the adjoining districts, thus adding greatly to the immorality of these places. This is very noticeable in the country districts around Oxford and Cambridge, more especially the latter. For the purposes of discipline at the Universities, large powers are entrusted to certain officers called proctors, part of whose duty is to prevent any intercourse between undergraduates and women of the town, the latter being liable to arrest and imprisonment if caught *flagrante delicto;* the result is that the majority of the women take up their head-quarters in the adjoining villages and towns outside the jurisdiction of the proctors, thus introducing an immoral element into places which would otherwise be comparatively free from taint. The other disadvantage is, that diseased women flock in from the free districts, to those under supervision, to obtain for themselves the benefits of medical inspection and hospital nursing, thus pressing unfairly on the resources of the district and the time of the medical staff. If all places were made subject to the same supervision this double evil would be avoided.

With regard to the machinery to be employed, it is only natural that Captain Harris should incline to entrust the police with the carrying out of the Act, and they are no doubt the proper persons to perform the subordinate duties ; the public, however, are naturally, and it seems to me very justly, jealous of vesting administrative power in the police, who are, and ought to be, nothing more than servants of the executive ; and even if this were not so, it is at least a question whether so difficult

and responsible a duty could be safely remitted to the unaided discretion of police inspectors : they are, as a rule, undoubtedly worthy men,
but it is no disparagement to them to say that the person responsible
for the action taken should be of superior position and education ; and
I would suggest that the police should act under the orders of medical
officers, it being of the greatest importance to guard against tyrannical
and indiscreet behaviour in the performance of the difficult duties
created by the Act.*

It does not seem to me that the surveillance of any houses of ill-
fame, except accommodation houses, should be considered part of the
duty of the police, as for reasons that I shall give in another place, I
am inclined to think that, with this exception, such places should be
altogether repressed.† It is difficult to know what offences the assistant-
commissioner requires that a woman should be guilty of to justify her
registration as a prostitute, and it is to be regretted that his evidence
is not more explicit on this point, as the question what conduct is to
expose a woman to police surveillance is one of no small difficulty.

I subjoin here the presumptions of prostitution required on the Continent, before placing a woman upon the registry ; not that I wish it to
be supposed that I advocate their adoption *in toto*, or that I consider
that they afford the only or the best criterion to judge by, but because
it seems to me that I shall best assist the reader to form an opinion on
this difficult point—what course of conduct is to render a woman liable
to be placed on the police registry as a common prostitute—by placing
before him all the facts within my knowledge that appear to bear upon
it. The points, then, from which presumptions of clandestine prostitution are deduced on the Continent, are the following :—

" 1. When a girl is arrested in any public place or public road, giving
herself up to acts of debauchery with a man who declares he does not
know her, and will not bail her.

" In this case the offence of clandestine prostitution is complicated
with the offence of outraging public feeling and modesty, and often that
of vagrancy.

" 2. When a girl is arrested introducing into her house a man whom
she has met in the public streets, or place of public resort, and who
makes the same declaration as the above.

* The following answer to the Lords' Committee shows that the commissioners of
police are fully alive to the necessity of employing men of first-class character on this
service, as it is impossible for the commissioners to superintend the carrying out of the
proposed measure. I submit that this duty should be entrusted to gentlemen, and
not left to mere police inspectors.

" Great care is taken in their selection ; for, in addition to intelligence and temper,
we require good moral character, and, as a rule, married men are employed. Sir
Richard Mayne, the Commissioner of Police, recognised from the first the importance
of these qualifications, and yet we had one defaulter, a young man of great activity
and promise, who, yielding to temptation, married a brothel-keeper, thus sacrificing
his character and his place ; with this exception our men have done their work admirably. We enjoin upon them specially, forbearance and kindness ; and especially
point out that the law gives them no power to incarcerate or to deprive the women
of their liberty, unless under special circumstances. I will just mention to the committee that we have had through our hands 5,479 women, and out of that whole number, we have only had occasion to employ the penal clauses of the act in six cases."

† As to accommodation houses and brothels, see page 231.

" 3. When a girl is arrested in a furnished house or inn, shut up with a man who makes the same declaration as the above.

" 4. When in a short period the police have met the same girl in the streets, or public places, with different men, although each of them may have declared themselves to be her sweetheart or her protector.

" 5. When a girl has been arrested in a house of accommodation, or when the police see her entering or leaving a house of this description.

" 6. Associating with well-known prostitutes, or the mistresses of houses of ill-fame, is considered presumptive evidence of clandestine prostitution.

" In any of these cases, and on a written report signed by two policemen, the girl is summoned before the Bureau des Mœurs, by letter; and if she refuses to come she may be arrested and brought by force before the chief of the Bureau. She may then be examined as regards her family, her antecedents, her business, &c., and a letter is written to the mayor of the town in which she says she was born ; if subsequently it is found that she has renounced work, and has no other means of subsistence than prostitution, if found affected with venereal disease, and it is in vain to hope that she will return to an honest way of living,— permission is asked from the mayor or the prefect, to inscribe her on the register of public prostitutes."*

I regret to observe that Captain Harris is inclined to recommend that a card should be given to the prostitutes when registered; this has too much the appearance of the health ticket of the foreign *inscrite*, and if not intended to be used in the same way is certainly very adaptable to the purpose. The only reason for giving this card seems to be to facilitate identification by the police ; a little additional trouble on their part seems a good substitute for it. Captain Harris agrees that the licensing system is undesirable. It is imperative to avoid not only the reality, but also the appearance of it. It will be seen that more hospital accommodation is necessary for the extension of the Act, and even for the proper working of it in its present state, as the question of greater hospital accommodation requires attention, whether any change such as here suggested is made in the law or not. I shall deal with this subject hereafter in the chapter on amelioration, to whose pages it seems more properly to belong.

One serious objection presents itself at once to the mind of an Englishman, when measures of surveillance are suggested to him ; it is sufficiently well founded, to require to be fairly encountered and fully answered, or else frankly admitted to be fatal. The objection is, that such measures are invasions of private liberty, and therefore intolerable in the land which boasts itself to be the peculiar home of freedom. The slave who sets foot on English soil is free, and here the fugitive from tyranny finds refuge and shelter. We may go where we like, do what we like, say what we like, be what we like, so long only as we obey the laws. And these laws are framed with the object of securing to the individual the largest amount of liberty consistent with public welfare. This personal liberty, the birthright and heritage of every Englishman, purchased by our fathers' blood, and secured by

* Jeannel, p. 227.

the wisdom and labours of centuries, is a noble possession to be preserved by us undiminished, and by us transmitted to the after-time unshorn of any of its fair proportions. This is not merely a sacred duty, but an instinct in our nature, so that when any change is proposed that seems to encroach upon a right so precious, we may expect it to be regarded with suspicion, and encountered by resistance, and doubly so when the objects of its attack are mean, defenceless, and despised. Moreover, this English liberty includes the right to sin as much as we please, so long only as we do not thereby commit any offence cognizable at law, against the property or person of our fellow subjects. We may gamble, drink, and whore; the first must be done to a certain extent in private ; the second must not cause public commotion ; but the last may be done without any restriction whatever.

Every man is free to seduce a woman, take his neighbour's wife, or keep a mistress, without rendering himself obnoxious to the penal law. He may be a sabbath-breaker, atheist, or teacher of sedition, and yet incur no punishment. In like manner it is undeniably lawful for a woman to abandon herself for money if she chooses. This right of sinning, however, infinite though it at first sight appears, is subject to certain restrictions, and even actions, in themselves innocent, may fall under the scourge of the law if indulged in under circumstances prejudicial to the public safety. For instance, there is no harm in stone throwing *per se*, but if little boys, or others of a playful disposition, throw stones at railway trains, or in places of public resort, they by so doing render themselves liable to punishment ; and in the same way it is unlawful to let off fireworks in the streets, or to ride full gallop in Rotten Row. Again, there is no harm in selling goods at a shop—on the contrary, it is a very praiseworthy means of earning daily bread ; but the fishmonger who sells stale fish, the butcher who sells tainted meat, and the tradesman who uses false weights, are liable to punishment. And this, notwithstanding that it would be quite possible to do substantial justice between the dishonest trader and his customer, by leaving the latter to recover damages for the injury done to him in a civil action ; *caveat emptor* is a sound maxim, the buyer has his own folly to thank if he is taken in. And again, there may be no buyer at all, and therefore no one is actually taken in. The mere fact of endeavouring to trade with the bad fish, or meat, or the false weights, is an offence against the law. It will no doubt be objected that there is no parallel whatever between the case of a dishonest trader and a diseased prostitute—that the former is pursuing a lawful calling, and that people come to his shop with an honest object, and therefore that it is only right that they should be protected by the law ; while to the latter it is impossible that a man should go with an honest purpose, and therefore the law rightly extends protection in the one case, which in the other it withholds. There is, no doubt, much force in this observation ; it must not, however, be carried too far ; and it must be remembered that the gist of these offences is, in the one case, doing acts that may prove injurious to the public health, in the other attempting to obtain money under false pretences ; and the fact that any injury is actually done on the one hand, or any money actually obtained on the other, is not material to constitute the offence. The question remains, does the immorality of the transaction through which the injury must come in the case of the prostitute, place the infliction of the injury, or the attempt to inflict it, beyond the cognizance of the law? I think not, and will produce a case in point. Gambling is, in the eye of the law, immoral, and its public practice prohibited, so much so, that not only are public gaming tables suppressed, but even wagering on horse races is prohibited in the streets, and in public-houses. If any man, therefore, loses his money gambling, he has only himself to thank for his folly ; and had he not engaged in an immoral transaction, he would have been secure against the loss. So that it was through his own evil deed that the loss befell him ; and yet if money is unfairly won at games of chance, the cheat is liable to punishment for obtaining money under false pretences. The reason is obvious ; gambling, although a wrong thing, and a pursuit which, therefore, the law will not encourage, is very widely indulged in. It is quite impossible for the law to put it down ; it is plain that, in spite of any enactment that might be passed against it, men would still yield to the indulgence, and therefore the law punishes those who play unfairly. No man would willingly play with a cheat, neither would any man in possession of his senses knowingly go with a diseased woman. The cases are analogous ; why should not the law insist in both on fair play, that what is actually given should correspond with what is professed to be given ; and why should the law punish the individual taking advantage of human weakness in one case, and not in another ?

We have, then, in the law against unfair gaming the principle admitted that punishment may be meted out to those who in immoral transactions, which the law takes no other cognizance of, act in a manner injurious to others. Although the victims of the unfair play are themselves engaged in an immoral pursuit, and have thus exposed themselves, through their own fault, to evil machinations, those who take an unfair advantage of them are punished. But here again we find a difference ; the law does not interfere until the crime has been committed. The law attempts no surveillance of gamblers, but this is because the law will not attempt impossibilities, and it would be impossible for the police to exercise any surveillance over persons unknown to them. It may be objected that in the proposed registration of prostitutes, a whole class will be placed under certain disabilities, quite irrespectively of any given individuals comprising that class, being in such a state as in the particular case to make inspection necessary. To this it may, I think, be fairly answered that when persons commit themselves to a course of life which may, and in the majority of cases does, actually render them dangerous to the public health, the law may reasonably interfere with their liberty, so far as to insure that as little evil as possible may result to the state from their immoral practices ; in fact, we may go a step further, and say that it is only right that this should be done, and that personal liberty and personal rights must be in all cases subservient to the public welfare. Compulsory vaccination is a case in point : here the law interferes plainly and directly with the liberty of the subject ; parents may dislike to have their children vaccinated, and it may be that in nine cases out of ten the precaution is superfluous ; still there is a certain danger that must be guarded against, and private inclination and opinion must yield to the exigencies of public safety.

The laws for the suppression of betting-houses establish another principle, which is, that persons who will persist in doing an immoral thing, must not do it in such a manner as to place temptation in the way of the thoughtless and ignorant, and, by a parity of reasoning, the law may insist that if women will pursue the shameful trade of prostitution, they must do so in such a manner as not to place temptation in the way of those who might otherwise abstain from immorality. The laws protecting minors from dealing with their property or binding themselves by contracts, and married women from being sued for debt, or dealing with their property, except under certain conditions, furnish a further instance of protection being afforded by the state to persons in an otherwise defenceless condition. The young and inexperienced are peculiarly liable to yield to the temptations of harlots and to suffer the evils incident thereto : for their protection, therefore, if for no other reason, the law may rightly place restrictions upon prostitutes. Further than this, large numbers of the lower classes are, as we have seen, almost forced by circumstances into a vicious mode of life. Surely it is not too much to ask the law to protect them so far as possible from the evils attending the accident of birth. We have thus far argued the case, merely from the point of view of protecting others ; may we not add a plea on behalf of these unhappy women themselves ? Is it not a worthy object to force these wretched creatures to pay some attention to cleanliness and health, to bring healing and elevating influences within their reach, to raise them, if not to virtue, at least from the lowest depths of degradation, to bring to them relief from suffering and help in distress ? For the sake of these wretched women, no less than on behalf of the rest of the community, this act of mercy should, it seems to me, be passed. One other instance of interference for the public good with private liberty must not be unnoticed : the Habitual Criminals' Bill which, while these sheets are passing through the press, has received the sanction of the legislature, strongly asserts this principle. Under its provisions, persons may be committed to prison, not for overt acts of crime brought home to them by regular legal process, but because they are known to be leading lawless and predatory lives. No principle is more clear or more jealously asserted than that every man shall be presumed to be innocent until proved to be guilty ; but here the burden of proof is shifted, and guilt is presumed until innocence can be shown. This Bill, and especially, perhaps, the clause relating to receivers of stolen goods, is a far more arbitrary enactment than the measure that we are considering. The laws restraining nuisances and compelling unwholesome and noisome trades to be carried on in such places and in such a manner as to interfere as little as possible with the health and convenience of the community are clearly restrictions for the public good upon private liberty, as also are the laws permitting the compulsory surrender of private property for the public advantage. I think that I have now said enough to show that the principles involved in this measure are already sanctioned and acted upon in numerous instances. A paternal government, as it is called, is intolerable to English instincts, and will ever, I hope, remain impossible in this country. People must be left to a great extent to reap the bitter consequences of sin and folly, but the principle lying at the very root of the existence of society is, that for the common good and for the advantages obtainable by this means only, each member of the state must be content to be deprived of the power to do exactly as he pleases— that is, must surrender for the sake of social order a portion of his freedom. So much for the arguments that may be adduced against the proposed legislation on the ground of interfering with the liberty of the subject. But after all, what is this liberty? It is not liberty, but wanton licence. It is not freedom, but lawless indulgence.

"They talk, sir," says Dr. Guthrie, "of the liberty of the subject. Let no man confound the liberty of the subject with licence and licentiousness, and I hold that the worst enemy of liberty is he who does so confound them. Why, the liberty is all on the side of evil-doers. I know many parents in Edinburgh who tremble to send their young men, even on lawful business, through the streets at night ; I know of others who refused to live in certain parts of the town, otherwise most desirable, on account of the temptation thrown in the way of the younger members of the family. Why should this be tolerated ? Why should the liberty of the well-doing be encroached on and circumscribed by the licentiousness of evil-doers? Our magistrates should exercise the law—should clear the streets of every one of these infamous women, and make them at least decent, if they cannot make them moral and virtuous. On the Continent no such offence to decency is seen. These women are not allowed to walk the streets ; and as to saying, 'You might perhaps take up a good person in place of a bad,' the real truth, sir, is, there is not one of these wretched women in Edinburgh but is as well known to the police as the way to the police office—not one."*

With the objection that recognition and regulation make the law an accomplice in sin, I have already dealt ; I will only add this one remark. The law is cognizant of the existence of prostitution. It is known that thousands gain their bread by lives of infamy ; the evils incident to and arising from their calling, also, are well known. May it not be urged with at least equal truth that the law that permits without restraining is in reality an accomplice, and chargeable with the evils which it refuses to remedy. "Am I my brother's keeper ?" was the excuse for himself, offered by the first murderer, and is virtually said by all who see suffering and wrong, and pass by on the other side. Let us beware lest in endeavouring to avoid a sin, we do not fall into a greater. The suffering shame and ruin ascend from the pitiless streets and haunts of misery to the gates of heaven, and cry there for vengeance, not only on those who wring from broken hearts their guilty pleasures, but also on those who, wrapping close around them the cloak of self-righteousness, and shutting up their bowels of compassion from the sorrow that they needs must see, refuse to make even an effort to avert it, or to raise the arm, which if stretched forth, might save.

* "Daily Telegraph," 1st July, 1862.

After all, the question resolves itself to one of common sense. Does the Contagious Diseases Act, so far as tried, work well? I appeal with confidence to results. *Si monumentum quæris circumspice.*

Remarks on the cases admitted into the London Female Lock Hospital during the year 1867. *By James R. Lane, F.R.C.S., Surgeon to St. Mary's and the Lock Hospitals.*

" At the present time, when the propriety of legislative measures for the diminution of venereal disease is beginning to attract the serious attention of the public, some particulars respecting the patients admitted into the Female Lock Hospital during the past year may not be without interest.

" The hospital now contains one hundred and thirty beds, thirty of which are allotted to patients admitted in the ordinary way on their own voluntary application, this being the largest number which the funds of the hospital, derived from charitable contributions, enable the governors to support ; while the remaining hundred are maintained by the Government, and are appropriated to patients sent from the military districts of Woolwich, Chatham, and Aldershot, after compulsory inspection under the Contagious Diseases Prevention Act. At the beginning of the year, only forty beds were retained by the War Office for this purpose ; but the number was increased by degrees, till it reached one hundred in September, and will shortly be still further increased to one hundred and twenty.

" The total number of cases admitted during the year was 877, of which 169 were ordinary, and 708 were government patients. The practice of the hospital has, therefore, afforded a good opportunity of comparing these two classes of cases, between which, it will be seen, there are several points of contrast, exemplifying the effect of inspection, or the want of it, on the character of the disease, which are well worthy of attention.

" Of the ordinary patients, 158 have been discharged cured or materially relieved ; two have died ; and nine were still in the hospital when this return was made up (Jan. 31st). Of the two deaths, one was from pneumonia ; the other was from a sloughing bubo in an old and broken-down workhouse patient. Of the government patients, all have left the hospital ' free from contagious disease,' with the exception of four, who were discharged on account of their being in an advanced stage of pregnancy, and two who were still in hospital on January 31st.

" The period of residence averaged, on the whole number of cases, 34·5 days ; but the average of the ordinary cases was 50 days, while that of the government cases did not exceed 31 days.

" The cases may be separated into two principal subdivisions, headed syphilis and gonorrhœa ; the former comprising all ulcers of the genital organs, indurated or otherwise, suppurating buboes, etc., together with all secondary or tertiary affections ; the latter comprising uterine and vaginal discharges, warts, labial abscess, simple inflammatory swellings and excoriations of the labia, and their attendant non-virulent buboes. This division may not be free from scientific objection ; but it seems practically the most convenient for the present purpose. The proportion which these two classes of disease bore to each other in the two sets of patients was strikingly different; syphilis accounting for 80 per cent. of the ordinary, but for not more than 41·5 per cent. of the government patients. The average stay in hospital of the syphilitic cases was, in the ordinary patients, fifty-three days; in the government patients, forty-one days. The stay of the gonorrhœal patients was, in the former, thirty-six days; in the latter, twenty-three days.

" The syphilitic cases may be further divided into—

" 1. Primary syphilitic sores, more or less recently contracted, accompanied or not with suppurating bubo. Of these, there were 56 ordinary and 168 government cases, with an average residence in hospital of forty-nine and thirty-seven days respectively.

" 2. Chronic ulcerations of the genital organs, of long standing, and occurring for the most part in those who had long been leading a life of prostitution. Of these, there were six ordinary and 32 government cases, with an average residence of fifty-five and sixty-seven days respectively.

" 3. Secondary affections; viz., mucous tubercles, cutaneous eruptions, superficial ulcerations of mouth and fauces, iritis, etc. Of these, there were 54 ordinary and 77 government cases, with an average stay of fifty-six and thirty-seven days respectively.

" 4. Tertiary affections; viz., ulcerative skin-disease, deep ulcerations of the throat, affections of bone and periosteum, gummatous tumours, etc. Of these, there were 19 ordinary and 17 government cases, with an average stay in hospital of fifty-two and fifty-five days.

	Proportion per cent. of admitted cases.		Average number of days in hospital.	
	Ordinary patients.	Government patients.	Ordinary patients.	Government patients.
Syphilis	80	41·5	53	41
Gonorrhœa..................	20	58·5	36	23

" Further analysis of the syphilitic cases :—

	Proportion per cent.		Average number of days in hospital.	
	Ordinary patients.	Government patients.	Ordinary patients.	Government patients.
Recent primary sores ...	41·5	57·1	49	37
Chronic ulceration	4·5	10·5	55	69
Secondary disease	40·	26·2	56	37
Tertiary disease	14·	5·8	52	55

" It seems tolerably clear, from the facts above stated, that venereal diseases in women subjected to compulsory inspection are so far less severe than in women applying voluntarily, that they require only an average of thirty-one days' hospital treatment for their cure; whereas the latter require the much longer period of fifty days. But the difference is really greater than this; for the ordinary patients frequently leave the hospital by their own wish when their severer symptoms have subsided, or are made out-patients, in order to make room for others, in consequence of the urgent demand for in-patient accommodation; while the government patients cannot leave, under penalty of imprisonment, until the surgeon certifies them as being perfectly free from contagious venereal disease.

"It is also evident that, under a system of inspection, a very large number of women suffering from gonorrhœa—i.e., vaginal and uterine discharges—are isolated and placed under medical treatment, who, if left to themselves, would be pursuing their vocation, and spreading disease in all directions. Thus, of the government patients, 58½ per cent. were suffering from gonorrhœa, while of the others only 20 per cent. were so classified; and the latter were for the most part admitted in consequence of some complication, such as warts, excoriations, or inflammatory bubo, and consequently required an average of thirty-six days' treatment, instead of twenty-three days, which was found sufficient for the government cases. In the government cases, these complications were much less frequent—the majority of them being, with the exception of their discharge, in perfect health; and many were not aware that anything at all was the matter with them, until they were required by the police to submit themselves to examination. In fact, purulent discharges in the female are, as a rule, attended with so little pain or inconvenience, that the patient has but slight inducement to apply spontaneously for relief; or, if she does apply, she is treated as an out-patient, either by her own choice, or in consequence of the paucity of in-patient hospital accommodation. On the other hand, the much greater severity of gonorrhœa and its complications in the male render it of the greatest importance that females suffering from this form of disease should be discovered at an early period, and not only be subjected to proper treatment, but be prevented from doing mischief while their treatment is going on.

"Further, by an analysis of the syphilitic cases, it will be seen that recent primary ulcers formed a larger proportion of the government than of the ordinary cases, constituting 57 per cent. of the syphilitic admissions in the one, against 41 per cent. in the other class. With respect to constitutional syphilis, on the other hand, the preponderance was largely the other way; secondary disease forming in the ordinary patients 40 per cent. of the syphilitic cases, as compared with 26·2; and tertiary disease 14 per cent., as compared with 5·8.

"The primary sores were decidedly milder in character in the government than in the other patients. This is sufficiently evidenced by the shorter period required for their cure—viz., an average of thirty-seven days, as compared with forty-nine. It is also especially worthy of remark, that phagedæna, a complication arising for the most part from destitution or neglect of treatment, has been rare in the government wards; while in the general wards it has not only been more frequent, but also much more severe, and in one instance fatal. Suppurating buboes, again, have been much less frequent in the government than in the other patients.

" With respect to the chronic ulcerations of the genitals, which I have separated from ordinary primary sores, these occurred more frequently in the government than in the other patients, in the proportion of 10·9 to 4·5 per cent. Cases of this kind were an exception to the general rule, in being more severe in the government than in the other patients, occupying sixty-seven days, as compared with fifty-five days, for their treatment. They were characterised by extensive ulcerations about the entrance of the vagina, often at the urethral orifice, and extending along the urethral canal ; with œdema and hypertrophy of the labia and nymphæ, these parts being often marked with cicatrices, and perforated with old ulcerations, often accompanied by condylomatous excrescences and ulceration about the anus and rectum, and not unfrequently recto-vaginal communications. With the aid of rest, regular diet and habits, and suitable applications, these ulcerations gradually heal ; but, when the patient returns to her old occupation, the cicatrices give way, and relapses constantly take place ; so that many of these women have been admitted a third, fourth, or fifth time into the hospital. When patients from Woolwich were first sent to the Lock in 1864, I was greatly struck by the number of cases of this kind which presented themselves, as compared with what I had been in the habit of seeing ; and it would appear that they are more frequent in women constantly cohabiting with soldiers, than in others—I presume, on account of the more dissipated and vicious habits of this unfortunate class, and the difficulty which they formerly had in procuring proper medical treatment. I believe that these lamentable cases are almost entirely the result of neglect ; and that, under a system of inspection properly carried out, they would rarely occur, as they would be arrested by treatment at an early stage. They are certainly becoming much less common in the government wards of the Lock Hospital, and it may be hoped that by degrees the supply of them from the inspected districts will be exhausted. They are met with chiefly in the older women, or in women who, if not older in age, are old in prostitution.

" With respect to constitutional syphilis, it will be seen that the proportion was greatest in the ordinary patients. Taking secondary and tertiary disease together, it accounts for 54 per cent. of the syphilitic admissions in them, against 32 per cent. in the others. The secondary cases were also much more severe in the ordinary wards, occupying, on an average, fifty-six days, as compared with thirty-seven days, for their treatment. In fact, the secondary disease in the government patients often consisted only of slight mucous tubercles on the labia, which rapidly disappeared under treatment. The tertiary cases call for no particular remark. They were less frequent in the government patients, in the proportion of 5·8 to 14 per cent. ; but in the duration of treatment there was no material difference.

" It may be affirmed, then, that a system of compulsory inspection of women known to be prostitutes, associated as it must necessarily be with adequate provision for their seclusion and treatment when found to be diseased, is of the greatest advantage to the unfortunate women themselves ; that the early treatment which it necessitates has a most beneficial influence on the character and duration of their disease, that it saves many from local mutilation, and many from permanent loss of health.   On the other hand, women of this class, when left to shift for themselves, do not for the most part apply for relief till their disease has assumed serious proportions, or until it interferes with their means of obtaining a livelihood.   In the slighter cases of syphilis, both primary and secondary, and in cases of uterine and vaginal discharges, they can follow their profession for an indefinite period without any considerable pain or inconvenience.   In fact, many of the government patients professed to be quite ignorant that anything was the matter with them until it was discovered by examination.   Is it surprising, then, that venereal disease is rife amongst our population, when it is officially recorded that in London alone there are 6000 women known to the police as prostitutes of the lowest description, and classed by them with thieves and other bad characters (see *Blue Book*, entitled " Judicial Statistics," 1865) ; when this, on the lowest estimate, does not constitute half the number of those gaining their living on the streets, and when 150 beds represent the utmost hospital accommodation afforded in the whole of London for females afflicted with venereal disease (see Report of the Committee of the Harveian Society, 1867) ?

" It is satisfactory to know that, as a rule, the women do not regard their compulsory examination and detention with feelings of objection or dislike ; I have questioned many of them on this point, and I have found that for the most part they are well contented with the system. They have sense enough to see that it is greatly to their interest to have a refuge at all times open to them when they become diseased ; and, though they are often weary of their detention in hospital for what they believe to be trifling causes, they are easily satisfied when they are made to understand that no one is interested in detaining them a day longer than is really necessary.

" In the above remarks, I have endeavoured to point out from facts which have come under my own observation, how far the present Contagious Diseases Act is beneficial to the females subjected to its operation, by contrasting their condition with that of patients presenting themselves at the same institution under the voluntary system.   I am unable, from my own personal knowledge, to say how far it has been effectual in diminishing disease among the soldiers and sailors, for whose advantage it was mainly intended ; but it has been pretty clearly shown by the investigations of Mr. Berkeley Hill, recently published in this Journal, that, if it has not everywhere done as much as was expected of it, the fault has not been in the Act itself, but in the incomplete manner in which it has been carried out, and the too limited area of its operation."—*British Medical Journal, February* 15, 1868.

(This has since been enlarged to 10 miles.)

From discussing the advantages derivable from a systematic supervision of prostitutes, we pass on to the question how far it is possible to control their appearance and deportment in public.   In dealing with this part of my subject, I propose, first to consider what steps, if any, should be taken with regard to the various places to which they resort. These naturally divide themselves into two distinct heads — the first comprises the casinos, music-halls, and public gardens, such as Cremorne; the second, the class of places known as night-houses. I must here, again, remind the reader that prostitution must always exist, that it cannot be suppressed by law, and that no measures taken against it will be wise and beneficial which do not recognise this fact. It cannot be denied that the existence of places where prostitutes congregate is an enormous evil. The attempt to suppress them all would, however, be as impolitic and quixotic as the attempt to suppress prostitution itself. All that we can do, is to render the public haunts of prostitutes as little injurious to the public morals as their nature admits of. Although this is undoubtedly true, it does not follow that every place is to be tolerated. It will be seen that the two divisions above referred to are very different in character, the one existing for other purposes besides that of affording facilities to the practice of prostitution, the other for this purpose alone. I think that we may lay down and act upon the following principle, that all places of which the only use is to enable women to meet with customers should be rigorously repressed, but that such places as exist for other objects, such as music or dancing, although it may be true of them that they are supported mainly by base women and their associates, must be tolerated.* The first division, therefore, must be permitted to continue as at present.† With regard to the second, this again divides itself

---

* For reasons given (page 231) I except the places known as accommodation-houses.

† I have had so good an exponent of my views in the following article, that I re-produce it :—

"THE ARGYLL ROOMS.—Public decency is in a difficulty, and it seems that the remedy is worse than the disease. We appear to be in that condition which the Roman historian has described as the vice of a falling State—we can neither endure our vices nor their cures. Last year, in a transport of moral and popular indignation, we closed the Argyll Rooms because they were the focus and complex of all metro-politan vice. This year we open them, because, on the whole, it is better that the vicious population should be brought together than that it should be let loose on society. There is antecedently much to be said for either view of the moral question. A whole cloud of evidence was brought, on the recent occasion of the proprietor of the Rooms applying for a license, to show that the streets have been in a worse state since the lorettes of London were deprived of their customary home, than when they had a local habitation. And, had the evidence stopped here, it might have proved some-thing. But, unfortunately, the proprietor went beyond this. The justification of such an institution is that it is a moral cesspool. But it cannot be at the same time a cess-pool and a healing fountain. Evidence was tendered that the Argyll Rooms were frequented by respectable tradesmen and their wives. Five or six hundred noblemen and gentlemen are said to have offered, or to have been ready to offer, their testimony to the admirable way in which the Rooms were conducted. The music is of the most scientific character, order and decorum find their chosen home in Windmill Street, and the evidence at least suggests that casinos divide with the pulpit the duty of pre-serving the general social health of London. This is proving a little too much. Had the argument confined itself to the one simple ground that immorality must be, and that on the whole it is better that immorality and its haunts should be under decent and responsible management and control, we own to a growing conviction that it was right to grant the license—not because the Argyll Rooms are a moral institution, but because, so long as they are open under the care and responsibility of a respectable, or at least substantial person, public morality suffers less than when harlotry un-

into the night-house proper, such as Kate Hamilton's,* Rose Young's, Coney's, &c., &c., where refreshments are supplied without a license,

---

attached turns a whole quarter of London to an unlicensed Argyll Rooms and something worse.

"The Argyll Rooms, and casinos generally, are known to be the haunts of the *femmes libres* of society. This is, if fairly stated, their justification. The objection urged to licensing them is that we do evil that good may ensue—that we openly recognise, and so far authenticate and stamp with the authority of the State and Government, a flagrant violation of the moral law. It is said that we establish, and so far encourage, immorality as soon as we recognise it. Many fallacies are involved in this objection. To recognise a social evil is not to justify it. We know that many physical diseases are quite incurable ; but shall it be said that we authenticate them and welcome them because, utterly powerless to cure them, we do the next best thing, by diminishing their virus? Has the State moral duties or not? If it has, if it is bound to provide for public decency, it must, in the grave matter of sexual immorality, do one of two things—either attempt utterly to prohibit sins against the seventh commandment, and to enforce the prohibition, or so far tolerate them as at least to admit their existence by dealing with them. To talk of prohibiting prostitution and the like is absurd. What there is left for the State is to deal with this and other social evils so as to render them less generally noxious. By dishonestly affecting to deny their existence, we commit an offence not only against truth but against policy. The State is not as God, whose eyes are too pure to behold iniquity. The State is itself not a Divine institution, nor a partaker of the Divine nature. The creature and impersonation of facts and of society must deal with facts and society as they are. It may be quite right for an individual—and it is a safe rule for a single conscience—to take all consequences, and, instead of doing the least of two evils, to do no evil, whatever good may come of it. But the State is not an individual—it must provide the greatest good for the greatest number, and often this may only be by taking the least of two evils. Public morality is more confined in its range than individual duty. It acts upon motives necessarily less heroic—it cannot be so severe and austere in its consistency. If it cannot prohibit prostitution, its first duty is to make the best of it. We have made the worst of it by the impolicy of affecting not to see it.

"If, therefore, we are to accept the licensing of the Argyll Rooms as a public recognition of vice to the extent of placing it under public control, and as a step, not to the system of licensing immoral houses as on the Continent, but to the public and authoritative control of immorality, we should be disposed to accept with some satisfaction the decision of the Middlesex magistrates. What can't be cured must be alleviated. And if, as we have said, we must legislate for the greatest good of the greatest number, it is better that some hundred females of loose life should be entertained for a few hours in a single room, than that they should be encouraged to prowl about the streets. Whatever thins the loose population of the Haymarket and Regent Street is so far a social gain. We ought to regard the interests, not of the profligate, but of the respectable. At all events, when vice is concentrated in Windmill Street, men must go in cold blood to seek it out, while, flaunting on the *pavé* it tempts the young and unwary. Few except extreme profligates would go to the recognised haunts of vice ; but many fall under the public temptation of the streets who would avoid it in its own dancing and drinking saloons.

" At any rate, the lesson taught by the change of opinion on the part of the Middlesex magistrates since last year is, that it will not do to attempt a system of prosecuting these vicious places by instalments. There is already power in the common law to hunt down immorality by units and in detail. All immoral houses can be suppressed by the parochial authorities—all street-walkers may be arrested by the police. But to carry out the law is simply impossible. What is cut down in one street grows up in the next—the weeds are only transported from Norton Street to Brompton. It is of no use to prohibit—all that we can do is to regulate. We had rather not see a parochial crusade against immorality, for the evil will only be transferred to the other side of the boundary. Let authority deal with any offence against public decency ; let the magistrate, or the police, receive additional powers to repress public offences ; but the failure of the attempt to put down the Argyll Rooms shows that we are beginning to understand that to control is better than an abortive attempt to prohibit."
—*Saturday Review*, October 16, 1853.

and after the regular hours, and from which the police are so far as possible excluded, and the supper-rooms and cafés in and about the Haymarket from which the police are not excluded, and in which refreshments are not supplied without a license; it would be as unreasonable to deprive a prostitute of a place for obtaining refreshment as to close against her all places of amusement; these latter, therefore, must be left unclosed, at all events for the present. The case of night-houses, however, is very different; they exist only for the purposes of vice, and should be put down with the strong hand. We have already seen (page 76) how difficult it is for the police to suppress these places in the present state of the law. I submit that it would be well to deal with them in precisely the same way as by the Habitual Criminals' Bill the persons obnoxious to its provisions may be dealt with; there is no question as to their character, the only difficulty being, to obtain such evidence of it as shall amount to legal proof and justify conviction. It seems to me that if the principle of the Habitual Criminals' Bill were adopted in their case, and the burden of proof shifted from the police to the ostensible proprietor, their suppression would be easily obtained.

From the night-house to the house of ill-fame the transition is easy. This latter class comprises, as we have seen, two distinct species of brothel, the brothel proper, or dress house, where women are kept by the proprietor, and farmed for his benefit, and the accommodation house, where in return for a moderate payment the convenience of temporary shelter is afforded to chance companions. The first of these houses should, in my opinion, be utterly suppressed. I postpone, however, to the chapter on prevention, the discussion of this question. The second must, I think, be tolerated, and for the same reason that prostitution must be tolerated because their suppression is either impossible or attended with worse results than the mischiefs which they occasion. They are in fact rather the result of evil than the cause. True it is that in France they are viewed with more disfavour than the *maisons de filles*, but that is because the French system makes no efforts for the amelioration of the prostitute, but recognises prostitution as a necessary evil, and those who follow it as a calling, as persons forming a certain defined class whom it is necessary to render amenable in the greatest possible degree to regulation; it therefore directs all its efforts to producing centralization; this process is assisted by the *maisons de filles* with their confined inhabitants, and retarded by the *maisons de passe* with their floating occupants. In England we recognise prostitution as a necessary evil in the same sense only as we recognise poverty, crime, and disease as necessary evils. The object of those who advocate regulation in England is not to create a class bound down by hard and fast limits, whose life and development are blighted and ruined, for the supposed advantage of the state. We want no "martyrs to sensuality." We admit the fact that prostitution must exist, and admitting it, and

---

* The first-named has, I believe, been closed for some years past; I fancy that the others still survive; but however that may be, I mention notorious names for the purpose of indicating clearly not particular houses that may or may not have passed away or changed their names, but a class that certainly exists.

feeling its power for evil, we deprecate the policy of ignoring it, and demand that limits be fixed which it must not pass, and laws laid down for it that it must obey. We therefore suggest that those who are known to lead this life of shame, and to have no other means of subsistence than those afforded by prostitution, should be registered ; and as the only way of checking the fatal evils arising to the community from their mode of life, that those persons whose names are found in the register should be compelled to submit to inspection. We know that the class must exist ; we know the dangers to which by its existence we are exposed ; we desire to limit those dangers, and to deprive the class so far as possible of the power of inflicting physical injuries.

But we desire more than this, we desire to ameliorate the condition of the individuals comprising that class, and to lessen their numbers. We see that the life of prostitution is in the majority of cases temporary only ; we desire not to make it permanent. We see that prostitutes, (p. 49) as a rule, return to the ranks of honest people and become absorbed in honest society. We wish therefore to ameliorate their condition, to elevate their habits of thought and mode of life, so that their return may be assisted and accelerated, and that as little as may be of degradation may be absorbed in their absorption. The method, whatever it may be, by which our object can be best achieved, is evidently something very different from centralization. The motive, therefore, that makes the *maison de passe* in France peculiarly obnoxious to the law does not exist in England.

One other principle I may allude to here, which should be firmly held by all advocates of regulation, and should accompany the one that I have just stated, which is, that prostitution must so far as possible be kept a thing apart and by itself. Society must, so far as possible, be secured against its contaminating presence. We desire to give all possible access of good and helping influences to the prostitute, and to draw her back from her life of sin, but we must be careful in doing this not to give prostitution access to society. Fornication must not come to be regarded here as a *naughty* thing which everybody does.

I may now repeat and examine the proposition that houses of accommodation must be tolerated because their suppression is either impossible or attended with worse results than the mischiefs which they occasion. The main objections to them are the following : they afford facilities for the illicit intercourse of the sexes ; they keep in existence a class of people directly interested in the extension of prostitution ; it will be more difficult for the police to make complete registers, if places are tolerated to which women can take their customers, instead of having only their own houses to take them to. To the first objection I answer, that it proves too much. Prostitution being permitted to exist, houses in which prostitutes live must also be permitted ; to these they can take their customers, and it seems to me to make little difference whether the rooms to which men can be taken are regularly rented by these women, or by other people ; no greater mischief seems likely to arise (except that arising from the other objections that I have stated) to the woman, her customer, or the public, from the existence of houses of accommodation than from the existence of houses where prostitutes live.   The second objection is more serious ; it is no doubt most undesirable that any people should exist interested in the continuance and increase of prostitution, or that any persons should gain advantage or earn their livelihood from the sin of others.   On this subject, however, we are endeavouring to attain, not the desirable but the possible ; the only legislation for which we can hope, is a balance of evil.

Rigorous enactments against bawds and panders will enable us to prevent the keepers of houses of accommodation from turning them into dress-houses, or brothels proper, and from promoting the extension which they desire of an evil system.   While, as to the third objection, though we must regret any circumstance that may render more difficult the arduous duties which will, under the proposed system of regulation, fall to the lot of the police, we feel bound to say that any objections of this sort are of a secondary nature only ; that although they must, if possible, be obviated, when this cannot be done the difficulty must be cheerfully accepted and means found to meet it.

Having disposed of the objections that may be urged to the toleration of houses of accommodation, I may now consider the reasons that seem to render their repression impolitic, and these fortunately come within the range of experience.   We find that since the law has been put in force against these houses their number has been sensibly reduced ; on the other hand, hotels, restaurants, and coffee-houses have been to a large extent pressed into the service of prostitution ; thus is introduced the very mischief against which we desire to guard, namely that of bringing prostitution and society *en rapport*, so to speak.   However deplorable it may be that accommodation houses should exist, it is infinitely more undesirable that through their extinction every coffee-house should become a brothel, and that hotels and restaurants should be generally, and as a matter of course, used for immoral purposes.   In addition to this, any law for the suppression of these houses can be easily evaded, and in their absence means will be surely found to meet in some more irregular and objectionable way the requirements of vicious people.*   Legislation, then, on this point is at best useless, and should therefore be carefully avoided.

The regulation of prostitutes' appearance and behaviour in the streets is the only other topic to which allusion need be made in this chapter. The police have, as we have seen (page 75), power to arrest, if necessary, persons guilty of indecent and disorderly conduct in the streets. It seems hardly possible to interdict the prostitute from the liberty of using the public thoroughfares, which she naturally enjoys in common with the rest of the community, and it is a question whether the right can be denied to any one person of civilly addressing any other.   These natural rights, however, of using the streets and addressing the passers-by give rise to the evils of loitering and solicitation.

The condition of our streets—although a marked improvement seems

---

* This objection is not an imaginary one.   I understand that a limited liability company has already been started for providing its members with the accommodation they desire ; doubtless more will follow.

to have been effected in the interval that has elapsed since the appearance of the first edition of this work—is still far from satisfactory, and it is worthy of consideration whether, notwithstanding the right to which I have above referred, some further improvement may not be made in this respect. Of pertinacious solicitation there appears to be little or none, unless, perhaps, occasionally late at night. Against solicitation every man has the remedy in his own hands ; it is, no doubt, a nuisance to which he should not be exposed, but as the absence of rejoinder usually suffices to repress it, and in the rare cases in which it proves insufficient, an effectual appeal can always be made to a policeman, it seems better to leave things as they are, at all events for the present, than to run the risk of introducing by stringent enactments more serious evils. It is, moreover, a question of detail, fit rather to be dealt with by the Police Commissioners than worthy to be made the subject of legislation. This last remark applies with equal force to the question as to the best means of dealing with the mischief of loitering. It is to be met by applying to it some recognized principle rather than by direct legislation. I must, however, point out that certain localities are far worse than others : the question may arise whether in such of these as may happen to be merely bye-streets, any measures should be taken for the prevention of loitering, but it seems to me that all the principal thoroughfares should be protected from this nuisance, and this could be accomplished by a little firmness and tact on the part of the police.* Of one thing we must not lose sight, and that is, the necessity of giving no opportunity to the police of indulging in acts of petty tyranny. The majority of the force are, I believe, men of good temper and behaviour ; but no one acquainted with the streets of London can be ignorant that the instances of bullying and overbearing conduct towards unfortunate costermongers, applewomen, and others are far more frequent than could be wished.† The first thing necessary, therefore, is, that the police authorities shall tell off for the duty of preventing loitering, those men only on whom they can implicitly rely—men who will act up to their authority, but not exceed it, and who will perform their duties not only with firmness, but also with gentleness, moderation, and discretion. The next step is to give these men full instructions to prevent the obstruction of the thoroughfares. The duty is, no doubt, a somewhat difficult one, but the exercise of common sense will suffice in the majority of cases to prevent the commission of any grave errors. "I have often," the late Sir P. Laurie

---

* I may mention the street connecting Leicester Square with the bottom of Regent Street as a thoroughfare infested with loitering prostitutes from whose presence it should be freed, the Burlington Arcade as a place the policy of interfering with which is open to question.

† A case of very recent occurrence illustrates and justifies my anxiety that no unnecessary power may be intrusted to injudicious officers. A respectable married woman passing through a locality much infested by prostitutes, and ignorant of her way, asked a passer-by for direction ; she was immediately pounced upon by an over-zealous constable, and, despite her explanations and the remonstrances of the man to whom she spoke, was summarily walked off to the police station. What satisfaction to her for so gross an outrage was the severe censure ultimately administered to the policeman ?

once observed, " discharged unfortunate women against what appeared to be the reasoning of the police, that if a woman after having walked down Fleet Street dared to walk back again, she must be walked off to prison." And the worthy alderman was undoubtedly right. If some modern Dr. Johnson should propose to walk down Fleet Street, and having walked down should propose to walk back again, and should give like effect to the last proposition as to the first, and should repeat the operation a hundred times in the course of the day, " the active and intelligent officer" who should attempt to interfere with him would expose himself to the charge of being foolhardy and unreasonable. In the same way a cluster of the gentler sex round windows dedicated to the display of bonnets, robes, or jewelry should not be wantonly disturbed. If, in the place of the learned doctor on the one hand, and the fair cluster on the other, we find a portly harlot or a collection of vicious women, the same observations will hold good. The pavement is free to all: to use, however, not to abuse. The book-making fraternity are not allowed to pursue their avocations in the streets,—why should greater indulgence be extended to prostitutes ? The action taken against betting men perhaps supplies the rule of which we are in search ; and it may be safe to lay down that, making allowance for the difference of pursuit, the police should, in those cases in which they would interfere with these latter, interfere also with prostitutes, who should certainly be prevented from turning their promenades into short beats, and making any leading thoroughfare their daily haunt. The foregoing suggestions seem to me sufficient as regards the regulation of the streets in the day-time and evening. As the night advances, the number of disorderly characters present in the streets increases ; this is especially the case in those nearest to the places of amusement frequented by prostitutes and their companions. We have seen that the neighbourhood of the Haymarket has acquired an evil notoriety, and I think it is clear that the state of things existing in this and similar localities should not be tolerated. Although I have admitted that the liberty of using the streets should not be denied to women merely on account of their being prostitutes, there would, I think, be no harshness or undue interference with the liberty of the subject, in requiring such persons to withdraw from them within half-an-hour after the time at which the Argyll Rooms and similar places of amusement are usually closed. Some such measure as this seems absolutely necessary to prevent the continuance of a grave scandal, and we must not forget that if we make the streets less disreputable, we shall in doing so diminish both the opportunity for and the temptation to impure indulgence.

CHAPTER IX.

AMELIORATION OF PROSTITUTION.

THE amelioration of prostitution has a twofold operation. It should be directed to the healing and cure of prostitutes suffering from disease, and also to accomplishing their social and moral elevation. Up to a very recent period I had believed that this was the wish of all interested in the welfare of women in the United Kingdom. My readers may imagine with what deep regret I read in the last issued report (the 11th) of the Medical Officer of the Privy Council his official enunciation of the startling doubt " *Whether the venereal diseases of the civil population are henceforth to be deemed matter of public concern ?*"

From the latest report of the Committee of the House of Commons, on the Contagious Diseases Act we learn that this measure has been most successful. The report, dated July, 1869, says that—

4. "Although the Act has only been in operation two years and a half, and at some stations only seven months, strong testimony is borne to the benefits, both in a moral and sanitary point of view, which have already resulted from it.

5. "Prostitution appears to have diminished, its worst features to have been softened, and its physical evils abated."—P. iii.

Mr. Simon, while coinciding in the view " *that prostitutes having relations with soldiers in garrison towns should be supervised by government,*" is disinclined to extend the benefit of the Contagious Diseases Act to the civil population. He says :—

" Of the venereal diseases of the civil population, English sanitary law has not hitherto taken any special cognizance ; and whether this neutral state of the law ought or ought not to be abandoned is a separate question, of far more intricacy than seems to be generally imagined, and which on all accounts certainly deserves most careful consideration."—P. 11.

And after giving various reasons which, whatever their intrinsic value may be, are apparently satisfactory to his own mind, thus states the conclusion at which he has arrived :—

" The broad result in my mind from the various above-stated considerations is, that at present I very decidedly refrain from recommending any change in that neutral position which English law has hitherto held in regard of the venereal diseases of the civil population. So far

as my present knowledge enables me to judge, I believe that any departure from that position could do little but embarrass and disappoint."
—P. 16.

"Venereal diseases are, in principle, infections which a man contracts at his own option, and against which he cannot in any degree claim to be protected by action of others—the less so of course as his option is exercised in modes of life contrary to the common good; that thus, *primâ facie* the true policy of Government is to regard the prevention of venereal diseases as matter of exclusively private concern. *Caveat emptor!*"—P. 13.

And again, at page 18, he remarks :—

"Whether the venereal diseases of the civil population are henceforth to be deemed matter of public concern—*whether the civil fornicant may reasonably look to constituted authorities to protect him in his commerce with prostitutes*—is the principle which I conceive to be at stake."

From the above, and many similar passages to be found in this report, it would seem that Mr. Simon conceives the sole object, which people advocating the extension of the Contagious Diseases Act to the civil population have at heart, is to provide immunity from suffering for self-indulgent and vicious men. This narrow conception of the views entertained by others, and of the important issues really at stake, must tend to deprive this report of much of the weight, that might otherwise attach to it.

I must moreover enter my most emphatic protest against the method adopted by Mr. Simon, of stating the question. I feel sure that he would not willingly attribute to those from whom he differs motives which do not actuate them : nor do I believe that he would wilfully raise a false issue ; he has, however, in stating the principle which he conceives to be at stake, fallen into the error of treating as identical two propositions widely different. To the first proposition, and to that alone, we must look for the principle ; and for that I venture to solicit an affirmative answer; for the second, in common with Mr. Simon, and all right-minded men, I demand an indignant negative. The fallacy of stating these two propositions as identical is so transparent, that I should not have noticed it here only that it affords a striking illustration of the deep-rooted prejudice with which this question is unhappily interwoven, which confuses the understanding and judgment of men undeniably upright in their intentions, and possessed of undoubted ability. The first proposition presents us with "a question," to quote Mr. Simon's own words, "of far more intricacy than seems to be generally imagined, and which on all accounts certainly deserves most careful consideration." The second proposition has, so far as I know, never been put forward by any one, and is, in fact, nothing more than an inaccurate statement of one of the many considerations with which we have to deal in coming to our conclusion on the first ; and the proposition put forward by Mr. Simon may be fairly stated thus :—
"Whether the venereal diseases of the civil population are henceforth to be deemed matter of public concern, seeing that one necessary result must be that the civil 'fornicant' will in that case receive a certain amount of state protection in his commerce with prostitutes." Mr. Simon's

second proposition is, in fact, an exaggerated statement of the principal objection to his first. It is, perhaps, unfortunate that any steps taken to stay disease and to alleviate the many evils that are brought by prostitution upon the community must tend to make commune with prostitutes less hazardous; but the real question that we have to consider is whether, seeing the infinite mischief brought upon society by venereal diseases and the action of prostitution generally, such matters should not henceforth be deemed of public concern notwithstanding the comparative immunity from suffering thereby secured for men of loose habits of life. To make the path of sin less dangerous to the sinner is no wish of mine, but I hold that a course fraught with benefit to society and to thousands of miserable women should not be abandoned merely because it entails this consequence with the rest. Towards the conclusion of the article, Mr. Simon again indulges in language, that conveys both an odious imputation on his opponents and an unfair statement of the question at issue between him and them. When he considers " hospitals for prostitutes as elements in a machinery proposed to be constituted by law for giving an artificial security to promiscuous fornication."—Page 20.

Surely scientific vituperation cannot go further than this. Is this the language which one of Mr. Simon's supporters and critics has called vigorous? I trust my readers will agree with me that at least it is not convincing, and to them I confidently appeal to decide for themselves between the objections brought by Mr. Simon against " *State interference to provide for the disinfection of prostitutes,*" and the reasons which I give in this book for the extension of the Contagious Diseases Act to the civil population.

Before considering in detail the objections advanced by Mr. Simon and others to any state interference for the purpose of checking the spread of venereal disorders, it may be worth while to call to mind the principle on which the legislature acts in dealing with questions that concern the public health. I cannot do better than lay before my readers Mr. Simon's excellent statement on this point contained in his report on the " question of consolidating, and bringing into system the laws and administrative agencies which concern the public health," pp. 20 and 21. I shall thus answer Mr. Simon out of his own mouth, and we shall see how far he is himself prepared to support the principle on which in his report he mainly relies that venereal diseases are not *prima facie* matters of Government concern, and how far it is true that those who desire Government interference in the matter are seeking to introduce a novel principle into our legislation :—

" It would, I think, be difficult to over-estimate, in one most important point of view, the progress which during the last few years has been made in sanitary legislation. The principles now affirmed in our statute-book are such as, if carried into full effect, would soon reduce to quite insignificant amount our present very large proportions of preventable disease. It is the almost completely expressed intention of our law that all such states of property and all such modes of personal action or inaction as may be of danger to the public health should be brought within scope of summary procedure and prevention. Large powers have been given to local authorities, the obligation expressly imposed on them, as regards their respective districts, to suppress all kinds of nuisance, and to provide all such works and establishments as the public health primarily requires ; while auxiliary powers have been given, for more or less optional exercise, in matters deemed of less than primary importance to health ; as for baths and wash-houses, common lodging-houses, labourers' lodging-houses, recreation grounds, disinfection-places, hospitals, dead-houses, burial-grounds, &c. And in the interests of health the State has not only, as above, limited the freedom of persons and property in certain common respects : it has also intervened in many special relations. It has interfered between parent and child, not only in imposing limitation on industrial uses of children, but also to the extent of requiring that children shall not be left unvaccinated. It has interfered between employer and employed, to the extent of insisting, in the interests of the latter, that certain sanitary claims shall be fulfilled in all places of industrial occupation. It has interfered between vendor and purchaser ; has put restrictions on the sale and purchase of poisons, has prohibited in certain cases certain commercial supplies of water, and has made it a public offence to sell adulterated food or drink or medicine, or to offer for sale any meat unfit for human food. Its care for the treatment of disease has not been unconditionally limited to treating at the public expense such sickness as may accompany destitution : it has provided that in any sort of epidemic emergency organized medical assistance, not peculiarly for paupers, may be required of local authorities ; and in the same spirit it requires that vaccination at the public cost shall be given gratuitously to every claimant. The above survey might easily be extended by referring to statutes which are only of partial or indirect or subordinate interest to human health ; but, such as it is, it shows beyond question that the legislature regards the health of the people as an interest not less national than personal, and has intended to guard it with all practicable securities against trespasses, casualties, neglects and frauds."

We may see, then, from a simple syllogism that the position taken up by Mr. Simon in his eleventh report (that venereal diseases are not *prima facie* matters of Government concern) is, on his own showing, quite untenable. We will take for our major premiss Mr. Simon's proposition—" All such states of property, and all such modes of personal action, or inaction, as may be of danger to the public health, should be brought within scope of summary procedure and prevention." Our minor premiss will, I think, be admitted by all candid minds to be equally indisputable ; prostitution is such a mode of personal action as may be of danger to the public health ; and this being so, which conclusion is, I ask, the logical one ? Mr. Simon's, prostitution should *not* be brought within scope of summary procedure and prevention, or mine, prostitution *should* be brought within scope, &c. Again, the legislature " regards the health of the people as not less national than personal," and Mr. Simon cannot but agree with me that venereal diseases very seriously affect the people's health ; " but," says Mr. Simon (page 12), "*prima facie*, venereal diseases are not any concern of Government." Is this true ? Is it not clear as noonday that, *prima facie*, venereal diseases are the concern of the Government? It may be very true that certain considerations take the evils resulting from prostitution out of the general rule, but this is a separate question; all I wish to show at present is that towards these mischiefs the State has assumed an exceptional position—that they are excluded from the general rule, and that in the demands we make for action we are asking no new thing, but simply that the legislature should act in harmony with itself. If it were true that venereal diseases are, *prima facie*, not the concern of the Government—if in asking for their repression at the hands of the State we were requiring the legislature to adopt some novel principle, the onus of proving that the course so recommended was right and expedient, would rest on us; but if my contention is sound, that on Mr. Simon's own showing the attitude assumed by the legislature towards venereal disease is wholly anomalous, then with the opponents of the proposed action rests the burden of proving that the present state of things is justifiable. With those who support the exception lies the duty of showing that the exception is right. With all preventable forms of disease except the venereal, the legislature concerns itself, and therefore instead of the question so commonly asked, why should it deal with them? the question that ought to be propounded is, why does it leave them to themselves? That the supporters of the "neutral position" may be able to satisfy the public of its soundness is very possible, only let them begin at the right end of the controversy, and remember that it is not we who are desiring a harbour to be built for ourselves, but that it is they who have to justify the exclusion from the general haven of the most frail and tempest-tossed and utterly wrecked of all the many applicants for shelter and relief.

Bearing in mind that it is really for the advocates of the present exceptional state to show cause why they should not bring the law in this respect into harmony with itself, rather than for us to excuse our just demand, we may pass on to consider on what ground the exception from the general rule is, or may be attempted to be justified, and may remark in passing that the reasons offered must be sound and convincing, and that any such arguments as the following "that because there are not sufficient or properly appointed fever hospitals, no action against venereal diseases must be taken (page 17)," or that as the State cannot assist the wife of the gambler or drunkard, so it cannot protect her or her children against the consequences of the husband's debauchery (page 13), must be rejected as utterly futile.

OBJECTION No. 1.—Mr. Simon thinks "there are swarms of ratepayers who would object to see the prostitute kept in hospital at their expense for weeks or months, not necessarily from the exigencies of severe illness of her own, but essentially that she might be made clean for hire, lest any of her users should catch disease from her. They would remember in contrast that for themselves wonderfully little is done by authority to protect them against adulterations of food* or against false weights or measures; and they might regard it as a strange caprice of

---

* It appears from Mr. Simon's report quoted (page 238) that a good deal is done in this respect by the legislature.

law which should oblige them to contribute to the cost of giving an artificial security to their neighbour's looseness of life."

This objection assumes (among other things) that the "swarms" of ratepayers are all virtuous, and would neither for themselves nor their relations, such as sons or nephews, rejoice that life's temptations were made less full of pain and peril;—that, though so stern towards civil naughtiness, they do not object to the expense of relieving the immoral disasters of soldiers and sailors;—that the prostitute would not be sent to hospital on account of her own severe illness;—that she would be so sent "to enable her to hire herself out by being made clean."

Now this is really too bad, fathering as it does unworthy motives on those who desire to secure efficient hospital relief for the sick prostitute. The injustice of these two last assumptions is equalled only by the grotesque absurdity of the argument that the hospitals ought to be closed to prostitutes, because sufficient attention is not paid to preventing the adulteration of food and the use of false weights and measures. Can we not obtain, if necessary, legislation for the relief of both evils? To refuse to do one thing because something quite different requires to be done, can only be wise on the supposition that two wrongs make one right. But, after all our grumbling as taxpayers, we must bow to the voice of public opinion which, as some one has well said, does not depend upon the opinion of one individual, but flows from the combined judgment of the 200 able-thinking men who constitute the working majority of our constitution.

While on this point, however, I may deal with the different objections that may be urged against providing relief and assistance in their dire necessity to fallen women. It may be objected that the suggested provision for prostitutes during sickness will directly encourage immorality by making prostitution less hazardous, the risk of destitution ensuing on the contraction of disease being calculated to operate as a strong deterrent to persons meditating its adoption as a calling. This objection is plausible, but not, I think, well founded. Women do not as a matter of fact calculate chances before entering on a career of prostitution, or if they calculate at all, it is the calculation of the gambler who dwells only on expected gains, and dismisses from his mind, if ever indeed the unwelcome possibility should cross it, the anticipation of probable loss, or if he condescends to dwell for a moment on a contingency so remote, he trusts that the happy chapter of accidents will enable him in some unknown but yet expected way to tide over the season of disasters. The choice of prostitution as a means of living can not in my opinion be conceived even in this limited sense to be a matter of calculation; it is usually referable to accident, necessity, or vicious inclination. Such an objection, moreover, would be equally applicable to any attempt at ministering relief by private charity, and this even the most rigid of disciplinarians, including Mr. Simon himself (see page 20 of report), would hesitate to condemn. It may be further objected (as it has been by Mr. Simon) that such provision is an unfair tax upon the virtuous and well-conducted, compelling them to support the vicious and improvident, even against their will, and that such support, if given at all, should at least be given voluntarily. The plain answer seems to me to be this, the voluntary system has been fairly tried, and has been found wanting.   In spite of the efforts of private philanthropy, prostitution and its attendant disorders, social and physical, oppress us heavily, and, according to Mr. Simon, at least double the number of hospitals at present established are necessary to enable us to deal efficiently with metropolitan diseases.   It is time to check the evil. Diseased prostitutes can no longer be permitted to infest the streets and spread contagion and death at their good pleasure.   They cannot be kept off the streets except by being placed in confinement, and curing their diseases seems to be the necessary accompaniment of restraining their liberty.   It is, however, further urged that vicious men ought not to be preserved from disease at the expense of the virtuous.   If prostitution were an evanescent evil this objection would, I confess, have weight; but, seeing that its nature is what I have already described it to be, I reply that, striking the balance of evils, the fewest are attendant on a system of regulation and amelioration. No method of dealing with it that human ingenuity can devise can be an unmixed good, and we must only be content in this as in other things to take the rough with the smooth.   But beyond and above all ultilitarian reasons, one motive for adopting the course that I am now suggesting stands forth pre-eminent, and it is one that I commend to the careful consideration of all Christian readers.   It is this.   I have already shown that numbers of women have no choice fairly before them, except to join the ranks of prostitution, through the neglect, or even worse fault of society, rather than through their own deliberate sin—women who, if born under happier auspices, might have proved virtuous and faithful wives and mothers—find themselves vicious and despicable outcasts.   Shall we, the prosperous and respected, who indirectly permit or produce their fall feel under no obligation to seek for and apply the remedy.   I say that it is the plain duty of a Christian State to place within the reach of all its members, even the vilest and lowest, the means of obtaining health ; also, that it is its duty to place within the reach of all, so far as possible, the means of amendment and reformation.   From those who urge the hatred of sin as a Christian duty I claim the exercise of another Christian duty, the showing mercy. "Owe no man anything, but to love one another;" in other words, be just and loving.   Is it just to abstain from helping those to rise who had no chance or choice, except to fall ?   Is it love to join contempt for the sinner with hatred of the sin ?   Moreover, as I have said, providing for these poor lost women the means of regaining health is a step towards freeing them from a life of sin.   And it seems to me no less the duty of a Christian State to open the doors of virtue than the doors of health.   Does no memory of a former time survive, reminding these fallen ones of happier days, and raising thoughts within them of what might have been, and still might be ?   But what does it profit them ? How shall they retrace their steps or bridge the gulf that even in this world is fixed between the evil and the good ? they cannot cross it unless hope is present to guide and sustain them.   The memory, unless linked with hope, but makes their life more bitter and their course more reckless.   There are few human beings so degraded as to have no seeds of good left in them or desire for better things, but the seeds long neglected must fail to spring up and bear fruit, unless assisted by genial influences, while desire can effect nothing without effort, and effort is invariably bounded by the possible. It comes to this, then, if the good dormant in them is to be awakened and made productive, fallen women must be brought into contact with those who have the means and the will to help them—with those, in short, who can make them hope. And here we at once find ourselves in the presence of a great difficulty. Individual efforts to reclaim them are not wanting, but it is very hard to gain access to them, and even where access is gained and rescue from their life of sin appears achieved, to establish permanent reformation with our present machinery is hardly possible. On this point of gaining access to them we may listen with advantage to the remarks of one whose official duties at various places of amusement have thrown him amongst them, and who has related to me the result of his experience. He says :—" By a little, a very little, kindliness of manner towards them from myself, an official in a responsible position, and a willingness to render them any trifling assistance, and frequently advice, a sort of confidence was established, and they would unreservedly pour their troubles and their doings into my ear. I am convinced that by such means only one can obtain reliable information ; they are extremely jealous of any person questioning them out of mere curiosity, and it is only by tact, after confidence is established, that the whole truth and mysteries of their lives can be learned. Many a girl has told me that she knew no one whom she could go to or trust in if she were in difficulties, but if she kept her good looks and had health, she could always get plenty of money. I am bound to say that, although the majority of these women with whom I have come in contact are avaricious, depraved and lost to all sense of decency, I have seen very many instances of good feeling and kindheartedness shown to each other in sickness and trouble. My experience tells me that a girl cannot be very soft-hearted and tender if she is a prostitute ;—the very nature of her calling makes her otherwise : but the instances are rare in the better class in which all the traits of the true woman are entirely stamped out, and I have found no difficulty in bringing them to the surface."

OBJECTION No. 2.—Mr. Simon, however, further objects that even if advisable, the system would entail so enormous an expense for hospital accommodation as to render its rejection necessary. He says :—" To give a notion of the quantity of hospital accommodation which would be requisite to satisfy this programme, I may observe, for instance, that London is conjectured to have some 18,000 women whose living is gained by prostitution ;* and that, according to one of the secretaries of the society, on any given number of prostitutes, always about one-third may be assumed to be diseased.† If, instead of insisting on these colossal estimates, we take only half their total result, the plan would require for London alone the creation and maintenance of new hospital accommodation nearly equal to that which is now given

* Appendix of Association Report, page 22.
† Mr. Curgenven on the Contagious Diseases Act, p. 7.

by the twelve general hospitals of London for all bodily diseases put together ; accommodation, viz., for 3,000 patients. The charge of maintaining (independently of the cost of constructing) such lazarets as the above would, probably, be at least £100,000 per annum, and their construction would probably represent a first-cost of little short of half a million of money : beside all which there would be the considerable annual charges for police arrangements and medical inspections. This for London alone ! And the requirements of other large towns would probably be of like proportions."—Page 11.

Mr. Simon does not acquaint us, as I think he should, with the statistics and calculations by which he arrives at his estimate of the probable cost of dealing effectually with Metropolitan prostitution ; the only figures that he gives he has himself taken from others ; but these carry us a very short distance in the calculation—no further, indeed, than the starting point. Mr. Simon cannot assume that out of the given number of 9,000 prostitutes there will, under a system of supervision, be a perpetually recurring quantity of 3,000 diseased women. Such an assumption would contradict the result of all our recent experience, and be simply ridiculous. But it is useless to speculate on the process adopted by Mr. Simon ; I am unable to form any hypothesis from the facts and figures known to me by which his calculation can be supported. If his conclusion is the result of mere guess work, it would have been at least candid to say so ; if he is in possession of facts, figures, or other information not generally known to the profession, he should in justice to himself, the profession, and the public, produce them. It is, of course, impossible to tell beforehand the number of women for whom accommodation will be required in the first year, and afterwards from year to year. I endeavour at page 254 to form an approximate estimate on this question; for the present I will merely point out the expense per 1,000 that would be incurred ; this, taking the maximum cost per bed per annum at £40, and the average stay in hospital of each patient at one month, would be in round numbers £3,300. Again, Mr. Simon speaks of half-a-million of money as being probably required for the construction of these 3,000 beds. As will be seen hereafter, p. 257, I propose that, at the outset, many of the women should be accommodated in hospital ships, the use of which as they cease to be required for this purpose, could be discontinued, for in a short time, in accordance with what is witnessed in those of our garrison towns to which the Contagious Diseases Act has been applied, one half only of the original accommodation will be necessary, and this diminution will continue until, judging by the same standard as seen a little further on, one in six women only will be found diseased, and we may confidently expect, if the Act is applied to the whole country, to see the disease in course of time nearly stamped out.

OBJECTION NO. 3.—The next objection, which, if proved, would have great weight with the authorities and the public, is the statement made by Mr. Simon :—

" On the other hand, as regards our power of preventing venereal diseases by such a superintendence of prostitution as is proposed, it is certain that no appreciable good would be got except with much organization, and at very large cost of money ; and there are strong reasons for believing that the gain so purchased would, on analysis, be found to belong very predominantly to those kinds of venereal diseases in which the community has little or no permanent interest."—P. 14.

The real fact is, that it is *precisely these forms of disease in which society is most interested,* which have been most beneficially influenced by the system of inspection now in practice, and that it is on the slighter and less important forms that the least impression has been made. "The percentage of syphilis has steadily diminished. In the first period the proportion of syphilitic cases was 57·45. The percentage of syphilis decreased gradually during the succeeding periods, till it reached the number of 17·72 per cent. in the half-year ending March 31, 1869."— *Letter of the Devonport Surgeons to the Lords of the Admiralty,* p. 9.

In the London Lock Hospital, as previously stated (page 86), Mr. Lane reports that in 1867 42 per cent. and in 1868 only 35 per cent. of the prostitutes admitted laboured under syphilis, thus showing that the working of the Contagious Diseases Act has very considerably diminished the syphilitic average.

OBJECTION No. 4. — Mr. Simon doubts the success of the Continental system ; he says :—

"Then, as regards the preventability of venereal diseases, even the abstract question (abstract I mean from considerations of cost) is by no means an easy one. Especially we are in want of exact discriminative information as to the good which other countries have got from their sanitary superintendence of prostitution. I believe it to be the fact that, even under strict systems of police, prostitutes in very large proportions escape the intended supervision ; and that in their evasive traffic so large a dissemination of venereal disease may be kept up as to leave in net result very little apparent success to be boasted of."—p. 15.

My reply to this objection is, that I do not propose to apply to England the system in vogue on the Continent, but one apparently less obnoxious to the prostitute (that at present carried out in our garrison towns), and therefore likely to be in a far less degree the object of evasion.

No one can read the statistics I have furnished at pages 131, 139, and 142, without being convinced that the system has had the effect of immensely diminishing the severity and frequency of disease in the several European capitals. In speculating as to the benefits derived, or derivable, from a system of supervision, it must be remembered that the good achieved by it will be great in proportion as the area made subject to it is extensive. In Belgium, for example, the system is applied to the cities only, and the extra-mural districts are thereby left as focuses of disease, thus counteracting sensibly the good wrought by supervision.

OBJECTION No. 5.—Mr. Simon appears to infer that the Extension of the Contagious Diseases Act to the civil population would discourage early marriage by favouring fornication ; for he says :—

"I suppose it may be assumed that public policy is very decidedly in favour of marriage as against promiscuous fornication ; that the latter, however powerless may be laws to prevent it, is at least an order of things which no State would willingly foster."—p. 12.

And again :—

"The only state of things which can be regarded as essentially antagonistic to prostitution is the system of early marriages : which, in this respect, commends itself equally on moral and physical grounds ; for, in proportion as it is accepted, the promiscuous intercourse of the sexes ceases to excuse itself by circumstances, and the chances of venereal infection fall to the lowest level they can attain."—p. 19.

I was not aware before, that Government considered marriage in this sense. I thought that in the present state of crowded civilisation political economists had come to the conclusion that early marriage was an evil, and have always heard Ireland cited as an instance of its ill effects. Preceding pages (see page 148) show that Austrian laws, for instance, both civil and ecclesiastical, have done all in their power to check the extension of population by forbidding people to marry who could not prove that pecuniarily they were in a position to support a family.

In a medical point of view I have elsewhere shown* that early marriages are followed by the worst consequences to the rising generation. Premature procreation is bad for the male, injurious to the female, and detrimental to the children ; some of the arguments against it being reproduced at page 163 of this edition. But whatever may be the intrinsic value of early marriages, whether from a political, social, or medical point of view, the sufficient answer to this suggestion of Mr. Simon's is, that it is impracticable. As reasonable was the demand of the King of Egypt for bricks without straw, or the proposal of the French Princess that the people should have recourse to pastry who, from the scarcity of flour, could get no bread, as this recommendation to men to take wives who have not wherewithal to support them. If the only state of things essentially antagonistic to prostitution is out of our reach, we must discover and apply some less transcendental remedy. At the same time, it remains open to Mr. Simon to show, first, that early marriages will counteract prostitution ; and secondly, that the Government can, and will, by an improved system of emigration, or otherwise, place them within the reach of prudent men.

OBJECTION No. 6.—Mr. Simon doubts the moral results of Government superintendence on prostitution. That gentleman says :—

"Among arguments put forward to recommend a general superintendence of prostitution, there is one which seems to have gained for the proposal a considerable quantity of non-medical, particularly clerical, support. The report of the Association, namely, alleges 'that a collateral but not unimportant result which inevitably follows the establishment of preventive measures is the improvement in the moral and social condition of the women ;' and a memorial which was last year addressed to the then Lord President of the Council, by the President of the Royal College of Physicians, and others, supported the view 'that of the unfortunate women who are subjected to these re-

---

* See Author's work on the Reproductive Organs in Childhood, Youth, and Adult Age, p. 56.

strictive and sanitary measures, a comparatively large proportion have been reclaimed.' I believe it to be unquestionable that such women as have hitherto come under medical inspection have generally been influenced by it to become cleanlier in their persons, and that the brothels inspected by police are less apt than they were to be scenes of riotous disorder; changes, on which no doubt the users of those persons and places may congratulate themselves; but which cannot without extreme abuse of terms be described as of any moral significance. On the other hand, the last clause of the statement cannot fail to seem morally important to any one who accepts it without reserve. I fear, however, that such hopes as it at first sight would seem to justify, as to possible moral results of a government superintendence of prostitution, would on any large scale show themselves essentially delusive; not perhaps as regards individual reclamations to be effected, even from brothels, by pure and kindly human contact, but as regards the statistics of prostitution, broadly and practically considered."—Pp. 18 and 19.

Surely this is a rash assertion for Mr. Simon to make, immediately after the publication of the report of the House of Commons for 1869, a report which, I cannot too often repeat, contains most valuable information. It says;—

" Although the Act has only been in operation two years and a half, and at some stations only seven months, strong testimony is borne to the benefits, both in a moral and sanitary point of view."—P. iii.

The evidence I have adduced in the former edition of this book—that even when the English Government held a neutral position as regards prostitution, the prostitute had a tendency to withdraw herself from the paths of vice, and to settle down into a gradually regular life, till she became often a mother of a family—becomes of still more importance now that State interference interests itself on her behalf.

The partial Government garrison superintendence has, as I have just shown, had a most beneficial influence, and there is every reason to believe that if steps continue to be taken for further extending the Contagious Diseases Act, we shall have a beneficial change in the moral and social condition of the class such as nothing else can effect. If I have detailed correctly the career of the prostitute as delineated at page 39, my readers will have seen what strong inducements to attempt the amelioration of the prostitute are held out to the philanthropist, and how urgent the necessity that exists for State interference.

I verily believe that if I had not been convinced that a large number of the women who practise prostitution settle, and become valuable members of society, I should not have exerted myself as I have done to better their condition. To take advantage of and assist this tendency towards the marriage state, has been the object of much of what I have written. I have insisted over and over again in these pages that it is not my object to benefit the user of the prostitute, or, to again employ the language of Mr. Simon, " keep a prostitute in hospital that she should be made clean for hire, lest any of her users should catch disease from her."—P. 12.

In combating the introduction of the Contagious Diseases Act into civil life, Mr. Simon has entirely ignored this ultimate amalgamation of prostitutes with the population. If there are only 18,000 prostitutes in London, does it not become of the greatest importance that the State should first protect them, next cure them, and then assist an erring sister in forsaking what has become to her a vile occupation?

I cannot too often repeat that prostitution is a transitory state, through which an untold number of British women are ever on their passage. Until preventive measures, previously hinted at, to which I shall presently refer, shall have been considerately adopted—and thereafter, too, if needful, for I am no nostrum-monger—it is the duty, and it should be the business of us all, in the interest of the commonwealth, to see these women through that state, so as to save harmless as much as may be of the bodies and souls of them. And the commonwealth's interest in it is this—that there is never a one among all of these whose partners in vice may not some time become the husbands of other women, and fathers of English children ; never a one of them but may herself, when the shadow is past, become the wife of an Englishman and the mother of his offspring ; that multitudes are mothers before they become prostitutes, and other multitudes become mothers during their evil career. If the race of the people is of no concern to the State, then has the State no interest in arresting its vitiation. But if this concern and this interest be admitted, then arises the necessity for depriving prostitution not only of its moral, but of its physical venom also.

In combating, then, Mr. Simon's views, I have attempted to show in preceding pages that success has already attended the introduction of the Act, and I hope my readers will agree with me that the advantages of the Act have been so marked as to induce them to give it an impartial trial in England. From the disinclination to support brothels (in which girls are farmed out) in England, we may hope that our success will be even greater than on the continent, and I have a reasonable belief that if proper legislative measures are taken, clandestine prostitution will be robbed of many of its worst features, and although we may never be able altogether to prevent all its evil effects, we may so far ameliorate it as to render them much less detrimental to society, as well as to the female herself. Let our opponents recollect that if we do not eradicate prostitution, its consequences will remain as a deterrent cause to prevent promiscuous fornication, and this will be in the opinion of some, a great advantage to society.

One more answer to the general anathema of Mr. Simon against the extension of the Contagious Diseases Act to the civil population, and I take my leave of him for the present. I fearlessly assert the English Government can no longer maintain, in the words of Mr. Simon, "that neutral position which English law has hitherto held in regard of the venereal diseases of the civil population." Public attention has now been fairly roused to this important question. "We must lay aside that artificial bashfulness which has injured the growth, while it has affected the features, of genuine purity. Society has suffered enough from that spurious modesty which lets fearful forms of vice swell to a rank luxuriance rather than point at their existence,—which coyly turns away its head from the 'wounds and putrefying sores' that are eating into our system, because it would have to blush at the exposure."

Assuming that the necessity of State interference will be conceded, that the House of Commons will decide on extending the Contagious Diseases Act to the civil population, let us next consider how the Act may be best worked, by contrasting the past mismanagement with what should be done in future.

It is now many years ago since I called public attention to the error committed by philanthropists and medical men in treating prostitutes as out-patients. I regret to say that what I wrote and published twelve years ago, applies equally to the present day, regarding our civil hospital arrangements. I, however, now go further, and venture to question whether it is desirable for our civil hospitals to treat prostitutes as out-patients at all.

It is matter of very serious regret that the officers of the civil hospital are obliged, from week to week throughout the year (see p. 52), to make out-patients of a number of destitute women, whose segregation until cured is imperatively called for by every consideration of public health and morality. I need hardly say that this would not occur were the funds under their control as expansive as their anxiety to diffuse the blessings of the institution; but as it is well known that their large revenues are already fully bespoken and worthily expended, it would be unbecoming in me not to repudiate on their behalf the slightest suspicion of shortcoming. Out of the fifty-three applicants catalogued at pp. 52 and 53, no more than eighteen could be received into the hospital, and the other thirty-five either became out-patients, went off to seek admission elsewhere with infinitely less chance of ultimate success, or, more horrible thought still, after becoming out-patients, fell back in many cases upon their miserable avocation—to prowl the streets, to drink, to get worse day by day in spite of all our physic, and to propagate disease for gain, or perish.

The propriety and the utility of treating primary symptoms in prostitutes while they remain out-patients seem alike questionable. One, for instance, grievously afflicted, among the number catalogued above, attracted my particular notice by the superiority of her dress. She lived, she said, in her own lodgings in a street near the Strand. It is therefore clear she had no home to look to but the streets unless she paid her rent. In the course of the very same evening I was shocked to see this woman, accompanied by another, soliciting (as the Act of Parliament has it) in the street, and to reflect how frightfully she must contaminate any unfortunate man who might yield to her desperate entreaties. In dress and bearing she was by no means a female of the lowest class. No ordinary observer would have recognised her sanitary condition; but there she was—her rent, her food, her clothes to be earned—obliged to drink intoxicating liquor with every man who might offer it, dangerous alike to gentle and simple, the fast young man, or the tipsy father of a family who might be attracted by her pleasing face, and utterly heedless how much she was protracting, perhaps aggravating, her own sufferings. How comparatively futile our morning labours! how inefficacious the eleemosynary drugs!

Advocates of the "know-nothing" system, stand aghast! and ask yourselves if the toleration by society of this emissary of death in the occupation in which I saw her is reconcileable with society's duties (if duties it has) to God or man.

Here you see a woman who, patched up by voluntary charity in the morning, knows no other way—nay, whose only possible resource—to get her necessary food, or bed at night, is to sally forth into the streets. The ministers of charity eased her pain this morning ; they dressed her sores and gave her drugs. So they will again next Thursday. She may be worse then, or she may have made a little progress in spite of her drinking and her fornication. But in a month she will be no nearer soundness than had she been taken care of by the State within the walls of the hospital for one week ; and within that month what a scourge upon society will the surgeons not have kept afoot by their exertions ? Here is the power of charity again working to waste. I will not insult you by supposing that you would have had that creature, and the hundreds of whom she is the example, spurned from the gates of every workhouse and hospital, and kicked from every domicile in the name of religion, to perish how and where they might, by lingering, loathsome disease. That were too absurd. But what you do, virtually, is this : You who, if your principles have any worth in them, should protest against the Lock Hospital, proclaim the foul ward a misappropriation, and excommunicate all who relieve or sympathise with the venereal pariah—you neither protest, nor proclaim, nor excommunicate. You testify against none of these things on principle, but only against their extension—against exchanging for a useful flame that inefficient rush-light of private charity which now serves only to make misery visible.

If you consider it wicked encouragement of vice and countenance of immorality to feed, to clothe, to lodge the syphilitic, you will be satisfied that in these five-and-thirty cases the hospital administration steered clear of these greater sins. But, though you dare not go so far as to claim the entire dismission of these wretches down the winds of fate, you ought surely, in justice to your principles, to some extent to censure those who wrestled with corruption for their poor bodies, preserved them yet a little longer to defile the earth ; perverted charity from what you would allow to be proper objects, and as it were " threw physic to the dogs." In truth, we are at a dead lock, all of us—hospital authorities, social Radicals, and social Tories.

The same necessity of selection which is imposed upon the house-surgeon by the restricted number of beds at his disposition, works evil also in another way. As long as it is guided, not by philosophical considerations of public morals and public health, but by that sympathy for suffering humanity which animated the munificent founders of our hospitals, and the proper desire of the medical schools to secure the supervision of the most peculiar forms of disease, we shall take as in-patients only those most malignant and complicated cases, wherein the subject is practically incapable of getting about, and thus, by inference, of earning his or her bread. Thus competition among cases is as it were invited, the premium of a bed is held out for successful severity, and it is no exaggeration to say that the invitation is responded to, and the prize contended for, by the unfortunate out-patients who find themselves from week to week ' not eligible through seniority,' ' not yet bad enough ' to be taken into the house.   The devices, therefore, to which they frequently resort, in order to qualify, are, first to throw away the hospital medicines, and then, reckless of consequences to society, to pursue the best known means of aggravating disease—viz.,drunkenness,debauchery, and utter self-neglect.

If the British public could only once conceive the idea that the treatment, cure, and temporary segregation of the syphilitic, was as much a matter of public interest as that of the lunatic, whose seclusion all counties, towns, and parishes provide for with such remarkable alacrity, not so much out of love or respect for him as because he is a dangerous thing to be at large, I think I should not long be alone in wishing for equally public recognition of both complaints.   The attitude of society towards those afflicted must, of course, differ ; for, whereas upon the former we may properly, I think, exercise compulsion, we can do no more with the other than offer inducements and invitation to be made whole.

Were those inducements ample, in the shape of accommodation and treatment, and were the germs of pestilence sought out with more anxiety than the old neglected cases which are so interesting to the medical classes, we should in a few years have reduced the virulence of hospital syphilis to the level of that now seen in private practice, and of the latter, again, I have no doubt, to a corresponding extent.

I hold it to be the duty of the community to itself—in what form it provides the requisite money is immaterial, and the difficulty of this particular question is a contemptible excuse for inaction—to hold out by its public hospitals to all poor and common syphilitics the same facilities for being cured as the rich and genteel derive from their money and the skill of private practitioners.   Both classes are equally dangerous to society, in the first stages of the disease ; equally dangerous in the aggravated and neglected ones.   It may be relied upon that the propagation of syphilis affords no more personal gratification to the degraded pauper-harlot than to the man of means and position.   The one extensively commits the crime against society because it is inseparable from her only alternative against starvation ; the other seldom (I wish, for the honour of our sex, I could say never) knowingly, because it is not only cruel and disgusting, but often physically painful.   If we may not, under our present or any probable law, punish her for the crime, let us at least be wise enough, for the sake of society, to alter the circumstances which now almost drive her to its commission.

Admitting even that the means of granting indoor relief, now at the disposal of the London hospitals remained unamplified, I incline, on reflection, to the belief, and I would call the attention of the hospital surgeon of London to the fact that the reverse of the present system of selection would (so far as concerns syphilitic patients) be attended with advantage to the public health and to that of the majority of diseased prostitutes, without aggravating the sufferings of the remainder.

Were the slighter, because more recent, cases taken in hand as soon as presented, and the patients separated from the world, fed, lodged, and nursed until cured, it must be plain that infinitely more of them would be disposed of during twelve months, and a far less number of propagations be traceable to them, and the latter would in their turn become far less malignant. The broad sowing of syphilis, it must be kept in mind, is not so much due to the fearfully bad or complicated cases, which, besides generally betraying themselves, render fornication itself burdensome, as it is, among the higher order of prostitutes, to the inchoate or smouldering forms often unrecognised by the female herself, and, among the lower order, to the out-patient candidates for beds, who *must* and *will* live somehow and somewhere, to the greater or less damage of the commonwealth, according to the state of their particular cases. While the bed in the syphilitic ward of an hospital is occupied, for say six weeks, by one case of secondary or tertiary symptoms, the department might have nipped in the bud by active treatment three cases of syphilis primitiva, or gonorrhœa. The former, had it been kept as an out-patient, would have withdrawn to its garret, or its cellar, or its dark arch, and amended by degrees on its straw pallet or bundle of rags, under the care of some dispensary or parish medical officer. It would not have wandered a field for prey, and none of its fellows would have sought it from predilection. Its power of propagation would have been very limited indeed.

But neither of the three affected women, who by its admission into the hospital are kept upon the out-patients' list, are precluded from the practice of their avocation. They continue it, on the contrary, as a general rule, and therefore oscillate for months between progress and recovery, until patched up cases are perhaps in two or three months accomplished, or steadily get worse and worse, until absolute laying up becomes indispensable, and admission into the house a mere matter of seniority. Each of these three women being then, so long as she is afoot, a disease distributor, effective according to her unconsumed energy, it is a simple question, how much more the world would have benefited by their early recognition, and thereafter immediate separation and treatment in the wards of an hospital, than by the devotion of a precious bed for an indefinite period to one particularly malignant and interesting case?

It is now twelve years since I first published my opinion on hospital management—or, rather, want of management. The legislature has, we have seen, inaugurated a better system in our garrison towns, and secures the segregation till cured of all women found diseased within those districts, and with what happy results my readers will learn by turning to pages 245 and 254.

In another twelve years those who follow me may, I hope, have to chronicle that no prostitute in civil life will be treated week after week as an out-patient; but that she, like her sister in garrison towns and ten miles round, will, on the discovery of her diseased condition, be confined in hospital and restrained from infecting alike soldiers and civilians.

Till this time come, however, surgeons at hospitals (as they have only limited opportunities for taking prostitutes into the wards,) must select their cases; and I hope that, after reading this chapter, they will become convinced that they should only admit women labouring under chancres or primary symptoms, and that it would be well for them to receive particularly those girls who if not taken in would resort for a living to the streets.   In this way, the limited accommodation in our existing civil hospitals, would be made the most of, and the greatest benefit accrue to the public.   At present the hospital policy should be to let the sufferers from secondary symptoms and other non-contagious diseases, as well as uterine affections, remain as out-patients, strict injunctions being given to them at the same time not to expose themselves further to contamination.   Under such an altered system the present wards might be made more efficient, and the funds of the institution not thrown away, as they have too long and too often been from a mistaken and injudicious policy.

If, however, the experience we have gained from the evidence furnished by the medical officers of our Government Lock Institutions be not thrown away, we may next enquire if the few female civil hospital beds for prostitutes do much good.

We have seen, that, to confer any permanent benefit on society, and on sanitary grounds, when a woman is diseased, an early detection of her complaint is necessary, and that when discovered she should at once be placed in confinement, so as to prevent her disseminating the plague.   Moreover, she should not be allowed to leave the hospital till perfectly well and unable to contaminate any one she may have relations with.   Now our civil hospitals fulfil few of these conditions. The diseased prostitute is not sought after ; she applies only when the mischief she can cause is done, and many men have been diseased, and she finds herself unable any longer to carry on her trade.   If there be room in the wards to take the patient in, she occupies a bed say for many months, and even then society has no guarantee that she will remain till cured and do no more mischief.   On the contrary, as soon as she pleases, the girl of her own free will (and many do so) can quit the hospital long before the surgeon gives his sanction; hence society and sanitary laws are baffled, and instead of the hospital benefiting the girl and the plague of syphilis becoming checked, the propagation of the disease is aided by both the in- and out-patient hospital system of treating our prostitutes.

If (in spite of these remarks) prostitutes should still continue to be admitted in the present manner, would it not be well for the civil authorities in future, to exact on admission a promise from them ; that they will not of their own free will leave the institution till pronounced cured by the surgeons ?

It may be in the recollection of my readers, that some years ago it was given in evidence that prostitutes who were lying in hospitals suffering from venereal diseases, at Portsmouth, (on being sent for by the brothel-keepers) on the occasion of a ship being paid off, one and all left their beds to participate in the drinking and rioting that was a necessary consequence, to the no small detriment of her majesty's jolly tars, who of course became affected with the most serious forms of disease.   This, I may add, took place before the Contagious Diseases Act came into force, and compulsory residence in hospital (as now enforced) was carried out.

What happened, however, at Portsmouth will necessarily happen in any other place whenever the temptation occurs, or a like inducement is held forth to the patients.

Another objection to civil hospitals cannot and ought not to be concealed. Namely, in the wards of many, if not most civil hospitals, sufficient time and attention is not given to the treatment of such cases. Government seems to be becoming aware of this fact, and in the late inquiry before the House of Commons committee on the Contagious Diseases Act, the treatment of the patients by civil practitioners in Military Lock Hospitals is objected to by Government authorities, who, I think, very properly evince a greater disposition to place prostitutes when diseased in special institutions, under their own trained surgeons, who are responsible for the proper discharge of their duties to Government inspectors, and whose antecedents are a guarantee that every girl intrusted to their care will be properly examined and cured to the satisfaction of the authorities.

If this is the proper system, it follows that so far as society is concerned (not the individual prostitute who seeks aid at the civil hospital) the few beds now to be found in London hospitals might be almost as well dispensed with, and if Government hereafter should determine to extend the Contagious Diseases Act to the civil population, the beds in the civil hospitals now occupied by females may be devoted to the sole treatment of males who may contract syphilis. If public institutions do not offer greater facilities for the treatment of men labouring under primary symptoms or chancres, all the precautions now and hereafter to be taken to prevent syphilis spreading among prostitutes, will be foiled by unsound men going about diseasing them, (as appears from evidence, was the case at Aldershot before weekly health inspections were introduced among the soldiers, rendering perfectly futile the endeavours of the Government officers to check syphilis among the prostitutes at that camp). The results produced by Government in carrying out the Contagious Diseases Act, further prove that if it will more efficiently work the Act, it must have special hospitals of its own, and not depend upon adding Lock wards to the existing provincial institutions.

Up to this point the measures I have suggested have been voluntary, and I would make the attendance as easy as possible ; but supposing Parliament sanctioned the introduction of the Contagious Diseases Act into London, the authorities, having increased power given them, would send all unsound prostitutes to hospitals formed on the same plan as those established in the garrison towns.

Having thus brought the sick woman to the hospital, let us see what accommodation at present exists, and what is the number of beds really required in the metropolis.

At present, so far as I can ascertain, the beds given up to diseased prostitutes in the civil hospitals, which are wholly supported, let it be remembered, by voluntary contributions, amount to 155. These beds are thus apportioned :—

London Hospital accommodation for Venereal Patients.

London Hospitals.	Total of Venereal Beds.	Beds devoted to Females.	Females treated.	Beds devoted to Males.	Males treated.	Total treated.	Venereal Out-patients.
Lock (special) . .	41	26	..	15	..	..	5852
St. Mary's . . .	None	..	None	..	None	None	..
University . . .	None	..	None	..	A few	A few	..
King's College . .	None	..	No return kept	..	No return kept	No return kept	4000
Charing Cross . .	None	..	ditto	..	ditto	ditto	..
St. George's . . .	None	..	ditto	..	ditto	ditto	..
Royal Free . . .	26	26	..	None	..	..	{ 2 out of every 3 are believed to be venereal.
Middlesex . . .	20	8	..	12	..	..	465
London	15	15	44	..	No return kept	No return kept	Not reported.
Guy's	58	30	124	28	123	526	12,500 (an approximation.)
St. Thomas's . .	None	..	..	None	..	..	12,600 (an approximation).
St. Bartholomew's .	75	50	360	25	222	582	
Total . . .	235	155		80			

The insufficiency of beds I need not dwell on; but the first and most important inquiry becomes, how much accommodation is required? This preliminary question must be met by considering what is the accommodation in the other principal capitals of Europe.

To do this I have constructed the following table :—

City.	Years.	Population.	Number of Beds for Females.	Population of London.	Proportional number of beds there should be in London, according to the proportion provided in the five other cities.
London	1869	3,170,000	155	...	...
Berlin	1867	702,000	140	...	632
Brussels (exclusive of suburbs)	1866	164,000	80	3,170,000	1552
Hamburg	1867	222,000	120	...	1712
Paris	1869	1,890,000	470	...	789
Vienna	1863	560,000	400	...	2265

Supposing, therefore, (to allow for short returns), that 155 beds are constantly appropriated to *female* venereal patients in London, our shortcoming, as compared with

Berlin is	632	—	155	=	477
Brussels	1552	—	155	=	1397
Hamburg	1712	—	155	=	1557
Paris	789	—	155	=	634
Vienna	2265	—	155	=	2110

We infer, then, that if London had in round numbers 1,400 more beds, it would have equal accommodation to the five principal capitals in Europe. If, however, we wish only to equal the accommodation provided in the cities of Paris and Berlin, we should not require more than 800 beds.

I believe that 1,400 beds would more than suffice for the exigencies of London. In a few years we should not require so many in consequence of the frequency and severity of the disease diminishing, as it has done at Devonport, in proof of which I adduce the following evidence :—

Dr. Leonard says in reply to questions,

"496. *Dr. Brewer.*] How many women have been brought up to be examined who have not been diseased ?—Some of the weekly returns will show that at once ; I have the weekly returns for the whole of May, at Devonport ; the number of women brought forward for examination on the 1st of May, was 178, and the number found diseased out of the 178 was 29.

"497. Were they all prostitutes that were brought before the visiting surgeon ?—They were all prostitutes ; on the last day of May 211 were brought forward, and only 12 were found diseased, so that on repeated examinations the number brought forward exhibits a smaller amount of diseased."

Dr. Leonard, in his examination before the Committee of the House of Commons, put in a Table published at p. 90 of the Report, in which it is shown that out of 18,121 common prostitutes at all the stations under the Act, 12,297 were found free from disease, and 4,864 were sent into hospital as infected persons ; of these latter, 28 being pregnant, were not admitted. This tends to prove that about one in four prostitutes is diseased at present.

THE EXPENSE OF BEDS.

Dr. Leonard in reply to question,

"556. *Chairman.*] What is the average cost of each bed ?—It varies very much indeed. In London it is very moderate ; the cost being £25, that is the cheapest of the whole ; I do not know how they can manage to do it, but they do it. At Chatham it is about £40. At our own military lock hospitals it is £38."

Taking, then, the maximum expense at £40, and the required number at 1,400, the beds necessary for London would cost £56,000 a-year.

If only the smaller number of 800 beds would be required, then the annual expense would be £32,000.

If, however, we accept the minimum expense per bed, namely, £24 10s., then we require only £34,300 to defray the annual expense of 1,400 beds.

Let me remind my readers who may wish to compare these expenses with those in France, that the necessary data are given at page 115, where it is stated that in Paris the Lourcine Hospital, containing as it does 276 beds, was maintained in 1855 at an annual expense of £7,261, or about £26 per bed, a decrease of £12 on the highest English estimate.

I think, however, there can be no doubt that the estimate of £38 per bed per annum is excessive, and might by economical administration be considerably reduced, without any real diminution of efficiency.

The following Table shows the number of Beds in Lock Wards, number of Women admitted into Hospital, &c., in the different Garrison Towns in England where the Contagious Diseases Act has been introduced. (Condensed from the report of the Select Committee of the House of Lords, 1868).

DISTRICT.	Return of the Number of Prostitutes brought under the Provisions of the Contagious Diseases Act, for the week ending January 7th, 1869, in the following Districts.				Return of Men in Garrison, and Number of Soldiers admitted into Hospital suffering from Contagious Diseases, January 2nd, 1869.			
	Number of Beds in Lock Wards.	Number of Women admitted to Hospital on Certificates of Visiting Surgeon.	Number of Women examined and found free from Disease.	Total Number under the Provisions of the Act.	Total Number of Soldiers admitted into Hospital.	Strength of Garrison.	Average Number constantly under treatment.	Number of days lost to the Service.
Woolwich	40	16	28	44	34	1,933	25	175
Aldershot	70	20	60	80	...	12,776	128	...
Windsor	20	1	14	15	...	981	17	...
Shorncliffe	25	3	20	23	8	2,122	23	163
Chatham	75	11	45	56	26	4,335	44	208
Sheerness	5	4	1	5	3	2,433	13	88
Portsmouth	120	22	53	75	50	12,873	203	1,421
Devonport	162	42	106	148	31	9,099	115	805
Total	517	119	327	446	152	45,652	568	2,860

I am indebted to Mr. James Lane for the following statement as to the cost of beds in the London Female Lock Hospital during the year 1868:—

Expenses of maintenance of Female Lock Hospital, including salaries of house surgeon, secretary, matron, nurses, &c., but excluding cost of washing and clothing for Government patients while in hospital, which are separately allowed for by Government ; and excluding also cost of repairs of building ... £3177

Number of patients treated :—Government 1133
Ordinary 207

Total 1340
Average stay in hospital, 35·4 days.

Average cost per patient £2 7 5
Average cost per bed per annum, supposing it constantly occupied ... 24 10 0

The average annual cost of the Government beds is less than that of the ordinary beds, on account of the milder character of the cases, and the smaller amount of extra diet and stimulants consequently required.

The average stay in hospital was—Of the Government patients ... 32·59 days.
Of the ordinary patients ... 50·88 ,,

Showing a difference of ... ... 18·29 ,,

That is to say, it takes about 56 per cent. more time, and therefore costs about 56 per cent. more money to cure a patient who applies of her own accord, than to cure an inspected patient. The one, in fact, costs £3 8s. per case, while the other only costs £2 3s. 8d. per case. Each ordinary bed would thus only accommodate 7 patients annually, while each Government bed would accommodate 11. This is *one* of the many economical results which would be obtained by the legal inspection of venereal disease, as compared with the voluntary system, to which Mr. Simon wishes to adhere.

To those who would object even to the moderate expenditure which, if my information and calculations are accurate, would suffice, I would remark that it would be recouped by the sum saved in the army alone, as the following evidence relative to Aldershot will show :

Inspector Smith says in reply to question

" 1054. *Chairman.*] The number of troops, I think, has been about the same?—The average for the year was 12,090, from the 1st June, 1868, to the 31st May, 1869. I have not a return of the number of troops for the previous year. The number of days lost to the service was 54,222 for the year ending the 31st of May, 1869. That would be equal to 148·553 men's service : I have made a calculation of their costing, perhaps, £100 a year, taking in the expense of medical officers, and hospital sergeants and orderlies, and medicines, and I find that it would be about £14,855 6s. 10d.

" 1055. Mr. *Mitford.*] That would be saved if we could contrive to stamp out the disease, would it not?—If it could be stamped out, the whole of that would be saved."

The Table given at page 255 shows that we have nearly 46,000 men in the eight garrison towns mentioned in the table. I shall not be far out in stating that the money saved in the army, will recoup us the cost of maintaining these sick men suffering from a preventable disease, which would be, according to this calculation, annually upwards of £56,000.

PROBABLE STAY IN HOSPITAL.

Dr. Leonard in reply to question

"499. *Chairman.* Is it possible to strike anything like an average of the time it takes to cure an ordinary case of syphilis?—The average is stated in most of these returns. The average time required for cure at Portsmouth, during the quarter ending the 31st March last, was $40\frac{11}{64}$ days, or, in round numbers, 40 days. At Devonport the average time was about 31 days."

At the Royal Albert Hospital, Devonport, since March, 1867, the average detention in hospital has steadily diminished, the successive half yearly returns showing an average of 59·14, 49·90, 31·97, and 31·76 days, a minimum attained in the half year ending March, 1869.—*Letter to the Lords of the Admiralty, by the Surgeons of Devonport,* p. 9.

At St. Lazare, in Paris, the average stay in hospital is 45 days for the registered, 60 days for the clandestine prostitutes.

NUMBERS CURED ANNUALLY.

If we have 1,100 beds, and each patient occupies a bed one month, we may calculate on curing 14,300 women, or if 800 beds only are decided on, 10,400 annually. In either case the amount of relief afforded would greatly diminish the frequency of disease.*

As the increased demand for hospital accommodation will to a great extent be only of a temporary nature, we must look about us and see how it can be met without incurring Mr. Simon's half-million. I have well considered this subject, and I propose that additional accommodation should be provided in the Lock Hospitals already established in the different garrison towns—each such institution being worked by its present staff. In London, the central Lock Hospital could be so extended as to enable it to receive additional patients, and obviously as the provincial Lock Hospitals increased their accommodation, the central institution in London would be relieved. In addition to this, a few ships could be given up temporarily for the purpose of receiving the extra ordinary number of prostitutes that at first we should require accommodation for.

To satisfy myself as to the feasibility of adapting floating hospitals to this purpose, I consulted Dr. Rooke, the medical officer in charge of the Dreadnought at Greenwich. That gentleman kindly states :—

"In reply to your question respecting floating hospitals for the reception of prostitutes, I believe they would be a great benefit. I am certain that it would be the greatest blessing to the mercantile marine if the Contagious Diseases Act were extended to the port of London. Let us have power to hunt up the slums of Shadwell and Ratcliff Highway, to ship off the diseased prostitutes which abound there, and I am sure that not only the sailor but the ship owner will greatly benefit. Often sailors come to the Dreadnought for advice for venereal disease, they refuse to remain, saying their ship is to sail in a day or two. They sign articles and sail, and very often after being at sea a

---

* Thus, according to the calculations of page 254, the annual expense would not exceed £44,000, and might fall as low as £32,000 (even if all the beds provided were always occupied), instead of amounting to £100,000, as estimated by Mr. Simon.

few weeks become useless as seamen, and an expense to the owner for the remainder of the voyage. Again, sailors may be said to be the carriers of the disease, and its propagators throughout the world. The only way to stop this evil would be to make a medical examination of all merchant seamen compulsory before signing articles. These measures would, I feel certain, check the spread of disease. The expenditure in our hospital is large, on account of the expensive staff. If this item be deducted, each bed would cost about £30 a year. I believe that a floating hospital for prostitutes might be maintained at a cost of £25 a bed. We are very liberal in our scale of diet, as regards meat, a very expensive article, because sailors are accustomed to have at least one lb. daily when engaged in active employment."

Supposing the Government, at the suggestion of the Medical Officer of the Privy Council, refuse acquiescence in the proposal to extend the Contagious Diseases Act to the civil population, does not that gentleman see that on the Lock Hospitals in the different garrison towns will be thrown the duty of disinfecting all the prostitutes in England? If Mr. Simon, in his official position, does not foresee this, it remains for me, a civil practitioner, to show the Government that such must be the case, and for the following very natural reasons :—

Under the Amended Act at present in force, every suspected woman within a radius of ten miles from the garrison town must be summoned, arrested, examined, and, if diseased, sent to hospital, there to be kept till cured, as certified by the Government Medical Officer.

If hospital provision is not made for the prostitute living outside the naval and military districts, every parish officer, medical man, clergyman, or rate-payer, has but to recommend a sick girl to enter one of the garrison towns, and the Government inspector, always on the look out for such persons, will at once take charge of her; in the interest of the army, if not in that of society, and thus the expense will be shifted at once on the Consolidated Fund—and the rate-payer will no longer have to complain that he "pays the expenses of making prostitutes clean for hire."

So soon as this practice becomes general, as it assuredly will, these Garrison Lock Hospitals will be converted into great female Lazar houses, where all comers must be *admitted*, even if they are not *welcomed;* nor do I see what course the authorities can take to prevent such recommendation being given and acted on, or to avoid their own consequent liability. Regard for the health of the soldier will necessitate the examination of the girl ; who if found diseased, within ten miles of the garrison, will have to be treated and cured, according to law, for public opinion will not allow the sick prostitute to be sent back to the parish in which she was born, uncured—nor will there, I presume, be any dispute outside the walls of the garrison Lock Hospital about settlement when the girl is found diseased and destitute within the ten miles radius. As the admirable arrangements now made in our garrison towns become known generally to the women in different parts of the country, all the sick and maimed will crawl in, and it will be probably in this way that the Government will feel itself ultimately compelled to adopt the course which the medical officer of the Privy

Council, " as at present advised," does not recommend—namely, extend the Contagious Diseases Act to the civil population.

I have long foreseen the official difficulties in the way of the introduction of any general Act. In my evidence before the Committee appointed by Government, in 1864, I stated my opinions, and I have not shrunk from reiterating them on several public occasions, pointing out similar objections to those taken by Mr. Simon in his last report. But since I have become convinced of the desirability of extending the Act, I have attempted to adapt my views to the circumstances of the case, hence my present opinions, feeling certain that my protegée, the sick prostitute, is making, and must ultimately make her influence felt, , and that her condition will be ameliorated, in spite of " the hitherto neutral position of Government authorities on her behalf."

Having established hospitals, the next question is as to the alterations which may with advantage be made in some of their arrangements, and among other important reforms I would suggest that

Venereal Wards should not be public.—That it is desirable for a few pupils to witness all the forms of venereal disease met with among prostitutes, admits of no doubt ; I need not say how especially necessary it is that those who propose becoming attached to hospitals and prisons, as well as those who aspire to military, naval, or poor-law appointments, should be well acquainted with these affections. I, however, think it undesirable that the wards wherein a number of diseased unfortunates are confined should be open, as now, to all pupils alike. In lunatic hospitals, selected pupils are alone allowed to enter the wards, and precautions are taken against the abuse of this privilege, the wards being only open to these students, during the visit of the medical man, who gives lectures on the most interesting forms of disease.

In Paris the wards of the female venereal hospitals are so sealed to impertinent curiosity, that a pupil desirous of studying these complaints must become attached to the house in the capacity of *externe*, by special permission of the General Hospital Board, and on the recommendation of the surgeon. He gives his services, whatever they may be worth, in consideration of a daily mess and a stipend of eight francs a month, and has, no doubt, great opportunities of studying disease. An extremely limited number of men, and those selected, therefore, are seen at any time about the wards of the Lourcine Hospital ; and as they invariably exhibit the greatest delicacy and politeness towards the unfortunate inmates, such satisfactory relations are maintained between the patients and the doctor as make the word hospital, one of far less horror to French prostitutes than to those of the class in this country.

If no other change is practicable in the system of managing our civil hospitals, I might at least suggest that the crowds of pupils who frequent them should be only allowed to witness the treatment of a selected number of these cases. The inspection of a number of women whose cases present no marked features of interest, can be fraught with no advantage to science, and is painful and demoralizing to the unhappy patients.

Classification of Female Patients.—We might, I think, take with advantage another hint from our continental neighbours, by dividing the women who apply for the cure of venereal complaints into the following classes :—

1. The married, who, guiltless themselves, have been injured by their husbands. These are annually becoming more numerous in the London hospitals, and no less than six of them were discharged from the Devonport Lock Hospital in the five months ending May, 1869. To compel them, if they enter, to mingle with the hardened offenders, is a scandal to decency and morality, a cruelty to them if they submit to it, if they cannot, a withholding of the means of health.

2. Girls who have been recently seduced and defiled,—for their reformation is not hopeless, but often accomplished where proper classification takes place, as in the Lourcine, but is next to impossible if they are placed among the thoroughly vicious, who are too apt to pass their time in hospitals, even when strictly watched, in obliterating all trace of modesty from their less hardened fellow-sufferers.

3. Pregnant prostitutes, or those with children—for the child is a certain link between the mother and morality, during the existence of which her case is never hopeless ; and charity, placing youth by the side of corruption, has much to answer for.

4. The childless, barren, and confirmed prostitutes.

Among other plans for the amelioration of prostitution which I think it desirable to consider is that of

MIDNIGHT MEETINGS.

Various philanthropic individuals have tried the plan of holding midnight meetings in rooms contiguous to the haunts of vice. Sorry should I be to appear even to slight the efforts of any fellow-labourer, but truth compels me to say that of all the useless expedients adopted for remedying by private measures public wrong, this seems about the worst. Such public exhibitions and appeals to excited feelings are scarcely calculated to produce durable impressions.

That which midnight meetings seldom achieve, the proposed medical inspections and hospital detentions ensure, namely access, and in addition they afford the prostitute temporary repose from excitement and time for reflection. These are the very advantages that are attempted to be supplied by Lock asylums and penitentiaries. Notwithstanding the most constant and self-denying exertions of the managers of these institutions, comparatively few fallen women come under their cognizance, and of these very few are permanently reformed.

The following is an admirable description of a midnight meeting, from the *Star* of Feb. 23, 1868 :—

" THE MIDNIGHT MISSION.—The enterprises of philanthropy are as varied as its spirit is comprehensive—the means it adopts as flexible as its aim is fixed. The promoters of that new movement which takes the shape of a midnight mission to fallen women do not seek publicity for themselves ; but, as they must hope for support from public sympathy and approval, neither do they shroud their doings from the observation of such as may fairly claim to be eye-witnesses. It was at our own instance and request we were on Tuesday night permitted to be spectators of that second gathering at a West-end *restaurant* of which a brief account appeared next morning. We propose to describe exactly what we saw ;

and leave to our readers the formation of an impartial, though it cannot be an unsympathising judgment.

"The invitations distributed in the public resorts of that unhappy
class for which we have no name, one does not shrink from writing,
fixed twelve o'clock as the hour of meeting. Half-an-hour past that
time, passing up the Haymarket, one could observe a diminution of the
usual throng. Midnight is the hour of high-tide on that reef of ship-
wrecked souls. When the casinos and music-rooms close, their occupants—except the few whose broughams roll them westward to abodes
of more secluded vice—flood the adjacent pavements, and gradually
subside into the taverns, cafés, and supper-rooms, where paramours may
be found or awaited. To-night there was another and a purer meeting-
place open to as many as would enter. Round the door a group of men
and youths had formed—curiosity, let us hope, their worst motive and
sentiment ; for the most unmanned by sensuality would scarcely venture
to mock at, or hope to frustrate, the purpose of that gathering. Passing the strictly-guarded entrance, we find ourselves within a room,
lofty, spacious, and well furnished. On the tables are tea and coffee,
with light comestibles, and nearly every chair has its female occupant.
A hundred and fifty of the invited are already present. A dozen or
twenty gentlemen, all of mature age, and chiefly in clerical habiliments,
are moving about from table to table, and aiding the professional waiters
in their duty.

"A glance across the room would scarcely reveal the character of the
assembly. Are these the 'gay' and the 'unfortunate,'—the dashing
courtezans or the starveling prostitutes of the West-end ? They differ
very little in appearance and demeanour from as many women of 'the
middle and lower middle class,' to adopt Mr. Gladstone's discriminating
phrase,—taken promiscuously. With few exceptions, there are no extravagant dresses,—still less are there any symptoms of levity or indecorum. Gravely and quietly, with self-respect and silent courtesy, the
refreshments provided are consumed or declined, and new comers provided with places till not a vacant seat remains. There is one young
woman sitting apart, a patriarchal-looking gentleman bending over her,
endeavouring, apparently, to console her grief—which, did we not know
her vocation and his, we might attribute to the loss of that friend or
relative for whom she wears mourning. Here and there is one whose
veiled or averted face indicates something of shame or disquietude ; but
the great majority wear an aspect of cheerful gravity that sets the observer thinking painfully how hearts thus masked may be approached.
At least fifty more have entered since we first took note, and the room
is crowded to the door ; some of the later comers have an air of social
outlawry not so marked before, and bold-faced women in silk stand by
the side of fellow-sinners in humbler raiment. The disparity of age
strikes one more than before. Here are mere girls—girls of sixteen or
seventeen—girls who, if seen in pure and happy homes, would have
recalled the poet's image of innocent white feet touching the stream
that divides childhood from womanhood,—girls on whose fair faces
paint and drink have not yet replaced the natural bloom with streaks
and patches. Here are women of the age at which wise men seek loving
helpmates, and children are born early enough to be the pillars of house-

hold happiness. And here, too, are women in their ripened prime—women who should be rejoicing, under any burden of domestic care, in the strong arm of a husband's trust and the golden girdle of sons and daughters—but women whose still healthful frames and comely features speak but of a physical vigour invulnerable to twenty years of dissolute pleasure and precarious livelihood. It is a heart-saddening thought that the youngest of these two hundred women is already old in vice—has crossed the line that can never be repassed—has loosed that zone of purity which no power even in Heaven can re-clasp. But that to the oldest and most obdurate there is to-night to be offered such help as God or man can give—help that may make the past less terrible by making the future hopeful—it would seem a cruel trifling with human sympathies to collect these victims of irremediable error before eyes that look daily on virtuous wives, and on children that make visible the doctrine, ' heaven lies round about us in our infancy.'

" It is about one o'clock when the gentlemen whose activity we have described, gather in a central space on the floor, and one of them requests attention. It is the Hon. and Rev. Baptist Noel who does this—the man who threw up good chances of a bishopric to become a Dissenting pastor. ' My young friends,' he begins ; and he has no reason to complain of want of attention, though there are no signs of special interest. He tells his strange audience of that midnight meeting of the two Apostles and their gaoler—the earthquake, and the cry for salvation. He rapidly and plainly applies the story not so much to the conscience as to the consciousness of his hearers. If we had expected that the speaker would so err as to sermonize, we should be happily disappointed. He does not avoid these most deep-seated truths of human duty and destiny which are the basis of religious emotion, but he does not dwell on them. He speaks like a man in the flesh, though not like a man of the world. If he were the latter, he would scarcely warn these comfortable-looking, healthy women that ten years of their present life will send them all to the grave. But there is a hearty human and almost fatherly tenderness in the emphasis he lays on the unreality of their joys, the bitterness of their reflections, the vileness of their seducers, the unworthiness of their habitual associates. He contrasts all this with the possibilities, not only of what they have lost, but of what they may regain. He offers the means of instant rescue—a home, which he takes care to assure them is not a prison ; a home in which they shall be subjected to no indignity or privation, but from which they may emerge respected, perhaps beloved. He tells them of others who have thus been saved from all the misery of a sinful life. He refers to a letter from one who, forty years ago, escaped back into good repute, and has grown up in honourable married life. But all this, while he has spoken to an audience more attentive than interested, and certainly not affected. As by an afterthought, he mentions that, since their last meeting, some mother has sent him a photograph of her daughter, beseeching him to seek that lost one in this company. In an instant the sealed-up fountains are opened, and strong emotion replaces real or feigned indifference. They who heard unmoved of Divine love and human help are touched and shaken by the voice of a weeping mother. Some sob audibly in their tempest of awakened memory. Tears run down the cheeks of many. It seems as though every fallen daughter were asking, ' Is it my mother ? Is it my picture ?'

"Mr. Noel is either not an orator, and does not know the power he has gained, or he has reasons for not retouching the chord which so loudly vibrates. Perhaps he wisely desires to avoid any approach to the physical phenomena of revivalism. Yet he might surely use the only key that opens these hearts he so much desires to enter. He resumes his former tone of general exhortation—an impressive and persuasive tone, we should say, did we not see how soon these fair faces have resumed their calm insensibility. He gives way to the Rev. Mr. Bickersteth—a clergyman who cannot rid himself of pulpit phrases, but who speaks with an earnest humanity that should make any phraseology a power to melt and move. When he ceases, prayer is offered by Mr. Brock, another Baptist minister, and one whose very face is eloquent of kindhearted goodness. His supplication is surely not unaccompanied. Church congregations are not more decorous than this—let us hope, not more devout. Nearly every face is covered, and some knees are bent. It is such a prayer as every human being can join in—the fervent breathing, in homely words, of a heart that asks aid from Heaven to abate the sin and misery on earth ; the sin and misery here, close at hand.

"Another prayer is offered by Dr. Maclean—a layman, judging by his long white beard, but of apostolic soul. Mr. Brock then announces, with loud and cheerful voice, that fifty—a hundred, any number—who will at once quit their present way of life, may this very night be taken to a reformatory home ; and if any would return to parents at a distance, the means shall be provided. How many will go ? How many will *not* go ? we should rather say. Will not all embrace with glad gratitude this proffered rescue? Can any one of these girls and women, who have been for two hours at least restored to the company of good and honourable men and women (for two or three of the latter have aided)—can anyone deliberately go back to the trade and the society that debases and destroys ? Alas, yes ! Here is one, young and very fair, who replies with a firm though courteous voice, she has decided ; and she will not go with the real friends who are now earnestly talking, in groups or singly, with their departing guests. With one exception, and that instantly hushed by her companions, there has been no rude refusal—but there are many who hesitate, and hesitate till they are again lost. Every one going out seems like a captive carried off by the devil from good angels. But some twenty or more do remain, and over these, whatever chances and changes may await them on the hard road of repentance—over these may we not already rejoice, as does the good shepherd over sheep recovered from the wilderness to the fold ?"

THE LOCK ASYLUM.

My desire to visit the Lock Asylum was gratified by Mr. James Lane, surgeon to that institution, who kindly accompanied me through the wards, together with Mr. Carbonell, one of the governors who takes a deep interest in the subject. The buildings are large and lofty, situated a little out of town on the Harrow Road, having been rebuilt within comparatively a few years. It appears that an asylum is offered to all the girls who enter the Lock Hospital, or who are sent there by Government to be cured of venereal diseases under the Contagious Diseases Act. It cannot, however, be said that these poor patients show any great disposition to enter the asylum. In the year 1867, out of 877 patients 76 only entered the asylum, or in other words 8·09 per cent. Of these

169 Ordinary, 42, 24·8 per cent.
708 Government, 34, 4·7 per cent.

The women on admission to the asylum are placed apart in a probationary ward; as we entered this room we noticed fourteen sitting round a table, with the matron at the head, occupying themselves with needlework. In reply to my inquiries I was informed that the latest comer had only been a week in the institution, another had nearly worked out her full probationary period of three months, the rule of the institution being that those who conduct themselves well for that time may become permanent inmates of the institution, in which they can remain for a term varying from twelve to eighteen months, and at the end of it a situation is found for them. In answer to my further inquiries I was told that of twenty who had entered this probationary ward during the preceding six weeks, six had desired to be discharged. I can readily believe that the monotonous life of that ward must have been very irksome to the sort of female whose habits I have described in the second chapter of this work. The inmates are allowed to walk every day in a sort of courtyard behind the asylum, and are instructed in reading in classes, but I was told that writing is forbidden as leading to correspondence with the outdoor world. Once a month they are permitted to write to their friends, but their letters must be shown to the matron before being put into the post. In another large room we saw twenty-one women working at their needle. These had passed through their probationary period, and I was told might converse quietly as they sat at their work, provided they did not talk loud, another matron, who was seated at the table, constantly supervising them. My informants told me that the matrons objected to sewing machines, having so many human machines to do their work, though, judging from their manner of working, needlework seemed to form but a small share of attention in the institution. I was next taken to the laundry, which seems the staple business of the asylum. In a large, lofty, well-ventilated ground floor, we saw about twenty girls ironing.

Monday and Tuesday in the week, the clothes collected from private families in London are here washed, and at the time of my visit on Thursday the linen was being got up. The matron told me that she thought it took ten months to educate a girl to this business. I asked if there was not a great demand in all parts of the country for laundry women, having elsewhere heard that it is very difficult for county families to obtain such servants even at high wages, but it appeared that this was not the destination of these girls, who were placed out in small families, where their future career could be watched. It occurred to me, however, that the education of the laundry opened a good career for this class of women.

The Lock Asylum was, at the time of my visit, about half self-supporting. Government provided for ten beds by contributing £20 per bed towards the maintenance of the inmates. The dormitories are excellently constructed. They are lofty rooms, divided by partitions open at the top, and strict rules are laid down for preserving the privacy of each compartment. Whilst passing through the asylum, I asked myself what class of girls do these fifty-two that I see in the wards represent. In the first place, they are the picked and selected of a very large class. These fifty-two women voluntarily come into the asylum. They were the well-behaved, quiet, domesticated, but delicate-looking prostitutes. Making every allowance for the plainness of their dress, as a man of the world I should say that they were not likely to gain a livelihood by prostitution, and I asked myself, as I have done on more than one previous occasion, would not these girls, even if no asylum had been offered to them, have soon left the paths of prostitution and taken to some other calling, merely from their unfitness to undergo its hardships.

If, however, I am at issue sometimes with the authorities of these institutions as to the sort of girl who enters an asylum, I likewise occasionally differ from them as to the way they carry out their philanthropic mission. I was lately visiting a hospital, and the authorities told me that if the girl wished to return to her friends after being cured, not only was the wish seconded, but a policeman was sent with her to see that she really was remitted to the care of her parents.

The plan may be a very good one, to prevent the prostitute being waylaid as she left the hospital by some of her old associates, but it did not seem to occur to the would-be benefactors of the girl that the arrival of a parishioner in charge of a policeman creates a great sensation in a little country community. They did not seem to have contemplated the possibility of the fact that the villagers become curious to learn what Mary Smith has been doing at ———— ; I ventured to suggest to the authorities that the village gossips would probably over their tea hint at her gay doings, and that the young men would not long be idle in ferreting out her antecedents ; and the quiet village, notwithstanding all the care of the rector or aid of his good wife, would be made very disagreeable for the fair penitent who had once quitted her home on an evil errand, and it too often happens she will quit it again, no more to return to her native place.

These bucolic ways are very curious. Let a girl be seduced by one in her own rank, let her have a child, or even two, and her " misfortune "* may be overlooked, but the parish cannot forgive her having been a gay woman or a soldier's trull. Public opinion, even in a remote country village, has some very curious phases, and I venture to doubt whether its inhabitants cordially take to returned convicts or repentant prostitutes. Sudden reformation is again one of those popular delusions that I must expose. The consequences of vice are not thus to be got rid of. They may be put out of sight ; that is all that we can say of them.

* Scene a Hayfield. The clergyman addresses Mrs. Smith, who is raking behind the cart, " Well Mrs. Smith, how is Fanny ?" " La, sir ! why the baby is dead ! so now I says she is quite as good as she was afore." " *Quite !*" said the Rev. gentleman. This was poor Fanny's second *misfortune* as it is called, and so long as the child died, they considered it in this straw-plaiting village as no *misfortune*.

On the other hand, in a quiet country community, let a woman be married, and brought home as the wife of a good workman or labourer, her antecedents may be suspected, doubted, or even well known, but as she is the legal wife of one who is responsible for her acts, she is tolerated, and gradually amalgamates with the others, but even then when her female neighbour's wrath is up, she may be reminded of unpleasant truths, and it may be well that her children should be at school, and not hear more of their mother's antecedents than she is herself ready to tell them.

I must not leave this subject without considering a little more closely whether Penitentiaries and Lock Asylums are really calculated to produce any substantial impression upon prostitution. After my visit to the Lock Asylum, the details of which have been above given, I ventured to suggest to Mr. Carbonell, who for many years (I can testify from my own knowledge), has taken a deep interest in the well being of the Lock Asylum, a doubt whether this and kindred institutions were adapting themselves to the wants of the day. I admit that the public are under the greatest obligation to penitentiaries for having for many years past been the only institutions which have recognized and taken an interest in penitent women. After this avowal, it may seem ungrateful in me to question their utility, and to point out that very few women can be rescued in this way, and at a large expenditure of money ; but as a writer on this subject, I cannot refrain from expressing my doubts whether even this well conducted asylum answers the purposes for which it was created. I have often asked myself the question whether it is really necessary to confine a girl from twelve to eighteen months within the walls of an asylum. How many will remain for so long a time in the institution ? When they leave the seclusion which they have become accustomed to, are they better adapted than when they entered, for coping with the temptations outside? Are they not liable again to be tempted, and again to fall into evil ways. It should be remembered that selected as I have shown them to be, and admirably trained whilst within the walls of the institution, after leaving the asylum they have still to gain a position before they can marry, and amalgamate with the social ranks. I venture to entertain the opinion that many of the philanthropic persons who established these institutions years ago, did so without having previously studied the natural history, the habits, the wants, the tendencies, and the careers of these women. Now that we are better acquainted with all these circumstances, I must be permitted to express a doubt whether their complete segregation is likely to prove permanently beneficial. The upper class of prostitutes are never met with in asylums, nor are the lower. If there are 50,000 prostitutes in London, we need means to rescue not 100 or 1,000, but 12,000 annually, supposing that a prostitute only follows the calling for four years. My object is to assist the many in rescuing themselves and getting away in a few years from a calling that they must detest. My philanthropic friends, however, still maintain that eighteen months seclusion is required to eradicate the seeds of vice, and they cannot be induced to see that the money can be laid out better, or that any system should be preferred to the one adopted at the Lock Asylum.

I will only add that if the principle is right, no institution can more effectually carry out its objects than does the Lock Asylum. Cleanliness reigns everywhere—the ventilation is good—punishment, I am told, there is none—kindness towards the inmates characterises the officers—religious instruction is provided, and the girls are taught to consider that the Governors feel an interest in their future wellbeing—and persons who take a deep interest in the institution point to the statistics of the good work it has done with pride and satisfaction.

That a certain amount of good is wrought by these agencies, is undoubtedly true, and if people are willing to give their time and money for the sake of obtaining good results, however small, far be it from me to say a word to dissuade them, or in any way to retard their efforts, which have my fullest sympathy. It would, however, ill become me to allow my sympathy to obscure my judgment, or to make me refrain from giving full expression to the opinions which I have formed on a subject so important, seeing that they are the results of long experience and careful thought. I repeat, then, that midnight meetings are unlikely to prove productive of satisfactory results, because their voice cannot effectually reach the large body of prostitutes to whose relief the efforts of the philanthropist should be directed. Penitentiaries and lock asylums, supported and managed by private effort, are also productive of results wholly inadequate to the labour and money bestowed. The reasons seem to be obvious ; a gigantic evil cannot be removed by private irregular and unsystematic efforts. A little tinkering here and there, may here and there produce a little good, but the advantage obtained is accidental, partial, and transitory. What we want is combined effort and regular machinery, carrying out some well-considered, universally accepted and definite scheme. We must utilise our resources, and combine our forces. Of our present state it may be truly said,

> " The ways
> Were filled with rapine, here and there a deed
> Of prowess done, redressed a random wrong."

We are drawing our bows at a venture instead of taking deliberate aim, fishing with lines when we ought to be using nets, leaving scattered individuals to perform as best they can, duties which demand the care and concentrated action of the State. We have seen again and again that penitentiaries attract to their friendly shelter those only who would of themselves relinquish a calling for which they have become unfitted by loss of health, and strength, and personal attractions. Would I then withdraw from the reach of the sickly and failing and doubly unfortunate, the possibility of living, the hope of recovery ? Far from this ; I would shelter them as tenderly as ever ; but I would do more— I would show to the thousands now squandering in unclean and filthy living, their youth, and health, and beauty, the road to a better life, and open wide for them the portals of decency and hope. Further still, penitentiaries assist those only who have abandoned prostitution, or, at least, have professed their intention of so acting : more than this is necessary, the prostitute must be helped even in the days of her prostitution. Quixotic and hopeless enterprise ! So it may appear at first, so perhaps it is under the present system—or, rather, want of system.

But let those who uphold the penitentiary system consider for a moment whether my theory is more unreasonable than their practice ; they snatch their patients from scenes of excitement, to bury them in secluded, monotonous retirement, and what is the result ?   What wonder if these last forget the cruel bondage, the hazards, and the heartlessness from which they have escaped, the long dreary hours of loneliness, want, and despair, and remember only the flesh-pots of Egypt, the moments of pleasure and excitement.   What wonder if, wearied of a life of dull routine, they rush back from cold and passive virtue to sparkling, glittering ruin.   And what wonder if habits, the result of continuous action, cannot be abandoned on a sudden ?   Is it reasonable, I ask, to take women in moments of excitement and remorse, or in times of misfortune, and to hurry them in a fit of desperation, or, at least, without reflection, into a course of life directly opposite to that to which they have been accustomed, and which habit has made for them a second nature ?   I will present the supporters of penitentiaries with two alternatives, and whichever they choose will, I think, convict them of conduct as little in accordance with reason as my own " Quixotic and hopeless enterprise,"—either the women whom they receive are worn out, and could no longer continue their trade of prostitution, or they have come under the influence of some momentary impulse, and are liable to return to their wallowing as suddenly as they left it.   In the first case I will ask, why support paupers as interesting objects of charity because they happen to be vicious, whereas if they only added to the misfortune of poverty the disadvantage of virtue, they would be remitted to the tender mercies of the workhouse.   I ask is this reasonable ?   In the second case, they are expending valuable time and labour, and money, on persons whom they well know, or ought to know, will, in about forty-nine cases out of fifty, take an early opportunity of quitting the penitentiaries, or even, if they continue in them for the allotted eighteen months, will probably relapse into vice on their re-entry into the world again.   I ask is this reasonable ?   It may be right — in a certain sense I believe it is.   It certainly is not reasonable.   It is, in fact, putting it as favourably as I possibly can for the advocates of penitentiaries, lodging, boarding, and clothing a promiscuous herd of vicious women on the offchance that some few may really reform and succeed in breaking off old habits, and contracting new.   Is this reasonable ?   Inasmuch as it is right to extend help and opportunity of amendment to 100 on the chance of saving even one, it is right, and therefore reasonable—but reasonable only if no better and surer method of action can be discovered.   I recur now to my own theory, that the prostitute must be helped even in the days of her prostitution.   I am fully aware that the object which I have in view is one difficult to carry out, but I submit that its achievement is at least as easy as that of effecting reformation by means of the present penitentiary system.   That system proceeds, as I have shown, on the supposition that a sudden change of life can prevail to break off old habits.   It will be said, perhaps, that this is not true, because eighteen months' residence in the asylum is considered necessary to give time for old habits to die away and new habits to take their place.   But this is really begging the question.   Putting aside the difficulties which must await these recluses on their re-entry on the world, to encounter which successfully a life of retirement seems a poor preparation, I say that in taking them suddenly from the streets, and placing them in seclusion and under restraint, you are putting them into a position for which they have not sufficient strength of mind, or will, at least—that to find women of the town equal to the task imposed on them, must from the very nature of things be the exception, and not the rule. The principle of the advocate of this system has for its basis not the possibility merely, but the probability of sudden conversion. My plan proceeds, on the contrary, on the principle that change must be gradual, and that satisfactory reformation can only be accomplished not by suddenly transferring these women from one mode of existence to another, but by preparing them for a change of life by instilling gradually into their minds a change of thought and ideas. This can only be done by bringing them into contact with the ideas and feelings of that society which they have outraged, and by continually recalling to their notice the contrast presented by their own reckless, hopeless existence—to that pure and decent life, blessed by home ties and home affections, to which their sin makes them strangers—by bringing them into contact with men other than those with whom they usually consort, and making them feel that there are men who disapprove their mode of life, and refuse to find pleasure in their sins—by making them acquire habits of cleanliness, decency, and self-respect. The conviction that their mode of life is a fatal mistake, will thus gradually arise in their minds ; and if this growing conviction has for its companion the knowledge that a change is possible, we may expect with some confidence that the ideas thus gradually received will be abiding, and not transitory, and will ripen under proper care and help into true reformation. But how can this be done ? It clearly cannot be done by voluntary association, nor by disjointed efforts ; it must be done by a system supported and enforced by authority.

I apprehend that few people will find any difficulty in following me so far as this ; but now comes the difficulty, what machinery can we make use of, what system imposed and backed up by authority can be devised capable of doing all this ? I answer, the machinery is simple : the same men who examine the health of their bodies, may, if they will, do all this for them. But it may be answered this result has not been seen in France. I answer, that in France no attempt has been made to produce it.

We have seen that under the system as carried out in our garrison towns, something of this kind is being done. The women are at least taught to respect themselves, and they are already less dirty and less disreputable. If care be taken in the selection of the health inspectors, every prostitute who comes within the scope of the Act, will week by week find herself brought face to face with a man who disapproves and stands aloof from her life of sin, she will have the necessity of cleanliness impressed upon her, she will have the filthiness of her life imperceptibly brought to her notice. I would suggest that at the inspector's office papers should be kept, to be had on application, showing how those who desire to turn from a life of prostitution can have the means placed before them of doing so, and a notice should be fixed up in the office that such papers are there, and may be had on application. This would at least prevent the women who came for inspection, from supposing that their calling was either allowed or tolerated or considered necessary. The weekly inspections will, however, lead to something more, they will lead to the detention of numbers of these women ; the life in the hospital will give to all the very opportunities that now penitentiaries give to some, and give them in a far more judicious and salutary manner. It may be that many weeks of inspection will be undergone, and more than one visit made to the hospital, before the desired change is produced. But I have said that the method that I propose is gradual, and that the change to be real must be gradual. It may be that some better machinery can be found for producing this gradual change of ideas and habits, if so I should hail with satisfaction its appearance, but until then I commend to the attention of the thoughtful reader the institution of health inspections and hospital detentions, as a powerful means of preventing disease and effecting reformation.

It may be well to consider if, in future, the assistance of the Government board I have sketched out at p. 287 could not here come in, and aid the convalescent prostitute who has been relieved at the hospital. A very little pecuniary assistance and some sympathy might, at this stage of a girl's career, be of inestimable value. Say she will return again to a vicious course,—I dare say she will,—I maintain that is no reason why we should not aid her ; for sooner or later, give her but the chance, and she will willingly quit a life that has become distasteful to her.

One more word, and I may dismiss this portion of my subject : one mistaken notion, the fallacy of which I have already exposed, lies at the root of the penitentiary system. The old idea, once a harlot always a harlot, possesses the public mind. Proceeding from this premiss, people argue that every woman taken from the streets through the agency of penitentiaries, is a woman snatched from an otherwise interminable life of sin, whereas I have shown that the prostitute class is constantly changing and shifting, that in the natural course of events, and by the mere efflux of time the women composing it become reabsorbed into the great mass of our population—and, in fact, those whom the penitentiaries receive are those who are weary of, or unfit for their work, and in search of some other mode of life. The reasonable course to adopt is to assist the natural course of things ; to bear in mind that sooner or later the life of prostitution will be quitted, and that the duty of society is to accelerate so far as possible the change, and in the meantime to bring such influences to bear on abandoned women as shall enable them to pass through their guilty years with as little loss of self-respect and health as possible ; how to render the prostitute less depraved in mind and body, to cause her return as soon as possible to a decent mode of living, to teach her by degrees, and as occasion offers, self-restraint and self-denial, to build her up, in short—since join society again she will in any event—into a being fit to rejoin it, is the problem to be solved. Will not this be more easily and satisfactorily accomplished by subjecting all alike to supervision and bringing them into daily contact with healthy thought and virtuous life, than by consigning to wearisome and listless seclusion a few poor creatures snatched at haphazard from the streets ?

CHAPTER XI.

PREVENTION OF PROSTITUTION.

WE have seen that prostitution presents a threefold aspect ; it may be regarded as an evil condition that must always exist, and therefore a fit subject of regulation, and also as one capable of diminution both as to the intensity of the mischief produced by it, and the numbers of the people made subject to it, and amenable, therefore, to amelioration and preventive measures. Having already treated of regulation and amelioration, I may now say a few words upon the subject of prevention. Of the various causes to which I have attributed the presence among us of prostitution, three especially seem worthy of notice in this chapter, *seduction, evil training, and poverty*. It is difficult to obtain statistics sufficiently accurate or reliable to enable us to assign with any degree of certainty the proportions in which the causes to which I have adverted operate in the production of prostitutes. It is scarcely necessary for my purpose to attempt to do so. It seems sufficient to point out that these three causes exist, and to say that so far as prostitution can be traced to causes with which human laws can directly deal, it is traceable to them. We have then to consider how far the results of seduction may be made to fall short of a recourse to prostitution, by what means the early vicious training, with its attendant horrors, may be put an end to, and how far it is possible to diminish or relieve poverty and its consequences.

It is customary to argue, that the punishment of seduction cannot be apportioned in any but the present manner, namely, wholly to the female, unless where illegitimate offspring result from it, in which case the State imposes a fine of two shillings and sixpence per week upon the father. The grounds on which the legislature have decreed this state of the law are, that the woman, if not always the most active, is a consenting party. The result is practically that the consequences to the male being known and finite, thousands of men annually suffer themselves to be seduced—as the law has it—by designing women, who sacrifice not only their own future peace of mind and temporal prospects, but court the scorn of the world and bodily suffering to gratify inordinate passion. The unfortunate male is the victim, and by curious perversion the manufacture of prostitutes by female labour is

rampant. This is another painful fiction, which, had I the power, I
would attempt to dissipate. If I could not do so much, I would at
least endeavour to devise a means of strengthening the male resolution.
The next time the bastardy laws come up for consideration, I should
propose inquiry how, while in other respects the mental inferiority of
woman continues to be insisted on in all other particulars, she should
be held paramount in that of seductive powers. That this is false is
proved by the fact that the woman allows the sacrifices and sufferings
she incurs to equipoise with those of her seducer. She is acquainted
too well beforehand with both, to allow the hypothesis of her total
ignorance. In the majority of cases she has plentiful knowlege of pre-
cedents ; yet she falls. She must, therefore, either be temporarily
insane, or permanently weaker minded. Her very liability to siege
almost presupposes personal attraction, and personal attractions as
naturally ensure vanity. There is never a fair start between man and
woman *cæteris paribus*. Her side of the balance is always over-weighted.
Enough of vanity alone to kick the beam is in her scale ; yet because,
from the day when a man in real earnest first set his wit against her,
she was no more able to fly from his fascinating power than the quarry
from the falcon, or the rabbit from the snake, but rather met her fate
half-way, this strong-minded creature is by law considered the real
seducer, and a number of the most estimable people in the world are
ever ready to endorse without question this cruel article of the law's
belief.

And here, again, must physiology be invoked to help the lawgivers
and society to a more just conclusion. It will some day be taken into
account I hope, that as (I believe) Coleridge said, the desire is on the
side of man, love of approbation on the side of the woman ; and law
will be amended after deeply comparing the physiology of sinning men,
not with that of virtuous, but of fallen women. We have hitherto set
up for compassion an impregnable female *eidolon*, and because *she* was
adamant have declared men to be the seduced, not the seducers.

We are used to talk, and we have, in fact, legislated, as if the gates
of a woman's honour were of brass, and could not be opened but from
within ; and as if the outer force required to beat them down could be
calculated to a pound by an engineer. There are gates, it is true, and
modesty is their keeper ; but the keeper may slumber or be bribed, or
may make a fair fight against the foe and be beaten. But how does
the righteous world act ? Though the castle and the gate, the porter
and the enemy are all variable quantities—when the place falls, we
always hang the garrison.

I extract the following passage from one of the many letters to the
Editor of "The Times," evoked by the proposition of the St. James's
Refuge :—

"The law of 1834, which, in my opinion, brought this mischief on
society, was founded on a mistaken theory—namely, that women are
the best guardians of their own honour. This is inverting the order of
nature, and falsifying the common experience of all time. It is, in fact
splendid nonsense. The result is, that the law throws upon the weakest
of the two offenders all the consequences of a vice in which she at least

could only be a participator. There was, to my mind, something marvellously cowardly and unmanly in this. The best guardian of the honour of woman is he who, having gained her affections, has obtained a mastery over her judgment, and all that makes her respectable in society. But the days of chivalry are indeed past, since men become seducers by Parliamentary licence. It is, however, alleged that the Legislature has provided means for securing justice to the woman so betrayed, by allowing her to produce corroborative evidence. This is adding insult to injury. Why, Sir, between 300 and 400 of these cases come under my own observation every year, and I can affirm that in nine cases out of ten there is a total absence of any evidence whatever —and why? Because the men who practise these frauds are for the most part habitual seducers, and take all the precautions which such scoundrels are likely to invent. It is not an uncommon circumstance for two or three young women (mere girls, in some instances) to be with child at one and the same time by one man, and that man a married man, and yet the law has no remedy for this, because there is no corroborative evidence. But suppose it otherwise, what is a penniless girl to do against a fellow who can afford to fee counsel to browbeat and frighten her out of court?

" *Let every member of Parliament who voted for a law founded upon the Arcadian notion that every woman is the best guardian of her own honour apply it to his own daughters, and watch the result. Why, he gives the lie to it every day of his life, his anxious thought being how best to guard his children from the pollutions which surround even them.* If, therefore, the rich practically repudiate the notion, why apply it to the children of the poor, who on leaving home at an early age for service are deprived of the restraints and checks of kindred?

" It will then be asked, what are the remedies for such obvious evils? I answer that paternal governors should adopt the same course in their collective as they would in their individual character—namely, to distinguish between habitual profligates and a casual error ; to afford to the woman who appears for the first time in the character of a mother, a facility for affiliating her child which should be denied to her who commits a second offence. By this means a great end would be accomplished—viz., fixing the consequences where they ought to rest—on the actual seducer of the woman. Sterne, no mean observer of human nature, asked one hundred years ago—' Is there no difference between one prepensely going out of the way, and continuing there by depravity of will, and a hapless wanderer straying by delusion and wearily treading back her steps?' I ask the same question."—(J. B.)

I have taken the liberty of italicising, without farther comment, a passage which I should especially recommend to the consideration of our lawgivers and others whom it may concern. But the whole appears to me valuable, as conveying the impressions of a thoughtful and experienced man, who evidently is versed in a sphere other than metropolitan, and serves me to open, I think, not inappropriately, a few observations upon the bastardy laws, a change in which would be a considerable step towards prostitution prevention.

It cannot be denied by any one acquainted with rural life, that seduction of girls is a sport and a habit with vast numbers of men, married (as suggested by "J. B.," which I fully corroborate) and single, placed above the ranks of labour. The "keeping company" of the labouring classes, accompanied by illicit intercourse, as often as not leads to marriage; but not so that of the farmer's son, farmer, first, second, or third-class, squire, or squireen. Many such rustics of the middle class, and men of parallel grades in country towns, employ a portion of their spare time in the coarse, deliberate villainy of making prostitutes. Of these, the handsomer are draughted off into the larger communities, where their attractions enable them to settle; the others are tied to the spot of their birth and fall. Men who themselves employ female labour, or direct it for others, have always ample opportunities of choice, compulsion, secrecy, and subsequent intimidation, should exposure be probable and disagreeable. They can, for a time, show favour to their victim by preferring her before her fellows; they can at any convenient moment discharge her. The lower sort of them can often procure access to the Union for both her and her offspring; and the upper can scheme marriages of the nature alluded to at page 44. With these, and with the gentlemen whose *délassement* is the contamination of town servants and *ouvrières*, the first grand engine is, of course, vanity—the little more money that will get the poor girl a little more dress, admiration, and envy than her equals enjoy. Then, when the torch is set to the fire, woman's love of approbation helps her to her own destruction. Then cheap promises—promises of marriage—made to be broken— which, however, the strong-minded one of the Parliament's imagining is always ready to believe—and promises often taken down on the rolls of Heaven, whose breach must be a sin against the God of Mercy himself, of care for the woman and her offspring. But the latter are as easily snapped as the former, and the woman whom her neighbours call a scheming hussey for thinking of a marriage above her station, is called a silly fool for her pains if she fall, without inducements of ambition, before the assault of passion only. She may be with child, or she may not, but she has at law a remedy for her wrong. Yes, and what is it? Will the strong-minded one apply herself to it?—and how often? She loved too much, and she still loves overmuch, in nine cases out of ten, to dream of worldly wisdom, or, as she calls it, persecuting her child's father. The worldly wisdom that overcame, as the sham has it, the hardihood and modesty of the male, and turned his head, cannot get its poor owner into a court of justice, even when her parents are so minded, and funds are forthcoming for a breach of promise action. Her remedy is a farce so far; or rather it is a farce to say that it has any prophylactic or *in terrorem* value. But she has one more remedy —or her friends have; for her father, whom the law supposes to be charged with the maintenance of his children when derelict by the world, and therefore to have in return some presumed employer's right over them, may proceed at common law for loss of her services. But this he can only do if he has means, inclination to face the extreme of publicity and abuse, courage to meet a heavy preponderance of law and public feeling against him, and can adduce an amount of corroborative evidence which should suffice to carry a much more heavy conviction.

This machinery, which stands upon a fiction, is cumbrous, and its results are rare and generally ridiculous. It amounts, in fact, to no remedy for wrong; and the crime which it is supposed to check flourishes under its pleasant shade. There is, however, one tolerably certain method of enforcing law against a man who, having seduced, has deserted a woman and her child. When we have recited that, we may close the list of remedies. She may apply to a bench of magistrates for a summons. The summons is granted; and the man found, or not found, the usual result is " an order in bastardy," in pursuance of which the maximum sum of half-a-crown is due and payable by the father each and every week for the support and maintenance of the said infant, but for that of his strong-minded seducer—nothing!

Sighing,—or, it may be, smiling compassionately at the crest-fallen appearance of the strong one who has found hardihood to come before them,—the bench of justices regret their inability to do more for her. They would make an example if they could, they say in some instances; in others, they make an order for only 1s. 6d. or 2s. a week. The magistrate, who is a family man, and has perchance himself grown a crop of wild oats, gives a sad thought or two to the case as he jogs home; and has even been known to advocate in public some more extended protection of women. But the plague is for all that—as it may be when I, too, am passed away—yet unstayed. The days of chivalry are gone indeed, and the honour of all women but those of his own house is so much a bye-word with the Englishman—their bodies so often his sport—that the reform of the bastardy law, and the thence resulting check to prostitution, may chance to be deferred until a sense of common danger shall have made us all fellow-agitators.

If I could not get imprisonment of the seducer substituted for the paltry fine of half-a-crown a week, I would at least give to the commonwealth, now liable to pecuniary damage by bastardy, some interest in his detection and punishment. The union house is now often enough the home of the deserted mother and the infant bastard: and the guardians of the poor ought, I think, to have the right, in the interest of the community, to act as bastardy police, and to be recouped their charges. I would not allow the maintenance of an illegitimate child to be at the expense of any but the father. I would make it the incubus on him, not on its mother; and I would not leave his detection, exposure, and money loss in the option of the latter. A young man who now has a second or third illegitimate child, by different women, has not lived without adding some low cunning to his nature. It often happens that a fellow of this sort will, for a time, by specious promises or presents to a girl he fully intends ultimately to desert, defer making any payments for or on account of her child. If he can for twelve months, and without entering into any shadow of an agreement (and we may all guess how far the craft of an injured woman will help her to one that would hold water), stave off any application on her part to the authorities, her claim at law is barred; and she herself, defied at leisure, becomes, in due course, chargeable to her parish or union. But not thus should a virtuous State connive at the obligations of paternity being shuffled on to its public shoulders, when, by a very trifling modi fication of the existing machinery they might be adjusted on the proper back—permanently or temporarily, as might be considered publicly expedient. I would enact, I say, by the help of society, that, in the first place, the seduction of a female, properly proved, should involve the male in a heavy pecuniary fine, according to his position—not at all by way of punishment, but to strengthen, by the very firm abutment of the breeches-pocket, both him and his good resolutions against the temptations and force of designing woman. I would not offer the latter, as I foresee will be instantaneously objected, this bounty upon sinfulness—this incentive to be a seducer; but, on the contrary, the money should be due to the community, and recoverable in the county court or superior court at the suit of the Government Board; and should be invested by the treasurer of such court, or by the county, or by some public trustee in bastardy, for the benefit of mother and child. The child's portion of this fund should be retained by such public officer until the risk of its becoming chargeable to the community quasi bastard should be removed by the mother's marriage, or otherwise; and the mother's share should be for her benefit as an emigration fund or marriage portion. Persons acquainted with the country will bear me out, that many a woman not married by her seducer for economy's sake (which would satisfy justice), would, with a dower, even thus accruing, soon re-enter the pale of society through the gate of matrimony. I think that very useful knowledge of such a law as this would be rapidly diffused, and be found materially to harden men's hearts against female seductions.

Morality based on fear has, I grant, a most rotten foundation. But the reader must remember that the ear and heart of man, once barred by salutary caution against the charmings of•all save exceptional and ungovernable lust, would be much more accessible to the moralizing influence—the legitimate attachment—which I have proposed that society should simultaneously hold out at a cheaper rate. To the practical, systematic seducer—no uncommon character—upon whom moral argument is, and always will be, thrown away, this pursuit would, under such a *régime*, become a very first-class and most expensive luxury, demanding more money, craft, and time than many of us have to dispose of.

The careless man, who is, as the law now stands, supposed to be the secondary or passive party, finding that seduction, besides being neither so convenient nor so creditable as marriage, was nearly as costly—especially when often given way to—would cease to expose himself unguardedly to the illicit blandishments of womankind. It would be a hard matter for an intelligent girl to compass her own estrayal against the conscience that her pecuniary profit would be nothing, her public shame in the power of her neighbours, and that her intended victim was armed against her by a *chevaux-de-frise* of pounds, shillings, and pence, replacing, for their joint good, the trivial weekly half-crown, which is at present no defence to him—no check upon either his or her propensities. Supposing, again, for the sake of argument, that the sin and the gratification of a seduction are shared in common; few, I presume, will deny that practically, and in most cases, the female pays all the penalty? Are we not called upon, then, by common justice, if not by religion, to invite some such change in the law as shall help to guard the pair from the sin, and, at all events, secure a more equitable adjustment of the consequences.

I cannot close these observations without again drawing at some length upon the eloquent article in the *Quarterly Review*, to which I am already much indebted. The quotation, even if the passage be well known to them, must be welcome to all men of feeling who take an interest in the subject, and doubly welcome to those who are yet unaware what pure hearts, powerful minds, spirit-stirring pens have preceded me in this agitation :—

"The third needed change in social ethics is this : that the *deserter*— not the seducer—shall be branded with the same kind and degree of reprobation with which society now visits the coward and the cheat. The man who submits to insult rather than fight ; the gambler who packs the cards, or loads the dice, or refuses to pay his debts of honour ; is hunted from among even his unscrupulous associates as a stained and tarnished character. *Let the same measure of retributive justice be dealt to the seducer who deserts the woman who has trusted him, and allows her to come upon the town.* We say the deserter—not the seducer : for there is as wide a distinction between them as there is between the gamester and the sharper. Mere seduction will never be visited with extreme severity among men of the world, however correct and refined may be their general tone of morals ; for they will always make large allowances on the score of youthful passions, favouring circumstances, and excited feeling. Moreover, they well know that there is a wide distinction—that there are all degrees of distinction—between a man who commits a fault of this kind under the influence of warm affections and a fiery temperament, and the cold-hearted systematic assailer of female virtue, whom all reprobate and shun. It is universally felt that you cannot, with any justice, class these men in the same category, nor mete out to them the same measure of condemnation. But the man who, when his caprice is satisfied, casts off his victim as a worn-out garment, or a damaged toy ; who allows the woman who trusted his protestations, reciprocated his caresses, shared in his joys, lay in his bosom, resigned herself to him, in short,

'In all the trusting helplessness of love,'

to sink from the position of his mistress to the loathsome life of prostitution, because his seduction and desertion have left no other course open to her—who is not ready to make any sacrifice of peace, of fortune, of reputation even, in order to save one whom he has once loved from such an abyss of wretched infamy — must surely be more stained, soiled, and hardened in soul, more utterly unfitted for the company or sympathies of gentlemen or men of honour—than *any* coward, *any* gambler, *any* cheat ! . . . .

"When once the morality of the world has recovered a healthy tone on this subject, and desertion is branded as unmanly and dishonourable, seduction will become comparatively rare ; for men will be chary of contracting obligations which they feel must cling to them for ever.

All men will feel then, as the ingenuous and kind-hearted feel now, how sad a mistake it is to suppose that the chains of illicit love are at all lighter or weaker than those of more public and legitimate connexions. 'It never happens,' says one of our chief novelists, 'to a man of just and honourable feeling, to make a woman wholly dependent on himself, and to shut on her the gates of the world, without his discovering, sooner or later, that he has not only encumbered his conscience, but has more effectually crippled his liberty, and more deeply implicated his peace, than by all the embarrassments of the Church.'"

If only to reduce the sad total of unfortunates yearly driven to prostitution as their last resource, it seems to me that some system worthy of the name should be adopted for dealing with the victims of seduction ; but its consequences end not with the ruin of the unhappy mother, two cognate evils—illegitimacy and infanticide—spring from her fall. I wish to call attention a little more at large to these last-mentioned topics, deeming them worthy of notice both on account of their own inherent interest, and as affording additional reasons for the systematic treatment of cases of seduction.

The numbers of illegitimate children yearly brought into the world are very considerable.

" STATISTICS OF ILLEGITIMACY.—The number of children born in any country, out of wedlock, is not exactly known. A comparison, however, can be made of the number of children in different countries who are registered in such a manner as to disclose their illegitimacy. Statistical investigation has shown that there are many causes which may account for the differences that exist in the proportion of children born out of wedlock in various foreign countries, among which may be mentioned that of the legitimation of children born before marriage. England stands almost alone among the civilized nations of Europe in refusing legitimation, even at the wish of the parents, to offspring born out of wedlock. In England the percentage of illegitimate births to total births has declined from 6·7 in 1847 to 5·9 in 1867, while the number of persons married to every 100 of population has increased from 1·586 in 1847 to 1·672 in 1867. In Scotland, where many of the children registered as illegitimate are legitimated by the subsequent marriage of their mothers, the percentage of children born out of wedlock to total births was 8·5 in 1856 and 10·1 in 1866. In Spain the proportional number of illegitimate births was 5·6 in 1859, and 5·5 in 1864 ; but these results being derived from the baptisms of the children are very erroneous. The percentage for Italy in the year 1865, including foundlings, most of which are illegitimate, was 5·1 ; the number of illegitimate births in Italy, however, appeared incredibly small, being only 10,547 out of a total number of births of 865,387, affording a ratio of a little more than 1 per cent, a result manifestly erroneous. In Holland illegitimacy is very low, and the rate in 1859, which was 4·1 per cent., was the same (4·1) in 1864. In Belgium the percentage has decreased from 7·4 in 1859 to 7·0 in 1865. The returns for France, although they show a higher proportion than Belgium, indicate a slight improvement from 7·8 per cent. in 1858 to 7·5 per cent. in 1864. The rates for

France are comparatively low, but the social habits of the French may perhaps account for the small proportion of illegitimacy. In Prussia there is little variation in the proportion between the year 1858 (8.4 per cent.) and that of the year 1864 (8·1 per cent.). In Norway the proportion per cent. of illegitimate to the total number of births was 8·6 in 1850, and 8·4 in 1860. In Sweden the percentages are rather high—viz., 9·4 in 1855 and 9·5 in 1864. In Austria the rate of illegitimacy was 9·0 per cent. in 1851, and 10·9 per cent. in 1864, showing a marked increase of bastardy. In Wurtemberg the percentages were 16·1 in 1857, and 16·4 in 1864 ; and in Bavaria the high proportion was reached of 22·6 in 1857, and 22·5 in 1862.

"It should be remembered that in some of the European States marriage is prohibited until the parties can show they have the means of maintaining their offspring. In many cases concubinage results, and the children are illegitimate. Glancing at the returns for some of the European capitals, it is seen that Vienna had the highest ratio of illegitimate births to total births—viz. 51·7 per cent. in 1851, and 51·5 in 1866, so that more than one half of the children born in this city are illegitimate. This high rate may, perhaps, be chiefly owing to children being brought from all parts of the country to be placed in the foundling hospitals of the capital. Dr. Herz, assistant physician to the Vienna foundling institution, states that only unmarried females are received in the public lying-in hospitals, where they are delivered and their children are cared for in the foundling institutions, quite free of expense, until they attain their seventh year. If they do not wish to enter private houses as wet nurses, they are dismissed after about three months have elapsed. Thus, the children being well provided for, the temptation to commit infanticide is removed. One of the greatest advantages for the lower classes in Vienna consists in the *crèches* erected and supported by voluntary subscriptions, where children are received during the daytime and boarded for about a penny a day. In Vienna there are two large hospitals for children ; and of equal importance is a third institution which Dr. Herz calls dispensaries for children, of which there are six or seven in this city. In Paris the percentage of illegitimate births to total births was 26·4 in 1858, and 28·1 in 1867 : a distinction is made between illegitimate children recognized and not recognized. In Paris, as in Vienna, the high rate of illegitimacy may be chiefly accounted for by the large number of illegitimate births registered in the city not belonging to the resident population. In Berlin there is but little variation in the proportion between the year 1840 (15·0 per cent.) and that of 1863 (15·9 per cent.). In Edinburgh the ratio was 7·6 in 1856, and 10·2 in 1866. In London the percentage was the lowest—viz., 4·2 in 1857, and 4·1 in 1867.

"The facts from which the above calculations have been deduced are exclusive of 'stillborn.' With reference to the question of the legitimation of children born before marriage, the Registrar-General of England states that he does not wish to see it introduced into England and Wales. He does not approve of a man shortly before his death marrying a woman whom through life he has been ashamed to make his wife, and thus legitimating the issue of a long concubinage, altogether changing their *status*, and depriving of his supposed inheritance him who has for many years been brought up and considered as his lawful heir. It is—in the opinion of the Registrar-General—a power which immodest designing women should not be able to persuade weak men in their dotage to exercise. If the Scotch law legitimating issue *per subsequens matrimonium* were introduced into England, he points out that cases might occur in which a man in years would be empowered to make a selection from his aged paramours, and, by marrying the favoured one, make her eldest son heir to his extensive estates; and were he a marquis, all the sons and daughters of the family would become at once lords and ladies. The Registrar-General cannot approve the system; it may prevail in many countries as well as in Scotland, but in his opinion it should not be adopted in England."[*]

The accompanying table shows the number of legitimate and illegitimate children born in England and Wales, from 1845 to 1865, inclusive, according to the returns of the Registrar-General.

Years.	Legitimate Children.	Illegitimate Children.
1845	505,280	38,241
1846	534,096	38,529
1847	503,840	36,125
1848	526,812	36,747
1849	538,825	39,334
1850	553,116	40,306
1851	573,865	42,000
1852	581,530	42,482
1853	572,628	39,763
1854	593,664	40,741
1855	594,260	40,783
1856	614,802	42,651
1857	620,069	43,002
1858	612,176	43,305
1859	645,130	44,751
1860	640,355	43,693
1861	652,249	44,157
1862	667,462	45,222
1863	680,276	47,141
1864	692,827	47,448
1865	701,484	46,585

For children born under this condition there is no provision, save such as can be made by the unhappy mother herself, doled out by the parish, or wrung from the unwilling father. The first is precarious, the second inadequate and unfair to the ratepayers, while the third is limited to a maximum of 2s. 6d. per week. It is, of course, possible that the mother may have the means of supporting herself and her offspring, and in some, we will hope in many, instances the father will obey

[*] 'The Times,' January 28, 1869.

the obligations of nature. In the majority of cases the father refuses to provide for the mother and child the necessary support ; the mother is driven to the streets, and the child handed over to the workhouse, the hireling, or the grave. It is grievous that children should be born dependent for support on the caprice or good feeling of the father, and that men should be left at liberty to make harlots and breed paupers with impunity. This is the result of the present system. The evil does not end here—the offspring of unlawful love is to the mother, instead of a source of joy and an object of loving care, an intolerable burden and a cause of shame. Her natural desire is to hide her reproach from the world, and to rid herself of the burden ; hence come concealment of birth, baby farming, and infanticide. The procuring of abortion might, perhaps, be added to the list, but need not be here considered, as it is likely to be practised most by a class far removed from the very poor ; it is also a crime recognised as such by the law and by the law adequately dealt with ; it cannot be said to be a necessary result either of prostitution or seduction,* nor can any possible means of lessening the evil results attendant on a fall from virtue, and the birth of illegitimate children, mitigate or remove the temptation to this crime. With the three other evils which I have mentioned, the case is different. It is possible, by judicious legislation, to render concealment of birth less easy to accomplish and less desired ; baby farming may be regulated, if not suppressed ; infanticide, either caused by motives identical with those that lead to concealment of birth, or a result of baby farming, will yield to the influences by which the others are diminished. Very few words will, I think, suffice to show the gravity and the extent of the evils with which I am now concerned. Baby farming is a term lately introduced to describe a somewhat old practice. By it we understand the taking off the parents' hands of infants, by midwives and others, for a consideration. This consideration may consist of payment made either in a lump sum, or by instalments. The number of children that a woman may have under her care at any one time is unlimited. The receiver need not possess any qualification requisite for the due performance of the duties that she undertakes, she need take out no license, and is subject to no inspection or supervision. The women who adopt this calling are as a rule of unscrupulous character, and inhabit low and unhealthy neighbourhoods.

The facilities afforded by such a system, for the disposal of infant incumbrances, are at once apparent : the chances that the infants will receive fair play at the hands of their strange foster mothers are small indeed, when we consider that their gains are large in proportion to the number of children received, the shortness of the period over which they survive, and the amount expended on them during that period. It is difficult to ascertain with accuracy the number of the children in this country annually placed in the hands of baby farmers ; if I put it at 30,000 I shall probably be under the mark. Even at this computation it is frightful to contemplate the waste of life and the misery that

* The 'Judicial Statistics' of 1867, return eight cases only of attempts to procure miscarriage.

is going on year by year in our midst, without any serious effort being made to provide a remedy.

A glance at the returns made by the Registrar-General, of the causes of death among infant bastards, is sufficient to prove that a large proportion perish from neglect or improper treatment. Such headings as the following cannot fail to attract notice, and seem to point their own moral: "Accidental suffocation," "suffocated in bed," "lying on its face," "accelerated by cold," "want of maternal nourishment," "want of breast milk," "low vitality," "marasmus," "atrophy," "emaciation," "gradual wasting from birth," "exhaustion from diarrhœa."

The following instance of a baby contract shows the sort of terms on which the transfer of infants can be effected, and the sort of care that the adopting party can be reasonably expected to bestow.

"Mr. Bedford, the coroner for Westminster, held an inquiry at the Charing Cross Hospital, on the body of Fanny Williams, aged eight months. Mrs. Brown, the wife of a gilder, living at 1, Plough-yard, Crown-street, Soho, said that about four months ago she had taken charge of and adopted the child from its mother, a single woman, named Caroline Williams. On Thursday night last she was sitting in her room with the child on her lap, when it was suddenly seized with convulsions. She at once took it to Dr. Cooper, of Moor-street, who advised her to take it to the hospital. She did so, but on its arrival it was pronounced by the house surgeon to be dead. Caroline Williams, aged seventeen, the mother of the child, said she was a single woman. She was confined with the deceased child in June last. She had saved a few pounds in service, and being unable to attend properly to her child, she answered an advertisement she saw in a paper, from a Mrs. Brown, who desired to adopt a child. She saw Mrs. Brown on the subject, and after some conversation together, Mrs. Brown agreed to adopt her child for £5, and the following agreement was drawn up :— 'Received of Caroline Williams £5, for which sum I agree to take and adopt her child, Fanny Williams, and to bring it up in a respectable manner ; failing to do which I agree to forfeit and pay to the said Caroline Williams the sum of £20. The said child to be no further trouble or expense to its mother or friends—Ann Brown.' She had never seen her child since. The medical evidence showed that the child was brought in dead on Thursday last. It had died from convulsions, brought on by teething. There was no reason to suppose the child had not been properly nourished, or unfairly treated. The coroner having remarked upon the extraordinary document which had been put in by the mother, and condemned the system of advertising for children, a verdict of death from natural causes was returned."

I have said enough to show the horrors of this atrocious system. It would be to little purpose to accumulate anecdotes and instances. If the reader will apply to the plain statement of facts and results that I have given his own common sense and experience of human nature, he can picture for himself the evils that must of necessity result, especially when we remember that the moral and religious training bestowed upon such of these poor children as may survive in spite of neglect, cruelty, and privation, is likely to be on a par with the attention and care bestowed upon their physical and sanitary requirements. We may now turn to the other results of seduction and desertion to which I have referred—concealment of birth and infanticide—which though differing in degree, are in truth variations only of the same evil. A learned writer * has remarked upon the small amount of crime convicted when compared with the amount of crime committed. His remark is made with reference to forgers, thieves, and others who fall strictly under the designation criminal classes. It is, however, also true, though perhaps in a less degree, of the forms of evil now under consideration, that the amount of crime detected forms but a small proportion of the crime committed. We must bear this in mind when referring for information on the state of the public morals to the judicial statistics. Were it otherwise, we might read with some complacency that the cases of infanticide were in the year 1865, when the numbers of births of legitimate children amounted to 701,484 and of illegitimate to 46,585, only 83, and that the endeavours to conceal births were according to the same returns no more than 209 in 1867, 211 in 1866, and 222 in 1865. When, however, we pass on to the returns of the Registrar General, we shall find that the appearance of things is far less satisfactory. In the year 1865 no less than 119,810 deaths of infants under one year old are reported, or more than half of the total of infants perishing under the age of five years. Of these deaths, 183 are attributed to homicide, against 198 so perishing under five years; in other words, of 198 babies murdered before attaining five years of age, all but fifteen were less than a year old. Of these latter the total number of violent deaths occurring in 1865 is returned at 1698, of which 1447 are attributed to accident or negligence, and 165 are unclassed. In addition to these 1698 deaths confessedly violent, we find 699 under the heading, sudden causes unknown, and 2710 under the equally suspicious heading of causes not specified.† These returns will do much to modify any complacency that we may have contracted while perusing the judicial statistics, especially when we remember that the cases of concealment of birth are usually cases of infanticide also, but included in the milder category by the leniency of judges and juries.

It may be said that black as this list of deaths confessedly is, there is nothing to show that it is confined to the illegitimate, and that brutality is well known to be confined to no set of people in particular, and to be found among parents who have availed themselves of the rites of the church previously to living together, as well as among those who have neglected or despised them. A little consideration will, I think, suffice to satisfy the inquirer that a vast majority of the artificially accelerated deaths fall upon infants born outside the married pale. It will be remembered, that the proportion of bastard to legitimate children is about six per cent., that is, that for every child resulting from unlawful embraces, sixteen are produced by the marriage bed. Bearing these

---

* M. D. Hill, Repression of Crime, p. 7.

† These figures will not be found in the actual shape in which I have presented them, as the deaths of males and females are given separately, and the figures in the text are the result of the addition of the separate items. It is to be regretted that no separate returns of deaths of legitimate and illegitimate children are made.

figures in mind, we shall receive vast instruction from a perusal of the coroner's returns.

Turning to the judicial statistics for 1867, we find that in that year 1153 inquests were held upon illegitimate children aged one year and under, against 2960 inquests held upon legitimate children of like age, so that though the proportion of legitimate to illegitimate children exceeds 16 to 1, the number of inquests held upon the former are little more than double the number of those held upon the latter, thus presenting a ratio of inquests held on illegitimate children eight times as high as it ought to be, taking as our mean the number of the deaths occurring among the legitimate, though this mean is hardly the true one either, because misery and want are present in numberless instances, even when the parents have been duly married to bring about, if not the actual destruction of the offspring, at least the neglect that leads to the premature and sudden, if not violent death; in addition to all this, we may remember with what tenfold force the observations of the learned recorder to which I have already referred apply to the case of the illegitimate as compared with the case of the legitimate child, and we shall unavoidably come to the conclusion that even the enormous disproportion shown as the result of the coroner's inquest is very far below the real state of the case, and that we shall not be far wrong if we take the violent, and sudden, and unaccountable deaths returned by the Registrar General as the untimely fate of children unlawfully begotten, while if even a considerable proportion of that black list could be shown to belong to married life, it would not weaken, but on the contrary strengthen our apprehensions as to the untimely and miserable end that in the majority of cases falls to the lot of so-called "love children." A little further examination of the figures at our disposal seems to place almost beyond the possibility of doubt the supposition that a large proportion of the illegitimate children brought into the world meet with a violent, or at least premature end. We find that the number of inquests held on illegitimate children of the age of one year, but under seven, amounted to 2960, while the number held upon legitimate children of a like age reaches only to 201. There is here a preponderance of illegitimate deaths striking enough to call forth suspicions of foul play, but as compared with the discrepancy exhibited by the earlier period, the proportion has fallen off from one half to one fourteenth. Clearly the time of the strongest temptation to tampering with the life of the infant is during the earliest stage of its existence. It is at the outset of the baby's life that the mother has to answer for herself whether she can bear the shame that must inevitably occur to her from that infant life. During that evil time, also, it becomes apparent whether or no the father will support the life he called forth, and whether, if he fails to take the burden on himself, the mother can make up by her exertions for his default. Let the first gust of shame pass over, the first difficulty of providing for the babe be faced and overcome, and it is reasonable to suppose that the chances against its life being preserved are little greater than those against the attainment to maturity of the offspring of married life.

The results, then, of seduction and desertion are to force the mother to take to prostitution, and to tempt her to make away with her child either by her own hand or by means of baby farmers, thus giving rise to an amount of crime fearful to contemplate, while if the children survive the neglect and ill-treatment of their early years, can it be hoped that they will do otherwise than swell the ranks of the pauper and criminal classes?

The following letter from the Assistant Overseer of Marylebone, which appeared in the *Daily Telegraph* of the 24th of September, 1862, seems worthy of perusal from the ample experience of the writer. He says :—

"My attention having been drawn, both from the reports in your journal and from cases coming under my own observation, to the alarming increase of child-murder, I am induced to offer a few remarks, in the hope that another session may not be allowed to pass without some Act to check, if possible, this fearful crime. It will be found that this offence has gradually increased year by year since the passing of the Act 7th and 8th Vic., c. 101, on August 9, 1844, which makes the mother alone responsible for a bastard child; and the 7th section of which prohibits any board of guardians or their officers 'to conduct any application to make or enforce an order, or in any way to interfere as such officer in causing such application to be made, or in procuring evidence in support of such application, under a penalty of 40s.' It too often happens that when a young girl finds herself pregnant her friends and relatives turn their backs upon her. She then, becoming destitute, applies to a parish, and all that can be done is to admit her into the workhouse, and there keep her and her offspring; and unless some friend assists her with the necessary funds for the summons, &c., the putative father entirely escapes, and leaves the burden on the ratepayers.

"The remedy for this appears to be to put illegitimate children, so far as parish relief is concerned, on the same footing as legitimate ones, giving power to boards of guardians to issue process and recover from the putative father (where the mother has sufficient corroborative proof) the cost of the confinement, maintenance, &c.—not the present absurd 2s. 6d. weekly, but at a rate which should be fixed by the magistrate according to the position of the father. Another precaution which appears to be necessary is to enact that every unmarried woman who shall find herself pregnant shall, before the end of the sixth month of her pregnancy, register herself at an office to be appointed for that purpose in each parish, and her neglecting to do so should subject her to a penalty as for a misdemeanour.

"My experience, arising from numerous applications, shows me the want of some institution where the 'first child' only of a young unmarried woman could be received, so as to give the unfortunate mother an opportunity of regaining her position in society; the cost of the child's maintenance in such institution to be enforced as above-mentioned against the putative father. It is a remarkable fact that in this mighty city of London there is only one so-called 'Foundling' Hospital, and there the first and principal rule is, 'that the mother shall make the application for the child's admission.'"

We have in a previous chapter noticed the difficulties which at the present time beset and hinder all attempts made to effect the reform of fallen women, who must for the most part be left to run their course until opportunity favours their re-entry into the ranks of decent life, or the workhouse or grave receive them. We see also that under the present bastardy laws, all the burden of supporting her illegitimate child falls upon the mother, the father escaping scot free, or at the worst with a light payment of 2s. 6d. a week fastened upon him, which ceases on the child attaining the somewhat unripe age of 13 years. We have seen that this system in many cases tempts to murder, and in the great majority compels to a life of prostitution, that it encourages a trade hardly less infamous than prostitution, that of baby-farming; that it leads to a terrible waste of infant life, with a worse result if death does not intervene, than even death itself, hardship and want, evil associations and bad example being the portion of the luckless children, while such of them as are not reared by vile mothers and their hirelings find shelter only in the workhouse, and thus become chargeable on the ratepayers. It seems to me that it is a disgrace and foul blot on this Christian land of ours that all these evils should exist, and that on a scale of such magnitude, without any adequate means of dealing with them being proposed, or so far as I can judge, even looked for. I have already suggested in a paper read before, and subsequently published in the Statistical Society's Journal for December, 1859, (and the same view is supported in the letter that I have quoted above) that the obligation of supporting illegitimate offspring should not be left only with the mother, but that the father should be made responsible to the greatest possible extent. I submit that the questions how to deal with seduction, with illegitimacy, with prostitution, should all be considered together, as forming only separate branches of the one great question how can we best deal with immorality and its evil results. The victims of seduction and its female offspring go far towards providing the supply of prostitutes which infest our streets and public places. How can we save the children and their mothers? For the latter there are the Lock Asylums and Penitentiaries, for the former the Foundling Hospital. With the adequacy of the Penitentiaries I have already dealt; it behoves me now to consider very shortly the case of the Foundling Hospital.

THE FOUNDLING HOSPITAL.

I would refer those who desire full particulars concerning it to the Report of the Charity Commissioners made therein in 1837. It will be sufficient for my present purpose to state briefly and concisely my reasons for alleging that it is an unsatisfactory and comparatively useless institution.

The object of its foundation, which is an exceedingly rich one,* is to provide the means of saving fallen women from despair and its consequences, and their offspring from destruction; its field of usefulness should be as extended as possible, its benefits conferred without stint

* This hospital has a revenue of the present value of £11,000 a-year, and an assured income within the present century (according to the Charity Commissioners) of £40,000 a-year.

or favour, and in such a way that the benefactions it bestows may be real boons to the recipients and to the country. But it only relieves a class, and a small one, who have but little need of relief. Moreover, the method of relief is cruel, separating the mothers for ever from their children; inefficient, supporting and educating very few children at a vast expense (after causing the deaths of a great many), for the ultimate purpose of rearing expensively a class of persons whose only wish must be to forget their early education and surroundings, illegally, since it was founded by Charter and Act of Parliament for an altogether different purpose, and its present system has never been sanctioned by any adequate authority.

Now, to what conclusion do the matters considered in previous pages lead us? I think to this, that we ought to have some institutions with ramifications all through the country for the express purpose of dealing systematically and authoritatively with the different evils to which I have referred. Inseparable from such a proposal is the amount of expense it would entail, and the means of meeting it. The wealth of this hospital would provide the proposed institution with funds, the perversion of its wealth would justify the transfer.

The Foundling Hospital was founded by Captain Coram towards the end of the 17th century. On its endowment he bestowed the savings of his lifetime, literally beggaring himself in the hope of providing relief and sustenance for children more to be pitied even than orphans. The result of his charity proved not to be in accordance with his expectations, as far from decreasing the misery caused by profligacy, it only increased it. Parents abandoned their children in greater numbers than before, crowds being sent in from remote parts even of the country, and left to starve and die about the streets from lack of room to receive or means to support, if received, the crowds of the deserted. The mischief became in course of time sufficiently serious to attract the attention of Parliament, and by its action the scope of the charity was greatly modified. Even if we admit, for the sake of argument, that the intention of the founder as modified and altered by Parliament (which, however, is not the fact), was now being actually carried out, no case would be thereby made out which would bar the right of Parliament to interfere in the management of the institution, and give such fresh scope to it, and direct such different distribution of its funds as should seem wise and best calculated to promote the general welfare. But if the facts are as I believe that the intention of the founder has been entirely departed from, and that the enactments of the legislature are habitually disregarded, then I submit that Parliament not only has the right, but that it is its bounden duty, to interfere and to appropriate the funds on the cyprès doctrine to such object analagous to the founder's intention as shall produce to society the greatest amount of benefit. It remains for me to show that the institution, the foundation of which I propose, has for its end objects analogous to those for whose promotion the Foundling Hospital was instituted. I propose the establishment of a Government Board, or other competent authority to whom application may be made in cases of pregnancy by the woman herself or her parents, or master or mistress, or other responsible person whose duty it shall be to investigate the truth of the statements on which such applications may be founded, and if satisfied of their truth to take charge of the pregnant woman thrown out of a situation, affording her work and assistance until confinement, and during her lying-in. It should further be the duty of the Board to settle at the time of the application the question of paternity, and if the seducer have left the neighbourhood, to discover and fix upon him the duty of providing for the child when born. In doing this, it would be obviously necessary to guard against affiliating the child on the wrong person, and to see that the mother did not profit by the money obtained from the seducer, for this were no better than opening a regular and profitable market for female honour. The Board suggested should apply at their discretion the funds accruing for the keep and education of illegitimate children. Were the institution a recognised and a public one, I think the profession will bear me out that for a good proportion of the mothers situations might be found as wet nurses, and an opportunity thereby afforded them of recovering a respectable position. The situation of wet nurse would be acceptable and open to many thousands of women, were they cared for, from the time of their condition being discovered until their confinement, a period most trying to the unfortunate, and neglect during which leads too often to her permanent ill-health and to the birth of so sickly an infant that the mother loses all chance of being taken as a wet nurse.

Further, I believe that if the women were thus relieved, a large number would be rescued from their position by marriage with their first paramours, when the latter were persons in the same rank of life with themselves. By applying such natural remedies, I think that illegitimacy might certainly be checked, and its sad consequences much softened to the unhappy mothers. This board could also materially alleviate, if not altogether remove, the evils attending on baby-farming. We have seen that the great evil of this system is that it places the lives of children in the hands of unscrupulous women, leaving them absolutely at their mercy, there being no power to prevent possession of the infants being obtained, or to enforce the bestowal of proper attention on the duties thereby undertaken. Now just as properly qualified and duly licensed persons only are allowed to take upon themselves the charge and management of lunatics, so those only who are properly qualified and duly licensed should be permitted to take upon themselves the charge and management of infants. I propose that the power of granting licenses and exercising supervision over all baby-farmers should be vested in this board. All persons wishing to adopt this calling might be required to send in their names and testimonials to it, and to receive a license from it on showing themselves to be fit and proper persons to receive one; such license should be renewed annually, and a small payment might be made as duty thereon by the recipients. The names of all persons licensed might be registered; the number of babies to be received should be limited, and the receivers should be required to make a return to the board of all infants confided to them, with such particulars as it should seem from time to time necessary to require; and their houses should be at all times open to inspection by

the officers of the board.   It should also be made illegal for persons t
adopt any children without first satisfying the board as to their ability
to maintain them when adopted.   It is impossible to compensate the
young for the loss of parental care ; supervision by means of a Government board seems to present the best substitute within our reach ; their
physical wants would be at least provided for, and moral and religious
training, and a decent start, secured to them ; and wherever marriage
of the parents took place, the children could be restored to them. Youthful criminals are almost as great a perplexity to the moralist and the
legislator as prostitutes ; no one can walk the streets of London, or any
large town, without feeling that the neglected state of the children is
a reproach to us, and that if society would only take one half the pains
to prevent the increase of the criminal class that it takes to repress and
punish crime, a vast amount of suffering, loss, and shame would be
averted.

If even half of the 46,000 bastards annually brought into the world
grow up to adult years, how enormous must be the accession yearly received by the criminal and prostitute classes from this source—how
great the saving, could we but cut off, or seriously diminish, the supply
thus arising.   Surely it is worth a trial.   It may be urged that if the
evils resulting from Captain Coram's philanthropic scheme were so extensive and so marked, a recurrence to his scheme must be mischievous
and injudicious, and no doubt the objection is plausible.   Let us, however, examine it a little more closely, and see whether it is a mere
wreck buoy, warning us to avoid altogether the dangerous rock, or
whether it may not be more accurately likened to the chart that shows
the dangerous places, and the channel through them, which may be
safely followed.   Captain Coram's hospital was the only institution of
the kind in England ; it was to be expected, therefore, that all who had
children to dispose of, and could reach it, would flock to it with their
burdens.

The same thing is observable in Vienna, its enormous proportion of
illegitimate children, 50 per cent., being due in great measure to the
fact that all the bastards of the country flow into the haven provided
by the capital.   Again, his scheme was limited to saving the children ;
it provided no systematic check on seduction, or help to its victims.
According to the plan which I am now suggesting, the whole country
will be divided into districts, in each of which there will be a subsidiary
institution, to say nothing of the private licensed houses, so that the board
in London, though directing the efforts made throughout the country, will
have to provide in the Metropolis only for metropolitan wants.   It may be
said that the facilities thus afforded for disposing of children will tend
to increase the number, not only of seductions, but also of improvident marriages, because the knowledge of the provision for distress will
make people more careless and self-indulgent.   This objection will, I
think, be considered to be satisfactorily disposed of when it is remembered that the board will number among its duties not merely receiving
the child and helping the mother, but also compelling the father to
defray the expenses, according to his means.   By yielding rights you

impose duties, is the language of the seducer; he will be somewhat startled when he finds his words more true than his intention; and it may be, the experience may serve as a salutary check upon his future proceedings. When the hardened conscience, dull intellect, and indulgent will, case up the man as in triple brass against moral persuasion, an appeal to his pocket is not unlikely to prove an irresistible argument.

By the aid of this compensating medium, it is not unreasonable to expect that my proposal, so far from inducing mischiefs greater than the disease, will, if adopted, prove an unmixed good and a marvellously moralising agent.

Before I pass on from the question of seduction, I may make one further suggestion. Under the present bastardy laws the mother must, as we have seen, be the applicant for redress, and the interference of others, either in her interest or in that of the ratepayers, is not tolerated; while the right allowed her of claiming, previously to the birth of the child, the assistance of the magistrate, is seldom or never acted upon, and virtually a dead letter. The advantage that would accrue from the exercise of this right is self-evident; so great is it, that it should not merely be permitted as a right, but imposed as an obligation. That the person interested in concealing the birth, and desirous of screening the father, even to her own and her infant's hurt, should be the only one by whom action can be taken, is a gross absurdity. If the injury consequent on her silence recoiled on herself alone, it might be unfair to take from her the opportunity for self-sacrifice; but she cannot suffer alone; her helpless babe, and the whole community, suffer from her mistaken lenity. The right to set in motion the machinery of the law against the father should be extended to other persons. There are few women more exposed to temptation to immorality than domestic servants, especially those serving in houses where men servants also are kept; if the pregnancy of any such servant comes to the knowledge of her master, he should have the right allowed to him of making her condition known to the magistrates, and taking the steps necessary for insuring the detection of her paramour—nay, more, the adoption of this course should be made obligatory upon him, and he might be made answerable for any miscarriage of justice arising from his wilful default by being himself made chargeable to the same extent as the putative father would have been but for his neglect. The same principle might be adopted in the case of shopkeepers and other employers of female labour. Such a course would obviate the evils arising under the present system; a woman found pregnant is usually dismissed from her employment without a character; and yet the adoption of this course is ruin to her, and affords her seducer an additional chance of escaping the consequences of his wrong-doing. Were her dismissal accompanied by the further action here suggested, her first false step would be no longer irretrievable, and the author of her shame would be made a partner in her responsibilities. We are too apt in this utilitarian and self-seeking age to forget that incidental, as well as direct, duties attend the different social relationships. The duties of man to man, the personal obligations and mutual responsibilities of life, formed beautiful and attractive features in the feudal system. We may rejoice at our freedom from the bondage and tyranny incidental to and inseparably connected with it; but we should not forget the kindly feelings and righteous sentiments inculcated by its spirit, by which its rigour was softened, dependence ennobled, and the insolence of power restrained. Now that man is no longer inseparably linked to man, this idea is weakened, and masters are tempted to imagine that if they pay their servants' wages, and provide them wholesome food, they have done all they ought to do. Labour is free, and service optional; based upon contract, and defined by law, the letter of the bond is carried out, and no further duty recognised. The rights of man are remembered, the duties of man forgotten, each man getting for himself all he can, and giving only what he must, till willing service and kindly rule have almost passed away, and the old family servant has become as extinct as the old English squire; while, by a strange anomaly, class hatreds and class distrust grow with the growth of freedom. This isolation of the individual is deplorable, and a strange comment on the watchword of liberty, *fraternity*, and equality, by which it has been introduced. The exaggeration of freedom may land us in evils as pernicious as the worst form of tyranny; the lessons of the past are vain, unless they enable us, while abandoning the evil which degraded, to preserve the good which ennobled, the days that are gone. Not merely, then, from utilitarian motives, but from obedience to the principle that men should watch over and assist those who serve them, I recommend the adoption of this proposal.

I would even carry a step further the right of third parties to apply for bastardy orders, and on the principle that every man has a right to provide so far as he can against apprehended liabilities, I would concede to ratepayers the right to set the law in motion for their own protection, subject only to such restrictions as may be found necessary to avert the danger of charges being preferred unless with sufficient cause.

Closely akin to the relief of the seduced woman and the prevention of her further fall is the amelioration and reformation of the prostitute. As I have already indicated, I have little faith in the efficacy of lock asylums and penitentiaries; nor from the agency of enforced seclusion do I anticipate reformation, but from the gradual instilling of sentiments of self-respect and self-restraint. I therefore do not advocate the establishment of penitentiaries on a large scale, but " by line upon line, and precept upon precept, here a little and there a little," good may be done to these unfortunate outcasts. It is the only plan, gradually to educate them back to a sense of decency. Practical men devoting their time and thoughts to the carrying out of a special object, and learning from the experience and from the mistakes no less than from the successes of the past, wisdom for the future, are more likely to hit upon the means of solving a difficult problem than mere theorists or amateurs. I would, therefore, intrust to this board the carrying out of the Contagious Diseases Act, and vest in it power to make such provision as should from time to time seem expedient to assist in the paths of reformation, such women as on leaving the hospital, or from any other cause, should desire to abandon prostitution. The funds of the board would consist of the property held at present by the Foundling Hospital, and of such further sums raised either by parliamentary grant or parochial rates, as might be necessary. The funds thus vested in it, and the sums recovered from the fathers of bastards, together with the profits arising from the employment of the women received into the institution, would go far towards defraying its expenses, and any additional sums required would contribute to lighten the public burdens in other ways, and therefore form no additional charge upon the ratepaying and taxpaying population. If we can by this means, or in any other way prevent seduced women from becoming, and their daughters from growing up into prostitutes, we shall, if our position be true—that the supply stimulates and increases, and to a certain extent creates the demand—have taken a great preventive step ; there is more, however, that we may do—we may take care that so far as possible no persons shall be permitted to follow any calling that makes them interested in the continuance and increase of prostitution, and the procuring a supply of prostitutes ; further, that prostitutes shall ply their trade in a manner as little degrading as possible. For these two reasons the trade of a brothel-keeper must be resolutely put down.

One argument only in support of houses analogous to the Continental *maisons de filles* seems worthy of serious notice, and that is the sanitary one. It is on this ground that their toleration in Paris is excused, it being considered easier for the police to exercise the desired supervision of prostitutes when collected in these houses than when isolated and scattered through the town.

Jeannel (page 252) testifies to the freedom from disease attained in these houses :—

"At Bordeaux I have remarked that in the houses of the 1st Class the proportion of syphilitic women has decreased to 1 per 500 examined. In one house, where the number of girls was eight, no one has been diseased during the last four years, that is to say, no one was found diseased, although 1,864 examinations were made."

Lecour also mentions that in the Medical Service of the Dispensary, for September, 1867, only two cases of syphilis were found amongst 100 women in the registered houses, and one case only in 200 of *filles isolées*.

At the International Medical Congress in Paris, in 1867, Mr. De Meric gave an account of the diseases to which the women were subject at a notorious French brothel in London, from 1862 to 1867. It appears that the mean number of women was 7 ; during the five years 109 different females passed under his notice ; 1,848 examinations were made with the speculum—73 of these women resided from 8 days to 6 months in the establishment, 9 resided from 6 to 12 months, the remaining 27 lived from 12 to 30 months in the house ; their ages varied from 16 to 25 years ; the contagious diseases under which they suffered occurred in the following ratio—blennorrhagia, simple chancre buboes, depending upon simple or purely inflammatory chancres, infecting chancre, general syphilis. Among the 109 women, only 32

cases of contagious diseases were noticed during 66 months ; 38 inmates never presented any sign of disease ; urethral blennorrhagia
occurred only once ; simple chancre was met with three times ; buboes
occurred thrice ; only one case of indurated chancre was discovered ;
general syphilis was noticed in 21 cases. Of these 21 syphilitic cases
16 women were more or less affected at the time they commenced their
trade in the establishment, in five others the disease occurred after they
had entered the house. Mr. De Meric mentions that these 16 women
had become contaminated while they were carrying on a system of
clandestine prostitution previously. Of these 16 sick women six were
immediately sent back to their country as soon as their condition was
discovered, four were drafted into the Royal Free Hospital, and the six
others presented such slight symptoms, that their cases were treated
while in the establishment. Mr. De Meric states that during five years
only two complaints on the part of the frequenters of the house were
made—one that he had contracted a urethral discharge, and the other
a chancre. "This last case," he adds, "was problematical, for the soft
chancres of which I have spoken existed on the forefinger."

"It is evident," adds Mr. De Meric, "that I cannot entirely depend
upon accurate figures ; what I wish to prove is, that in an establishment
where examination is far from being obligatory, where sequestration is
still less so, but where medical intervention has always been prompt
and well followed up, infection of the male has been extremely rare.
What would happen then—(my remarks refer only to houses of accommodation, and do not apply to women plying in the public streets)—
what would happen, I repeat, if the visits were made three times a
week, and the sequestration obligatory ? I ought to say, nevertheless,
that if all the uterine catarrhs were sequestrated, it would be necessary
to send to hospital nearly all the women, for these catarrhs seem to be
the necessary accompaniment of prostitution."

It appears on the whole that there is little risk of contracting disease
in a well-organised French brothel. Still, curiously enough, within a
fortnight after the reading of Mr. De Meric's paper, I attended two gentlemen, both of whom alleged that they had contracted the disease for
which I treated them in this very French house ; one of them, a man
of high position in a distant county, had come to London expressly for
the purpose of visiting this establishment, and he complained most
naïvely that, after travelling some hundreds of miles—and though introduced by an old client of the house, and paying most liberally, he should
have been allowed to contract a foul disorder. I mention the circumstance because it shows with what false security a young fellow enters
one of these houses ; and it may afford crumbs of comfort for those—
who assert that regulated prostitution contributes to the encouragement
of vice—to learn that even the best-regulated establishments cannot,
notwithstanding the assertions to the contrary, guarantee freedom from
disease. Did I believe that French brothels would ever be largely tolerated in London, I should point out many other objections to them.
The system of procuring young foreign girls for the *debauchées* of the
London market, which every now and then crops out in police reports,

suffice to point out the frightful scenes of female martyrdom to which women are exposed in this sort of establishment.

If any one wishes to hear an additional argument against the establishment or Government toleration of such dens of possible iniquity, let him turn to page 119, and see the cold-blooded way in which these French houses may be supplied with victims.

Conceding freely that comparative immunity from disease is secured by the brothel system, to the women who inhabit and the men who frequent such establishments, the question remains whether this freedom from disease is not too dearly purchased? Is it worth while to sacrifice to the pursuit of health every religious and moral consideration? I think not, and I believe that my readers will for the most part agree in this conclusion, especially when it is considered that by a judicious arrangement of health districts, according to the plan suggested at p. 291, all the prostitutes in the country may be made subject to supervision and the spread of disease infinitely reduced. It is as much my object to raise the fallen as to prevent their injuring society; and I cannot too often repeat that the surest way of completing a woman's degradation, and rendering her reform impossible, is to confine her to the vile companionship and hopeless servitude of a brothel.

Having, in the chapter on " Causes of Prostitution," referred to the vice bred like filth, from the miserable herding of the lower orders, it becomes me also to number the improvement of their dwellings among preventive measures. The passing of the Common Lodging-house Act of 1851, rendering compulsory the registration of such houses and the compliance of their keepers with certain regulations demanded by decency and cleanliness, was·a step in the right direction; and the results thereby obtained are satisfactory as showing how much has been done— painful as showing what is still to do.

It is clear that the whole number have not yet been brought under supervision. This must be a work of time; but enough good has resulted hitherto to encourage us to proceed in what is obviously the way of right.

A step above these common lodging-houses are the so-called private dwellings, where each chamber is let to a separate family. These are subject by law to none but health inspections; but their occupants being generally of a class to whom all decency within their means is as grateful as to the wealthiest, the promiscuous crowding is a source of pain to them that the public would farther its own interest by helping to alleviate. None can feel more acutely than the working classes of all grades the great difficulty of procuring wholesome dwellings near the seat of their labour. Many men live miles away from their work, in order to preserve their growing families from the moral and physical contamination of the crowded courts and alleys, in which only they could find lodgings within their means. The State by itself, or by energetically putting the screw of compulsion upon the municipalities, who are slow to avail themselves of permissive enactments, to love their neighbours as themselves, should hold out a helping hand to the working million, who are, for want of dwellings adapted to their use, drifting to and fro among the wretched London "tenements," or reduced to harbour in the common lodging-house.

This packing of the lower classes is clearly not yet under control, and seems liable to aggravation by every new thoroughfare and airway with which we pierce our denser neighbourhoods. While it prevails, who can impute the defilement of girls, the demoralization of both sexes, as blame to the hapless parent who does the best he can with his little funds, and procures the only accommodation in the market open to him ? It is preposterous, as I have before hinted, to attribute the prostitution so engendered to seduction, or to vicious inclinations of the woman. From that indifference to modesty, which is perforce the sequel of promiscuous herding, it is a short step to illicit commerce ; and this once established, the reserve or publicity of the female is entirely a matter of chance.

Among the preventives that we ought to consider before attempting the *cure* of prostitution, should be numbered an altered and improved system of female training. Some remarks on this point published in the *Times* many years ago, are still extremely pertinent.

" When we examine our system of training for girls of the poorer class, we see one very important defect immediately in it, and that is, that they receive no instruction in household work. Girls are taught sewing in our parish schools, and very properly, because, even with a view to domestic service, sewing is an important accomplishment ; but they are not taught anything about household work. We do not say that a parish school could teach this, for household work can only be really learnt *in* a house ; the schoolroom can provide napkins and towels, but it cannot supply tables, chairs, mantelpieces, and carpets for rubbing and brushing ; and, the material to work upon being wanting, the art cannot be taught. But this is only explaining the fact, and not altering it. Household work is not learnt, and what is the consequence ? The department of domestic service in this country is hardly at this moment sufficiently supplied, while crowds of girls enter into the department of needlework in one or other of its branches, and of course overstock it enormously. Add to this a sort of foolish pride that poor people have in the apparent rise which is gained in rank by this profession,—for, of course, every one of these girls is ultimately to be a ' milliner,' which has for them rather a grand sound. The metropolis, sooner or later, receives this vast overplus of the sewing female population, and the immense milliners' and tailors' and shirtmakers' establishments hardly absorb the overflowing supply of female labour and skill, while, of course, they profit to the very utmost by the glut of the labour-market. A vast multitude of half-starving women is the result of the system ; whereas, had household work formed a part of their instruction, besides a better supply of the home field of service, what is of much more consequence, the colonies would take a large part of this overplus off our hands.

" What is the natural remedy, then, for this defect in the training of girls of the poorer classes in this country ? The remedy is, of course, that they should be taught, in some way or other, household work. At present, in the absence of any such instruction as this, it must be admitted that, however incidentally, the sewing which is taught in all our parish schools is simply aiding the overflowing tide of needle labour, which is every year taking up such multitudes of young women to the metropolis, and exposing them to the dreadful temptations of an underpaid service. And how is household work to be taught? Well, that is, of course, the difficulty. There are, as we have said, great difficulties in the way of our parish schools taking it up. The experiment, however, has been tried, in different places, of special institutions for this object ; and, in the absence of any formal and public institutions, the houses of our gentry and clergy might be made to supply such instruction to a considerable extent, and without any inordinate demand on private charity. Extra labour, as every householder knows, is often wanted in every domestic establishment ; it is even wanted periodically and at regular intervals in a large proportion of our good houses. It would be of great service to the country if a practice, which is already partially adopted, were more common and general—that of taking parish girls by turns for these special occasions. This might be done, at any rate in the country, to a large extent, and even a few days' employment of this kind in a well-furnished house, occurring at more or less regular intervals would be often enough to create a taste and a capacity for household work. The profession of household service might thus be indefinitely widened, and a large class be created that would naturally look to such service as its distinct employment, and be ready, in case of disappointment at home, to seek it in the colonies."*

I shudder as I read each jubilant announcement of " another new channel for female labour." Each lecture, pamphlet, and handbill, that calls attention to some new field of competition, seems to me but the knell of hundreds whose diversion by capital from their natural functions to its own uses, is a curse to both sexes and an hindrance of the purposes of our Creator. No more impious *coup d'état* of Mammon could be devised than that grinding down against one another of the sexes intended by their Maker for mutual support and comfort.

Free-trade in female honour follows hard upon that in female labour ; the wages of working men, wherever they compete with female labour, are lowered by the flood of cheap and agile hands, until marriage and a family are an almost impossible luxury or a misery. The earnings of man's unfortunate competitor are in their turn driven down by machinery until inadequate to support her life. The economist, as he turns the screw of torture, points complacently to this farther illustration of the law of trade ; the moralist pointing out how inexorable is the command to labour, too seldom and too late arrests the torture. He only cries enough when the famished worker, wearied of the useless struggle against capital, too honest yet to steal, too proud yet to put up useless prayers for nominal relief at the hands of the community, and having sold even to the last but one of her possessions, takes virtue itself to market. "And thus," as Parent-Duchâtelet says, "prostitution exists, and will ever exist, in all great towns, because, like mendicancy and gambling, it is an industry and a resource against hunger, one may even say against dishonour. For, to what excess may not an individual be

* "The Times," May 6th, 1857.

driven, cut off from all resources, her very existence compromised? This last alternative, it is true, is degrading, but it nevertheless exists."

But if the national education of women is not to be confined to reading, writing, and needlework, what are we to do with them? The ready answer is—TEACH THEM HOUSEWIFERY; and the rejoinder, how and where, was well met by the sensible and practical suggestion in the newspaper article above quoted, " that household education should be incorporated to a much greater extent than at present, with the discipline of union houses and schools."

The parochial clergy and well disposed gentry of the country have ample opportunities, if they would embrace them, of diverting to household pursuits the crowds of young women who annually jostle one another into the ranks of needle-work. The hall, the parsonage, and the parish school would be the best of normal schools for cooking, scrubbing, washing, ironing, and the like. Their owners would gladly, I fancy, impart gratuitous instruction in exchange for gratuitous service, and every housekeeper will bear me out in saying that the knowledge of the business once acquired, the market for properly qualified domestic servants is ample and not half supplied, while that for every description of needlework has long been overstocked. The vanity of girls and mothers must, it is true, be overcome, but the greater economy of the proposed domestic education would go some way to carry the day in its favour ; and if a true appreciation of the happiness that waits on colonization, and of the essentials to its success, were once to get well abroad among our people, their mother wit would lead them soon enough to grasp the comparative value, of the domestic and needlework systems of training.

Prostitution, though it can not be directly repressed, may yet be acted upon in many ways, and in proportion as the social system is wisely administered will its virulence be abated. We cannot put it down, but we can act indirectly on both the supply and demand. A judicious system of emigration will direct into healthy channels the energy that in overpeopled countries finds an outlet in riot, wickedness, and crime. Still, in advocating emigration as helping to prevent the spread of prostitution, I am far from advising that single women should be sent to the colonies alone and unprotected.

I cannot better show the evils attendant on indiscriminate and carelessly directed emigration than by appealing to the experience of an eye-witness of the evils thereby occasioned, who published the result of his observations in the *Melbourne Argus* of the 7th of May, 1859. He says :—

"After careful inquiry, I find that a very large proportion of the prostitutes now in Melbourne were free emigrants, and persons of loose character when they were selected by the Government agents at home. Others, previously virtuous, have been seduced on board of vessels, while a third class have been contaminated by their companions on the voyage. Government ships are now, however, under much stricter regulations than formerly ; the matrons appointed are responsible for the conduct of females under their charge, and the consequence is that cases of seduction are comparatively rare. The discredit mostly lies with private ships, over whose passengers there is exercised little or no salutary control. On board some of these vessels after nightfall, scenes may be witnessed well calculated to deter fathers, brothers, and lovers, from venturing the honour of any they hold dear, in such keeping. Indeed one of the most fertile sources of prostitution is to be found in the contaminating influences to which unprotected young women are subjected on the voyage hither; for, even should they manage to leave the vessel's side unscathed in honour, the indolence and enervation contracted during three months of unwonted ease and abandonment of all self-reliance often meets with so sudden a shock on facing the stern realities of their new position as to compel them, sooner or later, to seek a livelihood by means unfortunately far too facile. Deprived of the advantages of a home, and the counsel and wholesome restraint of parents or guardians; charmed with her newly-acquired freedom, and possibly indulging in the expectation of matching herself with some rich colonist (as the immigrant has been led to believe by English writers on Australia will be her most probable lot), she refuses to go into servitude, or, if she does, is speedily disgusted with it, and either indulges her vanity by accepting a situation of an equivocal character, or passes at once into the gaudy flaunting ranks of open prostitution. To say the truth, there are many employers who make the lot of their servants as little palatable as can be imagined, and who often, by their harsh and ungenerous treatment, break down the last barriers of virtue which remain in the heart of the poor creature who has to apply to them for the means of an honest subsistence. The chief blame, however, in this colony, must be attached to servants themselves.

"Young women of all classes of society and degrees of education and refinement come out hither, or are dispatched by their *friends* in Britain just to get them out of the way. Others find their way to Australia to fulfil long-standing contracts of marriage, but owing to the instability of colonial employment, and other mutations of fortune and residence peculiar to the place, too often find their intended husbands unable to support them when they arrive, if they do not learn to their great dismay that their recreant lovers have gone to the diggings, or are already married. There are large numbers of married women now in Melbourne and its suburbs, who, in consequence of their husbands having betaken themselves to the diggings and giving no note of their whereabouts, are compelled to resort to prostitution as a mode of obtaining a subsistence. An instance of a somewhat similar character recently came under my notice, and I am afraid it is but the type of a class. A gentleman who, on the date of his holding a Government appointment, had married a respectable lady, suddenly found himself deprived of the means of subsistence, not by any misconduct of his, but by a necessary reduction in the staff of his department. For months did he make the most strenuous efforts to obtain the only class of employment for which his education and habits fitted him. The diggings were the last resource, and his successes there were so indifferent as not to enable him to remit to his wife more than a tithe of her requirements. Unable to remove her to the gold-field on which he was engaged, or to support or

I appeal with confidence to every one acquainted with London life, and ask if this statement is not strictly true? but in that case, what becomes of the notion that the mischief, if left to itself, will work out its own cure? I appeal to those who fear God, and reverence His laws, and who therefore refuse to recognise, lest by so doing they should be supposed to countenance, vice, and I ask them to consider whether this attitude of indifference is not open to a construction far different to that which they themselves would put upon it. May not those who follow evil courses say, "We know that our lives are obnoxious to censure, that the finger of scorn is pointed at us, but the law will not touch us, and why? because it dare not; and it dares not, because whatever good people may think or say to the contrary, our sin, if sin indeed it be, is committed in obedience to natural laws; surely nature's teaching is at least as good as that of religion."

And so it comes to pass that men consider the sin as a thing that everybody practises, though nobody talks much about it, until to abstain is looked upon almost as a mark of want of manhood, and the natural consequence is that what everybody does nobody feels ashamed to acknowledge participation in, and if such is the state of public feeling, who can be surprised at the condition of things to which attention is called by the article above quoted. Now, I say the time has arrived when serious men should give to prostitution serious thought. It can no longer be ignored the evils attendant on it are too great and too much on the increase. Evil agents are active and stirring, and those whose lives are pure, who love their country and their fellow men, must show an equal diligence. The field of inquiry may be repulsive, the problems that meet us difficult of solution, and my fellow labourers must expect for a season at least to have only their labour for their pains, and for their only reward an approving conscience. But we may trust that the time is approaching when the justice of our cause will be acknowledged. It cannot be that the people of this country will for ever ignore the misery to be found in their midst. Nor even to human ears can "the crying of the poor and the sighing of the needy" for ever appeal in vain.

It is absolutely impossible to exaggerate the suffering entailed by a life of prostitution. Instead of the scorn so freely lavished on the poor lost daughters of shame and misery, I plead for a little pity—nay, far more than pity, I plead for justice. If unequal laws between man and woman compel to a shameful and a hated trade the helpless and shuddering victim of seduction, whose fall, though it has soiled and stained, has not utterly polluted her, I charge those laws with cruelty, and I say further that her blood is on the head of those who know the injustice of such laws yet will not help to alter them. If human beings are left to herd together with indecent indiscriminacy, because in this rich and luxurious city they can obtain no more fitting shelter; if they are allowed to grow up from childhood to youth, and from youth to adult years amid scenes of depravity and sin, I ask on whose shoulders does the blame really rest; whether on the victim's, reared to a life of infamy, or on society's, that leaves them to a fate so awful. If in this wide world, teeming with abundant supplies for human want, to thousands of wretched creatures no choice is open save between starvation and sin, may we not justly say that there is something utterly wrong in the system that permits such things to be. If the traffic in human flesh and female honour is not repressed by the arm of the law, may we not justly accuse the law of falling far short of its duty? And if all this be true, is there not abundant cause of prostitution that is capable of removal? Is it too much to say that by amending the bastardy laws, by improving the dwellings of the poor and keeping the young from haunts of vice, by encouraging and promoting emigration, and resolutely putting down so far as possible the great body of night house keepers and brothel keepers throughout the country, the number of prostitutes will be greatly decreased? Prostitution we cannot prevent, but we can mitigate the misery entailed by it, and can do much, if we will, to prevent women becoming prostitutes. The evil can not be done away, but it may be lessened, and that to a very great extent. We cannot do all we wish : is that a reason for doing nothing? Let us do what we can. The mischief that must always exist will have more or less intensity according as we regulate it, or leave it to itself. The women will become more or less depraved, according as good and healing influences are brought to bear upon, or withheld from them. The numbers who resort to a shameful trade will lessen or increase according as the causes of prostitution are removed or neglected. The neutral position has been fairly tried, but the nation is certainly not improving. Let us assume a position at once more manly and more humane. The evils to be overcome are too intense for individual effort to cope with, but the good which scattered philanthropists, earnest and self-devoted though they be, cannot achieve, is not beyond attainment if wise, discriminating and concentrated power is enlisted in the cause. While men stood with folded arms aghast at the evil which appeared of too long standing, and too stupendous for human power to cope with, the filth of the Augæan stables continued to accumulate, but when resolute will, high intelligence,· and manly courage took the task in hand, and let loose upon the filthy stalls the cleansing waters, the mischief was removed. Laugh not, neutral reader, at the old classic tale, *"mutato nomine de te fabula narratur."*

THE END.